Inside Computer Music

Inside Computer Music

Michael Clarke, Frédéric Dufeu,
and Peter Manning

OXFORD
UNIVERSITY PRESS

OXFORD
UNIVERSITY PRESS

Oxford University Press is a department of the University of Oxford. It furthers
the University's objective of excellence in research, scholarship, and education
by publishing worldwide. Oxford is a registered trade mark of Oxford University
Press in the UK and certain other countries.

Published in the United States of America by Oxford University Press
198 Madison Avenue, New York, NY 10016, United States of America.

Library of Congress Cataloging-in-Publication Data
Names: Clarke, Michael, 1956– author. | Dufeu, Frédéric, author. | Manning, Peter, 1948– author.
Title: Inside Computer Music / Michael Clarke, Frédéric Dufeu, Peter Manning.
Description: [1.] | New York : Oxford University Pres, 2020. | Includes bibliographical references and index.
Identifiers: LCCN 2020005410 | ISBN 9780190659646 (hardback) | ISBN 9780190659653 (paperback) |
ISBN 9780190659684 (epub) | 9780190659677 (updf)
Subjects: LCSH: Computer music—History and criticism.
Classification: LCC ML1380 .C53 2020 | DDC 786.7/609—dc23
LC record available at https://lccn.loc.gov/2020005410

9 8 7 6 5 4 3 2 1

Paperback printed by LSC Communications, United States of America
Hardback printed by Bridgeport National Bindery, Inc., United States of America

In memory of Jonathan Harvey

Contents

Acknowledgments

nside Computer Music and the accompanying software are the result of the research project "Technology and Creativity in Electroacoustic Music" (TaCEM) funded by the United Kingdom's Arts and Humanities Research Council (AHRC) from 2012 to 2015, with additional support from the Universities of Durham and Huddersfield. The project's aim was to investigate the relationship between technological innovation and creative imagination through the detailed examination of nine case studies—nine groundbreaking works in the history of computer music, all exhibiting, in different ways, significant technical and musical developments. We are greatly indebted to the composers of these nine works: John Chowning, Barry Truax, Philippe Manoury, Hildegard Westerkamp, Francis Dhomont, Trevor Wishart, Jonathan Harvey, Cort Lippe, and Natasha Barrett. All were unstinting in their support and advice, and happily made available whatever documentary evidence they had of the creative and technical process. In several cases this included extended audio archives which they have permitted us to use and make available to readers as part of the interactive software that accompanies this book. The composers also took part in videoed interviews which are incorporated into the software and provide readers with an opportunity to see and hear them discussing the music and their creative process. Sadly, the one exception is Jonathan Harvey, who died just as our project was starting. We were able to discuss the project with him in advance and the analysis we were proposing of his *Fourth String Quartet.* Even though very ill, he spent a whole day discussing the piece and providing us with copies of his sketches and much valuable information which has informed our study of the work. Harvey was a leading figure in pioneering the creative potential of new digital technologies and this book is dedicated to his memory.

Our study of these works was in many cases also aided by discussions with and resources from those who helped with their production. We wish to express our gratitude to Arshia Cont, Cort Lippe (who worked closely with Philippe Manoury on *Pluton,* as well as being the composer of another of our case studies), Markus Noisternig, Gilbert Nouno, Miller Puckette, and Olivier Warusfel. Videos of our discussions are again incorporated into the relevant software. We also wish to thank Yann Geslin, who helped us initiate our investigation of the materials kindly provided by Francis Dhomont for *Phonurgie.*

We are grateful to IRCAM and in particular Cyril Béros for allowing us to use the simulation program and materials for the study of Philippe Manoury's *Pluton,* and to Durand-Salabert-Eschig for giving us permission to use the score of *Pluton* in the context of our project. We wish to thank Jacqueline Schaeffer for granting us kind permission to use an excerpt of Pierre Schaeffer's *Étude aux objets* in the software for Francis Dhomont's *Phonurgie*, as well as François Bonnet and Jules Négrier for their help with this case study. We are most grateful to the Arditti Quartet and IRCAM for allowing us to use a recording of the instrumental parts of Jonathan Harvey's *Fourth String Quartet* in our software, and to the Paul Sacher Foundation for permission to print extracts from Harvey's sketches of this work which are now part of their collection. Our thanks also go to Faber Music who have kindly allowed us to reproduce extracts from the score of the *Quartet*, and to Jean-François Denis who kindly allowed us to use and reproduce audio materials from Hildegard Westerkamp's *Beneath the Forest Floor* and Francis Dhomont's *Phonurgie,* both published by empreintes DIGITALes. And we are grateful to Melvyn Poore who allowed us to use his tuba recording for Cort Lippe's *Music for Tuba and Computer.*

We would like to acknowledge the important contribution made by the advisors to our project: Roger Dannenberg, Simon Emmerson, Évelyne Gayou, Xavier Rodet, and David Zicarelli. Their feedback and wise suggestions have greatly enhanced our research. We are also most grateful to our project associate, Alex Harker, whose advice was of significant help in the development of the accompanying software. Our thanks to Elizabeth Manning for voicing the demonstration videos accompanying this text.

Finally, we would like to acknowledge that preliminary and intermediate versions of our work were presented in many international conferences related to computer music and music analysis; we are very grateful to the many colleagues who responded to our work and offered helpful comments and advice on later developments.

The generosity of all these people and organisations has enabled us to bring together a wide range of creative and technical information in our investigation into how these factors are combined in the realization of innovative musical works.

About the companion website

www.oup.com/us/insidecomputermusic

Oxford has created a website to accompany *Inside Computer Music*. Material that cannot be made available in a book, namely demonstration videos for each chapter and links to the software, are provided here. The reader is encouraged to consult this resource in conjunction with the book. Examples available online are indicated in the text with Oxford's symbol ⊙ .

Technology and Creativity in Computer Music

Combining text and software to explore computer music from the inside

This publication (the text and the software) aims to explore the relationship between new technical innovations in computer technology for music and the creative practice of composers employing these new techniques. It asks the following questions: Does the new technology lead to new sounds and new ways of structuring music, and if so how? What are the creative options, sonic and structural, presented by new software and hardware? How can these be manipulated and shaped to form music? How have particular composers developed successful working methods in using this technology?

To answer such questions, a set of case studies has been examined in depth, involving specific works in which composers have adopted new techniques, whether developed by themselves or by others. Each of these works has been researched from a number of different perspectives: the technical and musical background, the technology employed in the particular work, and, through music analysis, the musical outcome. Innovative approaches have been employed both in undertaking and presenting this research. On the one hand, it has been important to find appropriate ways of presenting the musical potential

2

of what are often highly technical processes. On the other hand, it has been necessary to find ways of analyzing music that often evades even the most basic fundamentals of traditional music analysis: notes, harmonies, or instruments.

The approach taken has been to adopt, and very significantly enhance, techniques of interactive aural analysis.[1] In essence this approach closely links text and interactive software. The software allows users to engage with emulations of the techniques used by the composers. In this way, readers can learn about the technology and its musical potential for themselves, and perhaps gain some insight into the issues and challenges faced by the composers as they worked. Software also enables the musical analyses to be conducted in the medium of sound itself. This is especially important for musics, such as those of our case studies, where traditional notation and verbal analytical terminology are not ideally suited to the sounds and structures of the works. Software also makes possible the incorporation of video recordings of interviews with the composers and/or technical innovators involved in a composition, sometimes illustrating their ideas with live demonstrations. Again, this is something that could not be achieved simply on paper.

Each of the nine case studies has its own dedicated software application, addressing the musical materials and structures, compositional processes, and technologies with interactive presentations that are inevitably specific to the composer and work being studied. However, these nine applications have been developed with a unified design and common overall architecture. For each case, the interactive aural presentations are either "explorers" or videos organized around specific aspects or topics, and the succession of interactive explorers is globally ordered as follows: the first explorer is always a representation of the work as a whole, enabling users to navigate aurally the entire musical structure, explore the categories of materials or processes, and get familiar with the significant components of the piece. Then, the examples that follow present simple instances of the technologies used by the composer, introducing their fundamental properties and sound potential. The subsequent examples then grow in complexity, inviting the reader to learn incrementally, from simple principles to their actual implementation in the context of the studied work. Where relevant, some interactive analytical charts are also provided, as well as emulations of the systems used at the time of composition.[2]

It is important to underline the fact that, even though the focus of this publication is on the role of technology in musical creation, the software applications are meant to be entirely accessible, and any reader can easily engage with these resources. No particular technological knowledge or skills are needed to explore the nine case studies interactively.

Demonstration Video 0.1 is an introduction to the accompanying software, showing its general architecture, modes of use and navigation, and examples of interactive aural presentations. In each chapter, the reader is directed to more specific demonstration videos that develop the considerations in the written text while showing how particular aspects of the software operate, and readers are strongly encouraged to engage further with these interactive resources. ▶

Technical innovation is therefore employed in order to investigate technical innovation, and hopefully to demonstrate something of the creativity this facilitates in the works of the composers studied. Text nonetheless plays a crucial role in articulating ideas, and the integration of text and software is vital. In this book, therefore, there are frequent links to video demonstrations of the software relevant to a particular point being made in the text, as with Demonstration Video 0.1. These short videos act both as illustrations of such points and also as mini-tutorials to guide readers in how to use the software. Although the videos will provide some insight into the potential of software, to gain the most out of it, and to learn in greater depth, it is important to download the software and use it interactively. The learning then becomes open-ended: in many cases additional material is provided relating to the work, which it was not possible to incorporate fully into the textual discussions. So readers will be able, if they wish, to extend their research into particular case studies beyond what is presented here.

The pursuit of new perspectives in the analysis of electronic and computer music

The generic descriptor "electronic music" embraces an abundance of sound production and manipulation techniques, explored in an equally extensive range of creative contexts. Whereas acoustic music is associated with general typologies that are well understood by those who take an interest in the classical repertory, such as orchestral music, chamber music, folk music, opera, or jazz, the same or even a suitably equivalent sense of identity cannot be assumed in the case of music that makes use of the electronic medium. The evolution of rock and popular music provides a good example of the problems that are often encountered in such a context. For many listeners it is the more immediate sonic characteristics of the associated works that determine the limits of their engagement with the underlying technical and musical processes. As a result, many of the contributing components in both contexts that have led to specific classifications, such as electronic dance, industrial, techno, hip-hop, and ambient music, are only superficially understood by the wider public.

The implications of this dichotomy are considerable, not least for those who wish to gain an informed understanding of electronic music, and it is thus especially important to introduce the reader to the key issues that have shaped and influenced the research project that led to the production of this book, as well as the accompanying software and related audiovisual materials.

4

Other analytical approaches to this repertoire can be found in *Electroacoustic Music: Analytical Perspectives*, edited by Thomas Licata (1982); *Analytical Methods of Electroacoustic Music*, edited by Mary Simoni (2006); *Expanding the Horizon of Electroacoustic Music Analysis*, edited by Simon Emmerson and Leigh Landy (2016); and *Between the Tracks: Musicians on Selected Electronic Music*, edited by Miller Puckette and Kerry Hagan (2020).[3] For those readers who wish to study the medium in a wider context, attention is drawn to three books also published by Oxford University Press, which have a useful role as companion texts: *Electronic and Computer Music* by Peter Manning (2013); *The Oxford Handbook of Computer Music*, edited by Roger Dean (2009); and *Composing Electronic Music: A New Aesthetic* by Curtis Roads (2015).[4]

There are some important differences between the genres of music that have explored the possibilities of purely acoustic resources over the years and those that have been based on sounds produced by an electronic means. While the development of both Western and non-Western music has taken place over many centuries, the evolution of electronic music has occupied a much shorter time span. Although speculative predictions on how sound might be manipulated in a future domain date back as far as those made by Francis Bacon in his visionary work *New Atlantis* (1626),[5] for all intents and purposes the birth of the medium extends back no further than the pioneering work of Thomas Edison on the practical uses of electricity during the latter part of the nineteenth century, preparing the ground for the introduction of the thermionic valve in 1906 and all that was to follow in terms of the development of electronic resources for sound production and audio signal processing.[6]

Progress over the subsequent decades leading up to the Second World War was limited in the first instance to a diverse series of individual initiatives that engaged with the technical and musical considerations necessary to underpin what was essentially a journey into entirely uncharted territory. In a technical context, one of the more notable outcomes was a succession of electronic musical instruments conceived as additions to the existing repertory of acoustic musical instruments. These included the Theremin (1924), the Ondes Martenot (1928), and the Trautonium (1930). The Hammond organ (1935) was an exception to this trend, being specifically designed as a direct replacement for the pipe organ, and in due course as an alternative to the conventional acoustic piano. Crossing boundaries from the conventional to the unconventional in terms of electronically produced sound, however, required the evolution of musical aesthetics that embraced new creative horizons, and here the diversity of pioneering ventures is quite remarkable, ranging from the revolutionary ideas of the Futurists and Ferruccio Busoni to those of Edgard Varèse and John Cage.[7] The intervention of the war interrupted these preparatory steps toward establishing such a new medium of musical expression. However, the rapid advances in communication technologies during this time were to prove of material practical significance for future developments.

By the termination of the war in 1945, the stage had been set for a series of important initiatives both in Europe and the United States that finally established the development of a composing and performing medium that was to become generally known as electronic music. These initiatives were based in the first instance on analog technologies, ranging from individual hardware devices that could be used to generate and manipulate audio signals, such as laboratory oscillators and filters, to facilities for mixing and recording sound materials via the medium of magnetic tape. Although in Europe these developments were primarily concentrated in studios funded by national broadcasting corporations, notably in Paris, Cologne, and Milan, a somewhat more diffuse series of both collective and university-based initiatives was to emerge in the United States.[8] During the 1950s the scope and level of activities continued to gather pace, not only in Europe and the United States, but also further afield, notably in Japan, and by the end of the decade the general public was starting to become aware of the world of electronic sounds, embracing applications ranging from simple sound effects to complete artworks. Access to suitable facilities for aspiring composers, however, remained for the most part restricted to those fortunate enough to gain access to an established electronic studio.

This emphasis on exclusivity was to change during the mid-1960s with the production of commercially produced analog synthesizers from manufacturers such as Moog, Buchla, ARP, and EMS (London). This development made suitable facilities available to a much wider spectrum of creative artists, and also signaled the start of a major revolution in its own right concerning the use of electronics as a resource for a rapidly expanding world of rock and pop music. As the medium of electronic music continued to develop during the 1970s, its creative possibilities were explored with increasing intensity and diversity. The positive trajectory of the associated technical developments continued well into the early 1980s, changing direction as the decade advanced into one of progressive decline as alternative technologies based on digital engineering became more generally available. By the end of the 1990s the design and manufacture of analog equipment for electronic music had all but ceased, and gradually the term "computer music" came into general use.

The implications of this material change of circumstances were not immediately grasped. Many practitioners assumed that the new era of digital engineering would simply subsume and enhance the key features of the older technologies, thus ensuring continuity with former ways of working with electronic resources. To a certain extent such aspirations were indeed possible. However, the digital domain soon opened up new avenues for exploring the creative possibilities of the medium, focusing attention away from preserving the unique practical ways of working with analog equipment. Obsolescence was thus fast becoming a significant consideration.

During the early 2000s other concerns arising from the passage of time were to surface. Whereas formerly a significant proportion of those who had contributed to the development of the medium since the Second World War could provide personal and highly informative insights into its evolution, these direct lines of communication were starting to diminish as, one by one, the individuals concerned passed away. A similar situation was to materialize in terms of access to the legacy of completed works. Here there are some important differences to be noted between electronic and acoustic compositions. The conventionally notated scores associated with the latter repertory provide definitive reference points, both for a detailed study of each work and also for the production of subsequent performances and recordings at any point into the future. In addition, the physical nature of the score ensures a significant degree of sustainability, unaffected by the passage of time. Recordings of electronic music, however, are problematic in a number of respects. Early electronic music works created in studios were recorded on magnetic tape, with commercial works released on vinyl. Over the years, many of the original master tapes have degraded to the point where they can no longer be played. As a result, the works concerned are lost for eternity. Although the advent of the compact disc in 1982 signaled the start of a digital recording revolution that was ultimately to transform the world of music production, distribution, and preservation, a significant number of electronic composers continued to master their works on magnetic tape. The key to a wholesale move to digital recording lay in the development of recording facilities for the personal computer, but these only reached maturity after the turn of the century.

In the current environment of highly sophisticated digital technologies, it is thus important to recognize the significance of three legacy issues that arise from the above observations: (1) how to secure continuing access to the repertory of works composed over the years, (2) how to secure and sustain access to the various technologies that have been used in their production, and (3) wherever possible to enhance our understanding of these works by directly interrogating both the composers concerned and those responsible for the design of the resources they used to create their works. In many respects the latter objective is the most elusive, for self-evident reasons. However, the potential insights arising from such engagements provide powerful incentives for such inquiries.

Much has been written on electronic music from a variety of perspectives, from the early pioneering era to the present day, and it is important to appreciate that the resulting production of books, articles, and allied materials have collectively made important contributions to our knowledge and understanding of the medium as it has developed over the years. Nonetheless, for the reasons discussed earlier, there is some way to go before such lines of inquiry achieve their full potential. Particular attention has been paid in more recent years to the practical techniques that can be used to study the key features of individual works, and significant progress has been made in terms of developing different approaches to sonic analysis, ranging from feature analysis using subjective criteria applied through listening to analysis of the spectral content using software for digital signal processing. There is, however, a further question that has to be addressed: What is the scope and nature of information being sought in such contexts, and why and to what extent will the outcomes assist our understanding of the work concerned? The issues arising in this context are necessarily complex and embrace a multitude of different perspectives and objectives. These circumstances make it especially important for the authors of this book and the accompanying materials to introduce the reader to the specific rationale that underpins the choice of composer and the associated detailed study of an associated work in each of the nine chapters that follow.

A useful starting point in this context concerns the reasons why the authors were motivated to embark upon this program of musical and technical research, consolidated in the arguments put forward to secure funding from the UK Arts and Humanities Research Council. A fundamental objective was the development of suitable ways and means of addressing key aspects of the legacy issues identified earlier, and in so doing provide new insights into both the creative and technical characteristics of the medium of electronic music. The following questions were identified as key elements of the proposed methodology:

- How far has technology had an important impact on the musical creativity of electronic music composers?
- How do the resources of music technology and the creative processes of composition interact in individual works, and what is the musical significance of this interaction?
- How far is the use of technology here guided by particular aesthetic/creative principles?
- How is the musical structure formed in these works, and how far and in what ways has the technology enabled new creative possibilities in terms of shaping sounds and/or forming musical structures?
- How does a specific work relate to the composer's practice more generally, and what is its contribution, in the broader context, to the development of electronic music?

In order to embark on such far-reaching investigations, it was first necessary to identify a group of works upon which to base a suitably focused program of research. The criteria used in this context need some explanation, since the choices made have of necessity materially influenced the scope and nature of the perspectives that have emerged. A primary decision made at the outset was to focus specifically on works that have contributed to the evolution of computer music as a domain in its own right—hence the title of the book. As noted earlier, the transition from analog to digital technologies has materially transformed the creative environment for composing electronic music, with the consequences embracing both art and popular genres. Furthermore, although

8

the full impact of this step change was to take a number of years to come to fruition, the pioneering phase of computer music dating back to the late 1950s established the key methods of digitally generating and processing sounds that are widely employed today. This strategy facilitated a further set of questions based on issues that hitherto have only been partially explored:

- Can software, with interactive aural examples, articulate technical issues in a more musically meaningful way for a nontechnical audience?
- Can the discussion of music that exists primarily as sound and is essentially temporal and transitory in nature be facilitated by software that incorporates interactive manipulation of sound examples?
- Can software provide a means of demonstrating the interrelation of the musical and the technical in a manner that is more meaningful to an extended range of end users?

Nine case studies from the history of computer music

The starting point for this journey is the birth of the digital computer—a fascinating study in its own right.[9] In the same way that World War II resulted in a major stimulus for the technologies necessary to underpin the development of analog electronic music, the increasing demands for facilities capable of processing large quantities of information data spurred pioneers to investigate the possibilities of developing ways and means of converting the techniques of early mechanical calculators into an electronic, and in due course fully programmable, environment.[10]

Parallel initiatives establishing the design principles associated with the development of digital computers gathered pace during the early postwar years in a number of countries, notably the United States, the United Kingdom, and Australia, but the key to their future lay in attracting the interest of commercial manufacturers. Although credit here is due to Remington Rand for its pioneering 409 model, launched in 1949, it was the entry of IBM into the field in 1953 that marks the start of developments that were to prove of lasting significance to the evolution of computer music, starting with the pioneering work of Max Mathews and his associates at Bell Telephone Laboratories (aka Bell Labs) from the mid-1950s onward. Chapter 1, focusing on the work of John Chowning, and in particular the composition of his work *Stria* (1977), using software originally developed by Mathews, provides an insight into this early phase of computer music, based in the first instance on the resources provided by large mainframe computers. Chowning's contributions to the development of the medium have been considerable, not least in the context of his pioneering work with frequency modulation (FM) synthesis, a powerful and versatile method of generating sound material for computer music that is still widely used today.

One notable distinction between the early years of computer music and concurrent developments in electronic music based on analog technologies was the exclusivity of the former domain, limited to a handful of pioneers able to gain access to institutional computers.[11] Allocations for processing time were at a premium, and this further restricted the opportunities for aspiring composers and researchers, both at Bell Labs and elsewhere. The first tentative steps in the latter context were taken by the universities of Princeton and Columbia during the early 1960s. By the early 1970s, developments started to gather pace, extending to the Massachusetts Institute of Technology (MIT), Stanford University, the University of Illinois at Urbana-Champaign, and the University of California at San Diego (UCSD). By the middle of the decade, advanced facilities for computer music were being developed at a number of leading institutions. Stanford, for example, established the Center for Computer Research in Music and Acoustics (CCRMA) in 1975, and this development was to prove especially important for the continuing work of Chowning.

In the same year the Institut de Recherche et Coordination Acoustique/ Musique (IRCAM) purchased a dedicated mainframe computer, pending the official opening two years later of this major new research center in Paris, under the direction of Pierre Boulez. The particular importance of IRCAM in shaping the development of computer music from the late 1970s to the present day will become evident in due course, impacting both directly and indirectly on the work of many of the composers who have made significant contributions to the development of the medium over the years. At the same time, it is important to recognize that a wider perspective on the evolving genre embraces many other notable achievements in both technical and creative contexts, and these contributions are reflected in the choice of composers selected for closer study.

The progression from the exclusivity of mainframe computing to the extensive range of powerful resources for composing computer music that are now available to the individual in a personal computing environment is a fascinating subject of study, and key elements of this evolutionary process will emerge in successive chapters. The first stages in terms of technological change were already well underway by the end of the 1960s. A key driver in this context was a growing demand for computers that could be produced at a significantly lower cost, thus balancing increased accessibility by a wider community of potential users with the consequences, at least initially, of having to accept a reduced functionality. As the years progressed, advances in computer design ensured this differential in performance became increasingly reduced, assisted to no small extent by the development of specialist fast "front-end" processors that could handle the heavy processing requirements of audio and video applications. Indeed, the commanding advantages of mainframe computing were already facing increasingly significant challenges from other quarters. Few could have predicted, for example, that the invention of the microprocessor in 1972 and subsequent developments based on its technology would in due course materially challenge and ultimately replace the technology of traditional computing architectures.

The first stages in this process of progressive miniaturization, from mainframe to minicomputer, are charted in Chapter 2, which considers the circumstances that led Barry Truax to compose *Riverrun* in 1986 at Simon Fraser University (SFU), British Columbia. Truax has become well known for his pioneering work with granular synthesis, a technique investigated by Curtis Roads in the early 1970s. He first came into contact with a minicomputer at the Institute of Sonology in Utrecht in 1971, his two-year period of study at this important center for computer applications in music leading him to develop some of the very first programs to generate sounds directly from a computer in real time. Hitherto the programming environment of traditional mainframe computers required all such materials to be generated in a non-real-time mode, the sonic results being accumulated in a digital format as a data file for subsequent playback directly via a digital-to-analog converter. Truax's acquisition at SFU of a physically smaller but more powerful minicomputer and a pioneering front-end digital signal processor to speed up computation in 1981 facilitated the development of a fully interactive and real-time environment for composing works by means of granular synthesis, of which *Riverrun* is a striking example.

Attention then turns to developments at IRCAM, and in particular the pioneering work of the composer Philippe Manoury. As mentioned earlier, a notable feature of IRCAM was the initial emphasis on mainframe computing applications. Although significant use was made of this technique, for almost a decade a number of researchers chose to concentrate instead on developing facilities that were specifically designed for real-time computer music synthesis and signal processing. As was to prove the case with Truax, a particular incentive was the prospect of working with such resources interactively, not merely in a composing context but also in terms of live performance. As a background to the study of Manoury's *Pluton* (1988) these IRCAM-based initiatives are studied in detail since they were materially to influence the development of some of the most significant resources widely used today for both the composition and performance of computer music.

The next chapter studies the work of Hildegard Westerkamp in the context of her work with soundscape composition, a distinctive genre of computer music that concentrates on exploring the creative possibilities of naturally produced sound materials. Born in Germany, Westerkamp emigrated to Canada in 1968 and studied at the University of British Columbia, before joining the World Soundscape Project at Simon Fraser University, at the time led by Raymond Murray Schafer. Westerkamp has since become a leading composer, radio artist, and sound ecologist.[12] The piece of Westerkamp to be studied in detail, *Beneath the Forest Floor*, was completed in 1992 in Toronto, toward the start of a decade that was to prove of particular significance in the evolution of computer music as the speed of both technical and musical development gathered pace.

In Chapter 5 the chronology now returns to developments in Paris, and the work of composers associated with the Groupe de Recherches Musicales (GRM), a major center of creative activity originating from the pioneering work of Pierre Schaeffer in the late 1940s and 1950s, in the first instance developing his concepts of *musique concrète*. This school of composing and its associated aesthetics exemplify a musical style that over the years has progressed from analog to digital technologies and been explored not only by members of GRM but also by other composers, working elsewhere, not only in Europe but also America, notably in Canada. Although for many years GRM was reliant on analog technologies, the transition to the digital domain resulted in a suite of composing resources that have proved to be unique and highly influential in the wider context. A study of the work of Francis Dhomont provides a significant insight into these important musical and technical developments, leading in turn to a detailed study of his work *Phonurgie*, completed in 1998.

At the start of the 1990s the true potential of the personal computer as a self-contained and increasingly powerful resource for composing computer music had yet to be fully grasped, but by the end of the decade it was becoming clear that the desktop environment would eventually replace even the powerful computer workstations that had been developed for high-end processing applications during the 1980s. It is thus all the more remarkable that a UK initiative dating from 1986 should have established a notable benchmark in this context at such an early stage. Known as the Composers Desktop Project (CDP), the associated group of pioneers set out to create composing resources that could match the capabilities of those provided by the major computer music institutions, but at the same time be affordable for individuals. This development is considered in the next chapter, which focuses on the work of Trevor Wishart in this context, both as a technical innovator and also a major composer, leading in due course to the composition of *Imago* in 2002, which is studied in detail.

Wishart's pioneering work with the CDP was materially influenced by the formative experiences he gained working at IRCAM as a visiting composer, an association that was to develop further as the years advanced. Another UK composer, Jonathan Harvey, was similarly to establish close links with IRCAM, resulting in a series of works that have been major contributions to the computer music repertory. His engagement with the medium is located within a creative locus that significantly embraces the world of conventional composing with acoustic instruments, thus drawing together many different aspects of contemporary composition and musical thought. The work chosen for special study, Harvey's *Fourth String Quartet* (2003), made significant demands on the real-time signal processing facilities available at IRCAM, and the ways in which these were creatively explored merit close scrutiny.

Although Harvey's direct interaction with developments in computer music were based primarily in European contexts, an important American dimension followed his appointment as professor in composition at Stanford University in 1995, creating significant opportunities for him to engage with developments at CCRMA. This highly productive cross-fertilization of perspectives is encountered again in Chapter 8, which studies the work of Cort Lippe, both as a composer and as a software developer. Having gained early experiences with the possibilities of computer music in the United States, he relocated to Europe, following in the footsteps of Truax a decade later to study at the Institute of Sonology. However, instead of then returning to the United States, Lippe moved to the Center for the Study of Mathematics and Automation in Music (CEMAMu), Paris, in 1982. Four years later he moved to IRCAM, remaining there until 1994, when he returned to the United States to take up a post at the University at Buffalo, New York. Although his initial status at IRCAM was as a visiting composer, he soon joined the staff as a technical assistant, becoming directly involved with the development of the facilities for producing sound materials in real time, including those extensively explored by Manoury. In a similar context he also came into contact with Harvey during his early exploration of the possibilities of live signal processing at IRCAM. In a creative context Lippe's repertory has focused in particular on the composition of works for live instrumental performers and digital electronics, leading to a series of software applications that are specially crafted for individual works. The work selected for detailed study, *Music for Tuba and Computer* (2008), provides a useful perspective on the technical and creative advances that have been made in such contexts over the years.

The final chapter studies the work of Natasha Barrett, paying particular attention to her use of advanced techniques for the spatialization of sound materials in performance spaces. Interest in the use of multiple loudspeakers dates back almost to the dawn of electronic music, and a variety of techniques have been developed over the years. These range from live diffusion techniques at the mixing desk in concert performance to the advanced mapping of sound images at the composition stage to multiple playback channels. Although significant progress was made in both contexts during the 1970s and 1980s using purely analog technologies, as computers became progressively more powerful, attention soon turned to the possibilities of developing advanced and highly sophisticated algorithms for the control of spatial imaging. Barrett took a keen interest in exploring such techniques at an early stage in her career, becoming in due course one of the leading practitioners in this regard. A particular landmark in this context has been her work with the advanced spatialization facilities developed at IRCAM, and a study of *Hidden Values*, completed in 2012, provides a revealing insight into this important aspect of computer music.

This book and the accompanying online materials are designed to offer the reader several different levels of engagement with the perspectives that emerge.

For those who wish to limit their further inquiries to the key technical and musical features of the works studied, the accompanying videos of interviews with composers, and with the developers of the software tools they used, will prove especially useful in this context. For others who wish to engage more directly with the associated methods of composing, the downloadable software includes programs that model the actual techniques used in each case. The reader can also directly explore the associated techniques for themselves, and in so doing gain not only unprecedented access to the underlying creative processes, but also explore their further potential.

The study of just nine works from the computer music repertory can only provide a selective window into the world of computer music, focused in the first instance on important works that have resulted from pioneering developments over the years. However, the methodology thus used is extensible to the works of other composers and the associated technologies they have employed, and it is hoped this initiative will encourage others so to do.

John Chowning
Stria

Contexts for *Stria*

Max Mathews and the beginnings of software for computer music

John Chowning's contributions to computer music have materially influenced the development of this medium, from the 1960s to the present day. In paying particular attention to his earlier work, up to and including *Stria*, it is important to appreciate that this critique embraces just a segment of a long and distinguished career in this regard. In a pioneering context Chowning is especially notable for two developments, the first being his research into the possibilities of digitally controlled sound spatialization, an important technique to be considered in depth in Chapter 8, and the second a distinctive and powerful technique of sound synthesis still widely used today, known as frequency modulation (FM) synthesis. These investigations took place at a time when analog methods of generating and shaping sound materials were ubiquitous, and the potential of the computer to provide a much more powerful and versatile resource for such purposes had yet to be realized.

Computer-based techniques of digital sound synthesis were pioneered by Max Mathews at Bell Telephone Laboratories, New Jersey, working with a team of co-researchers that included John Pierce, James Tenney, and Jean-Claude Risset. During the 1950s the acoustic research division of Bell Labs became increasingly interested in exploring ways and means of increasing the density of communications that could be transmitted via the telephone network. In the

16

first instance this research focused on the transmission of speech quality data, but in due course investigations extended to the more demanding requirements of music.

Up to this point, audio could only be transmitted in an analog format, with limited possibilities for multiplexing different telephone calls down a single data cable.[1] Attention soon turned to the possibility of transmitting such signals digitally, using analog-to-digital and digital-to-analog converters at either end of the line to code and decode the audio information. It occurred to Mathews that the development of computer software that could directly generate audio data in a digital format might provide an effective means of testing the performance and fidelity of such a system.

Such a proposition was far from straightforward, given the embryonic state of the computer industry at this time. The first commercial computer, the UNIVAC, appeared in 1951, and it was not until 1953 that IBM made its debut with the IBM 701, followed in 1954 by the IBM 704. All these early machines were based on valve technologies, of enormous physical proportions, and they were slow and unreliable.[2] In 1955 Bell Labs gained access to a 704 computer located in the IBM World Headquarters, New York, and it was with this machine that Mathews synthesized his first digitally generated study in 1957, *The Silver Scale*, a seventeen-second sequence of triangle wave tones composed by a colleague, Newman Guttman, using a nonstandard musical temperament.[3]

Known as Music I, this simple program signaled the start of a design revolution that was to underpin the future course of digital music technology. Although this sketch was a landmark achievement the limitations of the program as a composing tool were self-evident, in particular the lack of any functions to control both the volume and the attack and decay characteristics of the individual tones. In 1958 Bell Labs acquired its own computer, a faster and more powerful IBM 7094, based on the newer technology of transistors. This facilitated the development of Music II, a more versatile program that allowed the generation of four-part polyphony with a choice of sixteen different waveforms and a facility to control their dynamic characteristics. These enhancements, however, came at a price in terms of the complexity of the coding that was required to create these textures, as well as the extra demands made on the computer itself. Mathews realized that significant improvements had to be made to the design of the software if the computer was to achieve its true potential as a facility for synthesizing music.

The starting point for a more detailed study of the techniques employed in achieving this goal involves an understanding of the mathematics involved in the representation of audio signals in a digital format. The associated principles were first articulated by Claude Shannon and Warren Weaver in 1949 and these provided an important reference point for Mathews.[4] The schematic shown in Figure 1.1 provides a useful overview of the procedures involved in converting

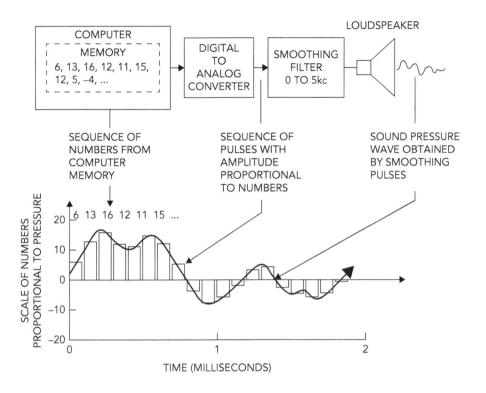

FIGURE 1.1

Schematic diagram depicting the conversion of a sequence of numbers stored in a computer memory to a sound pressure waveform. The sampling rate is 10,000 numbers per second to yield a bandwidth of 5,000 cycles per second [Hz] for the sound wave.[5]

a digitized waveform into an equivalent analog signal, ready for audition via an amplifier and loudspeaker.

The crucial considerations here in terms of the resulting fidelity are the frequency of the individual samples representing the waveform and their numerical accuracy. Put in the simplest terms, the speed of sample generation, referred to as the *sampling rate*, determines the maximum possible audio bandwidth (50 percent of the frequency) and the numerical accuracy of the individual samples determines the quality of the resulting sounds.[6] To give a present-day example, a conventional CD contains digital audio sampled at a rate of 44,100 samples per second, allowing a maximum audio bandwidth of 22,050 Hz, with each sample quantized to the maximum resolution possible from the binary coding of sixteen-bit sample values, which can embrace integer values from +32,767 to –32,768. This equates to a basic signal-to-noise ratio of about 98 dB.

These fidelity standards have proved generally acceptable to the audio industry and the listening public, although several techniques have been employed to improve the quality further, such as using oversampling techniques to improve the accuracy of quantization. It is important, however, to appreciate that such conditions were well beyond the reach of the early pioneers of computer music. Before the era of microchip technology, converters had to be constructed from discrete electronic components and resolutions of just ten or at the most twelve bits per sample were the order of the day, as were sampling rates that rarely exceeded 20,000 samples per second.[7] A closer look at the frequency setting of the smoothing filter in the above schematic, for example, indicates an audio bandwidth of 5 kHz, which in turn is associated with a sampling rate of just 10,000 samples per second, as stated by Mathews in the accompanying caption.

From a present-day perspective it is difficult to appreciate the significance of the challenging conditions faced by composers during the early days of computer music. Quite apart from these fundamental problems of music fidelity, access to computers was generally restricted to a select few individuals working in large scientific institutions, and the high cost of using these resources materially constrained the allocation of computing time. The associated data processing demands of music synthesis invariably consigned such tasks to time slots scheduled in the late hours of the night. To make matters worse, the special offline technical facilities necessary to convert the results from a digital to an analog format were often in locations remote from the main computer, requiring the physical transfer of digital sound files recorded on magnetic tape from one site to another. By the time Mathews started work on Music II, both the computer and the associated converter system were located in the same building, but this was not the case for his earlier work developing Music I, which required time-consuming journeys across New York each day.

A further constraint was the time required to compute the synthesis instructions, often proving to be many orders of magnitude greater than the duration of the resulting sounds. As a consequence, even when it became possible for individual users to submit synthesis tasks directly via a computer terminal for immediate computation rather than overnight, significant delays waiting for the calculations to complete were the rule rather than the exception.[8] Mathews realized that if composers were thus to be isolated from the processes that generate sound, it was necessary to develop a symbolic coding environment that could be readily understood and engaged with working entirely offline. Accordingly, the concept of the "orchestra" and the "score" was developed for what became generically known as the Music N family of programs. This arrangement draws on the familiar environment of an orchestra, consisting of a series of individual instruments that are activated by performance data, provided in an accompanying score.

At the heart of this coding environment, the building blocks for constructing instruments are known as *unit generators*, a repertory of core algorithms that embrace both synthesis and signal processing functions. The composer selects and configures the generators for each instrument, with further assistance where required from a set of mathematical functions that may be used to modify data passing from one algorithm to another. This transfer takes place at two levels, first in terms of the flow of audio data, and second in terms of the flow of control data. This dual method of linking sound-producing functions was conceived before a similar design strategy was adopted for the voltage-controlled analog synthesizer, launched by Robert Moog in 1966 at the start of a commercial revolution that was to embrace several other manufacturers before the end of the decade, including Buchla, ARP, and EMS London. Although the technology in the latter instance requires the physical interconnection of the individual hardware components, the architecture shared many features in common with that associated with software-based digital unit generators, notably a modular design approach where different devices, such as oscillators, filters, and envelope shapers, can be freely interconnected in the manner described above.

The functional similarities between voltage-controlled synthesizers and the facilities developed by Mathews for the Music N series of programs were noted by a number of contemporary commentators, including Mathews himself.[9] At the same time, some important differences may be identified. For example, the former provide a fully interactive working environment, generating sound in real time, whereas the latter offered essentially the converse. Furthermore voltage-controlled synthesizers could be purchased commercially as self-contained ready-to-use systems. By the time Mathews had completed an initial version of Music III in 1960, the foundations for the subsequent significant advances in digital technologies were firmly in place, but the exclusive nature of computer music systems at the time ensured that the latter remained relatively isolated from mainstream developments in the world of electronic music for several years.

Initially Mathews's associates at Bell Labs were primarily engineers, working at the forefront of developments in digital communications. In addition to Guttman, the head of his research unit, John Pierce, also composed a series of pioneering computer music studies during this formative period, including *Five against Seven—Random Canon* (1961) and *Variations in Timbre and Attack* (1961). It was the involvement of composers, however, that was to provide the extra dimension necessary to ensure the software fully achieved its creative potential.

The first composer to engage directly with the work at Bell Labs was David Lewin, a junior fellow in composition and theory studying with Milton Babbitt at Harvard.[10] During 1960–1961, following a course of instruction from Mathews on the principles of coding, Lewin prepared a series of synthesis tasks, sent by post from Harvard to Bell Labs for processing and subsequent return as audio recordings. Two short studies were produced before Lewin moved on to a teaching post at the University of California, Berkeley, to pursue different interests. He was followed by James Tenney, who joined Bell Labs in 1961. Having previously studied at the Julliard School of Music and Bennington College, Tenney transferred to the University of Illinois in 1959 to study algorithmic composition techniques with Lejaren Hiller, leading to an MA degree completed in 1961. Fortuitously, his subsequent move to Bell Labs allowed him to engage directly with the final stages of refining Music III, producing a series of six pioneering compositions, including *Analog #1: Noise Study* (1961) and

Five Stochastics Studies (1962). He also produced a detailed description of the program, published in 1963.[11] Although the subsequent development of Music IV by Mathews, completed in 1963 with assistance from Joan Miller, is generally better known, the basic design principles for the latter version were established with Music III.

Figure 1.2 provides an illustration from Tenney's description that provides a useful introduction to the key principles involved in the design of a Music III instrument. The example comprises a simple tone generator (described here as a timbre waveform generator) consisting of a wave table (P10) with two input controls.[12] The input on the left-hand side controls the amplitude of the output waveform, that on the right its frequency. The envelope generator uses a special amplitude function (F2), read through once for each new sonic event. The two inputs for the envelope generator, the (maximum) amplitude and the overall duration, are triggered via an associated note/event score command. The frequency value for the timbre generator supplied via the same command is also subject to dynamic variation via the vibrato generator. The function for the latter consists of a sine wave (F1), the associated amplitude control determining the depth of the vibrato and the frequency control the associated speed. The intermediate function (known as an "add" unit) combines two inputs: the core frequency of the note thus to be generated, and the vibrato function that is to be superimposed. Ironically, this early example of a Music N instrument also illustrates the basic principles involved in FM synthesis, the technique to be studied more closely in due course in terms of their subsequent implementation for the composition of John Chowning's *Stria*.[13]

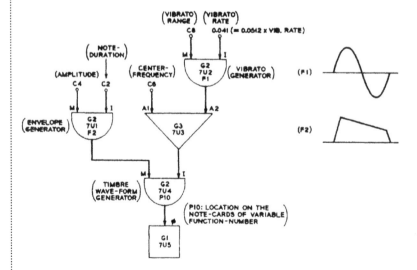

FIGURE 1.2

Design of a Music III instrument, illustrating the parameters involved in FM synthesis.[14]

The unit generators and mathematical functions available for Music III and Music IV provided a useful repertory of modular building blocks for both synthesis and signal processing tasks. The original Music IV library (1963) provided the following functions:[15]

1.	OUT	output unit
2.	OSCIL	standard table-lookup oscillator
3.	COSCIL	table-lookup oscillator with no phase reset
4.	VOSCIL	table-lookup oscillator with variable table number
5.	ADD2	add two inputs
6.	ADD3	add three inputs
7.	ADD4	add four inputs
8.	RANDI	interpolating band-limited noise generator
9.	RANDH	sample-and-hold band-limited noise generator
10.	MULT	multiply two inputs
11.	VFMULT	table-lookup unit
12.	RESON	ring-modulation resonant wave generator
13.	FILTER	second-order all-pole band pass filter
14.	LINEN	linear envelope generator (trapezoidal)
15.	EXPEN	single-scan table-lookup envelope

One of the biggest challenges during the pioneering era of computer music was a basic requirement to write all software in a code that was unique to the computer concerned. Known as an assembler language, this consists of a processor-specific instruction set, which had to be completely rewritten should the program be subsequently transferred to another computer either by choice or as a matter of necessity following a change of model. Fortunately, in the case of Bell Labs, the IBM 7094 remained in service for almost a decade, allowing Music IV to enjoy a relatively long and useful life span as a composing facility. Princeton University took a keen interest in Music IV, and in 1963 a copy of the program was transferred to a similar IBM 7094 on the campus by a team of researchers that included Hubert Howe, Godfrey Winham, and Jim Randall. It subsequently proved possible for this team to implement a number of improvements and additions, resulting in a version known as Music IVB.

By this stage it was becoming clear that writing software in low-level code not only limited its portability, but was also very time-consuming. In many instances the solution lay in a new generation of higher-level compilers, essentially interpreting programs that convert instructions written in a common language into the machine code specifically required by the host computer. Unfortunately, these advances came at the expense of overall computing efficiency, which could only be mitigated by continuing to write any time-critical processes in assembler code. Although such hybrid approaches require additional work developing suitable protocols for communicating between the two machine operating levels, the subsequent benefits were often to prove significant.[16] During the 1960s and early 1970s the language of choice for scientific users was FORTRAN (FORmula TRANslation), and a subsequent version of Music IVB completed in 1967 at Princeton, known as Music IVBF, used FORTRAN for the interpretation and compilation of synthesis instructions and assembler code for their execution.

During the mid-1960s Mathews became increasingly concerned with the development of a truly machine-independent version of Music IV that could be ported from one computer to another with the minimum of difficulty. The forthcoming replacement of the IBM 7094 by the much more powerful IBM 360 at Bell Labs, requiring the use of an entirely different assembler language, made this issue a matter of pressing importance. The initiative here was taken by Arthur Roberts at the Argonne Laboratories, Chicago, who developed a pilot version known as Music IVF in 1965. However, Mathews completed the definitive, all-FORTRAN version in 1966, known as Music V, subsequently installed in a number of institutions worldwide. The inevitable loss in processing efficiency, however, left others at the time less than convinced that this was necessarily the best way forward.

By the end of the decade other institutions had taken an interest in acquiring Music N software, notably the Massachusetts Institute of Technology (MIT) and Stanford University, and in both cases optimizing processing speed was considered the greater priority. As will be discussed further below, Stanford took the initiative producing Music 10, specially configured for the DEC PDP-10 mainframe computer in 1966. In a similar vein, Barry Vercoe, working at MIT, completed Music 360 for the IBM 360 in 1969. Fortunately, both of these third-generation computers remained in service worldwide until the early 1980s, and the subsequent IBM 370, introduced in the mid-1970s as a replacement for the 360, used the same assembler code.

The 1970s had also seen the introduction of the PDP-11, a minicomputer that was to prove especially important for several computer music initiatives, and some of these will be discussed in later chapters. This product of a new generation of more affordable and physically smaller computers opened up the possibilities of computer music to a number of institutions for the very first time, and Vercoe was quick to grasp the significance of this rapidly expanding market. Accordingly, he developed a version of Music 360 written in Macro-11, the PDP-11 assembler code, releasing Music 11 in 1976. Conversely, during the late 1970s, Richard Moore and Gareth Loy at the University of California, San Diego (UCSD) developed Cmusic, written for the DEC VAX, the computer that replaced the PDP-10. Like Music V this was written entirely in the higher-level programming language C, which has become one of the key resources for developing computer applications. The steady improvement in computing speeds since the late 1960s mitigated the consequential loss in processing efficiency, and this continuing trend encouraged Vercoe to release a C-based version of Music 11 in 1986. This program, Csound, finally secured the legacy of Mathews' pioneering work in computer music for use by future generations. Freely available via the Internet, this facility embraces an extensive repertory of synthesis and signal processing tools, available to all and still actively maintained by an extensive worldwide user community.

A material issue associated with the pioneering years of computer music relates to the continuum that extends from quasi-instrumental styles of composition, based on traditional methods of working with "note/events," to more abstract concepts of timbre, embracing the multitude of ways in which the associated spectral components can be creatively manipulated. In terms of balancing familiarity with the unknown, the significant time delays experienced between submitting a Music N task for computation and auditioning the outcome provided a powerful inducement for composers to embrace more imitative approaches rather than engage proactively with the unfamiliar. It was the particularly imaginative approach taken by Jean-Claude Risset, appointed as composer in residence at Bell Labs in 1964, that was to prove of material significance in overcoming more conservative attitudes in this regard.

Jean-Claude Risset and timbral synthesis

Risset was trained as a physicist and mathematician at the École Normale Supérieure, Paris, studying also piano with Robert Trimaille and composition with André Jolivet.[17] This combination of studies provided strong foundations for his subsequent engagement with the creative possibilities of computer music. As a student in the 1950s it is reasonable to assume that he would have engaged with Pierre Schaeffer's pioneering work with *musique concrète*, but this was not the case.[18] Risset offers the following explanation:

> I wanted to increase the functional part of timbre in my composing. Yet I resisted turning to electronic music—in Paris, it was mostly Pierre Schaeffer's *musique concrète*. I felt that electronic music yielded dull sounds that could only be made lively through manipulations which, to a large extent, ruined the control the composer could have over them. On the other hand, *musique concrète* did open an infinite world of sounds for music—but the control and manipulation one could exert upon them was rudimentary with respect to the richness of the sounds, which favored an esthetics of collage. Both techniques seemed to me to rely on ready-made objects or processes, which the composer could only warp for his purposes.[19]

These observations are revealing. Of particular interest is his initial rejection of techniques that were central to the aesthetics of Pierre Schaeffer and his associates. His views, however, were materially to change when he discovered that the digital computer could provide the degree of control and manipulation he was seeking, not only in terms of synthesis from first principles, but also in the processing of acoustically generated sounds.

Prior to the early 1960s, knowledge of the work being carried out by Mathews at Bell Labs had not extended significantly beyond those directly associated with the institution. This situation was to change in 1963 with the publication of a landmark article by Mathews on his work in the journal *Science*, with an international readership that extended to a much wider research community, including Risset.[20] This article was to prove a major stimulus for Risset in terms of seeking ways and means of directly engaging with the possibilities of computer music, and having secured sponsorship from a French research funding agency he arrived at Bell Labs the following year. His preoccupation with timbre led him to analyze the complex characteristics of acoustically generated instrumental sounds in terms of the individual spectral components, using the data to resynthesize the sounds using Music IV. His work modeling brass tones, notably trumpet sounds, was especially significant in this context, and, as will be seen in due course, his discoveries were to prove of special interest to Chowning.

Compulsory national service required Risset to return to France, 1965–1967, and by the time he returned to Bell Labs work on Music V was already well advanced. Nonetheless he was able to contribute a number of useful refinements to the software while at the same time starting to explore its creative potential as a composing resource.[21] His first work, *Little Boy* (1968), was based on a play by Pierre Halet recalling the dropping of the first atomic bomb on Hiroshima in 1945, seen through the mind of the pilot.[22] The transformations of timbre that are used to underpin the musical argument here established an important repertory of synthesis and signal processing techniques for his subsequent compositions, including procedures such as the manipulation of harmonic arpeggios and spectral processing of selected parameters within individual sounds while retaining the key characteristics of others. His work in the latter context anticipated the repertory of techniques based on the principles of linear predictive coding and phase vocoding that were to be extensively explored by computer music composers in subsequent decades.

The most significant piece to emerge from Risset's work at Bell Labs was *Mutations*, completed in 1969 just before his final return to France. This was a commission from Groupe de Recherches Musicales (GRM) in Paris, and in many respects it represents an extension of ideas initially pursued in *Little Boy*. The following comments by the composer provide a helpful perspective on his emerging thinking at this time:

> [The works] implement the scientific developments that made it possible to imitate acoustic instruments—such as brass, clarinet, piano and percussion—and to compose the internal structure of sound, in particular by:

- synthesizing gong-like or bell-like tones composed as chords with a prescribed harmony, hence prolonging harmonic control within the realm of timbre
- dispersing in time harmonic components that usually sound together, just as a prism disperses white light
- intimately transforming "inharmonic" sounds, that is, sounds made up of non-harmonically related components. By changing the amplitude envelopes of the components, I could leave the underlying harmony unchanged but influence the listener toward either focalized, synthetic perception (hearing separate sound objects or events) or distributed, analytic perception (hearing textures)
- implementing pitch paradoxes. For the compositions mentioned above, I manufactured tones with fractal structures (in other words, tones that look similar when examined at different scales) that seem to glide indefinitely up or down in pitch, or seem to go down in pitch but end up much higher than where they started.

Mutations, for example is a metaphoric journey from discontinuous pitch scales into a continuum of pitch. This transition happens through going to higher harmonics separated by narrowing intervals.[23]

These works were arguably the most advanced and insightful computer-generated works to emerge from the 1960s, very much establishing the shape of things to come, not least in the context of exploring the creative potential of the complementary techniques of analysis and resynthesis, where a study of the spectral characteristics of naturally generated sounds can provide not only a detailed understanding of their spectral content, but also the data necessary to create entirely new variations and transformations.

Whereas Risset's work at Bell Labs was predicated in the first instance on the study of acoustic instrument sounds, the transformations he achieved in terms of composing works such as the above were undoubtedly ground-breaking. Perhaps the most significant legacy of his work at Bell Labs was an *Introductory Catalog of Computer-Synthesized Sounds*, completed in 1969, complete with the Music V orchestras and scores required to reproduce them. One further characteristic of *Mutations* is of particular significance at this point. In terms of the repertory of synthesis techniques employed, it was the very first substantive work to make use of John Chowning's pioneering algorithms for FM synthesis, and it is to these important developments that our attention is now turned.[24]

John Chowning and the evolution of FM synthesis

John Chowning's career started with a period of military service during the early 1950s, including studies at the US Navy School of Music. In 1956 he enrolled at Wittenberg University, Springfield, Ohio, completing a music degree in 1959. A scholarship then took him to Paris to study with Nadia

Boulanger, thus bringing him into direct contact with the forefront of developments in contemporary music in Europe, including the emerging genre of electronic music.

On his return to the United States in 1962, Chowning commenced post-graduate studies with Leland Smith at Stanford University, completing his doctorate in 1966. Like Risset he first became aware of developments at Bell Labs via the earlier-mentioned article on computer music by Mathews published in *Science* in 1963, resulting in a visit to Mathews at Bell Labs in the summer of 1964. He returned with a copy of Music IV coded as a deck of punched cards. After some internal negotiations he was able to install the program on an IBM 7090 in the computer science department at Stanford, using a shared data disk facility to transfer the output files directly to a small PDP-1 computer located in the artificial intelligence department. The latter included an X-Y plotter display that could be configured to convert digital audio into an analog format for reproduction via a conventional loudspeaker.

This arrangement was not entirely satisfactory. In particular, the data conversion facilities only provided a monophonic output of limited fidelity. Work soon commenced on a matrix of four digital-to-analog converters specifically designed by Joe Zingheim for audio applications. This facility, completed in 1966, created for the first time a multichannel composing environment for computer music. Each of the four output channels offered twelve-bit sample resolution at a maximum speed of 25,000 samples per second. In a related context the installation of a DEC PDP-6 computer provided a powerful incentive for the development of a new version of Music IV, written specifically for this computer by John Chowning and James Moorer. The PDP-6 was soon replaced by a PDP-10, which became a popular mid-range computer for a number of research institutions worldwide. Fortunately, it also used essentially the same instruction set as the PDP-6, and with assistance from David Poole, Music 10 was completed in 1966. The award of Chowning's doctorate in the same year led to a position as a member of the faculty, along with the start of an intensive period of personal research into the development of synthesis algorithms for computer music.

Although he was aware of Risset's work during the early 1960s investigating the modeling of instrumental sounds by means of additive synthesis techniques, Chowning did not directly pursue these possibilities at this time, further progress on Risset's part, as noted earlier, being suspended while he returned to France for national service. Instead Chowning started to explore other ways of generating music, including the technique outlined in James Tenney's earlier article on Music III discussed above, that of applying vibrato to pitched sounds.[25] Although initially unaware of the true significance of this methodology, a sequence of events led him to discover the possibilities thus created for synthesis by means of frequency modulation.

His most important first step in this context came about as a result of a simple data coding error.[26] It was a chance mis-keying of a vibrato speed of one hundred cycles per second instead of ten cycles that led him to discover that at higher speeds of pitch, modulation frequency sidebands are generated either side of the primary pitch. The functional characteristics of frequency modulation in mathematical terms were already well known to the telecommunications industry in the context of broadcasting television and radio signals, but their significance when applied directly to frequencies within the audio spectrum was almost unknown.

Whereas analog frequency modulation techniques were already being explored by composers using commercial voltage-controlled synthesizers (and there are some notable earlier precedents in this context that can be identified in the works of leading pioneers of electronic music, such as Karlheinz Stockhausen), such composing environments did not permit the refinement of parameter control possible in the digital domain. Crucially, the mathematics of frequency modulation facilitate the generation of a rich and varied repertory of dynamically varying timbres, the sophistication of which is determined by the scope and nature of the functions used to regulate the modulating characteristics. Such a measure of control was only possible in a fully programmable digital environment.

In 1973 Chowning published what has become universally acknowledged as the standard reference text on the implementation of frequency modulation in the audio spectrum, and the following summary of the key features discussed in the article provides useful foundations for the subsequent study of *Stria*.[27] The diagram in Figure 1.3 illustrates the organization of a pair of oscillators to create a basic FM generator (the "P" values refer to the fields containing the data values on the score card used to activate the associated instrument at the designated point in time).

The significant components here are the carrier frequency, known in FM theory as the "c" component; the modulating frequency, known as the "m" component; and the deviation component, known as the "d" component. If the modulating frequency is very low, say eight to ten cycles per second (hertz) then the effect will be perceived as a pitch vibrato, the depth of which being determined by its amplitude. If, however, the modulating frequency is increased beyond about 20 Hz, the ear can no longer perceive the pitch variations as a function of time. Instead, a series of discrete side band frequencies are generated either side of the carrier frequency, at frequency intervals and individual amplitudes controlled by the values of the "m" and "d" parameters. As already noted, the deviation value is the amplitude input to the controlling oscillator, but since this parameter determines how far the modulated frequency will fluctuate either side of the central, or carrier frequency, its numeric value directly translates into a frequency parameter. Thus, if the carrier frequency is,

28

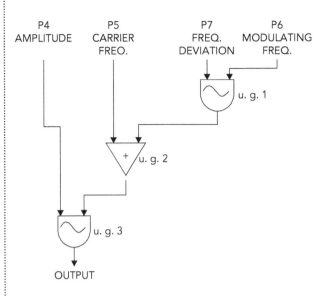

FIGURE 1.3

Diagram of a basic FM
generator.[28]

say, 400 Hz, and the numeric value of amplitude input to the controlling oscillator is 50, the modulated frequency will fluctuate between c + d and c − d, that is 450 Hz and 350 Hz.

Whereas these three variables determine the nature of the frequency modulation as a function in time, it is the consequential generation of frequency sidebands and the nature thereof that is of particular interest. Chowning discovered that sidebands are produced either side of the carrier frequency in the sequence c + m, c + 2m, c + 3m, etc., and c − m, c − 2m, c − 3m, etc. Most significantly, the associated deviation (amplitude) value not only determines how far this sequence of sidebands extends either side of the carrier frequency, but also the amplitude values of each sideband. In so doing a proportion of the amplitude of the carrier frequency is stolen and redistributed to the sidebands, the resulting timbre being determined by the frequency and amplitude of the sidebands thus produced. In terms of regulating these characteristics, a key concept here is that of the modulation index, known as "I," which is defined mathematically as the value of "d" divided by the value of "m" (I = d / m). Thus, if "d" has a value of 20 and "m" has a value of 20, the index is 1, whereas if "d" has a value of 90 and "m" has a value of 30, the index is 3. Whereas "d" will determine the frequency spacing of the sidebands either side of the carrier frequency, the index value "I" will determine the number of sidebands and their respective amplitudes, along with the residual amplitude of the carrier frequency (see Figure 1.4).

Varying "d" while maintaining "m" will keep the sideband frequencies constant but vary the number generated and their relative strengths. Varying "m" while maintaining "d" will fix the number of sidebands and their relative strengths but vary their frequency spacing. Varying both values will lead to

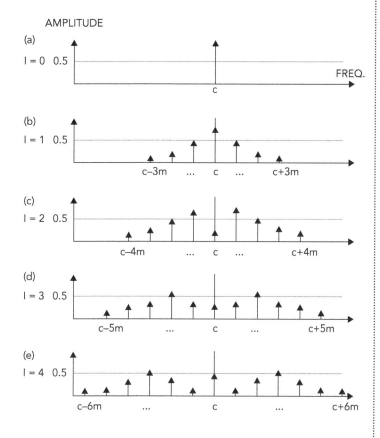

AMPLITUDE

FIGURE 1.4

Amplitudes of carrier and sidebands for modulation indexes ranging from 0 to 4.[29]

further complexities in terms of the resulting timbres. For example, increasing or decreasing "m" and "d" in a fixed ratio, thus maintaining a constant index value, will fix the number of sidebands and their relative strengths, but vary their frequency spacing.

Presentation 4 in the interactive software accompanying this chapter includes a demonstration of simple frequency modulation. Using this software, you can adjust the parameters ("carrier frequency," "modulation frequency," and "modulation index," or "deviation") in real time to hear the aural results. The software also provides a visual representation of the sidebands generated. You can, for instance, by setting the carrier frequency to 800 Hz, the modulation frequency to 100 Hz, and then changing the modulation index from 0 to 4, recreate the diagram above. There is also an option to display the frequencies of the sidebands numerically. Demonstration Video 1.1 shows the software in action. ⏺

The ways in which the distribution and individual amplitudes of sidebands change according to the index is determined by what are known as Bessel functions, and the diagram in Figure 1.5 illustrates their nature.

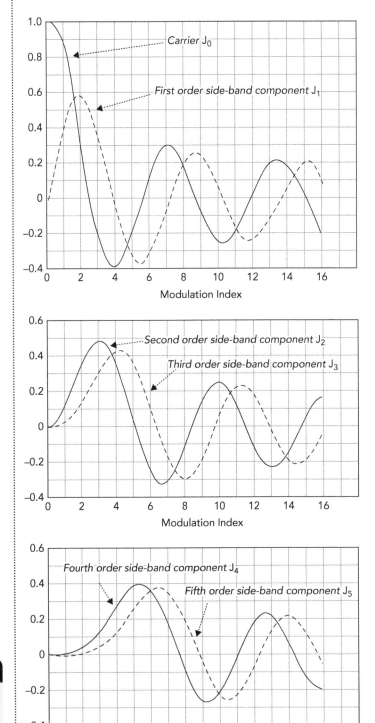

FIGURE 1.5

Bessel functions determining the amplitudes of the carrier and the first five sidebands according to the modulation index.[30]

Although Chowning carried out his initial investigations using Music 10, the examples of more fully developed FM instruments provided in the article were written in Music V to make it easier for others to explore their creative potential.[31] The following schematic provides a useful starting point for exploring

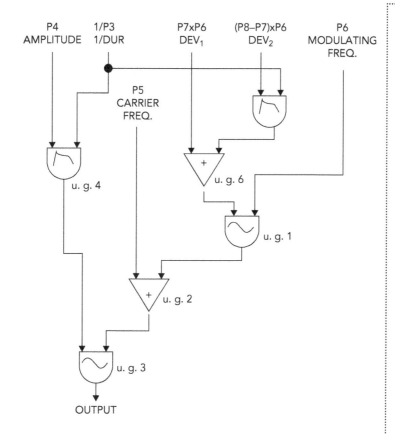

P4
AMPLITUDE

1/P3
1/DUR

P5
CARRIER
FREQ.

P7xP6
DEV₁

(P8–P7)xP6
DEV₂

P6
MODULATING
FREQ.

u. g. 4

u. g. 6

u. g. 1

+ u. g. 2

u. g. 3

OUTPUT

FIGURE 1.6

Diagram of an FM generator, incorporating envelope shapers.[32]

the characteristics of FM in more detail. In essence this is a simple modification of the basic configuration given above to incorporate envelope shapers both for the modulated wave and the amplitude (= the deviation "d") of the modulating wave (enabling these parameters to be varied dynamically so as to shape timbres over time), demonstrating further similarities with the Tenney example provided earlier (see Figure 1.6).

The "P" values, as before, refer to fields on the activating "score" data card. P3 is the overall duration of the event and 1/P3 thus provides the value necessary for the envelope shapers for both control oscillators to cycle through the respective envelope functions precisely once. The slightly more complex configuration for determining the deviation of the modulating wave arises from Chowning's research into the most productive ways of dynamically controlling the resulting timbre. Here he discovered the value of linking together the envelope function used to regulate the amplitude of both component oscillators so that the brightness of the resulting spectra is directly proportional to its overall loudness, the variation thus applied to the former tracking between two index values, P7 (index 1) and P8 (index 2). Such a characteristic closely matches the dynamic response characteristic of a number of acoustic instruments, notably the trumpet.[33]

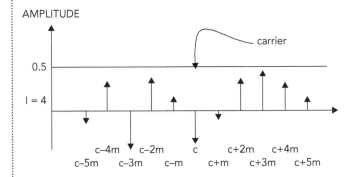

FIGURE 1.7

Sidebands with out-of-phase components represented below the X-axis.[34]

Such dynamic variation of FM timbre was essential for John Chowning in composing Stria. *Presentation 7 in the accompanying software shows this in action. You can see the envelopes progressing through time and see and hear the effect of this on the timbre in real time. The detail of this in relation to* Stria *will be described later, but for now Demonstration Video 1.2 provides an illustration of dynamically evolving FM in action.* ▶

One further characteristic of FM synthesis deserves particular attention in this consideration of its key features, the phase of the individual sidebands. These components consist of sine waves, each associated with a specific frequency. If these are studied more closely it transpires that some of these are in phase with each other, whereas others are 180 degrees out of phase. Providing the operating conditions are such that all the sidebands have a frequency greater than zero, this detail from an audio perspective is of no consequence, since the ear cannot detect these phase differences. However, under certain conditions these characteristics can prove materially significant. Returning to the earlier chart of sidebands generated at different frequencies, with the phase component now added, the mapping of sidebands for an index of 4 is thus modified as show in Figure 1.7.

In situations where the sidebands are at frequencies less than zero, these are folded back into the audible spectrum, but with the phase reversed. In some cases, such folded-back signals reinforce existing positive frequencies. In other cases, where they have opposite phases, they can partially or totally cancel a positive frequency (see Figure 1.8).

In the above example, at an index of 4 with identical carrier and modulating frequencies of 100 Hz, the result is a tone consisting of a fundamental frequency of 100 Hz, plus five harmonics with the relative amplitudes indicated. Although this example is a special case, and other combinations of "c" and "m" values can produce similar coincidences, notably where "m" is a multiple or submultiple of "c," these complexities of phase in the case of negative frequency sidebands that are folded back into the audio spectrum take on a further dimension when

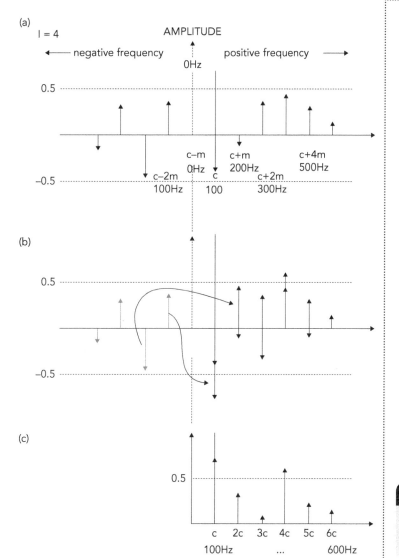

(a)

(b)

(c)

FIGURE 1.8

Phase inversion process
consequent to fold-back
from 0 Hz.[35]

consideration is given to dynamic variations of "c" or "m," where sideband frequencies move in different directions.[36]

> *Return to Presentation 4 in the accompanying software and select the option to "Display negative amplitudes." This will enable you to experiment with the features described above, changing parameter values and hearing and seeing the resulting spectrum, as presented in Demonstration Video 1.3.* ▶

The complexity of the relationships between the parameters used to control the processes of FM synthesis and the resulting sonic spectra and the significance of these for prospective composers should not be underestimated, as the subsequent study of *Stria* will show. Whereas in the case of alternative techniques such as additive synthesis it is possible to work directly with the characteristics of individual spectral components, this is not the case here. Initially Chowning was thus faced with significant challenges in terms of determining how best to develop the technique in a musically meaningful manner, but his perseverance led him to unlock the true potential of this powerful synthesis technique and explore its creative possibilities to the full. Here the contributions of Risset were to prove especially important.

Chowning first became acquainted with Risset's work modeling instrumental sounds following a visit to Bell Labs in December 1967, but it was a further two years before the true significance of these investigations in the context of FM synthesis became clear to him. The gateway to this deeper understanding was Risset's discovery that the timbre of acoustic trumpet sounds varies according to the volume of the instrument, brighter characteristics being associated with louder sounds, and vice versa. Indeed, closer scrutiny of his findings led Chowning to design the FM instrument studied earlier, where the modulating index directly tracks the volume of the generated sound. The realism of the result can be verified by recreating the instrument in a suitable Music N program such as Csound or a modern version of Max/MSP using the control data values provided in the 1973 article.[37] In addition to introducing the reader to the parameters necessary to generate brass sounds, Chowning also provides the data necessary to generate woodwind and percussion sounds, the latter including pitched instruments such as tubular bells.

Having thus developed a basic library of FM instruments, the time was now ripe to explore the creative possibilities of this synthesis method. The initiative here was taken by Risset, who, as noted earlier, included FM-generated sounds in *Mutations* (1969), followed by Chowning who composed *Sabelithe* (1971), and *Turenas* (an anagram of "natures") (1972). Both pieces provide a valuable introduction to the techniques used in *Stria*, demonstrating the subtleties and transformations of timbre that can be dynamically produced in this manner. In considering these works it is important to bear in mind the implications of the non-real-time environment on the composing process, in particular the need to work in a definitive manner, with little or no scope for experimentation. As a consequence, the resulting musical argument is especially persuasive in terms of the ways in which the contributing materials are articulated and combined with significant attention to detail. In *Sabelithe*, for example, an engaging dialogue develops between nonpitched percussion sounds and those of a brass instrument. As Chowning notes:

> At various points in the composition there are timbral transformations, but the most dramatic is near the end where a short, noisy, discontinuous percussive sound is gradually transformed into a Risset inspired brass tone. The carrier/modulation frequency ratio begins at 1:1.414, producing an inharmonic spectrum and a large index of modulation causes aliasing and thus noise. With each repetition of the element, the ratio converges toward 1:1 and the index reduces to one appropriate for

a brasslike tone. It is a compelling example and demonstrates the value of having a large timbral space controlled within a small parameter space.[38]

Whereas *Turenas* was composed using the same basic repertory of FM instruments used in *Sabelithe*, the piece is slightly more fluid in terms of the interactions created between the contributing components. Once again transformations of timbre between pitched and nonpitched sounds are distinctive components, and a notable feature is the computer-controlled projection of sounds in space, using the four digital-to-analog converters to create a quadraphonic listening environment. As noted earlier, his interests in this aspect of computer music composition predated his work on FM synthesis, and provided the motivation for the design and construction of his four-channel digital-to-analog converter system back in 1964. Spatial manipulation also features in *Sabelithe*, albeit working within the more modest constraints of a stereo environment. As discussed further in Chapter 8, Chowning was one of the first composers to explore techniques for spatial projection in a digitally controlled environment, and some aspects of his work in this context will be considered in the analysis of *Stria* that follows.[39]

The early 1970s were associated with some significant developments affecting the fortunes of both Chowning and Stanford. Whereas at an institutional level there was considerable uncertainty at the start of the decade as to the future of Chowning's work on FM synthesis, this was resolved in 1974 via a licensing agreement secured with Yamaha for ten years, granting the company exclusive rights to the manufacture of synthesizers using a hardware-based, real-time implementation of the algorithm. This development secured the commercial path toward the DX7 and its successors, spearheading a design revolution that was materially to transform the technologies of electronic and computer music. By this time Stanford was also being actively consulted by Pierre Boulez over proposals to establish a leading international research center in Paris to be known as IRCAM (Institut de Recherche et Coordination Acoustique/Musique), and Chowning and his associates were to prove highly influential in shaping its early development. In 1975 its status was further enhanced by the establishment of the Stanford Center for Computer Research in Music and Acoustics (CCRMA), bringing together the interests of musicians and technologists with additional funding to support a range of new and important research initiatives. The stage was thus set for the composition of Chowning's next work, *Stria* (1977), which will now be studied in detail.

Inside *Stria*

Like all the works featured as case studies in this book, *Stria* could not have been composed without digital technology. Indeed, the musical potential of technology is central to the way in which the work is conceived at every stage. On one level, this concerns the generation of timbres, produced exclusively using frequency modulation synthesis. On another level the computer facilitated the deployment of a new pitch scale and even a newly defined "octave." Digital technology also enabled the use of precise durational structures and the spatial distribution of the sounds. Using computer software meant that the composer could define the higher-level shape of the events that constitute the work, but also allow the detail of individual elements to be rendered using an algorithm he devised especially for this purpose.

Stria was composed in 1977 using two different software programs. As in the case of preceding works, Sabelithe and Turenas, the sound was generated using Music 10.[40] As discussed earlier, this program takes two data files as inputs that are named, by analogy with acoustic music practice, the "orchestra" file and the "score" file. As the name indicates, the orchestra file contains "instruments," and these can be built by the user from component unit generators. The "score" file plays these instruments. It contains "note" statements each with data, such as the start, duration, and frequency information, for notes to be played by a specified instrument. In the case of Stria, the orchestra file is relatively simple. It contains the definition of the FM instrument, described in more detail below, and defines the parameters that control it. There is also a global reverberation instrument.

Composers working with Music 10 or similar programs often write data into a score file entirely by hand. However, John Chowning created another piece of software for this purpose so that he could generate the data for individual notes, or "elements" as he names them, automatically. Chowning programmed this set of procedures using SAIL, the Stanford Artificial Intelligence Language, developed especially for the PDP-10. This program takes data provided by the user to define an "event," and on the basis of this information generates a sequence of notes. Although by the mid-1970s the speed of computers was significantly improving, neither Music 10 nor the SAIL program ran in real time. Indeed, especially with the process of sound generation, long delays could be involved, sometimes lasting several hours while the sound was calculated. From our discussions with the composer it is clear that he did not necessarily view this as a disadvantage. He valued the time for reflection and planning in between auditions.[41]

> You can use the accompanying software to watch videos of Chowning evoking several aspects of his creative process on Stria and beyond. Demonstration Video 1.4 presents this feature and shows an excerpt of the composer expanding on the waiting times involved in the computer-based sound generation. ▶

To accompany this text, we have produced an emulation of the whole process used to create Stria, both the SAIL procedures and those used for the sound generation. With today's technology our emulation can run in real time and as a single program. The data for the SAIL algorithms can be entered either by line commands in response to on-screen prompts, as in the original program, or in a more modern format using mouse control and number boxes. The sound generation part of the program is transparent and happens immediately after the data has been entered. We have also emulated the synthesis algorithm so that readers can experiment with its operation.[42] The main focus of the discussions in this chapter is on the shaping of the music through the use of the SAIL algorithms to create the musical events.

The golden ratio

The golden ratio plays an important role at many levels in this work. This ratio (1.6180339887 . . .), which is abbreviated to 1.618 by Chowning in the context of *Stria*, has been found to feature in many contexts, including the structure of ancient monuments, in nature and in music.[43] It is also related to the Fibonacci sequence (0, 1, 1, 2, 3, 5, 8, 13 . . .).[44] Successive pairs of numbers in this sequence approximate the golden ratio more and more closely as the sequence progresses. For some people this ratio takes on an almost mystical character, but as Chowning has said, he chose this ratio for purely practical reasons:

> It was an aural choice. I had read a little bit about the golden ratio in music . . . but that was not the driving force, it was the sound I was interested in.[45]

Having used other ratios previously, he wanted to try something different, and this one fit his requirements in that it could be used to generate rich timbres. The most striking way in which the ratio is used is in relation to the pitch structure of the work. Rather than use the traditional ratio of 2:1 to define an octave relationship, Chowning structured *Stria* around a new "pseudo-octave" defined by the golden ratio, 1.618:1. As will be seen in more detail later, this octave is then divided not into the traditional twelve semitone steps of Western music, but rather into nine or eighteen divisions. It is significant that this division bears no relation to the golden ratio or the Fibonacci sequence; it is rather another example of Chowning's pragmatic approach to compositional decision-making. This was the division he found worked best after a number of trials:

> I wrote a little SAIL procedure to sound all the tones of a cluster within a pseudo-octave, and I looked at the proximity of partials and chose a division that produced the fewest number of partial interactions that were above about 5 Hz—that critical band that produces roughness. . . . So, nine was that division, based on a couple of approximate trials, maybe seven, eight, nine, ten.[46]

The golden ratio also plays an important role in the structuring of temporal aspects of the work, both the timing and duration of individual events and the large-scale structure.

Timbre and FM synthesis in *Stria*

In acoustic music, timbre is to a large extent constrained by the nature of the instruments or voices employed. These instruments are preconstructed as physical entities and cannot be changed significantly. With computer music, however, the potential exists to build virtual instruments as part of the compositional process, and to define very precisely every aspect of their timbre, making timbral construction a part of the creative development of the work. Using FM synthesis to generate the timbres in *Stria* enabled John Chowning to shape the spectra he used, controlling precisely the partials present in each sonority. The composer built on the expertise he had already developed in FM synthesis and used in his earlier compositions *Sabelithe* and *Turenas*. *Stria* uses the same FM configuration throughout: a single carrier is modulated in parallel by two modulators. Using two modulators in this way greatly enriches the resulting timbre. The process can be thought of as in two stages. The first modulator produces a set of sidebands radiating out from the carrier frequency as with single modulator FM:

$$\left[\ldots \left(F_c - \left(2 \times F_{m1} \right) \right), \left(F_c - \left(1 \times F_{m1} \right) \right), F_c, \left(F_c + \left(1 \times F_{m1} \right) \right), \left(F_c + \left(2 \times F_{m1} \right) \right) \ldots \right]$$

where F_c is the carrier frequency, and F_{m1} is the first modulation frequency.

The strength of these sidebands and their aural significance depends on the modulation index, as described above.[47] The second modulator applies the same modulation process to all the frequencies (carrier and sidebands) generated at the first stage and produces sidebands around each of these, following the same principles. Table 1.1 illustrates this showing the derivation of the frequencies for the first two sidebands. Two-modulator FM synthesis therefore greatly proliferates the number of sidebands and the richness of the timbre. Chowning found that working with two modulators and using relatively low

TABLE 1.1

Frequencies of the first sidebands of a two-modulator FM synthesis

Modulator 1 Modulator 2	Sideband −2	Sideband −1	Original	Sideband +1	Sideband +2
Sideband +2	$F_c - (2 \times F_{m1})$ $+ (2 \times F_{m2})$	$F_c - (1 \times F_{m1})$ $+ (2 \times F_{m2})$	$F_c + (2 \times F_{m2})$	$F_c + (1 \times F_{m1})$ $+ (2 \times F_{m2})$	$F_c + (2 \times F_{m1})$ $+ (2 \times F_{m2})$
Sideband +1	$F_c - (2 \times F_{m1})$ $+ (1 \times F_{m2})$	$F_c - (1 \times F_{m1})$ $+ (1 \times F_{m2})$	$F_c + (1 \times F_{m2})$	$F_c + (1 \times F_{m1})$ $+ (1 \times F_{m2})$	$F_c + (2 \times F_{m1})$ $+ (1 \times F_{m2})$
Original	$F_c - (2 \times F_{m1})$	$F_c - (1 \times F_{m1})$	F_c	$F_c + (1 \times F_{m1})$	$F_c + (2 \times F_{m1})$
Sideband −1	$F_c - (2 \times F_{m1})$ $- (1 \times F_{m2})$	$F_c - (1 \times F_{m1})$ $- (1 \times F_{m2})$	$F_c - (1 \times F_{m2})$	$F_c + (1 \times F_{m1})$ $- (1 \times F_{m2})$	$F_c + (2 \times F_{m1})$ $- (1 \times F_{m2})$
Sideband −2	$F_c - (2 \times F_{m1})$ $- (2 \times F_{m2})$	$F_c - (1 \times F_{m1})$ $- (2 \times F_{m2})$	$F_c - (2 \times F_{m2})$	$F_c + (1 \times F_{m1})$ $- (2 \times F_{m2})$	$F_c + (2 \times F_{m1})$ $- (2 \times F_{m2})$

modulation indexes provided him with the timbral richness he was seeking while allowing him to retain careful control over the harmonic content of the timbre.[48]

The golden ratio in the context of FM synthesis

One of John Chowning's aims was to shape many different aspects of the music according to the golden ratio. A particular feature of this ratio in relation to FM synthesis provided him with the opportunity to create timbres, many of whose partials were related by this ratio: summing two numbers related by the golden ratio (GR) generates a third number also related by this same ratio. In other words: $GR^n + GR^{n+1} = GR^{n+2}$.

For example:

$$GR^0(1.000) + GR^1(1.618) = GR^2(2.618), \text{ or}$$

$$GR^1(1.618) + GR^2(2.618) = GR^3(4.236)$$

Similarly, with subtraction: $GR^{n+1} - GR^n = GR^{n-1}$
For example:

$$GR^2(2.618) - GR^1(1.618) = GR^0(1.000)$$

Since FM synthesis generates sidebands in the spectrum whose frequencies are the result of adding and subtracting the carrier frequency and the modulator frequency, if these frequencies are related by the golden ratio, then so will the first upper and lower sidebands in the timbre produced. This does not apply to later sidebands, and Chowning tends to use low modulation indexes, thereby focusing on the first sidebands. With the double modulator configuration used in *Stria*, it is possible to select values for both of the modulator frequencies and the carrier frequency that further exploit this feature of the golden ratio, and, not surprisingly, Chowning frequently takes advantage of this opportunity.

For example, in the very first event of the work, Chowning specifies the following relationships between the carrier frequency and the modulator frequencies (they are specified in the input to the SAIL algorithm in terms of ratios rather than actual frequencies, as the algorithm then generates a

TABLE 1.2

Relative frequencies of the first sidebands with golden ratios for modulator frequencies

Event 0 data: F_c = 1.0, F_{m1} = 1.618, F_{m2} = 1.618

	SB −2	SB −1	Original	SB +1	SB +2
SB +2	**1.000**	**2.618**	**4.236**	5.854	7.472
SB +1	**−0.618**	**1.000**	**2.618**	**4.236**	5.854
Original	−2.236	**−0.618**	**1.000**	**2.618**	**4.236**
SB −1	−3.854	−2.236	**−0.618**	**1.000**	**2.618**
SB −2	−5.472	−3.854	−2.236	**−0.618**	**1.000**

TABLE 1.3

Relevant powers of the golden ratio (1.618^n)

n	−1	0	1	2	3
GR^n	0.618	1.000	1.618	2.618	4.236

succession of elements at different pitches using the same FM ratios): carrier frequency = 1.0; modulator frequency 1 ratio = 1.618; modulator frequency 2 ratio = 1.618. Table 1.2 shows the first few sidebands generated by this data (in the format used in the above table). The numbers in bold are related to each other by powers of the golden ratio, see Table 1.3. Aurally, in most situations, it is the absolute value of the frequency that matters; negative values sound the same but with the phase inverted.

In this way many of, though not all, the partials of the timbres generated in *Stria* are related by the golden ratio.

Presentation 5 in the accompanying software provides an interactive version of this chart that allows you to see the results of using the data from the different events that make up Stria, *or to try out other data. The software also shows the strength of the different sidebands and how these vary as the modulation indexes change. As well as seeing the data you can hear the results. Demonstration Video 1.6 shows this in action.* ▶

Stria's synthesis algorithm

Bringing all these factors together, Presentation 8 in the accompanying software presents an emulation of the complete synthesis algorithm used in Stria. *This provides readers with the opportunity to experiment with the process used to generate sounds in* Stria, *trying out different parameter settings. Demonstration Video 1.7 illustrates this, showing the software in action.* ⏵

In composing *Stria*, however, John Chowning did not input data for individual elements. Instead, he created an algorithm to generate this data automatically. He defined "events," and the algorithm then produced the data for the "elements" required for each event. In its original version, *Stria* is made up of thirty-three events.[49] These events each comprise a variable number of elements. In most respects, elements might be thought of as equivalent to notes in a more traditional context. Chowning chose not to define every element by hand, but rather developed an algorithm in SAIL to calculate the data for each element. The composer specifies data concerning the shape of an event and the algorithm; the SAIL code then calculates the elements. The algorithm is determinate: providing the algorithm with the same input data will always lead to the same results. In theory these calculations could therefore be done by hand, but using a computer makes the process much faster, and it enabled Chowning to try out many alternatives.

There are twenty-six variables that define an event in the original SAIL program.[50] The function of each of these parameters will be described below but can be summarized as follows:

Structure of an event:

(Event type)
Number of elements
Number of recursions

Time parameters:

(Event begin time)
Event duration
Event attack time
Element duration factor

Frequency and timbre parameters:

Reset count in frequency table
Base frequency
Power for frequency space
Ratio for carrier frequency
Ratio for modulation frequency 1
Ratio for modulation frequency 2
Division of frequency space
(Constant lower or upper first sidebands)

Attack and decay:

Attack linked to frequency
Initial attack time
Final attack time
Initial decay time
End decay time

Spatialization/reverberation:

Reverb %
Distance
Initial angle

Functions:

Carrier amplitude envelope function
Modulator 1 envelope function
Modulator 2 envelope function

> As these parameters are described in turn below, you may wish to see and hear the effect they have on the construction of an event using Presentation 10 in the accompanying software. Twenty-three of the twenty-six parameters are operational in our emulation. The other three parameters, shown in parentheses in the above list, are not used in our graphic emulation but can be found in the emulation of original terminal user-interface described later.[51] Demonstration Video 1.8 introduces using our emulation in relation to the descriptions that follow. ▶

Structure of an event

Two variables determine the number of elements to be generated in an event. One specifies the basic "number of elements" to be generated in the event, and another sets the "number of recursions" to be created. Recursion takes the shape of an event and replicates it, inserting a variation of the event between two existing elements, thereby increasing the density of activity. In practice, in *Stria* this variable was only set to zero or one, resulting in either no recursion or just a single recursion.[52] When the recursion occurs, some of the parameters are set specifically for the recursively computed elements. For instance, the number of elements in a recursive call is theoretically equal to the number of elements in the original event, but limited to a maximum of nine elements. All duration-related parameters are reduced, and a specific base frequency is computed based on the carrier frequency of the preceding element. A new frequency space power is also computed, and always takes the value of either 1.618^{-1} or 1.618. The division for recursive events is always zero, meaning that the frequency space is divided into nine steps rather than eighteen. And the reverberation amount is set to 1.2 times the global event amount.

You might like to try adjusting the "number of elements" and the "number of recursions" using the emulation software to see and hear their effect. Presentation 10 takes the first event in the work as its basis. Try for example increasing or decreasing the number of elements. You can also introduce one or more recursions (but remember one recursion is the maximum used by Chowning in Stria).

Timing and duration

The next four variables determine the timing and duration of elements. The "event begin time" was used by Chowning so that he could enter data for several events, each starting with different offset times. You can find this option only in the terminal interface version of our emulation (this will be introduced later). The "event duration," as its name implies, sets the overall duration for the whole event. The "event attack time" specifies the time (measured from the start of the event) within which all the elements must commence. Within these specified parameters, the algorithm then calculates the start times and durations of the individual elements. A table of ratios (based on the golden ratio) is permutated to produce the required data, scaling these according to the event duration and attack times that the user has entered.

One more variable is found in this category, the "element duration factor." If this is set to one, all the elements have their duration calculated by a "proportion" procedure in the SAIL algorithm. It is again a deterministic procedure that uses a table of ratios based on the golden ratio. Reducing the "element duration factor" extends the calculated durations of the elements until, set to zero, the duration of all the elements is lengthened proportionately so they all finish simultaneously with the end of event. Using this option has the effect of progressively increasing the density of the sonority within an event, creating, at its extreme, a wedge shape of growing density.

You might like to try adjusting the "event duration," "event attack time," and "element duration factor" in Presentation 10 of the accompanying software to see and hear how they operate.

Frequency parameters

Another group of eight variables concerns the pitch and timbral structure of the event. The user defines a "base frequency" for the event. John Chowning chose to use the frequency of 1,000 Hz as the fundamental frequency for the whole work, and all the events in *Stria* have either 1,000 Hz or a golden ratio (GR) octave of that frequency as their base frequency (in theory, however, other frequencies can be used). The variable "ratio for carrier frequency" can be used to modify this frequency. Chowning uses only two values for this variable: 1.0, which leaves the frequency unchanged, and 2.618, which in effect shifts everything up two GR octaves (2.168 equals 1.618^2).

The next step is to choose the pitch range for the event. This range is defined in terms of the number of GR octaves above (+1, +2, +3 . . .) or below (−1, −2, −3 . . .) the base frequency. Mathematically this can be expressed as multiplying the base frequency by 1.618^n where n is the number of octaves above or below (when n is negative) the base frequency. This variable is therefore called the "power for frequency space." In events in *Stria*, Chowning uses ranges between one and four octaves above or below the base frequency. Next comes the decision whether to divide the specified range into nine or eighteen equal-tempered divisions. This is controlled by a switch called "division of frequency space." So, in effect, the pitch scale used in any particular event is a function both of the range chosen and its division into nine or eighteen steps—the wider the range the larger the steps will be. The smallest possible steps result from a division of a one-octave range into eighteen steps, and the largest from a division of a four-octave range into nine steps. There is therefore a significant variation in the density of the pitch space used in the course of the work.

Once the pitch information has been specified, the algorithm uses simple permutational procedures to determine the specific frequencies of the elements making up the event. In essence the permutation involves a table of ten ratios expressed as fractional numbers. This table is read forward then backward, then inverting the index for the data, and finally reading this inversion backward—this process is analogous to twelve-tone serial procedures of prime, retrograde, inversion, and retrograde inversion. The table is read successively in these different ways until it has produced as many values as are needed for the number of elements in the event. These ratios, scaled by the range, are then used to multiply the base frequency to give the final frequency for each of the elements.

Table 1.4 gives an example of this process in operation using one of the two tables employed in *Stria*.

The resulting data from these iterations is then used to set the carrier frequency of each element according to the following formula:

$$\text{carrier frequency} = \big(\text{base frequency} \times \text{ratio for carrier frequency}\big) \times \big(\text{frequency space}\big)^{\text{value}/9}$$

Table 1.5 is a graphic representation of the permutation process described above, showing the resulting *actual values* across the forty iterations from left to right.[53]

The variable "reset count in frequency table" determines whether or not the permutation process is reset to the beginning for this new event or continues from where it left off in the previous event.

The variables "ratio for modulation frequency 1" and "ratio for modulation frequency 2" are used to calculate the frequencies of the two modulating

TABLE 1.4

Permutations of table indexes across forty successive iterations; the actual values are themselves employed as indexes in a ten-element table containing ratios for frequency scaling

Original:

Iteration	1	2	3	4	5	6	7	8	9	10
Table index	1	2	3	4	5	6	7	8	9	10
Value in table	0	4	3	9	6	5	7	8	2	1
Actual value	**0**	**4**	**3**	**9**	**6**	**5**	**7**	**8**	**2**	**1**

Retrograde:

Iteration	11	12	13	14	15	16	17	18	19	20
Table index	10	9	8	7	6	5	4	3	2	1
Value in table	1	2	8	7	5	6	9	3	4	0
Actual value	**1**	**2**	**8**	**7**	**5**	**6**	**9**	**3**	**4**	**0**

Inversion:

Iteration	21	22	23	24	25	26	27	28	29	30
Table index	1	2	3	4	5	6	7	8	9	10
Value in table	0	4	3	9	6	5	7	8	2	1
Actual value	$9-0=9$	$9-4=5$	$9-3=6$	$9-9=0$	$9-6=3$	$9-5=4$	$9-7=2$	$9-8=1$	$9-2=7$	$9-1=8$

Retrograde Inversion:

Iteration	31	32	33	34	35	36	37	38	39	40
Table index	10	9	8	7	6	5	4	3	2	1
Value in table	1	2	8	7	5	6	9	3	4	0
Actual value	$9-1=8$	$9-2=7$	$9-8=1$	$9-7=2$	$9-5=4$	$9-6=3$	$9-9=0$	$9-3=6$	$9-4=5$	$9-0=9$

TABLE 1.5

Graphic representation of the frequency permutation process

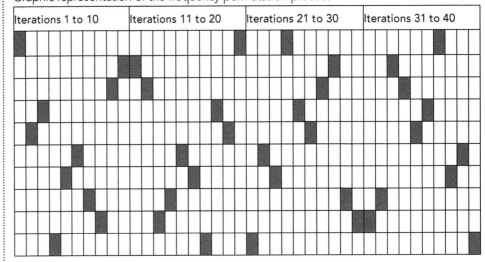

| Iterations 1 to 10 | Iterations 11 to 20 | Iterations 21 to 30 | Iterations 31 to 40 |

oscillators, and they play an important role in determining the timbre of the elements. These variables remain fixed throughout an event. Although in theory any value can be given for these, in practice Chowning uses only the following values, all powers of 1.618: 0.382, 0.618, 1, 1.618 and 2.618.

Another important factor in the creation of rich and lively timbres in *Stria* is the use of "skew." This is a subtle envelope function applied to every pitch in *Stria*, causing it to gently rise and then fall. Heard independently this change is barely perceptible, but when reverberation is applied the sound is enriched because the subtly different frequencies are sustained and overlap with each other. Furthermore, it means the relationship between overlapping elements subtly changes over time. The calculation of the skew factor is entirely automated within the algorithm and cannot be changed by the user from the terminal: its value is relative to the carrier frequency of each element.

You might like to try adjusting each of these parameters in turn using the emulation software to see and hear their effect.

Attack and decay

The user can specify the amplitude envelopes of elements in terms of their attack and decay times as a proportion (0.0 to 1.0) of the whole element's duration (as well as selecting the function to be used for the envelopes—see below). In each case the user provides an initial value ("initial attack" and 'initial decay") and an end value ("end attack" and "end decay"). The program interpolates between these values across the duration of the element. One further parameter, the "attack linked to frequency" switch enables the attack time of each element, relative to its overall duration, to be related to its carrier frequency.

You might like to try adjusting these parameters using the emulation software to see and hear their effect.

Spatialization and reverberation

The use of spatialization and reverberation in *Stria* is important but not as complex or significant as in some of John Chowning's other works, most notably *Turenas*. The basic reverberation algorithm remains unchanged for the duration of the work, and all the sounds are sent to a single reverberation unit (in the original Music 10 code, reverberation was implemented in a separate "global" instrument treating all the sounds in the same way).[54] What changes is the proportion of the sound sent to the reverberation unit. This is specified for each event using the "reverberation amount" variable and remains unchanged for all the elements in that event.

In his earlier investigations into spatialization, Chowning had discovered the significance of changing the ratio of direct to reverberated sound for spatial positioning. A "distance" scalar, which reduces the level of direct sound sent out, has an initial value set from the terminal, which either remains constant (if a negative value is typed) or decreases across the elements of the event (if a positive value is entered). An "initial angle" (azimuth) is also specified for each event. Starting from this angle, the SAIL algorithm (within the "azim" procedure) uses a simple function to calculate the positions of each element, according to the formula:

$$\text{deg} = \text{initial angle} + \left(360^{((n+1)/(N-1))}\right)^{0.2}$$

where deg is an angle in degrees with 0 left, 90 front, 180 right, 270 rear; n is the element index in the algorithm execution order (from 0 to $N-1$); N is the total number of elements in the event. With this formula, successive elements of one given event are distributed clockwise around the full two-dimensional circle surrounding the listener. The elements within an event each have a different spatial position, but in this work each element is in itself static.

You might like to try adjusting these parameters using the emulation software to see and hear their effect.

Envelope functions

Three envelope functions determine the amplitude envelopes used for the carrier and the two modulating oscillators, respectively. Alternative envelope functions are provided and can be selected for each of these functions using these three variables.

The "carrier amplitude function" shapes the overall amplitude of each element. The other two functions effectively shape the modulation indexes for each of the two parallel modulators, respectively. In *Stria* modulator 2 remains constantly set to function 4 for all the events. Modulator 1 uses function 3 almost exclusively except for events 0, 1, and 3, which use function 2. The fact that, as a result of using these envelope functions, the modulation indexes change over time is important in producing subtly evolving timbres.

> In the accompanying software in Presentation 8 you can change the envelope functions being used and see the shape of the function as well as hearing the results. Returning to Presentation 10, the software again provides the opportunity to try out the different envelope functions in the context of synthesizing a whole event and hear the results in that context. Demonstration Video 1.9 illustrates these options. ▶

The terminal interface

John Chowning entered data into the SAIL program one parameter at a time in response to prompts on the terminal interface. Presentation 11 is an emulation of this interface. It contains all the parameters described above including the three additional parameters not replicated in our graphic interface.

> Try out our emulation of the original SAIL command line interface using the accompanying software to get a sense of how the composer worked. This requires responses to a series of prompts, by either entering data or typing "return" to accept a default value. Please note that the parameters are here in a different order from that described above, but their function is identical. In our emulation, once the data has been entered the results are displayed graphically and can be played instantly. In the original version the output was score data that was then realized using Music 10 in non-real-time. Demonstration Video 1.10 shows this terminal user-interface in action. ▶

The shape of *Stria*

> Having explored the FM synthesis method used in the work and the SAIL algorithm, the accompanying software now provides you with an opportunity to investigate the shape of Stria. Presentation 10 allows you to recall the data for each one of the thirty-three events that make up the work. Having recalled an event you can see the data that produced it. You can also step through the stages by which the SAIL algorithm generated the elements from this data and see a visualization of the elements. You can hear this played and also adjust the data and hear how these changes alter the musical results. With any chosen level of visualization, you can also go from event to event and compare the data and resulting elements. Demonstration Video 1.11 illustrates these points and introduces using this aspect of the software. ▶

Another software tool provides a large-scale overview of the whole work. Presentation 1, "Interactive structural chart," displays all the elements on one screen. You can click on any element to hear it. The X-axis represents time. The display of the elements on the Y-axis can be changed to show the elements in respect of different parameters.[55] The initial display simply lists them in polyphonic order, from top to bottom, in the order they enter. This gives an indication of the changing density of the texture, a series of waves peaking toward the end of Section 3. Changing the Y-axis to "Duration" results in a roughly inverse pattern with increasing durations through many sections. Together these patterns reflect the increasingly dense textures as sections progress, with more and longer elements sounding simultaneously.

Perhaps surprisingly, changing the Y-axis to "Carrier frequency," which displays all elements sorted by their carrier frequencies as computed from the SAIL algorithm, does not show the simple falling and rising pattern (a "V" shape) often associated with this work.[56] The pattern is much richer and more complex. The two modulator frequencies do show patterns that fall and rise again, but again these are not simple "V" shapes—the Modulator 1 progression forms a "W" shape with two dips. The perceived pitch of the music, however, is not based on one parameter, especially as with FM, depending on the modulation ratios and indexes, a frequency other than the carrier frequency may be the most prominent.

Another feature of the software is that it enables you to identify the contribution made by the recursion option in the algorithm. There is an option to gray out the recursive elements on the graph.

In using this software, it is also possible to hear the contribution of different aspects of the synthesis process to the overall sound. You can choose to switch the reverberation unit on or off; likewise, the two modulators and the frequency skew factor can be turned off. It is also possible to identify elements with similar or identical settings for a particular parameter.

Demonstration Video 1.12 illustrates these features. ▶

Stria is therefore shaped by the composer by means of data inputted to the SAIL algorithm to define events. For each event the program then generates the parameters for the individual elements. The large-scale shape and structure of the whole work is a result of the ways in which these parameters change from one event to the next. As previously described, the algorithm is entirely determinist, and it is therefore possible to regenerate the work by inputting identical data.

Stria went through a number of different versions. You can hear the composer talking about these versions and the underlying reasons in the video of Presentation 12. In brief, the version premiered at IRCAM on September 29, 1977, was shortened immediately following that performance. These cuts were made by editing the tape recording of the work rather than by editing the source code. The stereo version released commercially on CD was inaccurate, and the correct final version is the quadraphonic version used in all subsequent performances (this was released on the DVD accompanying volume 31/4 of the *Computer Music Journal*).[57] There has sometimes been confusion about which is the correct version in previous analyses and reconstructions of *Stria*. In what follows here, and in our reconstruction, we are referring to the final quadraphonic version.

> *The accompanying software allows you to compare reconstructions of the different versions of the work. Using Presentation 1 you can select either of the two versions of the work (that premiered at IRCAM or the final quadraphonic version) and see and hear your choice. Demonstration Video 1.13 illustrates this.* ▶

The composer has described the inspiration for the overall structure of the work as being the inverted shape of a typical amplitude envelope of a sound. So, inverted, the gradually rising then decaying envelope becomes an initial descent followed by an ascent. The well-known diagram of the shape of the work produced in *Computer Music* by Dodge and Jerse illustrates this general outline in terms of the pitch of the work.[58] However, in reality the form of the work is much more complex and detailed. In Presentation 1 of the accompanying software, the visualization of elements sorted accorded to their carrier frequencies is calculated from the event data and shows the base frequency for each event after modification by scaling as described above (thick line) and its range, with internal lines to show the division of the space into nine or eighteen steps. The horizontal axis shows the start and duration of the events. However, it should be noted that there are further complications in depicting the musical shape. One is that FM synthesis can lead to partials other than the carrier frequency having preeminence (the complexity of Bessel functions means that this would need detailed calculation for each element and cannot be easily detected from simply looking at the input data), but because of the low modulation indexes used by Chowning, this factor is not normally very significant. Our software contains an option to switch off one or both modulating oscillators so that you can hear the difference modulation makes and the impact this has on the pitch structure. Another issue is the use, in some events, of recursion—which can lead to additional elements that lie outside the pitch space the composer explicitly defines for the event. The visualization found in Presentation 1 nonetheless provides a general outline of what the listener is likely to perceive as the overall pitch structure of the work.

Presentation 1 also depicts the temporal structure of the work. As with the pitch structure, this is a complex progression and not one that follows a simple linear path. In general, however, there is a tendency toward shorter events and elements toward the middle of the work and a return to longer events later.

A further important factor in shaping the work is the use of different functions to shape the amplitude envelope of the carrier (as noted above, the functions for the modulators remain largely the same). Although this is rarely changed (remaining mostly on function 2) on the few occasions it does alter (on four occasions changing to function 7 and once to function 8) it plays a significant role in articulating a change of character in the music. Functions 7 and 8 both differ from the gradual envelope of function 2 and introduce sharper attacks into the music. In a work that emphasizes homogeneity and slowly evolving structures, this provides one of the few marked changes between elements.

51

> You can hear John Chowning explaining more about the compositional and technical issues behind Stria and also discussing other aspects of his work in the video interviews included with the accompanying software. It is clear that Chowning is a composer for whom technology and creativity are inextricably linked, and his intimate knowledge of both the technical and the musical is central to his creative process.

Conclusions

John Chowning's *Stria* is a work that presents a distinct sound world with its own pitch and durational systems. The composer used software and algorithms he had himself devised to shape all aspects of the work, from the lowest level of the synthesis of new timbres to the large-scale formal structuring of the music. The timbral synthesis employed in *Stria* uses the composer's own frequency modulation techniques, in this piece also drawing on the mathematics of the golden ratio to provide a distinctive quality. Building on these timbres to create an entire composition, Chowning, as we have seen, did not assemble the work by hand, one note (element) at a time. Instead he turned once again to software, this time programming algorithms in the Stanford Artificial Intelligence Language. This enabled him to shape the music at a higher level, not in terms of crafting individual notes one at a time, but by prescribing the parameters to describe larger events. It is the SAIL algorithm that then determines the precise definition of the individual notes according to the input data provided for the event.

Software therefore plays a significant role at all levels of this composition. But although this might imply that the music is composed by computer, that is not the case. Both timbrally and formally, the computer is simply realizing the intentions of the composer through the intermediary of algorithms preprogrammed by the composer himself. The composer then determines the outcome by inputting data to these algorithms. The algorithms do impose certain constraints on the possible outcomes, but these have themselves been determined by Chowning in devising the algorithms in the first place. In other words, programming the algorithms was a part of the compositional process. In making decisions about the software, Chowning was making not just technical decisions but also musical decisions. Our software emulations provide you with the opportunity to experiment with different settings and experience the possibilities and the constraints for yourself. But, unlike the composer, you have to work within the compositional limits Chowning set for himself. *Stria* is one of a number of works discussed in this book in which it becomes clear that the divide between technical and creative invention has been blurred, if not eliminated altogether, the two aspects being fully integrated in the compositional process.

This is therefore a work permeated by the potential of digital technology, and as already noted it is a work that would have been inconceivable without this technology. Nonetheless, it is a work fully controlled by the decisions of the composer, and, as he himself makes clear, it was his ear and his compositional judgment that drove his decision-making rather than any dogmatic approach to the use of technology.

Barry Truax
Riverrun

Contexts for *Riverrun*

The birth and early development of granular synthesis

The contributions of Barry Truax to the development of computer music embrace not only an extensive repertory of works extending over forty years, but also a substantive contribution to an important and now widely used digital method of generating and processing audio material, known as *granular synthesis*. An additional dimension, which will be considered further in Chapter 4 (Westerkamp), is his important role in the development of the World Soundscape Project (WSP), concerned with exploring the relationships between people and the environment. The WSP was pioneered by R. Murray Schafer, who directed the project between 1965 and 1975 at Simon Fraser University, Vancouver, drawing together a team of co-researchers, including Truax. On Schafer's departure, responsibility for continuing SFU's role in the project passed to Truax, embracing both the preservation of the existing library of source recordings and also new additions to this important resource, which has been creatively explored by several composers, including Truax and Westerkamp. This in turn led to a powerful intersection between the aesthetics of soundscape composition and Truax's pioneering techniques of synthesis and signal processing that are the central focus of this chapter.

Today the technique of granular synthesis is encountered in a variety of software tools developed for computer music composition, both commercial and noncommercial, such as Csound, Max/MSP (since 2013 marketed simply as Max), Pd, and Reaktor. These various examples range from implementations of a relatively rudimentary nature to those of considerable sophistication, albeit only fully achieved in a creative context when employed by those who understand the inherent complexities of the underlying algorithms and how best to apply them.

The concept of coding and manipulating sound information in a granular format can be traced back to the theory of communication first put forward by Dennis Gabor in 1946[1] and further expanded by Claude Shannon and Warren Weaver in *The Mathematical Theory of Communication*, published in 1949.[2] In his paper Gabor noted that traditional approaches to wave analysis involve two distinct methodologies, the first considering the evolution of composite sound waves as a function of time, and the second concerned with their spectral content, measured in terms of the constituent frequency components and amplitudes at specific instants during the time continuum. Whereas each mode of analysis involves mapping just two variables at a time, combining the results to achieve a combined perspective requires a three-dimensional matrix, which creates several practical challenges when the resulting parameters are used for further study.

Gabor sought to overcome these difficulties by proposing an alternative method of wave analysis, based on the mathematical principles associated with quantum theory. Put in simple terms, this involves digitizing an audio wave function with respect to time as a series of grains, providing successive snapshots of the associated spectra, each lasting just a fraction of a second. In analysis terms, the primary variables are the duration and frequency of each grain, the nature of the amplitude envelope that is applied to minimize any discontinuities each side of the grain, and the density of grains in terms of the degree or otherwise of overlap between successively sampled grains, or conversely the time interval between grains. The significance of these variables and the ways in which they can be used to control the processes of granular synthesis will be studied more closely in due course.

The first composer to explore the possibilities of granular principles in the composition of music was Iannis Xenakis in the context of his pursuit of the possibilities of free stochastic music. Writing in 1954 in rejection of traditional notions of linear polyphony, he observed:

> When linear combinations and their polyphonic superpositions no longer operate, what will count will be the statistical means of isolated states and of transformations of the sonic components at a given moment. The macroscopic effect can then be controlled by the mean of the movements of elements we select.[3]

Although at this early stage of study it was not yet possible for Xenakis directly to explore the creative possibilities of such principles in a digital context, the foundations for pursuing such an aesthetic were established. The writings of Xenakis on his emerging ideas during the next decade can be studied further in his book *Formalized Music: Thought and Mathematics in Composition*, first published in French as *Musiques Formelles* in 1963, and subsequently in an English translation in 1971.[4]

The following extract from the latter provides a useful starting point for a study of the characteristics of granular synthesis:

> All sound is an integration of grains, of elementary sonic particles, of sound quanta. Each of these elementary grains has a threefold nature: duration, frequency, and intensity. All sound, even all continuous sonic variation, is conceived as an assemblage of a large number of elementary particles adequately disposed in time. So, any sound complex can be analyzed as a series of pure sinusoidal sounds, even if the variations of these sinusoidal sounds are infinitely close, short, and complex. In the attack, body, and decline of a complex sound, thousands of pure sounds appear in a more or less interval of time, Δt. Hecatombs of pure sounds are necessary for the creation of a complex sound. A complex sound may be imagined as a multi-colored firework in which each point of light appears and instantaneously disappears against a black sky. But in this firework there would be such a quantity of light organized in such a way that their rapid and teeming succession would create forms and spirals, slowly unfolding, or conversely, brief explosions setting the whole sky aflame. A line of light would be created by a sufficiently large multitude of points appearing and disappearing instantaneously.[5]

These visual analogies provide a useful gateway into a deeper understanding of the nature and function of acoustic grains. Without access to computing resources during this formative period of study, Xenakis had to devise purely analog means of generating such quanta. Indeed, the expected correlations here are not always immediately evident, since in many works it is the theories of granulation that inform the musical style of writing rather a more direct algorithmic implementation. The works from this early period that perhaps become closest to such an implementation are *Analogique A* (1958), scored for nine string instruments, and *Analogique B* (1959), an entirely electronic work. In the case of *A* the acoustic quanta comprise a blend of pizzicato and very short bowed sounds, whereas in the case of *B* they are composed of very short synthesized sine waves, extracted and juxtaposed using tape editing techniques.

A somewhat more refined and perhaps better-known electronic work from this period that makes extensive use of granulated materials is *Concret PH* (1958), which he composed for the Philips Pavilion constructed for the World's Fair held in Brussels the same year. Here the sound source is that of burning charcoal, where by extraction the individual crackles are manipulated in a granular fashion. The interest stimulated by this imaginative project led to the granting of access to an IBM 7090 computer, courtesy of IBM-France, providing him finally with the resources necessary to develop digital algorithms for generating performance data, and a resulting series of stochastic works, notably *ST/10-1, 080262* and *ST/10-3, 060962* (*Atrées*), both composed in 1962. In so doing he laid important foundations for the all-digital implementations of granular synthesis that were to follow.

Two composers are to be credited with pioneering the techniques of granular synthesis as we know them today, both inspired by the work of Xenakis; Curtis Roads and Barry Truax. Roads became interested in the possibilities of microsound during the early 1970s, his interests in the electronic medium being stimulated by an opportunity to access the studio resources at the University of Illinois Experimental Music Studio via a graduate student friend. At the time (1970–1971) this was a purely analog studio, based on a large Moog III modular synthesizer, an API mixing console, and a bank of analog tape recorders. Although he became aware of the functional characteristics of Music V, and managed to obtain a printout of the associated code, he was unable to access suitable computing facilities for exploring its creative possibilities.[6] As a first step in this direction, having commenced studies at Cal Arts in Los Angeles in 1972, he was able to install a version of this program on a Data General Nova 1200 computer. However, this computer had no audio converter and thus could not produce sound.

His creative interests at this time were strongly stimulated by the characteristics of rock-based styles of composition, reflecting his essentially nonclassical musical background. This aesthetic perspective was to prove highly influential in shaping his initial engagement with the creative possibilities of computer music, aspects of which were to become key features of his subsequent repertory of works. During the early years he was especially interested in exploring the characteristics of micromanaged rhythm, and this led him to engage directly with a new generation of artists furthering the techniques of electronica. In due course these developments influenced key genres such as intelligent dance music (IDM) during the 1990s, associated in turn with works by artists such as Aphex Twin, Autechre, and The Orb. Roads indeed collaborated with the British duo Autechre for two concerts, the first in Los Angeles in 2001, and the second in London in 2002.

Roads first became aware of the possibilities of granular synthesis in May 1972 when attending a course on formalized music at Indiana University, conducted by Iannis Xenakis, marking the start of an association that was to prove materially significant for him. While subsequently studying at the University of California at San Diego (UCSD) in 1974–1975, he was able to access a more substantial Burroughs B6700 mainframe computer. This machine provided the facilities necessary for composing computer music via Music V, the audio data files generated by the latter being subsequently realized acoustically via a twelve-bit digital-to-analog converter operating at 20 kHz. Using the programming language ALGOL, Roads developed a free-standing granular synthesis program known as PLFKLANG, used to generate note/event data, passed in turn to a Music V program for audio synthesis. The converter, however, could only operate in mono, requiring the subsequent use of analog mixing facilities to mix the component tracks necessary to create a stereo image. This facility resulted in his first granular study, *Prototype*, completed in 1975. The functional characteristics of his program merit further scrutiny, since they illustrate well the key principles of this synthesis technique.

The waveforms used by Roads for producing grains ranged from a simple sine wave to a band-limited pulse, thus establishing a palette of sources that embraced different degrees of sonic complexity. Each of the grains was of a fixed duration (twenty milliseconds), in turn subject to a simple amplitude envelope with a sustained peak. The permissible frequency range was between 40.4 Hz and 9,900 Hz, and the permissible amplitude range was between 30 dB and 70 dB. Control of the synthesis processes was regulated by the following set of variables:[7]

1. Beginning time and duration of an event
2. Initial waveform and waveform rate-of-change (slope)
3. Initial center frequency and rate-of-change of center frequency
4. Initial bandwidth (frequency dispersion) and bandwidth rate-of-change
5. Initial grain density and grain density rate-of-change
6. Initial amplitude and amplitude rate-of-change

The basic data mapping technique can be illustrated in a graphic format, as shown in Figure 2.1.

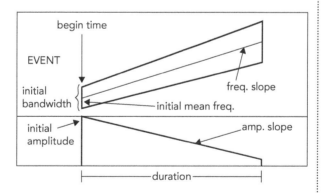

FIGURE 2.1

Variables for the control of PLFKLANG granular synthesis.[8]

Aside from the possible limitations of a fixed duration for each grain, the one drawback to this early implementation was that the system was non-real-time, requiring all the performance data to be provided in advance. Furthermore, this restrictive working environment, well known to the early pioneers of computer music, further isolated the composer from the processes of sound production. All programs and associated data had thus to be prepared using punched cards, subsequently placed in a queue for batch processing, where tasks that were least demanding in terms of computer resources were routinely given priority. Consequently, as noted in the previous chapter, sound synthesis applications would invariably be shunted to the back of the queue for overnight processing. Notwithstanding these challenging conditions, especially in the context of such a novel synthesis technique being explored for the very first time, Roads was able to make further progress with his pioneering software, producing a more sophisticated version of his program in 1981 that took advantage of a significantly improved array of digital-to-analog converters, offering up to four channels of audio with sixteen-bit resolution at a sampling rate of 40 kHz.

With the new decade the development of more affordable minicomputers opened the possibility of developing dedicated facilities for computer music, allowing for a much faster turnaround of synthesis tasks. However, as noted in the previous chapter, it was to be several years before such resources and their desktop-based successors could provide the processing power necessary to support real-time implementations of programs such as Music 11 and Csound. It was thus left to pioneers such as Roads and Truax to seek other ways of achieving such goals in the context of generating and manipulating granular sounds.

Further work developing the techniques of microsound led Roads to Paris in the early 1990s, and in 1993 he took up an appointment as director of pedagogy at the center established by Xenakis in 1966 for research and development in the field of stochastic music. Known originally as Centre d'Études de Mathématique et Automatique Musicales (CEMAMu), and subsequently as Les Ateliers UPIC, it was finally renamed Center for the Composition of Music Iannis Xenakis (CCMIX) in 2002. This direct association with the work of Xenakis acted as a major stimulus for the development of Cloud Generator, a granular synthesis program for the Apple Macintosh microcomputer, which he developed in collaboration with John Alexander and completed in 1995. Written in the programming language C, and with the enhancement of a graphical user interface, this versatile resource was to provide the kernel for Roads and others to extend the possibilities of the technique, in due course embracing a fully interactive real-time working environment.[9] The initiative for crossing this threshold, however, is to be credited in the first instance to Barry Truax, whose innovative work is the central focus of this chapter.

Truax's initial training was in physics and mathematics, studying at Queen's University, Ontario. However, childhood interests in music were rekindled during his undergraduate studies by coming in contact for the first time with synthesizers developed by Hugh Le Caine at Expo '67, Montreal.[10] After graduation, in 1969, matters came to a head for him, and instead of pursuing a purely scientific career, he chose instead to explore the musical applications of technology, transferring to the University of British Columbia, Vancouver, as a postgraduate student to study electronic composition. In 1971 Truax left his native Canada for a two-year period of study at the Institute of Sonology in Utrecht, bringing him into direct contact with the work of Gottfried Michael Koenig. During the 1960s Koenig had become interested in the creative possibilities of algorithmic methods of music production, developing ideas that were closely related to those of Xenakis.

Toward the middle of the decade, he started work on the first of two composing programs, PROJECT 1 (1964), soon to be followed by PROJECT 2 (1966). PROJECT 1 was inspired by his interests in the techniques of serial composition and their possible extension through the processes of automation, the associated software producing data for the construction of instrumental scores. The data parameters for each note thus produced are the choice of instrument, entry delay (= metric duration), pitch, octave register, and the dynamics. In the case of the pitch parameter, three-note groupings are generated from two source intervals provided by the composer, subsequently transposed to create a twelve-note row.

A key component of the data generation process is the use of random probability in association with a rule-based algorithm, the latter being chosen from a repertory of seven possibilities of varying orders of complexity. As was to be expected at the time, the development of the program required the services of the University of Utrecht's mainframe computer, an IBM 7090, written initially in ALGOL 60 and subsequently rewritten in an early version of the FORTRAN programming language, FORTRAN II. Tasks (or "jobs," as they were commonly called) had to be submitted for batch processing in the manner described above, and although as data generation programs they were not subject to the same order of delays as those producing fully synthesized audio data, the waiting times were still significant.

The same conditions applied to the early development of PROJECT 2. The latter program took these generative processes a stage further, expanding the choice of parameters to include modes of articulation and an expanded set of rhythmic components, including rests and tempi. The format of output data was also expanded to embrace groups of data of variable content in terms of the note/events and ensembles, created from selections of one or more of these groups. From a compositional point of view, the most significant difference is the change from an environment where score data is generated section by section to one where the processes are combined to create a generative model that is controlled by the composer in a "top-down" manner, changing parameters that influence the overall evolution of the associated algorithms but not directly determining the specific details of the resulting data.

The control functions provide different types of weighting to the selection procedures that determine the content of each group. The function called ALEA makes entirely random selections from a table of values, each element once chosen remaining eligible for reselection, whereas the function called SERIES removes values from the table after selection to prevent repetitions occurring. When all the available elements have been used up, this function may then be reprogrammed using a fresh copy of the table. Alternatively, the function RATIO makes weighted selections from an associated table. A different type of selection procedure is provided by a function called TENDENCY. This allows the composer to apply "masks" to the random-number generator, dynamically adjusting the range of values from which it may make choices.

In 1970 the Institute of Sonology purchased a PDP-15/20 computer with funds provided by Utrecht University. This was a notable development in the European history of computer music, matched at the time only by the acquisition of a PDP-15/40 computer for the Elektronmusikstudion (EMS Stockholm), funded by Swedish Radio in the same year, and two small PDP-8 computers acquired by Peter Zinovieff a year earlier for his private studio in London, to support his commercial company, EMS London.[11] In all three cases the primary purpose of these computers was to control synthesis hardware, leading to their classification as hybrid systems. In the case of the Institute of Sonology, however, the acquisition of a dedicated computer also stimulated further work on new versions of both PROJECT 1 and PROJECT 2, rewritten in FORTRAN IV. With the elimination of the delays routinely associated with batch processing, the time between submitting tasks and receiving the output data on a printer was dramatically shortened from several hours to a matter of minutes. This in turn raised the possibility of directly generating sound output from the computer via suitably designed digital-to-analog converters.

During 1972 Koenig and Stan Tempelaars developed the first version of the Sound Synthesis Program (SSP). In so doing they came directly into contact with the constraints of computers in terms of such demanding applications. Although the PDP-15 was a very new design, taking full advantage of the most recent advances in digital engineering, as one of the first generation of smaller computers it had only limited workspace—just 12K of eighteen-bit core memory.[12] Furthermore, the Institute of Sonology computer had no mass data storage facilities, significantly limiting the use of dynamic memory management techniques to expand this workspace. SSP was thus limited to the production of simple fixed format waveforms, producing a mono output, restricted in turn to the parameters of time, pitch, and amplitude supplied from associated data tables.[13] Although the software was capable of generating sound output in real time (that is, without an intermediate delay once a synthesis task was launched) it did not allow any direct composer interaction during execution. Any notion of performance control therefore seemed as remote as ever. With the arrival of Barry Truax, this Rubicon was finally to be crossed.

Truax's compositional imperatives on arriving at the Institute of Sonology were visionary in several important respects. Although well aware of the steady progress being made in the context of non-real-time computer music software such as the Music N series of programs in terms of an expanding repertory of synthesis and signal processing techniques, his creative imperatives were underpinned by a profound belief that the composer should be able to work with such resources in a truly interactive environment, directly influencing the processes of sound production. In an article subsequently published in the *Journal of Music Theory*, he argued the following:

1. That all computer music systems both explicitly and implicitly embody a model of the musical process that may be inferred from the program and data structure of the system, and from the behavior of users working with the system. The inference of this model is independent of whether the system designer(s) claim that the system reflects such a model, or is simply a tool.

2. That computer music systems form a source of data for the theorist in the form of program/system analyses, and records of user behavior (viz. protocols). In addition, such systems offer the facility to test (and therefore compare) theoretical models or concepts.

3. That real-time, interactive systems, together with composition programs of all kinds, are the most useful (i.e. observable) sources of data concerning musical activity and its modeling.[14]

4. That systems of any type will increase in their usefulness to the composer to the extent that they implement procedural musical knowledge and offer a significant learning potential for the user.[15]

The importance of the third precept to Truax, from the very outset of his career as both a composer and researcher, should not be underestimated. Nor for that matter should his concern to understand a consideration that lies at the heart of the research that has underpinned the composer studies that form the kernel of this book, which is the ways in which a composer can engage with composing software, and the influence of the latter on how it may be used:

How much of the user's strategy remains external to the program? How much of the process must be complete before the program is used, and how much continues after it stops? To what extent, then, does the system determine the user's strategy, and to what extent does it assist the user in formulating that strategy? Important for the user will also be the time taken before the results are audible, that is, before the feedback of information allows the user to modify his strategy and come closer to his goal.[16]

In rejecting from the outset the non-real-time environment of the Music N family of software, and opting instead for the rule-based approach being advocated by Koenig and others at the Institute of Sonology, he had to engage head on with this important issue in ways that were not being considered by advocates of the former approach. In situations where the processes of composition are so far removed from those of synthesis, the role of the computer is essentially passive, merely responding to a remotely entered set of instructions. This sense of detachment is further reinforced by the requirement to specify tasks in terms of a predetermined "orchestra" of individual "instruments," realizing a succession of performance events supplied as the associated data in an accompanying "score."[17] While such a classical approach is not without its merits, and indeed served Max Mathews and his associates very well during the formative years of computer music, such a working environment was far removed from that being sought by Truax.[18]

Whereas PROJECT 1 and especially PROJECT 2 were to prove the primary starting point for his investigations, Truax was also very much influenced by the prior work of Xenakis, in particular the concepts that had been embraced in his ST (= Stochastic) series of programs, discussed earlier. The characteristic of particular interest in this context was his use of probability laws to determine the evolution of sonic entities, notably those based on the distribution theory first advocated by the French mathematician Siméon Denis Poisson in the nineteenth century. For Truax the use of Poisson-ordered distributions of discrete sound events, each of a fractional duration, provided the basis for a novel means of composing directly in sound, particularly one that could not only generate the results in real time but also be interactively controlled. In the latter context he was able to draw on some key design principles associated with PROJECT 2, notably the use of "tendency masks," to regulate the frequency boundaries of the microsound events with respect to time. Figure 2.2 illustrates the general principles involved in the design of a mask.

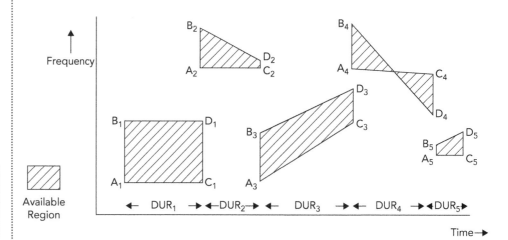

FIGURE 2.2

Tendency masks for the frequency of grains over time.[19]

The numeric data for each mask, using an integer format, consists of the following components: (i) the number of mask segments (maximum ten), (ii) the total number of events to be mapped in the distribution, (iii) the initial density in sounds per second, and (iv) the mask data for each segment (the values of A, B, C, and D in Hertz plus the duration in hundredths of a second).

The articulation of the microsound events within each segment is thus a function of their density and the pitch at which they are reproduced, the latter values being determined by random selection within the frequency boundaries prescribed by the tendency mask at the corresponding instant in time. Given the already mentioned restrictions on real-time computation, the audio output was necessarily monophonic, the density characteristic being simply a measure of duration of each component event. In this context Truax was to note:

> The Poisson distribution applies in cases where the density of events is sufficiently low (less than ten to twenty events per second), such that separate events may be identified, since a large density of events merges into a continuous distribution, just as high sound density results in a fusion of events into a continuous texture.[20]

This point of fusion was clearly regarded as an important boundary in operational terms. Proceeding in the opposite direction, techniques of granular synthesis, such as those that subsequently were to form the basis of his programs GSX and GSAMX, extend from the initial production of composite spectra to recognizable grains that can be individually perceived as discrete events. There are thus important similarities between the two methods of generating microsound, and this connectivity extends to the nature and content of the sounds themselves.

Truax developed three versions of his real-time synthesis program at the Institute of Sonology, known respectively as POD4, POD5, and POD6. Given the limited amount of memory available in the computer and the lack of mass data storage facilities, significant ingenuity was required to generate the constituent waveforms. The PDP-15, however, provided a limited but nonetheless useful amount of local data storage via a proprietary system known as DECtape, consisting of a pair of small magnetic tape spools that could be used to store waveform data. In the case of POD4, ten fixed waveforms of fifty samples each were provided, with the option of constructing a further eight derivatives that were user-defined. In the latter context the ability to audition the resulting waveforms in real time allowed instant evaluation and, where appropriate, modification of the sample selections made to construct these derivatives. In the case of POD5, a slightly different approach was taken. Instead of five times fifty sample versions, a single five-hundred sample waveform was used in association with an array of sixty different amplitudes that were in turn dynamically scaled. This technique made it possible to create smooth attack and decay envelopes for the resulting microsound streams. The extended sample length also facilitated the construction of a series of harmonic derivatives by cyclically reading every other, every third, or every fourth, etc., sample. It also allowed the construction of more elaborate user-defined waveforms and the use of amplitude modulation.

The control of frequency was equally ingenious, circumventing all the calculation overheads that are necessary when producing sound at a fixed sample rate. Indeed, had this method not been possible the POD programs could not have operated in real time. The solution came with the ability directly to microprogram the operation of both the real-time computer clock and the cycle time of the processor. Via a combination of repeated cycles of both timing variables, it became possible to produce a logarithmic table of pitch values with a resolution in excess of thirty steps per octave, in the case of POD5 working with a lower limit of 50 Hz and an upper limit of 8,000 Hz.[21] Most significantly, the technique allowed the normal correlation between speed and pitch, such as that observed when speeding up or slowing down the playback of an analog tape recording, to be completely decoupled. Such a facility was way ahead of its time, anticipating processing features that were to be embraced by more advanced implementations of techniques such as granular synthesis in more conventional processing environments.

Although the methods of waveform production described above were of primary importance for both POD4 and POD5, both programs allowed the use of externally generated waveforms, sampled via an analog-to-digital converter. Although the full potential of such a facility was not to be realized until more than a decade later in the context of GSAMX, the possibilities of thus embracing the subtleties of acoustically generated sounds were not lost on Truax. His ultimate quest at this time, however, was to embrace a technique that would allow the production of sounds that could vary dynamically in real time, not merely in terms of amplitude but also timbre. The solution here was to be provided by John Chowning, following a visit to the Institute of Sonology in 1973, when he introduced Truax to the principles of FM synthesis. Consequently, the first real-time implementation of this important technique came into being as POD6, requiring simple changes to the underlying processes of computation that in turn were to lead directly to the development of GSX and the composition of *Riverrun.*

As described in Chapter 1, all that was required in this context at the most basic level was a single sine wave providing a carrier frequency "c," in turn modulated by another sine wave of frequency "m" and amplitude "d," where the modulation index "I" is the ratio of "d"/"m". In this context the sine wave was simply stored as a table function of 512 values, from which both modulation components in terms of their frequency and amplitude can be dynamically extracted in the manner described for POD4 and POD5. Up to thirty different pairs of FM-configured oscillators could be used at any one time, each controlled in addition to the values of the primary FM parameters in terms of the amplitude envelope and a maximum permitted value for the modulation index.[22] Truax discovered that significant subtleties in the resulting timbres could be unmasked by randomly distributing the sounds between two mono channels. By varying the relative amplitudes and binaural time delays fed to each loudspeaker, each component could be positioned at one of seven locations between the two extremes. Such techniques were to become a major feature of his granular synthesis programs, illustrating yet again the important links between the POD programs and both GSX and GSAMX.[23]

Overall control over the selection of sound object data that comprises all timbral values is exercised via one of four statistical processes, known respectively as ALEA, RATIO, SEQUENCE, and TENDENCY. These were originally developed for PROJECT 2 by Koenig, although in the latter context they were used to generate score data, whereas in the case of the POD programs they are used to select the individual audio events. ALEA is an equal probability function making an aleatoric selection from the waveforms that have been assigned as available. RATIO is a weighted probability function based on integer ratios provided by the composer as applicable for the selection process. SEQUENCE is a fixed sequence of choices made in accordance with an ordering provided by the composer in advance. In this case there is no random probability component to the selection process. TENDENCY is a tendency mask very similar to that used for the Poisson-ordered distribution of event frequencies and densities described earlier, combining both the waveforms available at any one point and the weighting ratios to be applied to their selection (see Figure 2.3).

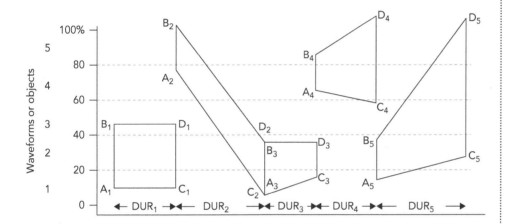

FIGURE 2.3

Tendency masks for available waveforms and their weighting ratios.[24]

In this context the vertical coordinates are expressed in percentage terms, since the total number of waveforms available will be determined in advance by the composer and vary from context to context.

In 1973 Truax returned to Vancouver, taking up a post combining teaching and research in the newly created Department of Communication Studies at Simon Fraser University.[25] In the latter context his primary interests focused around the further development of his work at the Institute of Sonology, and he was immediately faced with the challenges of modifying his POD programs to run on a different computer. Although the high-level commands were written in FORTRAN, for which a compatible compiler was available, the time-critical synthesis routines had been written in low-level assembler code, specific to a PDP-15. During 1974–1975 he modified the programs to run on a Hewlett-Packard 2116 machine, taking advantage of the slightly larger memory (16K of sixteen-bit memory rather than 12K of eighteen-bit memory) and, most importantly, both a disk unit and a mass storage magnetic tape unit. In 1978 he transferred his work to a NOVA 3 computer with non-real-time synthesis on a Varian computer located in Computing Science, and finally in 1981 to a PDP (LSI) 11/23, the first computer that could be dedicated to his personal research.[26]

A primary concern during this transitional period was the enhancement of POD with the ultimate objective of facilitating real-time generation of polyphonic textures. Unfortunately, the computer technology available at SFU still had some way to go before such a goal could be realized. A partial solution was identified from an ongoing collaboration with EMS Stockholm, where a near-identical PDP-15 computer could be used to operate a bank of digitally controlled analog FM synthesis oscillators. Truax was thus able to produce a hybrid polyphonic version of POD6 that could work in real time at EMS. However, back at SFU, his only option was to develop a non-real-time version, known as POD7. In accepting the consequential time delays as individual voices were synthesized and incrementally recorded, he developed an interactive audio file management system that allowed enhanced facilities for producing synthesis data and interactive feedback once the results were computed (see Figure 2.4).

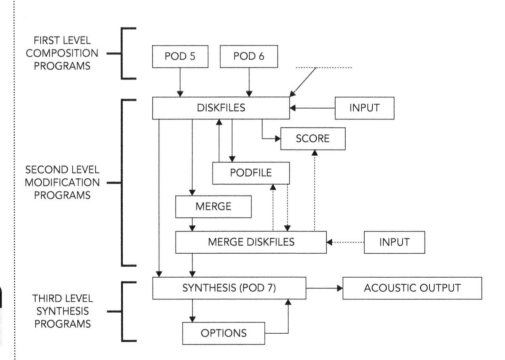

FIGURE 2.4

Program structure of the POD system.[27]

Having accepted the necessity of changing to a non-real-time synthesis environment, Truax used the opportunity to enhance the quality of the sound output, concentrating now almost exclusively on the FM synthesis technique introduced with POD6. The new program, for example, used a wave table of 8,192 discrete values, a substantial improvement on the 512 values of the earlier programs.[28] It also facilitated for the first time the direct generation of spatially distributed sounds within a stereo listening field.

By the end of the decade the production of POD-generated works was gathering pace, including *Sonic Landscape No. 3* (1975), *Sonic Landscape No. 4*

(1977), *Androgyny* (1978), and *Aerial* (1979) composed by Truax, and works by other composers who had opportunities to use the POD software, including *La mer à l'aube* (1977) and *Heliograms* (1977–1980) by Jean Piché.[29]

Notwithstanding the additional composing facilities provided by POD7, Truax still yearned for a system that could synthesize polyphonic voices in real time. The breakthrough came with the acquisition in 1981 not only of the PDP-11/23 computer, but also, a year later, a fast front-end digital signal processor, the sixteen-bit DMX-1000, manufactured by Digital Music Systems and first released commercially in 1979. The latter device is distinctive in several respects. First, it was designed specifically for synthesizing and processing audio data. Second, it used two high-speed memories operating in parallel. One memory stored up to 256 programming instructions, the other stored the associated data, both under the management of the host control computer. Third, it was microprogrammable, allowing the use of fully optimized signal processing instructions. The basic machine instruction cycle was just 200 nanoseconds, and this speed allowed audio processing several orders of magnitude faster than that possible with a PDP-15 or PDP-11 computer.[30] The memory stored a maximum of 4K words, and this restriction had implications for the storage of wavetables. This limitation, however, was significantly offset by the superior performance of the processor.[31]

The DMX-1000 was shipped with a software synthesis program known as Music 1000, developed from Music 11, the version of Music N written by Barry Vercoe at MIT specifically for the PDP-11. Although it was possible to execute the program in real time, it still required the preparation of a traditional "orchestra" and "score" in advance, with no opportunity for live interaction. For Truax the attraction of the DMX lay in the power and versatility of its signal processing facilities, finally making it possible for POD programs to generate polyphonic textures in real time. Whereas the control environment, written using a high-level compiler, could be hosted by the PDP-11/23 computer with relative ease, the synthesis kernel had to be entirely rewritten in DMX-1000 microcode.[32] The rewards for this extra work were considerable. For example, a reworking of POD6 as POD6X facilitated the generation of six voices of FM simultaneously in real time. In a similar vein, a similar reworking of POD7 as POD7X created a highly responsive system for creating, storing, verifying, and merging sound data in real time, in the latter context using a subroutine known as CONDUC.[33]

The early 1980s was to prove an important watershed in the development of Truax's POD-based compositions, starting with his four-channel work *Arras* (1980). His growing interest at this time in exploring the timbral possibilities of polyphonic FM textures required extensive use of POD6 and POD7, building up the textures layer by layer. The first compositions to be realized using the new DMX-1000-based system were *Wave Edge* (1983), followed by *Solar Ellipse* (1984–1985), two FM works inspired by the Chinese

Book of Changes, more generally known as *I Ching*.[34] What amounted to a quantum leap in terms of the available computing power, however, was leading to a reappraisal of the techniques being used for real-time synthesis, not least in terms of the range and versatility of the tools that could now be provided for interactive composing.

It has already been noted that a key feature of the POD systems was their engagement with the creative possibilities of microsynthesis, building up textures from aggregates of individual sonic elements. Hitherto, as noted earlier, Truax had regarded the point where these elements cease to be recognizable as discrete events as a boundary in terms of their minimum duration that could not usefully be crossed. A growing awareness of the underlying significance of Gabor's "Theory of Communication," however,[35] and the ways in which it usefully underpinned the principles of granular synthesis being explored by Roads, led him to look more closely at the way in which POD generated microsounds.[36] He concluded that the POD system of generating grains was not capable of managing a truly granular environment. Hitherto the restrictions had been a matter of necessity, since in a pre-DMX-1000 era it was impossible to provide the necessary dynamic control of individual grains at densities that exceeded these boundary conditions. The aural effect was thus one of essentially static textures of limited musical value. Now this was no longer the case, and it became possible to investigate the possibilities of building up textures from aggregates of individual sonic elements lasting just a fraction of a second, first realized with *Solar Ellipse*.

The key to overcoming this hurdle lay in harnessing the significant increase in computing power provided by the DMX to control the generation of grains at much higher densities, combining and overlaying several granular streams or voices simultaneously. Furthermore, a key requirement was that the improved system also had to operate in real time, allowing the composer to interact directly with the parameters controlling the processes of synthesis. Two versions of his new granular software were developed during the mid-1980s, GSX and GSAMX, supported in due course by GRMSKX, an additional control facility allowing the implementation of tendency masks in a manner similar to those offered by POD. GSX allows two basic modes of synthesis, fixed waveform and frequency modulation, whereas GSAMX uses sampled sounds as the source material.

Although the techniques of granulation used for the GS programs share features in common with those of Roads, the control environment develops several characteristics a stage further. The minimum duration of individual grains that could be controlled by the PDP-11/23 was approximately eight milliseconds (ms) per voice (125 grains per second), the number of simultaneous voices being limited by the speed of the DMX-1000 synthesis engine. In the case of fixed waveform and sampled sound synthesis, a maximum of twenty voices can be produced, resulting in in a total grain density of 2,500 grains per second. In the case of FM synthesis, the maximum number of voices reduces to eight, with a corresponding grain density of 1,000 grains per second. From the composer's point of view, it is the nature of the grains for individual voices that are of paramount importance, and it is from this perspective that the key operational characteristics of the programs will now be considered in more detail.[37]

The following basic parameters define the nature of each grain:

1. The waveform of the grain
2. The amplitude of the grain[38]
3. The frequency of the grain
4. The frequency range of the grain
5. The duration of the grain
6. The duration range of the grain
7. The delay between the end of the grain and the start of the next grain

The minimum duration of each grain, as noted above, is 8 ms, and the maximum is 120 ms, whereas the delay between grains can be varied between 0 ms and 120 ms. It is interesting to compare the upper limits of these two parameters with the earlier cited POD limits of approximately no more than ten to twenty events per second for each event to be individually perceived. The maximum grain duration of 120 ms corresponds to slightly more than eight events per second, well within this perception boundary. If an element of delay between grains is also introduced, this process of differentiation becomes even more marked. In theory there is no reason why these two limits should not be extended further; however, for all intents and purposes, the 120-ms limits adopted by these programs for these duration parameters are more than adequate for the purposes of granular synthesis. The ability to modulate both the frequency and the duration of each grain using an associated random probability algorithm is a powerful enhancement to the granulation processes, the significance of which will be returned to and discussed in more detail later.

One further key parameter that must be set at the outset is the linear amplitude envelope for each grain. In place of the fixed envelope used by Roads, Truax uses symmetrical attack and decay envelopes that can be varied between 1/2 the duration of each grain and 1/16 the duration of each grain, with a default value of 1/4. In practical terms, sharper envelopes may produce audible sidebands according to context, which can be usefully manipulated if so desired by using gentler envelopes. Figure 2.5 shows how Truax illustrates these basic grain characteristics.

In the case of sampled sounds, two approaches were adopted. The first required the sound extract to be loaded into the memory of the DMX-1000. This, however, could only store a maximum of 4K words, a total of 4,032 samples. Accordingly, the maximum sample length was limited to approximately

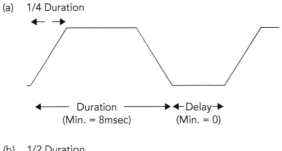

FIGURE 2.5

Grains with variable attack and decay envelopes.[39]

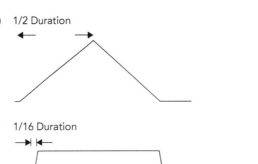

150–170 ms, thus allowing only very brief fragments of externally sampled material to be granulated. Notwithstanding the practical restrictions thus imposed, Truax successfully used this mode of sampling for his first work to use GSAMX, *The Wings of Nike*, completed in 1987. This was composed entirely from granulations of just two phonemes. The second approach, subsequently implemented, was altogether more satisfactory, providing the basis for the extensive repertory of works based on sampled sounds that was to follow. In place of the fixed preloaded sound extract, he was able to use an external hard disk drive for the PDP-11/23, offering a maximum capacity of five megabytes, which even at a sampling rate of 40 kHz could accommodate sounds lasting more than a couple of minutes. In this arrangement the internal memory of the DMX-1000 is constantly updated with new data from the disk, using internal buffering to maintain a smooth flow of audio for granulation.

There are some additional parameters that are specific to the mode of granular synthesis. In the case of fixed waveform synthesis these include the number of voices for each of the three possible waveforms (chosen from a library file of twenty). In the case of FM synthesis these extend to the average modulation index (the basic c/m ratio is specified separately) and index range, and the number of voices (maximum eight). In the case of sampled synthesis, in place of a frequency parameter an offset value relative to the start of the sampled sound and a speed of output parameter (default value one) that provides pitch/time transposition must be specified, along with the number of voices (maximum eight). In terms of the parameter variables that can be preprogrammed in advance using GRMSKX, these are limited in the case of tendency masks to frequency (fixed waveform synthesis or FM), offset (in the case of sampled synthesis), duration, modulation index (FM only), and, in the case of envelopes, amplitude and delay time.

In practice, given the significantly enhanced real-time control environment, Truax only made limited use of GRMSKX, choosing instead to use an alternative interactive performance control facility using ramp files to control the rate of change of parameter settings within user-specified limits.[40] The characteristics of this latter mode of control feature strongly in the work that will now be studied in depth, *Riverrun*, composed in 1986. This was the first work to be composed using GSX, and the analysis that follows provides a detailed introduction to Truax's work with granular synthesis, providing also a useful basis for further study of these techniques in later works, including those composed using GSAMX.[41]

Inside *Riverrun*

Riverrun: Technique, form, and structure

In investigating *Riverrun* in more detail, we will first look at the overall structure of the work. This is followed by an examination of the granular synthesis techniques and the GSX software that are so important to the work. Finally, we will look at how these are used to shape the music. Throughout, the text will be enhanced by the accompanying software, which contains video recordings of the composer explaining his approach and demonstrating the original GSX system in his studio, along with interactive explorers we created for this project. The explorers provide you with the opportunity to try out the techniques for yourself to deepen your understanding of their potential and the role they play in *Riverrun*. You are encouraged to download the software, as this facilitates full access and interactive engagement with these materials. Short video demonstrations of the software in use are also provided to give a quick taste of what the software has to offer.

The musical shape and structure of *Riverrun* are intimately connected to the technical means of its production—the granular synthesis techniques devised by the composer and realized using the GSX software that is employed exclusively in the composition. The work is constructed from a series of grain streams generated one at a time using the software and then superposed (using an analog multitrack tape recorder) to form sections of the work. The composer's own documentation of the work identifies five sections in *Riverrun*, and these are clearly identifiable aurally in the work as well as from examining the source materials (published by the composer on DVD and generously made available by him for use in this project).[42] There are occasionally brief overlaps from one section to another, but nonetheless the section breaks are always clearly delineated.

A distinctive feature of this work, relating both to its aesthetic and its means of production, is the fact that the work is made up out of relatively few compositional units. Each of the five sections comprises between two and four superposed *sequences*. Each of these sequences comprises four superposed stereo *strands*.[43] It is these strands that are the basic building blocks of the work, each the result of a single unedited take, performed on the computer live in the studio and recorded onto tape. There are fourteen different sequences, including a recurrence in the case of Sequence M, so the whole of this twenty-minute piece is made up of a total of just fifty-six sound recordings. Furthermore, on many occasions the different strands that make up a sequence are almost identical, with minor variations being used to add richness and depth to the texture. This is in marked contrast to many other approaches to composing computer music in which a work is formed out of very many different short sound objects. This is thus a work concerned with the juxtaposition and superposition of large-scale processes rather than small-scale motivic manipulation. Figure 2.6 provides an overview of the structure of *Riverrun*.

In the accompanying software, Presentation 1 provides an opportunity to explore the large-scale structure of the work in more detail. An interactive chart shows the sections that make up the work and the sequences and strands of which these sections are comprised. You can play the component parts separately or together. Demonstration Video 2.1 provides a short example of how to explore Presentation 1. ▶

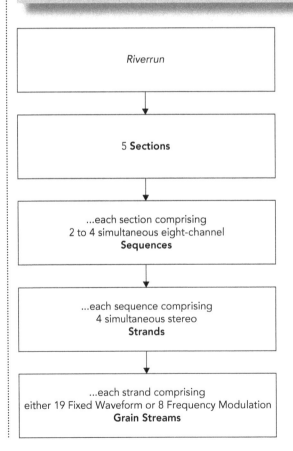

FIGURE 2.6

Overview of the structure of *Riverrun*.[44]

Granular synthesis in *Riverrun* and the GSX system

Going into further detail, any one strand is based either on grains employing *fixed waveforms* (stored in a wavetable) or using *frequency modulation*. If a strand uses fixed waveforms it can have a maximum of nineteen simultaneous streams of grains. If it uses frequency modulation, the maximum is eight streams. These limits were determined by the computing power available at the time, as described earlier. Each stream is a stereophonic succession of grains: successive grains follow each other, the next grain starting after the duration of the previous grain has elapsed plus any delay time. All the streams within a strand are generated together in real time in response to the same set of data inputted from the computer terminal (see Figure 2.7).

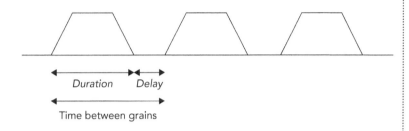

Duration   Delay

Time between grains

FIGURE 2.7

Successive grains within a stream.[45]

The parameters "duration" and "delay" as well as the "frequency" of the grains can be controlled by the user. In addition to specifying fixed values for duration and frequency it is also possible to specify a "range" for these two parameters, and the values for these parameters within the given range are chosen randomly by the algorithm. The range is centered on the initial value given for that parameter.

> *Presentation 2 in the accompanying software provides a simple introduction to real-time granular synthesis and to these fundamental parameters. You can play a strand of nineteen voices of fixed waveform granular synthesis and adjust frequency, duration, their random ranges, and delay, as shown in Demonstration Video 2.2.* ▶

The frequency modulation model contains many of the same features as the fixed waveform model, and introduces the "modulation index" parameter, along with an associated "range."

> *Presentation 3 in the accompanying software introduces the frequency modulation model of granular synthesis, as shown in Demonstration Video 2.3.* ▶

In the GSX implementation of real-time granular synthesis, other parameters allow for further flexibility and expressivity. The total number of streams or

74

voices can be varied within these limits using the "total # of voices" parameter (from zero to nineteen with the fixed waveform model, from zero to eight with the frequency modulation model). With the fixed waveform model, it is possible to enrich the texture by using up to three different stored waveforms and to allocate several voices to them. For both models, parameters are changed by hand using the keyboard—the original system does not have a mouse—to select and change individual parameters one at a time. Further options that facilitate the performance of the system include the use of *presets* and *ramps*. Saving and recalling data as stored presets enables quick movement between different configurations. An alternative to entering parameter changes individually by hand is to change them by triggering a ramp. Ramps increment or decrement values by a set amount at regular intervals. Each variable parameter can be given a plus or minus sign—no sign indicating no change for the parameter concerned—and an integer value by which it will be changed at each step. The time between steps is set by a global "ramp" parameter, in milliseconds. This ramp time can itself be changed or indeed ramped. There is also an overall increment value ("inc") that acts as a global multiplier of the individual parameter increment values. A negative value inverts all the ramps.

Figure 2.8 shows the list of parameters for the fixed waveform model as presented on the GSX computer screen interface.

> Presentation 4 in the accompanying software contains a video of Barry Truax demonstrating these features, using the fixed waveform version. Presentation 6 also allows you to work with this software for yourself using our emulation of the GSX system. Demonstration Video 2.4 provides a demonstration of how the software operates. ▶

Figure 2.9 summarizes the parameters available with the frequency modulation model.

Here the allocation of voices to different waveforms is replaced by controls for modulation index and the range within which this index can vary.

> Presentation 5 in the accompanying software contains a video with the composer demonstrating the frequency modulation version. Again, you can work with this version for yourself using our emulation of the GSX system in Presentation 6. Demonstration Video 2.5 illustrates these options. ▶

Much of the rich potential of granular synthesis comes through the desynchronization of the grains. Initially, when the GSX system is launched, all the grain streams have the same grain durations. As the user changes settings,

Inc	Freq	Freq Range	Dur	Dur Range	Delay	Ramp	# Voices Wv #2	# Voices Wv #3	Total # Voices

FIGURE 2.8

Parameters for the fixed waveform model of GSX.[46]

Inc	Freq	Freq Range	Dur	Dur Range	Delay	Ramp	Mod Ind	MI Range	Total # Voices

FIGURE 2.9

Parameters for the frequency modulation model.[47]

including the duration range, the streams become de-synchronized, adding depth and richness to the resulting texture. Even if the duration range is later reduced to zero again, although the streams have the same periodicity, they are never fully synchronized until the system is restarted. In our emulation, stopping the playback automatically resets the synchronization, making this easier to achieve.

> Demonstration Video 2.6 shows Presentation 7, containing a video excerpt in which Barry Truax demonstrates the significance of de-synchronization using the original GSX system. You can also try this out for yourself using our emulation in Presentation 6. ▶

These processes and the way the GSX system was designed and used by Truax had a crucial impact upon the way *Riverrun* was formed. The main means of shaping the music is by forming large-scale transformational processes, and this is done by controlling the parameters of individual strands of grains in real time. It is through the juxtaposition and superposition of these processes that the overall shape of the work is produced. Certain basic parameters cannot be ramped, such as the carrier/modulator ratio in the frequency modulation model, the grain envelope shapes, and the different available waveforms. Other parameters, as has been shown in the above demonstrations, can be changed dynamically during the "performance." These live studio performances of individual strands are then combined, sometimes after modification, on a multi-track tape recorder to form the final work.

Tape techniques

Granular synthesis and the GSX system are the major tools used in the creation of *Riverrun*. However, the use of analog tape techniques does play a small but significant role in the work. For example, Sequences A and L were recorded onto tape and then played in reverse. Because grains are symmetrical, this doesn't change the grains in themselves, but only affects the overall shape of the sequence. This reverse playback was used because of the impossibility, discussed above, of bringing grain streams back into synchrony once the duration range has been employed. Truax wanted this section to end with all the grains coming into synchronization, having previously been scattered. He therefore recorded the sequences in reverse, starting with synchronicity, then introducing random variation, and played them backward to achieve his desired effect. The other tape manipulations he used include doubling the speed of playback (Sequences M and J) and repeating a sequence (Sequence M in section 5).

Presentation 8 in the accompanying software allows you to simulate these operations digitally, using either recordings of these sequences, other sequences from Riverrun, *or any other sound files. You might even try to recreate the original sequences using our GSX emulation software, recording the result into a file and then applying the relevant tape transformation to this file. Demonstration Video 2.7 presents these features.* ▶

Spatialization in *Riverrun*

Analog tape techniques also played a role in the mixing of the individual streams and their spatial distribution. As streams are generated by the computer, they are placed alternately to the left and right channels of a stereo pair. This adds to the spatial depth of the sound and ensures that channels are decorrelated. Streams remain fixed spatially so there is no dynamic spatial movement within a stream and there are no intermediary positions permissible between extreme left and right.

The mixing of streams to form sequences was done using a multichannel analog tape recorder. When Truax combines four strands to form a sequence, the four stereo pairs (strands) are distributed across eight channels, interleaved to enrich the spatial experience when the work is performed as intended in this format. Spatialization is therefore used in this work, not to create dynamic spatial movement or spatial gestures, nor for the most part to counterpoint different materials in space (the interleaving of channels counts against this), but rather to enrich the texture and to envelope the listener within a complex multilayered sonority. Figure 2.10 shows the spatial distribution of stereo pairs for four strands.

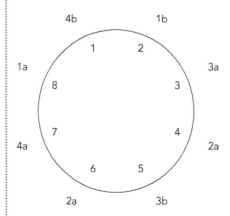

Channel distribution of four stereo strands.[48]

Sections and streams

The following commentary provides an outline account of the musical shape of *Riverrun*, section by section, showing how the different sequences help form this shape. At the end of each section an introduction to the relevant accompanying software is provided to enable you to engage with this material interactively and aurally.

Section 1

Section 1 lasts for 5′38″. It develops gradually over this time from relatively sparse grains, audible as separate events at the opening of the work, to a dense, complex texture. The growth of the texture, which can be thought of as representing the evolution of a great river from droplets of water, forming into streams before merging into a large river, is achieved both by the successive entry of the three superposed sequences that form this section, and by the changing parameters of each individual sequence. At the end of the section a regular beat emerges from within this texture.

The three sequences in this section are, in order of entry, A, L, and M (as labeled by the composer in his documentation). In the final mix all three sequences are played in a modified version, differing from how they were originally generated by the computer. Sequences A and L are played in reverse, while Sequence M is at double speed (and therefore an octave higher). Note that Sequences A and L are here described as heard in the work after reversal.

Sequence A is the first to enter. Its four strands are in turn faded in as part of the slow textural growth. Over the five and a half minutes, two of these four strands move from their initial rhythmic patterns of separate grains to faster and faster grains, eventually the separate grains merging into a continuous texture. The other two strands also begin to accelerate, but then the grains become gradually more regular in rhythm and are synchronized so that, toward the end of the section, a pulse at approximately 240 beats per minutes (BPM) emerges.

Sequence L is the next to enter, after approximately 1′10″. Its entry is noticeable because it introduces higher frequency regions to the overall texture. The four strands of this sequence all follow a similar transformational path but are at different, harmonically related frequencies, centered around 250, 500, 1,000 and 1,500 Hz, respectively. The sequence begins and ends gradually by increasing/decreasing the number of voices being generated. It opens with a relatively sparse texture with individual grains perceptible. The richness of the timbre grows by increasing the FM modulation index and its range before decreasing again. The density of grains then increases and, toward the end, the frequency range narrows, in each case by means of ramps.

The final sequence to enter in this section is Sequence M, starting at approximately 2′35″. It introduces an even higher frequency range to the overall texture, in part because it is played at double speed, raising the frequencies originally generated on the computer by one octave. Unlike the previous sequences that have a clear trajectory toward a goal, Sequence M follows a cyclical pattern. Each of the four strands has the same pattern, but starting at a different point in the cycle. Frequencies for the strands rise and fall between 5,000 and 9,000 Hz (which are doubled on playback), and the frequency range varies in proportion, increasing as the frequency rises. The duration also follows a cyclic pattern. This sequence creates a high shimmering component to the overall texture, gently fluctuating in the background.

> There are several different ways in which you can use the software to interact aurally with the sequences in section 1, for example:
> - You can return to the Interactive Structural Chart to play the original recordings of the individual sequences or strands separately or together (Presentation 1).
> - You can use interactive graphs of Parameter Evolutions to see visualizations of the parameter changes described above and hear the results of these on the sound (Presentation 11).
> - For Sequence L, you can watch a video of Barry Truax explaining the way the sequence is shaped and demonstrating it on the original GSX system (Presentation 10).
> - You can use our emulation and the increased power of modern computing to recreate the individual sequences (Presentation 12) or the whole section (Presentation 13) live, performing the original using preset data or modifying the data to explore other possibilities.

> All these options are introduced in Demonstration Video 2.8. ▶

Transition from section 1 to section 2

Section 1 merges into section 2 as follows: At 5'36" Strands 1 and 2 of Sequence A end with a "resonant" tail, and at 5'38" Sequence M stops. At 5'39" the "footsteps" (at 240 BPM) from Strands 3 and 4 of Sequence A stop and are succeeded immediately by the start of a new sequence: Sequence N, belonging to section 2, which has a similar pulse but at 60 BPM. It is as if the steps have simply changed gear. This overlaps with remaining strands from Sequence L that end at 5'41" The "footsteps" of Sequence N continue and at 5'43" are joined by Sequence D, a deep, rich, sustained pedal on the pitch D1 (slightly sharp).

> Presentation 1 in the software allows you to listen to this transition and listen to tracks individually. Demonstration Video 2.9 provides an opportunity to hear this. ▶

Section 2

Section 2 therefore begins fully at 5'43" and lasts until 8'48". Four sequences make up section 2: N, D, E and F.

Sequence N, as already noted, starts with rhythmically regular, synchronized grains at approximately 60 BPM. Gradually the duration range is increased leading the grains to go out of synchronization. The frequency range decreases at the same time and the average length of grains increases. These changes continue throughout the sequence, accelerating over time. After about a minute the sense of a synchronized pulse has completely disappeared, having transformed into an irregular sequence of grains in terms of both rhythm and frequency. The increasing duration of the grains is more noticeable by 2′30″. At approximately 3′00″, which corresponds with the end of section 2 (Sequence N overlaps into section 3), the now long grains begin to fade slowly in and out in eerie long envelopes contrasting with the brief, sharp attacks that opened this sequence. The timing of these envelopes is different for each strand, but otherwise the strands take the same transformational path, but with different timbral characteristics. Sequence N therefore follows a clearly directional trajectory. Otherwise section 2 is predominantly symmetrical in shape.

Sequences D and E essentially follow the same pattern, both consisting of a rich pedal note. During the section this pedal becomes somewhat blurred by an increasing frequency range and longer delays between grains before refocusing once more on the original pedal note at the end. The four strands of each sequence represent different harmonics of the pedal note: Strand 1: D1, Strand 2: D2, Strand 3: A2, and Strand 4: D3 (all slightly sharp). What distinguishes Sequences D and E is their timbre: D uses the fixed waveform model, whereas E uses FM synthesis as the basis for the grains.

Sequence F also follows a symmetrical pattern, as can be seen clearly in the parametrical display included in Presentation 11 of the accompanying software ("Parameter evolutions"). Again, its material is based around the pitch D (300 Hz—a little sharp) with each strand based on a particular octave: Strand 1: D3, Strand 2: D4, Strand 3: D5, Strand 4: D6. As the software example shows, the frequency range of all these strands widens to include higher frequencies but with the lower boundaries decreasing only slightly. The texture changes, therefore, from a unison pitch to a succession of grains spread across a wide range. The wedge reaches its apex in each strand at around 7′31" before contracting back toward a unison D.

As with section 1, you can engage with these sequences and the means used to produce them in a variety of ways, interactively and aurally, using the accompanying software to explore the larger structure (Presentation 1), to recreate the sequences (Presentation 12) or the whole section (Presentation 13), or to study the parametric evolutions (Presentation 11). The software also includes a video of Barry Truax showing how Sequence F was formed (Presentation 9). Demonstration Video 2.10 introduces some of the possibilities thus opened up. ▶

Section 3

Section 3 is also predominantly symmetrical and features Sequences B, C, and H. Behind these persists the eerie overlap from Sequence N already mentioned.

Sequences B and C form another pair, identical apart from their timbre: B using the fixed waveform model and C using frequency modulation as the basis for grains (cf. Sequences D and E). The sequences are based on a low G1 (100 Hz) pedal. The grains here are of very short duration with no delay between successive grains. The granulation process therefore introduces audible amplitude modulation. The different durations for each strand result in modulation frequencies that are different subharmonics of 100 Hz: Strand 1: duration 10 ms, modulation frequency 100 Hz; Strand 2: 20 ms, 50 Hz; Strand 3: 30 ms, 33.33 Hz; Strand 4: 100 ms, 10 Hz. All follow the same path, essentially a wedge shape. This moves from unison to a wide frequency range with the low G still as the center frequency, the duration range also increasing, before contracting once again to a unison. This pattern is like that of Sequence F in section 2.

Sequence H enters a little later in a higher frequency region based around D5 (1,200 Hz). The different strands are all identical apart from distinct timbres resulting from different FM modulation ratios. This sequence also broadens and then contracts in frequency range. As the frequency range broadens a dense granular texture unfolds. The density then decreases and the frequency range contracts once more to a unison, but on this occasion it is a little less intense because of the now lower grain density.

Again, you can use the software to play individual components of this section, to view and hear the parameter evolutions and to recreate the sequences and the whole section.

Section 4

Section 4 begins at 10′55″ and lasts until 14′13″, overlapping with the next section. It comprises the Sequences I, K, and J—the latter played at double speed.

Sequence K comprises a repeating cycle of deep pitches. This is achieved using presets to store parameter settings that can then be recalled instantly. Sixteen presets are recalled in a repeating sequence. As in Sequences B and C, subharmonics together with the amplitude modulation that underlies this form of granular synthesis combine to produce rich, deep timbres. The strands are almost identical, with the following exceptions: Strands 1, 3, and 4 all have an FM carrier/ modulator ratio of 1:1, whereas the ratio for Strand 2 is 2:1, resulting in a different timbral quality. Strands 1 and 2 have a frequency of 200 Hz, whereas Strand 3 is at 150 Hz and Strand 4 is at 250 Hz. Superposed on the repeating sequence is an increase in the modulation index and its range followed by a corresponding decrease.

Sequence K provides the nearest thing there is in *Riverrun* to a traditional pitch structure, as opposed to sustained pedal tones or randomly chosen pitches.

Sequences I and J are more directional. Sequence I begins with a granular texture with wide frequency and duration ranges and a relatively long delay between grains. These parameters then all reduce, the texture increasing in density and the frequency becoming more focused. The timbre is enriched by an increasing modulation index that then reduces again before the sequence fades out. The strands, which are all FM-based, have different carrier to modulator ratios and use different carrier waveforms. They also have different harmonically related base frequencies (125, 250, 375, and 750 Hz, respectively). Aurally, these only begin to emerge as the frequency range decreases.

Sequence J, despite being played at double speed, and therefore an octave higher than generated by the computer, is another low pedal texture. The notional frequency at the start is 0 Hz, but each strand has a different frequency range, from 100 to 250 Hz. The grains are also very short (20 ms) again producing an amplitude modulation effect. The overall result is a rather rough texture with a somewhat vague, unfocused deep pitch. During the sequence this becomes even more blurred as the frequency ranges, durations, and duration ranges all increase along with the modulation index and its range.

> Again, you can use the software to play individual components of this section, to view and hear the parameter evolutions and to recreate the sequences and the whole section. For example, Demonstration Video 2.11 presents the parametric evolution of Sequence K with its distinctive cycle of subharmonic pitches. ▶

Section 5

The final section begins at 14′09″, Sequence M overlapping with the previous section. It comprises just two sequences, M and G. M is played twice, first forward, then backward, creating a palindromic structure. This section is relatively static, a quietening of activity as the end of the work approaches.

Sequence M has already been discussed in relation to section 1; it is the only sequence to recur in the work. Here it is an octave lower than in section 1, where it was played at double speed. This does not affect its intrinsic structure, but it does mean that it is more prominent in the texture and its cyclic nature can be heard more clearly. After one complete cycle it is played again in reverse. This has little effect on the timbre of the sequence, since grains in the GSX system are themselves symmetrical (non-retrogradable).

> *You might like to compare the use of Sequence M in section 5 with its occurrence in section 1 using the Interactive Structural Chart in Presentation 1 of the accompanying software. The parametric evolution displays in Presentation 11 also show clearly the characteristic ramped patterns that are also visible in sonograms of the work.[49]*

Sequence G enters after M and a few seconds after the end of section 4. It is yet another example of a pedal pitch that becomes blurred then focuses again on the original pitch, but in this case the overall shape is not quite symmetrical. All four strands are identical, apart from a subtle timbral difference arising from the use of different carrier waveforms for the FM synthesis. The frequency is 150 Hz (a sharp D) with a small frequency range. The grains are again short (20 ms), resulting in amplitude modulation at 50 Hz enriching the timbre. During the sequence the pitch at first becomes blurred by an increase in the frequency range. This then decreases once again, followed by more subtle changes resulting from increases and decreases in duration and duration range.

At the end of the work, Sequence G finishes first, leaving the high ethereal frequencies of Sequence M to drift away.

> *Again, you can use the software to play individual components of this section, to view and hear the parameter evolutions and to recreate the sequences and the whole section.*

Conclusions

In light of the above account of how *Riverrun* is formed using the software, we can begin to understand more clearly the relationship between technology and creative process in this work. Most obviously the composer developed his own software for granular synthesis and used this to create the work. Everything in *Riverrun* is generated using this software and the only post-processing is the mixing of the resultant tracks and, in some cases, the changing of the speed or direction of the recording. Going further we might ask: How far did technical innovation enable, or inspire, or perhaps constrain certain musical possibilities?

First, it is worth noting that this is a two-way process: the technology and the musical creativity influenced each other. Truax created his own software to suit his musical requirements, and conversely, working with the technology also shaped his musical thinking for this and later works. It is a genuine interaction. The most obvious way in which the technology facilitated this work is through granular synthesis, particularly Truax's own version of it. The form of granular synthesis used here is purely synthesized, not derived from sampled sound. Nor are tendency masks used—these things would come in his later works.[50]

The construction of music out of thousands of tiny fragments of sound, often lasting only a few milliseconds, is something that cannot be done effectively with traditional acoustic instruments; it requires digital technology. The concept of the "note" as the basic building block of a work, or even of the sound object or sonic event as in much acousmatic music, is gone. So the very starting point for musical composition has changed. The fundamental element here is no longer something that can be meaningfully heard or shaped in its own right. The significance of a grain is the part it plays within the process of an evolving grain stream and it would not make sense, either practically or aesthetically, within this context to attempt to shape each grain independently. Compositional thinking here is in terms of process rather than event.

Furthermore, the GSX software offers a distinctive approach to granular synthesis, with unique compositional features. In 1986 it was unique in offering granular synthesis in real time—this was largely down to Truax's programming skills and the specialist hardware he obtained. So he was able to shape strands of music as he listened to them, performing them live and responding to the sound. Performing the system is an essential part of Truax's creative interaction with technology in *Riverrun*, even though the final work is not a live performance but a prerecorded, fixed media piece.

However, he could only create one stereo strand in real time. So to build the rich and complex textures of *Riverrun*, he needed to superpose multiple layers using an analog multitrack tape machine. This method of working imposed some restrictions on what he could do in terms of flexibility, certainly compared with how one might work today. Nonetheless, Truax's technical setup, including the analog recorder, is key to the understanding of the way the work is shaped, using many superposed layers of sound. Often, as we have seen, two or more strands within a sequence use very similar parameter settings and follow similar transformational paths. The purpose is not to create counterpoint between these strands but to enrich the texture by superposing related material. For example, on several occasions the same material is presented simultaneously in different versions, one using FM and the other fixed waveform synthesis; we are thus presented with two different timbral perspectives on the same material. Additionally, of course, the fact that each strand was performed separately and played live in the studio leads to further small but enriching differences.

Another musically significant feature of Truax's granular system is that it is based on streams of grains, and these streams have a potential for regularity, even if this is often hidden by random variation. Unlike some systems, which generate random grains within prescribed boundaries and sometimes independently of any concept of a stream, with GSX randomness is presented to the user as deviation from a central value. This applies to all the randomized parameters. With duration, for example, the user specifies a central value and then a range within which grains can deviate randomly. Likewise, for frequency, the range can be set to zero, in which case there is no random variation and the values are as specified and predictable. In part at least, this is simply about the way in which the parameters are presented to the composer. But the musical significance of this is that there is a sense of underlying order, and the software facilitates, indeed encourages, movement between fixed order and random fields. As we have seen, this is something Truax makes significant musical use of throughout the work: one of the main ways in which *Riverrun* is shaped is through the use of passages that feature movement toward or away from order in one or more of the parameters.

As we have seen, granular synthesis is not so much about the individual grains in themselves, but rather about the patterns and shapes formed by large groups of grains. Truax's software is designed to facilitate the shaping of sound in long evolving processes. Indeed, using the GSX system it is probably easier to do this than to create short gestures or events. Both the synthesis algorithm and the user interface encourage users to set up initial parameter settings and then transform the texture using ramps that progressively increment or decrement one or more parameters over time. The musical result is a piece that is about large-scale process. It is music of slow, subtle, textural changes, sometimes arriving at or departing from distinctive landmarks (e.g., frequency unisons or rhythmic pulses), but otherwise more concerned with transformational process than individual sonic objects. This is compounded by the superposition, at any one time, of several similar processes, as we have already seen. It is, therefore, a form of "process music," but very different in sound and aesthetic from minimalism, and the processes are applied not to the pitches and rhythms of notes, but to parameters of grains of sound.

In summary, therefore, technology and creative practice are inextricably bound together in *Riverrun*. The same creative mind produced both the software and the music, and it is not always possible to delineate where technological development was driven by preexistent creative goals and where, conversely, technology discoveries inspired new musical approaches. Truax's real-time granular system was designed to allow him to shape grain streams in real time, performing the transformations "live" in the studio and then form sections of music by superposing the resulting strands. The system encouraged the composer to think in terms of long evolving processes in which the interplay of regularity and random variation plays an important role. Regularity features, for example, as pitched pedal notes and rhythmic pulses, while randomness leads to complex rich textures. Superposition is used both to layer minor variations on the same texture, adding further richness to the sonority, and to counterpoint different processes with different trajectories.

There is a contrast between material that has clear, although slowly evolving, teleological trajectories and material that is cyclical or symmetrical in its temporal structure. Spatialization plays an important role in articulating and adding depth to these many-layered textures. What is clear is that *Riverrun* could not have been conceived without granular synthesis, or indeed the specific form of granular synthesis Barry Truax himself devised. Technological innovation and creative practice in this work thus go hand in hand.

> *The software contains further video material of Barry Truax, including interviews about Riverrun and the composer discussing other aspects of his work, and of granular synthesis more generally. Demonstration Video 2.12 introduces these resources.* ▶

3

Philippe Manoury
Pluton

Contexts for *Pluton*

First steps in the development of technologies for live computer music

There are several similarities that can be highlighted between Philippe Manoury and Jonathan Harvey, two of the composers selected for special study in this critique, and these features in common provide useful insights into their respective contributions to computer music. Both have produced a rich and varied legacy of works written purely for acoustic instruments, with these experiences proving highly influential on their respective engagement with the possibilities of digital technologies. At the same time, neither has become significantly engaged with the technical development of the resources they have used in this context. In this respect they both differ markedly from composers such as Barry Truax and Trevor Wishart, highlighting the diversity of approaches to be considered. A further connection between Manoury and Harvey arises from their work at IRCAM as visiting composers at key points in their respective careers. A key feature of Manoury's exploration of the medium over the years has been the use of real-time signal processing techniques in ways that were very much at the leading edge of contemporary developments.

The first significant steps in developing real-time modes of composing computer music date back to the late 1960s and a series of initiatives in Europe and America that used dedicated computers to control hardware-based facilities for audio synthesis and signal processing, notably GROOVE, developed by Max Mathews at Bell Telephone Laboratories; MUSYS III, developed by Peter Zinovieff in London; and EMS 1, developed at the Swedish EMS studio in Stockholm under the direction of Knut Wiggen. Known generically as hybrid synthesis systems, the sound-producing resources were predominantly analog in nature, although the EMS system included a pioneering bank of digital oscillators.[1]

The overriding constraint on such initiatives was the lack of computing resources sufficiently powerful to engage directly with real-time synthesis and signal processing applications, and it was to take a further decade before material progress was made in this context. These conditions make the early real-time synthesis experiments of Barry Truax at the Institute of Sonology in Utrecht, 1971–1972, generating sound directly from a PDP-15 computer, especially significant.[2] His pioneering work in this context coincided with the birth of the microprocessor, leading in turn to the microcomputer and a design revolution that was to challenge and ultimately surpass the development of minicomputers based on more traditional architectures. Such developments, however, were to take many years to come to fruition, and even the most advanced minicomputers available at the start of the 1980s lacked enough processing power to engage directly with real-time modes of high-quality audio synthesis other than on a very limited scale.

The key to material progress in the latter regard was the development of high-speed digital signal processing systems that could be controlled via a conventional computer. One of the earliest of these systems, the DMX-1000, was discussed in Chapter 2 in terms of its role as a key component of the pioneering real-time computer music system developed by Truax at Simon Fraser University, Vancouver. By the early 1980s, however, time was ripe for further progress to be made in the design of high performance "front-end" audio processors, and it is in this context that the Institut de Recherche et Coordination Acoustique/ Musique (IRCAM) was to play a major role with a series of important initiatives that merit closer study.

The pioneering contributions of IRCAM

The foundation of IRCAM was the result of an invitation in 1970 to Pierre Boulez from Georges Pompidou, the president of France, to establish an international center for music research. The main construction of a purpose-designed building for the institution, located underneath Place Igor Stravinsky in Paris, was completed in 1973, allowing work to start on a series of multidisciplinary research projects in music and both the physical and the cognitive sciences.[3]

In 1977 IRCAM was officially launched to the artistic community, opening its doors to the first tranche of visiting composers. During the early years creative activity focused primarily on facilities offered by a dedicated PDP-10 mainframe computer, making extensive use of Music V, the last version of the Music N series of programs to be produced by Max Mathews and his associates at Bell Labs, and its derivative Music 10, developed by John Chowning and James Moorer at Stanford University, California. Particular attention was paid to the possibilities of extending the capacity of these resources to embrace the processing of externally generated sounds as well as the direct production of computer-generated materials. Work was transferred in the early 1980s to a physically smaller but more powerful DEC VAX-11/780 computer, which continued in service until it was replaced by a network of high-performance workstations toward the end of the decade.

Even before the official opening of IRCAM, however, foundations were being laid for a series of initiatives that were to place the institution at the forefront of developments that established important new areas of creative practice in computer music, exploring real-time and increasingly interactive modes of audio synthesis and signal processing. Other leading research centers, such as Stanford (CCRMA) and MIT, were soon to follow suit, but in terms of pioneering the technologies necessary to facilitate such methods of working, a strong case can be made for highlighting IRCAM's special role in this regard. Before studying the key features of the systems that resulted from these initiatives it is helpful to understand the reasons why the essentially non-real-time working environment associated with the pioneering era of computer music continued to prove especially attractive for a number of years.[4] In artistic terms it transpired that a number of composers still preferred to work one step removed from the synthesis process, developing the associated coding of instructions completely in advance and then refining these where appropriate in the light of aural feedback and evaluation of the results. The early computer-based works of Jonathan Harvey are a case in point, and the specific characteristics of this method of composing and his reasons for so doing are discussed in Chapter 7. There was, however, a more fundamental and purely practical reason why non-real-time modes of synthesis were to remain so important for some time.

At the heart of the matter is a technical consideration that was significantly to exercise the thinking of those responsible for developing real-time computer music systems at IRCAM and elsewhere. This concerns how best to guarantee the quality of digital audio in situations where the associated data is subject to extensive digital signal processing that involves significant changes of amplitude, the argument being put forward from several quarters that a higher degree of numerical accuracy can be preserved when using floating point rather than integer representations of audio data.[5] At the time, conventional computers could not process more complex floating-point instructions and audio data in real time, and time delays between the input of instructions and the audition of the computed results were thus inevitable.[6] During the early 1980s the performance of the VAX/780 was usefully enhanced by adding a high-powered front-end FPS-100 floating-point array processor, but the resulting environment was still not wholly conducive to real-time modes of working.

During the late 1970s several researchers at IRCAM came to the view that the world of computer music urgently needed a floating-point digital signal processor that could meet the enhanced operational requirements of advanced real-time audio computing, but such technical advances could not be achieved overnight. This hurdle was finally overcome in 1989 when Intel released a high-performance floating-point processor, the i860, leading to the design of a prototype version of the IRCAM Musical Workstation (IMW) based on a modular configuration of i860 processor boards, in turn controlled by a NeXT computer. The prototype was completed in 1990 and released commercially as the IRCAM Signal Processing Workstation (ISPW) by Ariel in 1991. In both technical and musical contexts, nonetheless, integer-based DSP developments over the intervening period at IRCAM merit closer study at this point, not least for their significance in facilitating the realization of the original version of Manoury's *Pluton*.

This transitional phase of development at IRCAM was underpinned by an extended engineering project directed by Giuseppe (Peppino) di Giugno, leading to the construction of four real-time digital signal processing systems, known respectively as the 4A, the 4B, the 4C, and the 4X. Di Giugno's interest in computer music dates back to 1971, when a chance meeting with Robert Moog during a visit to Cornell University inspired him to investigate the possibilities of developing a digital control system for an analog synthesizer. At the time he was an associate professor in the physics department at the University of Naples specializing in particle physics, and this new area of interest led him to establish a research group in acoustics and electronics (ACEL), specializing in speech and music analysis, synthesis and coding, and digital signal processing. Having completed this initial project, his attention turned to the possibilities of developing facilities for sound synthesis that were not only based on all-digital architectures but also capable of operating in real time. Luciano Berio, director of the *département électroacoustique* at IRCAM took an interest in his work and invited di Giugno to join his personal research team in 1975, marking the start of an association with the institution that was to continue for more than a decade.

The development of the IRCAM 4X synthesizer

A preliminary version of di Giugno's first synthesizer, the 4A, was completed just before his move to IRCAM. The enhanced support facilities at IRCAM, not least the notable engineering skills of Alain Chauveau, led to a much-improved version of the 4A, completed in 1976. This was a complete digital additive synthesizer on a single wire-wrapped card, providing 256 oscillators at a 32 kHz sampling rate, controlled in turn by a microprocessor-based version of the PDP-11, known as the LSI-11.[7] The 4A synthesizer was succeeded by the 4B, completed in 1977. The latter design, the result of a partnership between di Giugno and Hal Alles at Bell Labs, New Jersey, introduced the possibilities of

FM synthesis based on a smaller bank of sixty-four oscillators and the added control flexibility of thirty-two envelope generators. This development was inspired at least in part by a recognition of the practical complexities of working in a purely additive synthesis environment and the potential of frequency modulation techniques of sound production that had been productively explored in non-real-time contexts using programs such as Music V.[8] Whereas both synthesizers operated in real time, they were still relatively complex to program, limited to a 16 kHz audio bandwidth (half the 32 kHz sampling rate), and an integer data resolution of sixteen bits.

Some important improvements were implemented in the next version, the 4C, completed in 1978, which brought together contributions from di Giugno, Alles, Chauveau, Peter Eastty, and James Lawson. Three different versions of the 4C were constructed, the most elaborate version being developed by Eastty, using a PDP-34 computer as the host controller. Although the sampling rate and the size of the FM oscillator bank remained the same as in the case of the 4B, a major step forward in terms of digital signal processing was the step change from a conventional sixteen-bit data format to one that used the significantly improved resolution of a twenty-four-bit integer format. This technical enhancement significantly closed the gap between floating-point and fixed-point (integer) modes of processing in terms of fidelity, to the extent that twenty-four-bit integer formats were subsequently to become ubiquitous as a widely used standard within the audio industry. Despite this important advance, the ever-increasing expectations of composers were already discounting the enhanced possibilities created by the 4C. Curtis Abbott had made significant improvements to the operating environment by introducing a high-level command language known as 4CED, but di Giugno realized that a major review of the underlying hardware architecture was necessary if creative expectations were to be fully met. This led to the design and construction of the 4X, the last and by far the most significant of the di Giugno synthesizers.

The first version of the 4X was designed and built by di Giugno in 1980 with assistance from Michel Antin, and following a number of design modifications the final version was released as a commercial product in 1984, manufactured by Sogitec.[9] Although the 4X was significantly more powerful than the 4C, its design was more of an extension of the basic architecture associated with the former than the outcome of a more radical design review. Thus, it was still constrained by the limitations of a sampling rate of just 32kHz, but now taking advantage of the superior performance of a hardware architecture that was based on bit slice technologies.[10] A total of eight DSP cards, known as 4U units, were constructed using these processors, specifically for use within IRCAM.[11]

Initially, master control of the 4X was provided via a PDP-11/55 computer using a Motorola 68000–based communications interface and an associated terminal keyboard and graphics display. For the commercial version of the 4X, the PDP was replaced by a physically much smaller and more powerful Sun

2/130 workstation, and this soon also became the control computer of choice at IRCAM.[12] Sixteen digital-to-analog and sixteen analog-to-digital audio converters were provided for real-time synthesis and signal processing. In the former context each DSP card could generate up to 129 waveform components, offering the possibility of synthesizing up to 1,032 additive synthesis components or 516 suitably paired FM oscillators. In the latter context the system could be used to process externally generated audio information in a variety of ways, including filter functions to implement fast Fourier transform (FFT) and linear predictive coding (LPC) techniques of analysis and resynthesis, and feature detection applications such as pitch tracking. The diagrams in Figure 3.1 provide an overview of the commercial version of the 4X.

Despite these major technical advances, the 4X still posed significant challenges for potential users in terms of the initial lack of suitable software for aspiring composers. Various tools were developed by the research team in due course, such as the 4XY compiler written by Robert Rowe and Olivier Koechlin. This could be used to program the 68000 control processor dynamically in real time in application-specific contexts such as FM synthesis and audio sampling. These tools consisted of extensions to the underlying C programming language in a run-time environment and offered useful opportunities to simplify the complexities of programming compositional algorithms. In terms of external control devices a comprehensive control surface known as PACOM was constructed, providing 108 control devices, including twenty-four faders of different sizes, two multi-turn potentiometers, two joysticks, a track ball, and seventy-two switches, supported by an array of display facilities including 168 LEDs, two bar graphs, and fourteen alphanumeric LED displays.[13] Another tool developed by Patrick Potacsek, known as the 4X Patch Language, provided a downloadable interpreter that could be accessed via an external interactive graphics interface. As 4X applications grew in complexity, the need for such tools became ever more pressing, but in many situations the software necessary to achieve the associated creative objectives had still to be written, essentially from first principles (see Figure 3.1).

Notwithstanding the continuing challenges to be faced in terms of programming accessibility for the wider composing community, the 4X provided a powerful and influential tool for several major projects during the 1980s, each exploring in significant depth the extensive possibilities of real-time computer music applications. Perhaps the best known of these is *Répons*, by Pierre Boulez. Boulez started work on this piece in January 1980, working initially with the prototype version of the 4X. The compositional process proceeded in a series of stages, the first performance of an initial nineteen-minute segment, commissioned by Southwest German Radio (Südwestfunk), taking place at the 1981 Donaueschingen Festival.

The first performance of a second version, about thirteen minutes longer, took place almost a year later at the BBC Promenade Concerts in London in

93

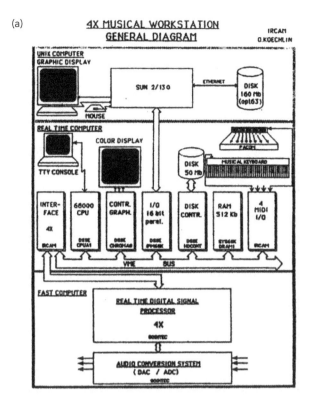

94

September 1982. Further revisions were to follow, starting in 1984 with a forty-minute version performed first in Turin and then Paris, in turn subject to further modifications in 1985.[15] Written for twenty-four instrumentalists, six soloists, and spatially diffused multichannel signal processing of the latter contributions, the resources of the 4X were stretched to the limit right from the outset. By the time the work was performed in 1984, even the most recent commercial version of the system was materially challenged by the technical demands of the latest revisions, which, instead of using the 4X in a purely responsive mode, processing sounds from the soloists in a predetermined manner, now embraced more proactive techniques of live interaction and feedback.[16]

Other composers who explored the creative possibilities of the 4X during the early 1980s included Brian Ferneyhough, Tod Machover, Tristan Murail, and Robert Rowe, and by the middle of the decade research in interactive techniques of composition and performance had become a significant focus of work at IRCAM. Whereas the PACOM control interface facilitated useful investigations into the direct control of live synthesis and signal processing, other researchers took an interest in using the system as an extension of traditional modes of performance via conventional musical instruments. Boulez thus was far from alone in exploring such possibilities in works such as *Répons*. Moreover, these investigations were to draw together a unique combination of internationally sourced talent and individual vision that was to have consequences that materially shaped the development of key resources for the medium that are widely used today.

A key contributor, indeed arguably the most significant pioneer in these processes of evolution, was Barry Vercoe. Having studied music and mathematics at an advanced level in his native New Zealand, Vercoe moved to the United States in 1962, where he encountered the possibilities of computer music for the first time. After completing doctoral studies at the University of Michigan at Ann Arbor and a series of short-term university posts, he took up a permanent appointment at MIT in 1971. Although perhaps best known for his pioneering work advancing the possibilities of the Music N family of software, starting with Music 360 (1970), followed by Music 11 (1973), and finally Csound (1986), he was also to make material contributions to the development of live synthesis techniques, especially in the specific context of using the computer as an extension of instrumental performance.[17] His initial interest in the possibilities of human-computer interaction led to the composition of his piece *Synapse* for computer tape and viola in 1976, which in turn established the research objectives he was subsequently to pursue at IRCAM. He discussed this in an interview conducted some years later:

> You can tell from the name *Synapse* that I was very interested in the real "touchy-feely" contact between the live acoustic instrument and the computer. . . . At that time, human-computer interaction, or the relation of the two forces, was strictly

on the shoulders of the live performer. This obviously deserved some attention, so when I went over to Paris [on the Guggenheim Fellowship] to work with Pierre Boulez and his group, I developed an automatic synthetic following system. Notice that I describe that as a *following* system, since I regard the human performer as the leader and the computer as responding with accompaniment. I have never really successfully modeled, nor even had very much faith in, the notion of the computer leading the way. It doesn't seem very appealing to me. It might occasionally be an interesting thing to experience, but I still have primary interest in humans as the entities I'm communicating with and hearing from.[18]

Vercoe took up his two-year fellowship at IRCAM in 1983, and started working closely with the flautist Lawrence Beauregard, who sadly died before the project was completed. Although, as is clear from the above quotation, his interests were firmly situated in the reactive possibilities of intelligent synthetic accompaniment, his work laid important foundations for the more interactive applications of real-time computer music that were eventually to follow. Interestingly, his work was to complement that of another composer/researcher, Roger Dannenberg, who also, and quite independently, had started work on a computer accompaniment system at Carnegie Mellon University. Although to a certain extent these ventures were competitive, they were subsequently to prove of mutual benefit, to the extent that Vercoe's final version of his system was able to take advantage of some useful tracking refinements originally developed by Dannenberg.[19] These developments were to provide a stimulus for several other composers seeking to work interactively with such synthesis tools, including Cort Lippe, whose notable contributions in this context are considered elsewhere.[20]

The challenge then, as is still very much the case today, was to develop pitch-tracking software to detect and analyze the acoustic output of an instrument, in this case the flute, and match these event characteristics accurately to a predetermined accompaniment. For his very first experiments, working with Beauregard, Vercoe used the sounds of a synthetic harpsichord, which were generated by the prototype version of the 4X, controlled in turn by the PDP-11/55 computer.[21] Such a task involves not only tracking the onset and ending of individual notes, but also other intrinsic characteristics that are required for generating a convincing accompaniment, such as variations in tempo, dynamics, and phrasing. Although the primary tracking process was based on a real-time acoustic analysis of the flute sound, input via a microphone and analog-to-digital converter, even the 4X could not always decode the required information fast enough for the accompaniment generator to response sufficiently promptly and/or accurately. The solution adopted here was to fit optical sensors to the keys of the flute itself, providing a very fast initial approximation of the pitch, which was then refined using techniques of audio analysis.[22]

Although this system achieved the initial intentions, Vercoe was aware that significant improvements had to be made both to the efficiency and functional characteristics of the control software for it to become a more attractive composing and performing tool. Accordingly, in 1985 he invited a former student, and by then a member of the research team at MIT, Miller Puckette, to join him at IRCAM to work on this important aspect. The key to progress in this context lay in improvements to the algorithms responsible for event scheduling in response to incoming performance data. Although the 4X remained the primary focus of attention in terms of the synthesis engine for the accompaniment, Puckette also investigated an alternative option that had recently become available, the Yamaha DX7 synthesizer.[23] The DX7 was the first all-digital MIDI synthesizer to be commercially manufactured following the introduction of the MIDI 1.0 communications protocol in 1983, and this new avenue of investigation was in due course to prove highly significant.

A key starting point for Puckette was the scheduling program developed by Max Mathews in 1981 for the Crumar General Development System, or GDS, the commercial outcome of a digital oscillator system developed by Hal Alles at Bell Labs in 1979.[24] Known as RTSKED, the attractions of this control system had already influenced Curtis Abbott in the development of his high-level command language 4CED for the 4C, and this experience provided useful underpinning for Puckette's work. Within a year he had developed the control interface for Vercoe's flute + 4X system to the point where it could be reliably explored as a real-time composing and performing tool for computer music. The reliance on a hybrid key sensor/acoustic tracking system, however, still presented some significant practical challenges, and it is at least partially for this reason that Puckette became interested in the possibilities of developing a MIDI-based control system.

A key issue here was the even greater problems associated with the detection of polyphonic rather than monophonic performance events. In this context, acoustic-based sensing techniques were at best unreliable and at worst impracticable, and it was here that the underlying architecture of RTSKED was particularly helpful. Puckette had already carried out preliminary work in this context at MIT before transferring to IRCAM, starting work on a prototype control system known as Music 500 for a bit-slice array processor manufactured by Analogic in 1982. Although this project was never completed, the design principles thus explored were embedded in the software subsequently produced to control the 4X. Named from the outset as "Max" in honor of this founding pioneer of computer music, this programmable control facility was to undergo a number of transformations before Max (and in due course its extension, Max/MSP), as known and widely used today, was finally completed and released to the community as a commercial product.[25]

A frustration at the time was the lack of a suitable graphics user interface for use as an extension of Puckette's programming system. Consequently, all instructions had to be entered using conventional alphanumeric command lines. The solution came with the installation of an Apple Macintosh computer at IRCAM in 1987. This turn of events was not without its critics, the idea of using such a ubiquitous, commercially produced facility being a source of concern in some quarters, but for Miller Puckette and his associates the acquisition was timely. It facilitated the development of a graphics-based 4X system, unencumbered by the complexities of the PDP-11/55 or indeed its immediate successor the UNIX-based Sun workstation, control now being exercised via a Macintosh II desktop computer.[26] To take full advantage of this new control environment, Max was entirely rewritten using the programming language C, eventually leading to the now familiar graphics-based control and command environment that it provides for composing and performing.

These developments were significant technical milestones, made possible in the first instance by the processing power and versatility of the 4X. What has yet to be considered is their impact on the development of live computer music at IRCAM. Two works may be identified as being especially significant in this context, the first having the status of being the first major work to be produced using the Vercoe/Puckette flute and 4X system, the second being the first work to be produced using the graphics-based Max and 4X system. Both were composed by Philippe Manoury.

Philippe Manoury: The background to the composition of *Pluton*

In terms of musical training, Manoury's early studies from the age of nine embraced classical techniques of harmony and counterpoint at the École Normale de Musique de Paris, and piano with Pierre Sancan. In the early 1970s his interests in composition were cultivated by Gérard Condé, who brought him to the attention of Max Deutsch, leading in turn to further studies in instrumental composition with both Michel Philippot and Ivo Malec. His interests in computer music date from 1975, stimulated by an initial study of the techniques of computer-aided composition with Pierre Barbaud. As in the case of both Roads and Truax, the pioneering work of Iannis Xenakis proved particularly influential in this context, starting with his computer-generated scores for *ST/10-1, 080262* for instrumental ensemble, *ST/48-1, 240162* for large orchestra, *Atrées* for ten solo performers, and *Morsima-Amorsima* for piano, violin, cello, and double bass—all composed in 1962. By the early 1970s Xenakis was experimenting with multimedia works involving the live control of performance parameters via a computer, notable examples including *Polytope de Cluny* (1972–1974) and *Diatope* (1977), and these later developments were of interest to Manoury.

A further influence at this time was the discovery of the music of Karlheinz Stockhausen, in particular his works involving the live processing of instrumental sounds, notably *Mantra* for two pianos and ring modulators, composed in 1970. Although the electronic devices used in these works were based on analog technologies, the creative possibilities thus opened up laid important foundations for Manoury's subsequent engagement with the possibilities of live digital signal processing.[27] By the middle of the decade his career as a composer of international standing was firmly established, including major works such as *Cryptophonos*, written for the pianist Claude Helffer and premiered at the Festival de Metz in 1974. It soon became clear to him that his growing interests in the possibilities of combining acoustic instruments with live electronics could only achieve their true potential via an engagement with those working at the leading edge of computer music research.

Here the groundbreaking work of IRCAM was to provide the all-important conduit to such advanced resources. In 1978, before departing for a visit to Brazil, Manoury submitted a proposal for a project investigating the properties of inharmonic sounds. This led to an invitation to join IRCAM as a researcher on his return in 1980 specifically to explore the possibilities of computer-based techniques of sound production. During his first year he concentrated on a project subsequently titled *The Principles of Correlation between Musical Components*. His primary preoccupation at the time was the nature of the relationships between notation and the aural perception of the associated acoustic realizations. The following observations establish the context for his lines of inquiry:

> It goes without saying that notation in Western music is not simply a way of fixing an idea or a means of dealing with a problem. Very often, notation may condition an idea, shade it and modify it. But most often in my case it has been phenomena taken from day-to-day experience or drawn from other disciplines that have sparked me off in one direction or the other. And at root, there has always been a question of the type: when one perceives a phenomenon, is one's attention drawn by the totality of the perceived form or does one rather appreciate the details which go to make up this form? Or perhaps: does the perceptual pregnancy of an event depend on the context in which it has been introduced or on the time during which it unfolds?

The key concern underlying his early investigations at IRCAM embraced what he identified as two poles of perception, the one based on synthetical perception, the other on analytical perception. The perception of time was a central component of his thesis:

> Time is the prime condition of all perception. But more than any other discipline, music is subject to it in irrevocable ways. The passage of time, its non-reversibility, are familiar phenomena which have excited the imagination of a large number of poets, philosophers and scientists; but it is still necessary to separate subjective content from these physical laws and see how time is perceived.

Another was what he describes as "instantaneous perception":

We have known for a long time that what we call "timbre" in music is a result of the perception of certain physical values and their evolution as a function of time. The time necessary to recognize such "forms"—and I am speaking here of forms bequeathed to us by experience and tradition, like traditional timbres—is generally shorter than the phenomenon in question. The sound of an oboe which lasts only a quarter of a second is nonetheless recognizable from the moment of attack, because the behavior of transients is sufficient cause for recognition. The case of artificial sounds however is different. Electronic sounds are "unheard" (in the etymological sense of the term), and the composer, who no longer has a fixed and finite instrumentarium, must operate with different criteria. The very short time lapse which allows us to recognize a traditional timbre no longer applies here. The composer must work on the spectral envelope and on its evolution in time. While the computer allows us to work on the small details of this evolution, it is also probably one of the reasons why composers are attracted towards a form of musical thought which favors the sound continuum. But in either case we enter a unique category of temporal perception. It is the time of the present, the time of recognition (in the case of traditional sounds), and of identification or contemplation (in the case of "unheard" sounds). The former are probably perceived less "consciously" because, obviously, the listener does not need to go through a sequence of conscious recognition of the type: "this is a flute, this is a cello etc.," and on the other hand, as we have seen, recognition only needs a fraction of a second, too short, perhaps, for one to be conscious of it. Electronic sounds are certainly perceived more attentively, because through their very novelty in relation to what is the norm they invoke a more contemplative state, linked to a greater psychological alertness. What is not yet assimilated holds our attention fatally more than what already is. But in both cases this category is based on the present, and offers a unique revelation of the nature of the phenomena in play.[28]

The issues arising in these contexts led to the composition of his first work at IRCAM, completed in 1982, which explored the relationships between these musical components: *Zeitlauf,* for twelve voices, thirteen instrumentalists, live electronics, and tape.

The critical commentary on the composition of *Zeitlauf* that accompanies the above observations provides a valuable insight into Manoury's creative thinking at that time. Defined as his "principles of correlation," his starting point concerned an analysis of timbre, followed by processes of resynthesis to create a spatial perspective within which his timbres could evolve, using partials that are entirely inharmonic. Having first produced various groupings of partials, ranging from those based on equally spaced frequencies to mathematically produced clusters, he developed software that would manipulate these configurations to extract further groupings, in turn distributed within the frequency spectrum to create centers of focus that could be clearly identified perceptually. At the same time, he explored the interrelationships between the essentially harmonic spectra of acoustic instruments in polyphonic contexts, exploring our ability readily to distinguish between instrumental components from different instruments in differentiated registers, and the more integrated perspectives associated with identical or very similar components within the same register, where component timbres can coalesce.

In the case of the electronic tape, he made use of an IRCAM program known as ALLONG, which allowed short segments of sampled vocal sounds to be isolated and extended, in effect pausing the natural evolution of the associated timbre, a technique subsequently to become well known to users of commercial MIDI samplers. These samples were then subject to two compositional procedures, one multiplying the frequency (pitch), the other the duration, resulting in a sequence of contributing segments. The pitch functions were either gradients up or down or fixed at the level associated with the end of the previous segment. Figure 3.2 shows the pitch multiplication factor in the vertical axis, and the duration of each segment in milliseconds in the horizontal axis.

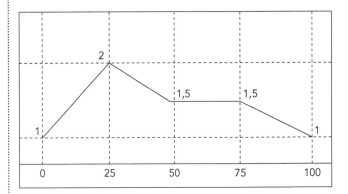

FIGURE 3.2

Envelope for pitch multiplication over time.[29]

In addition, three more traditional methods of synthesis were used in the composition of the tape component: (1) additive synthesis; (2) frequency modulation synthesis, based on the well-established principles of John Chowning; and (3) wave table synthesis. The latter mode of analysis and resynthesis opened the possibilities of creating a continuum between the naturally produced spectra of the sounds of acoustic instruments and those associated with those of his synthetic sounds based on inharmonic spectra.

It is, however, in the context of the live processing component of *Zeitlauf* that important foundations were laid for his subsequent work with the 4X, reflected in his following observations:

> The techniques that I used are almost all of the same sort, common to most electronic transformation: that of adding to or enriching the sonic material. It was

necessary to simplify the density and combination of such elements, in comparison with other parts of the piece, so as not to strain the perceptual mechanism in two directions at once. . . . A brief glance at history indicates that Western musical culture, more than any other, has been based on research into continually more complex polyphony and harmony (for instance the acceptance of the use of all intervals as equally valid). This is precisely because at the same time sound itself was consistently purified. For a westerner, the paragon of sonic beauty, of perfect instrumental technique, is the ability to produce the minimum variation of spectral envelope, equality among elements, elimination of parasitic noises related to the mechanical system, in a word the abandonment and suppression of a mountain of acoustical phenomena. Sounds that tend to a minimum of complexity can become part of more and more complex systems. . . . By accepting a larger range of timbres in Western music thanks to electronics, we must also accept a lesser degree of possible combinations. This is for the two reasons that I have already mentioned above: the non-recognition of forms (groups of fluid timbres) tied to the loss of the polyphonic dimension.

The transformation set-up consisted of three ring modulators, three frequency shifters, one vocoder and a reverberation unit. The role of this equipment was, on the one hand, to create a greater cohesion with certain tape sounds, and on the other to represent compositional relations between different versions of the same musical structure transformed according to a principle which I will discuss below. The three ring modulators and three frequency shifters correspond to the three orchestral and choral groups. They are either used with a fixed modulation frequency for a particular section or with a sequencer which is triggered by instrumental or vocal impulses. In the latter case I used a series of modulation frequencies where each step was triggered by an abrupt variation of amplitude by the modulated group of singers or players. The output of each tape of transformation is sent to a specific fixed loudspeaker so that it is as recognizable as possible.[30]

Although Manoury used conventional synthesizers to achieve the live electronic transformations, working essentially in a reactive manner according to predetermined settings of the device functions and the nature of the acoustic sources, the experience stimulated his interest in the possibilities of exploring a more versatile and genuinely interactive environment for the manipulation of such materials.

The catalyst for what was to prove a significant engagement with the medium of live computer music was provided by the arrival of first Vercoe and then Puckette at IRCAM, thus opening up the possibilities of using score-following software. These developments led to a long-standing association between Puckette and Manoury and the composition of a suite of four works by the composer, known collectively as *Sonus ex machina* and all composed in the first instance for the 4X: *Jupiter* for flute and 4X (1987); *Pluton* for piano and 4X

(1988); *La Partition du ciel et de l'enfer* for flute, two pianos, orchestra, and 4X (1989); and *Neptune* for three percussion instruments and 4X (1991). In terms of embracing new technologies for the very first time, the circumstances that led to *Jupiter* and *Pluton* are especially significant.

His intentions for *Jupiter* raised significant challenges both for Manoury and Puckette. Indeed, the piece was subsequently to undergo a number of revisions as it was modified and extended first for the IRCAM Musical Workstation (ISPW) in 1992 using Max/FTS,[31] and then for an entirely machine-independent environment using Pd (Pure Data), an alternative to Max/MSP developed by Puckette in the mid-1990s.[32] Our interest here, however, lies with the very first 1987 version of the piece. Thus, it was Vercoe's pioneering investigations into pitch-tracking and score-following for a specially modified flute that led directly to a major work of lasting significance.[33] In addition to Puckette, Marc Battier and Cort Lippe acted as technical assistants, working with the flute soloist, Pierre-André Valade. In recognition of Lawrence Beauregard, *Jupiter* is dedicated in memory to his name, and indeed embraces a specific pitch matrix based on musical equivalents to his surname.[34]

A useful perspective on the composition and purpose of *Jupiter* is provided by the following extract from Manoury's own notes on the work:

> *Jupiter* is the first part of a cycle to come, whose aim is to explore the interaction between different instruments and a system for processing and digital synthesis in real time. How does this happen? Firstly, in that the machine becomes more and more human by nature (in this case a musician). That is to say it listens, waits for an event, and then reacts when the anticipated event occurs. This obviously involves simulations, but in my view simulation, as imagination, is an art in its own right. It provides a part of what a conductor would contribute when working with a soloist. In truth the machine is smarter; it recognizes and follows the dialogue that has been requested (providing it has been instructed in advance). I am concerned that the piece evolves as a consequence of instrumental playing without external intervention. Thus, all that is generated from the synthetic or processed components will be triggered or derived from the actions of the flautist. External processes are used to mitigate possible errors and control the distribution of sounds between the four loudspeakers.[35]

The following extract from a contemporary IRCAM studio report provides a useful introduction to the methodology thus used:

> The 4X *listens* to what the musician is playing and compares it to what he is supposed to play, and then plays in consequence its own part, that can consist of both some processing of the sound of the flute and of synthesis scores. In the piece, Manoury uses Max to perform a lot of tasks, for instance for detection of rhythmic sequences played by the flautist. These sequences are memorised and interpolated

from one to another. Other typical uses of Max are playing chords, counterpoints, and arpeggios around the melody of the flute, or placing a spectral envelope at the pitch played by the flute, to shape a complex additive spectrum.[36]

This was the brief for Puckette in terms of developing the pitch detection and scheduling algorithms for what was to be the very first version of Max. The lack of a graphics interface at this time materially influenced the way in which the work had to be constructed, an underlying characteristic being the use of alternating sections where the control commands for the next section were loaded while the flautist was performing a section that was essentially unaccompanied. A drawback was the complexity of the text-based coding that was necessary in order to structure the various subroutines that were required to control both pitch detection and score following, and the playback of synthesized materials.

What may be described as the digital "orchestra" comprised several components, grouped in three categories: (1) sampled sounds (up to eight voices) based on flute sounds, both pitched and percussive, tam-tam strokes, and a vocoder-based cross-synthesis between a piano chord and a tam-tam sound; (2) An array of synthesizers, including twenty additive synthesis voices with a choice of eight different waveforms, a further twenty-eight additive synthesis voices with the added possibilities of applying individual amplitude envelopes to each component, and a further bank of eight voices based on formant synthesis; and (3) an array of signal processors, including delay lines, a frequency shifter, a noise modulator, a four-channel spatial diffusion system, and a reverberation facility. In addition, a phase modulation facility was provided for directly generated flute sounds.[37]

Manoury's experiences in composing *Jupiter*, combining techniques of pitch detection, score following, and composing algorithms, were to prove axiomatic in terms of the repertory of works integrating acoustic and real-time electroacoustic components that was to follow. A key concept, originally formulated during 1986–1987 and then further refined over the following decade, was that of virtual scores:

> It is not a method of composition itself, with its rules and laws, but rather a composition design in a fairly general sense. The term *virtual score* seems to have been delivered for the first time by Pierre Boulez in conversations I had with him in the 80s. It was not until 1986–1987 that I started to define the meaning I give [it] today. I do not pretend, in this, I have finally solved the question of the integration of instrumental and electronic music, but have made a pretty good contribution to what should be, in my opinion, the composition when confronted with technology real-time.[38]

Central to his thesis was the nature of the relationships that may be established between instrumental music and electronic music, specifically in terms of the ways in which the unique characteristics of each domain ultimately determine the ways in which these intrinsically different worlds of sound can interact, whether by means of integration or confrontation.

A key consideration here in his view is the correspondences that can be achieved between writing for instrumental resources and the ways in which such materials can be processed and manipulated in an electronic environment. His concept of "virtual scores" was thus not so much a rule-based method of composition, but more of a design principle, to be applied in the wider context, concentrating in the first instance on the modes of representation that can be identified with musical expression in both domains. This in turn involves engaging with the function and purpose of notation, specifically the extent to which such representations are tangible and subjective or conversely virtual and objective, raising issues of varying uncertainty in perceptual terms. Key aspects of his emerging ideas in this context will be encountered in the detailed study of *Pluton* that follows.

The original 1987 version of *Jupiter* for the 4X used the UNIX-based Sun workstation as the host computer, and, as noted earlier, the associated control environment did not prove conducive to the development of a graphics control interface to meet Puckette's specific requirements. The much smaller but functionally more versatile Macintosh II computer thus proved an excellent replacement. Although Frédéric Durieux made use of a beta version of the software for a stage work performed in early 1988, "it was to be Philippe Manoury's *Pluton*, whose production started in the autumn of 1987, receiving its premiere in July 1988, that spurred Max's development into a usable musical tool. The *Pluton* patch, now existing in various forms, is in essence the very first Max patch."[39]

Known as the Patcher, the associated graphically configured environment for creating patches was developed by Puckette with assistance from Lee Boynton, Cort Lippe, and Zack Settel. Almost all the basic tools of the current commercial version of Max were made available right from the outset, the necessary extensions for handling audio as well as MIDI components being added in due course. The following extracts from a conference paper delivered by Puckette in 1988 provide useful corroborative evidence in this context, and usefully set the scene for the detailed consideration of *Pluton* that follows:

> The Patcher is a graphical environment for making real-time computer music, currently with MIDI-controllable synthesizers. . . . Max has hooks for patching a digital synthesizer, which may just be (as now) an interpreting program in the Macintosh or may (in future) be a plug-in signal processing card. As a part of the work of controlling a digital synthesizer, certain objects in Max create signal processing elements in the synthesizer. These objects can intercommunicate by means of signals, special messages through which the objects will arrange to pass a signal in the synthesizer from one element to another. . . . The Patcher presents a visualization

of an object in Max as a box in a window, showing some of the state of the object. Each box in the Patcher's window has some number of graphical *inlets* and *outlets*. A connection between two objects is represented by a segment from an outlet of one object to an inlet to another. You can create a new connection by selecting any outlet of any object and dragging to an inlet of another object: a segment appears between them. An outlet may be connected to many inlets and vice versa.[40]

The above quotation succinctly outlines the Max programming environment explored for the very first time in the composition of this musically and technically significant work.

Inside *Pluton*

In many regards, Philippe Manoury's *Pluton*, for MIDI piano and electronics, strongly contrasts with *Jupiter*, and the subsequent third work of the cycle, *La partition du ciel et de l'enfer*, for flute, two solo pianos, ensemble, and real-time electronics, explored the differences as a compositional principle:

[T]his work establishes a confrontation between the first two parts of the cycle, *Jupiter* and *Pluton*, which provide it with its solo instruments (flute and piano), its musical material and the electronic processes for real time synthesis and processing. Two worlds are continuously interrelated: that of *Jupiter* (reflective, luminous, peaceful) and that of *Pluton* (restless, dark). Throughout the work, these two worlds interpenetrate one another in different ways.[41]

Technologically, *Pluton* also differs from *Jupiter*. The degree of interactivity between the performer and the digital environment was developed significantly further, and the concept of virtual scores was being elaborated jointly with musical applications in several dimensions across the piece for piano, as described in more detail below. As Manoury writes:

[A]fter *Jupiter* . . . it was too tempting to push further the notion of interactivity between instruments and machines. The approach of *Pluton*, although grounded on the same conception, is much richer. The mode of communication between the instrument and the machine is not discrete anymore, but continuous: the instrument does not just trigger and stop the electroacoustic processes anymore, [it] also controls their internal developments.[42]

Besides, the exploration of the different techniques of sound transformations available was less systematically linked to the musical structure in *Pluton* than it had been in *Jupiter*, as the composer recalls in our interviews:

[With *Pluton*] I tried to surpass a situation that I felt was somewhat critical in the previous work, *Jupiter*. It seemed to me that it was too sliced, that is . . . each section

105

of *Jupiter* is centered on a particular technological orientation. There is a section based on rhythmic interpolations, a section based on a synthesis model with formant calculations, a section based on another synthesis model, a section based on processing, and so on. And each section was based on a specific processing model. For *Pluton*, precisely since we had the possibility, with the first version of Max . . . to plug anything with anything fairly quickly, I thought I should now blend everything.[43]

You can use the accompanying software to watch videos of our interviews with Philippe Manoury, where he evokes several aspects of his creative process on Pluton *and beyond. Demonstration Video 3.1 presents this feature and shows an excerpt of Presentation 2 with the composer expanding on the musical structure of* Pluton *as introduced above.* ▶

The global form and materials of *Pluton*

On its premiere in Avignon on July 14, 1988, *Pluton* consisted of four sections. Revisions followed and the current version, premiered at IRCAM on February 24, 1989, has a fifth section, conceived as a substantial extension of the materials of the beginning, changing the duration of the piece from about twenty-five to fifty minutes.[44] These five sections are described by Manoury as follows:

1. *Toccata*, a sort of strong introduction with repeated notes.
2. *Antiphonie*, where, as the name indicates, contemplative sounding periods are opposed to a second, more active, toccata.
3. *Séquences*, in which the piano generates and controls the whole sonic environment.
4. *Modulations*, where the quality of the synthetic sounds depends on the way the pianist interprets her or his score.
5. *Variations*, starting with a long, very virtuosic cadence on the solo piano, before a gigantic finale representing an outgrowth of the initial toccata.[45]

These sections are themselves divided into subsections:

- Section I has two subsections (noted IA and IB).
- Section II has four subsections (noted IIA, IID, IIE, and IIF).
- Section III is an open form with a short coda.
- Section IV has four subsections (noted IVA, IVB, IVC, and IVD).
- Section V has six subsections (noted VA, VB, VC, VD, VE, and VF).

According to Patrick Odiard, the materials of *Pluton* are derived from one seven-note melodic cell (see Figure 3.3), in which minor seconds are dominant (four instances, along with a tritone and a major third).

In his analysis, Odiard notes that "a melodic thread of one hundred and twenty-two notes, limited to these three intervals [minor second, major third, and tritone], is deduced from an arborescent network constituted with the twenty-four forms of the cell— the twelve transpositions of the original . . . and those of the inverted cell."[47]

FIGURE 3.3

Melodic formula intrinsic to the materials of *Pluton*.[46]

Many of these twenty-four forms are segmented, and the melodic thread is built by a navigation between segments via common intervals or common notes. The musicologist specifies that this thread is the basis for sections IA and VA; for instance, the toccata of the very beginning of *Pluton* "exposes the melodic thread in a didactic way":[48]

[It] is represented in the form of repeated notes or ascending/descending groups. Each change [from one form of the cell to another] is notified by a modification of the number of time subdivisions.

Another fundamental structural entity for *Pluton* is of harmonic nature:

After all the notes of the melodic thread have been presented, a new structural layer is added to the first one, in a partial way. Its complete presentation occurs in section VA, a development of the opening toccata; the original melodic thread gives birth to a harmonic thread made of seven chords which substitute for the notes of the initial cell . . . each chord, made of seven to ten pitches, contains the pitch for which it substitutes. . . . The seven substitute chords offer a precise intervallic potential, that outlines the harmonic path for subsequent developments. Chords I and II are based on the minor third, chords III and IV on the perfect fourth and the tritone, chords V and VI on seconds and thirds, the last chord on the major third [see Figure 3.4].[49]

I   II   III   IV   V   VI   VII

FIGURE 3.4

Harmonic chords, acting as substitutes for the notes of the original cell.[50]

An analysis of the pitch materials of *Pluton* beyond these introductory elements would be out of the scope of this study; the following paragraphs focus on the constitution of the electronic environment, its behavior, and its modes of interaction with the pianist.[51]

Constitution of the digital environment for the performance of *Pluton*

The computer program producing the electroacoustic part of *Pluton* is constituted with the following modules for sound generation and processing:[52]

Generators
- A sampler module, named "Trevor."
- Two groups of FFT-shaped oscillator banks, named "Gumbos."

Processors
- A pitch shifter, inadequately named "Harmonizer."[53]
- A frequency shifter.
- Two reverberation units.
- A spatialization module including its own reverberation, sending sound over four loudspeakers.

The Trevor sampler module

The Trevor sampler module, incidentally named after Trevor Wishart, is constituted of two identical banks of eight sample players, allowing for the simultaneous playback of sixteen recorded sounds.[54] In *Pluton*, the Trevor module is controlled and used in a variety of ways, depending on the chronology of the piece. At the lowest level, each sample player is controlled with seven variables: sample identifier, duration, pitch, velocity, onset, attack, and decay. The sample identifier selects the actual sound to play; the duration sets the overall playback duration in milliseconds; the pitch is a value in midicents,[55] in effect changing the playback speed and affecting the transposition; the velocity determines the playback amplitude; the onset is the initial position from which to play the sound; the attack and the decay set the durations of the initial and final segments of a linear attack-sustain-decay envelope. The sample identifier can set the Trevor module to play one of twenty-three prerecorded piano samples (numbered fifty-one to seventy-three in the Max patch), or a sound fragment recorded during the performance itself. As Manoury writes, this technical possibility was introduced specifically for *Pluton*: "This [Trevor] sampler, in contrast to the more classic sampler used for *Jupiter*, allows 'sampling on the fly,' that is to say the possibility of sampling and resampling in real time."[56]

On a higher level, the playback of the samples is controlled by several distinct mechanisms. First, there are metronomes. Each of the two banks of eight sample players is associated with three metronomes that trigger playback with a fixed velocity and no transposition at three different regular intervals, providing a three-level polyrhythm of samples. This use of the samplers is in fact the first to be heard in *Pluton*: through section IA, the metronomes are activated and deactivated five times, each occurrence being associated with a different prerecorded piano sample.[57] Section VE also entirely relies on metronomes, albeit with a different behavior: the two sample player banks access samples recorded during the performance itself, deploying some of the materials played by the pianist over time. Besides, the polyphony is, in section VE, constrained with a "no steal" parameter: this prevents the triggering command from playing a new sample if a previous sample is still being played; this feature has the effect of breaking the continuity of the flow generated with the metronomes.[58]

Another control mechanism for the Trevor module is the triggering of sample playback from previously written sequences of commands. The first occurrence of such sequences can clearly be heard in the fifth electroacoustic event of section IIA: the prerecorded sample numbered fifty-seven is played with nine different transpositions (8,400, 8,000, 6,900, 6,500, 6,600, 6,200, 5,100, 5,700, 6,800 midicents) in quick succession (respectively separated with durations of 100, 87, 92, 84, 90, 77, 100, and 94 milliseconds).[59] Other sample sequences appear in sections VB and, more prominently, in section VC.

In a text dedicated to the techniques used in *Pluton*, Manoury mentions an important singularity of the Trevor sampler:

> One of the most interesting features of the Trevor [sampler] is the disassociation of pitch transposition from lengths. Here, it is possible to play a sample in the high range while slowing it down, and in the low range while accelerating it. In other words, the pitches and the tempo are two variables which can be utterly independent of one another. [An example, at the very end of the final section of *Pluton*,] highlights a phrase played by the piano at a high speed, and its reappearance at a tempo approximately sixty times slower, without any modification of the recorded pitches. It is more or less the equivalent of cinematic "slow-motion."[60]

This process is achieved in a submodule named "Trevor-machine," which in effect generates playback commands in a granular fashion. The module is controlled with an initial offset, a speed of progression within the buffer, and a window size in milliseconds. A transposition command is available, but is not used in *Pluton*, where the Trevor-machine plays all grains of sound with normal speed. This module is used through most of the final subsection (VF).

Finally, the Trevor sampler module is controlled with commands generated with Markov matrices in sections II and III; these processes are described in more detail in a later paragraph.

You can explore interactively the Trevor sampler module by accessing Presentation 6, named "Trevor sampler," in the accompanying software. Prerecorded samples can be loaded and played back; you can also simulate the performance of extracts of Pluton, record them on the fly, and play them back with the different control mechanisms presented above. For metronomes, prewritten sequences, and the Trevor-machine, menus enable you to load parameterizations used in the relevant sections of Pluton. You can also listen to the use of samplers in the larger context of the work, with Presentation 1, named "Interactive structural map." Demonstration Video 3.2 shows how to operate these features of the accompanying software. ▶

Gumbos: FFT-shaped oscillators

Gumbos are the other type of sound generator in *Pluton*. Used in sections II and IV of the work, these are banks of oscillators shaped with a real-time fast Fourier transform analysis of the piano. In total, there are forty-eight oscillators. In the implementation of the work, these are made of four Gumbo objects, respectively named "gumbo1," "gumbo2," "gumbo3," "gumbo4," each containing twelve oscillators; on a higher level, there are two oscillator modules, named "fft-oscs1" and "fft-oscs2."[61] The first module corresponds to gumbo1 and gumbo2, the second module corresponds to gumbo3 and gumbo4. A module named "gumbo5" provides control over all forty-eight oscillators at once. The following description of the functionality of Gumbos only considers one Gumbo object, corresponding to twelve oscillators.

A Gumbo object can receive up to twelve frequency values in midicents, and it sends them to twelve oscillators in several possible modes. A simple output command sends all frequencies immediately to all oscillators.[62] A skew command outputs frequencies in successive steps determined by a duration value in milliseconds, resulting in an arpeggio. A slide command operates glissandi between the previously stored frequencies and the new ones. In *Pluton*, two slide modes are used. Mode 1 starts all glissandi simultaneously, but all glissandi have a different duration, set by the product of a user-defined value in milliseconds and the index of the oscillator.[63] Mode 2 triggers all glissandi, one after the other.[64] Finally, frequencies corresponding to the MIDI notes received from the piano can be sent through to the Gumbo oscillators during the performance.

The amplitudes of the twelve oscillators are controlled by the FFT analysis of the live piano input. The signal of the piano is permanently transformed into the frequency domain, and the resulting magnitudes of all frequency bins are written into a buffer.[65] In the default case, the frequency of each oscillator output by the Gumbo object is converted to a frequency bin index to look up the buffer containing the magnitudes of the live piano analysis; the amplitude value of the oscillator is then set to the value read at that index in the buffer. For instance, an oscillator with a frequency of 1,000 Hz will have an amplitude of 0 and therefore be silent if no spectral energy is found at the frequency bin corresponding to 1,000 Hz in the analysis of the piano sound, while it will have a great amplitude if a lot of spectral energy is found at 1,000 Hz in the analysis buffer. As Manoury writes:

> The advantage of this procedure, compared to that of spectral filtering synthesis [used in *Jupiter*], is of two orders. First, the relationship between what is played by the instrument and what comes out of [the] synthesis is temporally organic. If

nothing comes out of the piano, nothing comes out of the synthesis. The synthesis represents a spectral image of the piano's sound, while its frequency content (the collection of oscillators) can be completely different. There is projection and permanent tracking of the instrumental sound by the machine. Second, the way in which the oscillators will resonate will depend, to an extent, on the harmonic relationship between the piano frequencies and the synthesis frequencies. Consider a simple low "C" of the piano. The sound energy will [be] strongest in all the regions situated around the natural harmonics of this note (C, G, C, E, G, etc.). If certain oscillator frequencies are close to these regions, they will resonate. The further they are from these regions . . . the less they will resonate.[66]

Puckette highlights the versatility of Gumbos across the register of the piano:

High notes of the piano tend to be quite local. In their spectra, they tend to have a strong fundamental and not very strong partials, and the FFT can resolve their frequencies quite well. Low frequencies tend to be quite spectrum-filling. A nice low note of the piano, especially a nice pedal low note of the piano, just starts everything off.[67]

Manoury himself implicitly remarks that the Gumbo technique was particularly fruitful for his experiments in *Pluton*: "[T]his procedure is perfectly adapted to the sound of the piano, which covers a large spectrum. With a much more limited spectrum (that of the flute, for example), it would not provide any results."[68]

Several parameters enable the adjustment of the behavior of the Gumbo modules. A spectral transposition parameter, named "spec," stretches the mapping between oscillator frequencies and analysis data. When the spec value is set to 64, an oscillator with a frequency of 1,000 Hz will have its amplitude set to the value found in the analysis buffer at the bin index corresponding to 1,000 Hz. If the spec value is 127, the same 1,000 Hz oscillator will have its amplitude set to the value found one octave lower, at the bin index corresponding to 500 Hz. The spectrum of the piano is therefore stretched before being mapped to the oscillator banks. Spec values below 64 would have the opposite effect of compressing the spectrum but are in effect not used in *Pluton*. An averaging parameter, named "lpf," smooths the transitions between the values read from the successive FFT analyses. A lpf value of 127 corresponds to a quick reactivity, while lower values average transitions, reducing beating effects, but also decreasing the aural impression of a real-time mapping between the piano and the synthesis, as reactivity is less effective. An "amp" parameter simply sets the global amplitude of the synthesis module, and a "tab" parameter sets the oscillators to refer to different wavetables. The default and most commonly used wavetable is a simple sinusoidal function, but two other wavetables, numbered twelve and thirteen, contain several partials, providing a much richer sound.

These wavetables are only used with the first oscillator module, in sections IVA and IVB.

> Presentation 7 in the accompanying software is a video of Miller Puckette demonstrating the use of Gumbo oscillators in a Pure Data implementation of the Pluton environment. Additionally, you can explore Gumbos interactively by accessing Presentation 8. You can start exploring the modes for setting the oscillators frequencies, independently of the FFT shaping; you can then investigate the way the live piano input and the synthesis engine interact. Finally, you can also use Presentation 1 to listen to the Gumbo oscillators in the context of sections II and IV of Pluton, in which they are used. Demonstration Video 3.3 shows how to use these resources of the accompanying software. ▶

The pitch shifter module

The first processing module in the real-time environment for the performance of *Pluton* is the pitch shifter. Technically, this module is built around two out-of-phase windowed delay lines, for which the delay time varies continuously. The delay time variation is achieved with an audio-rate counter producing sawtooth ramps from 0 to w or from w to 0 at a frequency f in Hertz, where w is set by a parameter named "hwind" with values ranging from 0 to 128. In the studied implementation, the frequency f is derived from a higher-level parameter named "hfreq" with values ranging from 0 to 128, according to the formula:

$$f = -0.13 \times (\text{hfreq} - 64)$$

When hfreq has a value of 64, f has a value of zero and there is no variation of the delay time and therefore no transposition. When hfreq is less than 64, f is positive and the counter ramps from 0 to hwind, producing continuously increasing delay times, which transposes the input signal downward. Conversely, when hfreq is greater than 64, f is negative and the counter ramps from hwind to 0, producing continuously decreasing delay times, leading to an upward transposition of the input signal. In such an implementation, the transposition interval depends on two parameters: hfreq and hwind. A constant delay value, set via a parameter named "hdel," can be added to the varied value, and feedback is implemented so that some of the output of the pitch shifter goes back into its own input, leading to multiple iterations of the transposition process.

The pitch shifter can receive signals from the piano and all the synthesis and processing modules, except the spatializer.[69] Under a variety of settings, it is used through most of *Pluton*, except in sections I, IVC, and IVD.[70]

In Presentation 9 of the accompanying software, Miller Puckette demonstrates the use of the pitch shifter. Presentation 10 is an interactive explorer, enabling you to experiment with sound files and the parameters of the pitch shifter as available in Pluton. *And again, you can use the interactive structural map of Presentation 1 to observe the pitch shifter in the context of the piece, and the evolution of its parameters through different sections. Demonstration Video 3.4 shows how to use these interactive resources.* ⊙

The frequency shifter

Unlike the pitch shifter, the frequency shifter transforms the spectrum of its input signal as follows: given f, the frequency in Hertz of the modulating sinusoidal oscillator of the frequency shifter, and i, 2i, 3i, the frequencies in Hertz of three partials in the input signal, the two outputs f_{pos} and f_{neg} of the frequency shifter will be:

$$f_{pos} = i + f, 2i + f, 3i + f$$

$$f_{neg} = i - f, 2i - f, 3i - f$$

Three parameters are available for the frequency shifter used in *Pluton*: "fsfre" gives a MIDI pitch which is then converted to a frequency in Hertz for the modulating sinusoidal oscillator, while "fpos" and "fneg," with values ranging between 0 and 128, control the amplitudes of, respectively, the positive and negative output components of the module. As Manoury explains, the frequency shifter enables a play with inharmonicity, one of his early interests in the context of computer-generated or transformed sounds:

> [The amount of inharmonicity], which provokes a loss of perception of the tonal pitch, is a function of the harmonic relationship between the fundamental frequency and the modulation frequency. Thus, a simple relationship such as the octave (or unison), will produce no inharmonic alteration of the spectrum. The fourth and the fifth produce slight [inharmonicity]. Complex relationships, such as the second, the seventh, or the augmented fourth, will create a strong inharmony which will render the perception of pitch opaque. One of the benefits of this procedure is that it breaks the melodic linearity, since each note, in function of its modulating frequency, will have a different weight. It is, in a more controlled form, what John Cage attempted with his *Sonatas and Interludes* for prepared piano.[71]

Like the pitch shifter, the frequency shifter of *Pluton* receives signals directly from the piano, or from any of the synthesis or processing modules. It is also used in most subsections of the work, apart from IIA, IVB, and IVC.

You can watch a video excerpt of Miller Puckette demonstrating the frequency shifter in Presentation 11 of the accompanying software and experiment yourself with sound files and the process in Presentation 12. To explore the frequency shifter in the context of Pluton, *you can go back to Presentation 1, as shown in Demonstration Video 3.5.* ▶

The reverberation modules

Two identical reverberation modules are used in the work. Each reverberation unit sends its input signal through a series of six short-time delay lines for early reflections, and four additional delay lines with feedback are used for the broader hall effect. Only three parameters are accessible from the higher-level program: "rgate" is the amount of the input signal sent into the unit, "revfb" is the amount of feedback, and "rout" is the reverberation output level.

A typical use of reverberation in Philippe Manoury's electroacoustic music since *Jupiter* is the implementation of infinite reverberation: using the parameters mentioned above, a short excerpt of the input signal can be captured into the module by raising rgate for a brief period, and this excerpt can be frozen by setting the feedback to its maximum value of 127. This effect is used as soon as the first event in section IA of *Pluton*, where the sound of the live piano is captured and held by the infinite reverberation on several successive iterations.

The first reverberation module can receive signals from the piano and all the synthesis and processing modules, apart from the other reverberation unit and the spatializer; it is used through the entire piece, except in section VE. The second reverberation module only receives signals from the piano, the pitch shifter, and the frequency shifter; it is used as a complement to the first module in sections IB, at the beginning of section III, and in sections VB, VE, and VF.

Presentations 13 and 14 of the accompanying software include a filmed demonstration and an interactive explorer for the reverberation modules of Pluton, *as shown in Demonstration Video 3.6.* ▶

The quadraphonic spatialization module

All the synthesis and processing modules can send their signals to some other modules, and to two categories of output: the stage output,[72] which simply passes its monophonic input signal to two loudspeakers located on the left and right sides of the stage, facing the audience; and the quadraphonic spatialization module, which ultimately sends its four signals to four loudspeakers located around the audience.[73]

The positioning of the incoming signal within the quadraphonic field is made with three coordinates: x, y, and a radius. In fact, the x-y pair sets an angle, and the radius value sets the magnitude from the center of the circle. When the radius value is zero, the signal is positioned in the center regardless the values of x and y. An automated system enables a higher-level control of x and y at once: when on, the input signal moves in circles around the listener. An increment parameter sets both the speed and the direction of these rotations.

A further reverberation unit, identical to the two autonomous reverberation modules, is integrated with the spatializer; in addition to the gate, feedback, and output amplitude parameters, a distance parameter gives control over the balance between dry signal and reverberated signals—both signals are then summed and positioned across the four loudspeakers.

Presentations 15 and 16 include a filmed demonstration and an interactive explorer for the spatialization module. Demonstration Video 3.7 shows how to access and operate these presentations. ▶

Mapping the piano performance to the real-time environment

The modules constituting the real-time environment are interconnected, parameterized, and activated in many ways through the performance of *Pluton*. The behavior of the overall digital environment and of its components is highly versatile. It is also, at least in principle, autonomous from any external intervention other than the performance by the pianist her/himself; no performer or operator is required for handling the settings of the program during the concert.[74]

The score follower: A virtual listener to the pianist's performance

During the performance, the piano continuously sends MIDI information to the software. This information (pitches, velocities, durations deduced from time deltas between note-on and note-off messages) is matched against a MIDI representation of the score, stored in the environment.[75] This enables the program to update itself according to *events*, represented on the score by Arabic numbers surrounded by circles. Typically, a subsection contains a certain number of events—for instance, section IVB has eight events, while section VE has as many as forty-four events; when detected, an event of the score is passed to a "qlist" object, which contains ordered sets of instructions destined to the synthesis or processing modules or to higher-level control mechanisms. By way of example, the contents of a qlist for events 3 and 4 in section IA is shown in Figure 3.5.

When event 3 is detected, the value 129 is sent to a receiver object tagged with the keyword "tto2," setting the level of the signal sent by the samplers to

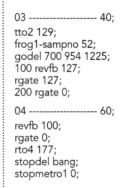

Contents of a qlist object for events 3 and 4 in section IA of *Pluton*.[76]

116

```
03 ------------------ 40;
tto2 129;
frog1-sampno 52;
godel 700 954 1225;
100 revfb 127;
rgate 127;
200 rgate 0;

04 ------------------ 60;
revfb 100;
rgate 0;
rto4 177;
stopdel bang;
stopmetro1 0;
```

the stage output to a high value (129), the sample index for the first polyphonic Trevor sampler ("frog1-sampno") is set to 52, and "godel" turns three metronomes on to trigger the sample with the three periods in milliseconds provided as arguments (700, 954, 1225). The value 100 at the beginning of the next line indicates to wait for 100 milliseconds before executing the following instructions: set the first reverberation module feedback ("revfb") to its maximum value of 127, set the input signal amount of the unit ("rgate") to a high value (127), wait for 200 milliseconds, then set the rgate value to zero—these final three lines for event 3 are the procedure for implementing an infinite reverberation, as described in the previous section. When event 4 is then detected by the score follower, the feedback is decreased slightly (revfb 100), the rgate value is left to zero, the level of the signal sent by the reverberation unit to the spatializer ("rto4") is set to the value of 117, and the two commands "stopdel bang" and "stopmetro1 0" turn off the metronomes activated in event 3.[77]

Events can contain few or many instructions. They are not the only procedure to trigger commands from the piano notes. For instance, the two commands "trec60" and "trec602" do not have an immediate impact on the electroacoustic production; rather, they open or close gates that enable the MIDI note 60 (middle C) to trigger the recording of the live piano sound into the buffers of, respectively, the first and second Trevor samplers.

Integrating the performance into the development of electroacoustic processes

As evoked in the introduction to this analysis of *Pluton*, with this work Manoury wanted to provide to the pianist an intimate control over the electroacoustic production, beyond triggering and stopping processes. On several occasions, the velocity values received from the live performance are mapped to the parameters of some synthesis or processing modules. This concerns the spectral transposition and amplitudes for the four banks of Gumbo oscillators, the frequency and window size parameters for the pitch shifter, the frequency of the frequency shifter, and, for the quadraphonic spatializer, the x and y positions as well as the speed for the spatial automation of circles around the audience. The mapping of the velocity values, ranging from 1 to 127, to the concerned parameters is made with tables such as the ones represented graphically in Figure 3.6.

You can look at the Parameter Envelopes in Presentation 1 to see where the velocity of the piano is mapped to specific modules, as shown in Demonstration Video 3.8. ▶

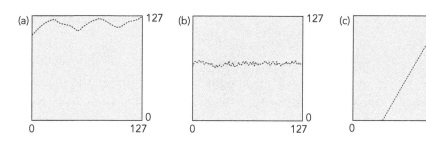

FIGURE 3.6

Tables for mapping velocity values (x-axis) to the pitch shifter parameter values (y-axis) in *Pluton*. From left to right: window size, frequency (table 1), and frequency (table 2).[78]

Markov sequences: Generating virtual scores from the piano performance

The use of Markov sequences to generate musical material with the real-time environment is typical of Manoury's electroacoustic work.[79] *Pluton* is his first piece in which this formalism was implemented to record data from the instrumentalist's performance and use it to generate recombined musical materials. As the composer specifies:

> [Until *Pluton*] the scores which "fed" the sampler were of a deterministic nature—which is to say that they contained a finite number of elements. Even if the rhythms were calculated in real time, in the case of *Jupiter*'s rhythmic interpolations, the collection of melodic elements was determined in advance. The process [introduced in *Pluton*] is based on the idea that a score can proliferate based on its own elements. It consists of a virtual score in which nothing is determined in advance (besides certain successions and linking conditions which regulate the interrelationships of elements). This formalism is the Markov Chain.[80]

The behavior of the Markov module can be described schematically as follows: if the pianist plays successively A, B, A, C, and if this sequence of notes is recorded in the Markov matrix, then the subsequent playback of the Markov chain will start with A, the first note of the sequence. Then, the transition probabilities from A are 50 percent for B and 50 percent for C. If B is played, then the only possible transition is toward A, which will in turn be followed again by either B or C with equal probabilities. If C is played, no transition exists, and the playback stops; a "restart" feature in *Pluton*'s implementation enables to trigger the sequence playback from the beginning again when a zero-transition case is reached.

The two Markov matrixes used in *Pluton* each contain eighty-eight memory spaces—one for each note of the piano—and the transition probabilities are weighted according to the velocities of the notes: the louder a note is played by the pianist, the higher the probability for it to be played by the Markov module. Considering the example above again, if B had been played with a greater velocity than C, A would have been followed by B more often than by C.

The MIDI-formatted notes (pitches, velocities, durations) output by the Markov matrix correspond to the MIDI values played and recorded by

118

the pianist, but are not used to play the corresponding piano notes; instead, they are sent to the Trevor sampler, and the MIDI information is used as described in the section previously dedicated to that module—most importantly, the pitch determines the transposition factor for the playback of the sample. Depending on the considered section, the sample itself can be a prerecorded sound file or a sound recorded from the piano during the performance itself. The MIDI values of the Markov sequences can also occasionally affect the parameters of some processing modules, rather than the sample playback: in section IIF, the Markov-generated pitch values are mapped, via tables, to the x-position of the spatialization module (during event 21), and to the y-position of the spatialization and the frequency of the pitch shifter (with three different tables across events 21, 22, 24, 25 and 26).

Presentation 18 of the accompanying software enables you to explore the Markov chains, by recording MIDI data from excerpts of Pluton or with a virtual keyboard. Presentation 17 is a video interview where Miller Puckette demonstrates its use in Pluton; in Presentation 19, Philippe Manoury exposes some of his musical ideas with this technique. Demonstration Video 3.9 shows how to access and use these interactive resources. ▶

The interactions between the piano and the computer through the musical work
Section I: Toccata

Divided into two subsections, IA and IB, the opening toccata introduces the materials of *Pluton* with the solo piano, playing increasingly forceful repeated notes. After about half a minute, the piano plays a fortissimo chord, triggering the first electroacoustic event of the piece: the chord of the piano is captured into an infinite reverberation, and simultaneously a complementary prerecorded piano chord (the sample numbered fifty-one in the Trevor module) is played with three asynchronous metronomes. The sound produced by the samplers is directly sent to the stage loudspeakers, while the infinite reverberation is spatialized around the audience, in relatively slow circular motions.

On event 2 the metronomes stop and the reverberation decays quickly, leaving the piano alone again. This effect of freezing the harmony, with both repeated samples and infinite reverberation, is repeated through all of section IA (events 3 and 4, 5 and 6, 7 and 8, 9 and 10). Across these events, the elements of variation of the electroacoustic part are the sampled chords themselves, the tempi of the metronomes, and the speed of the spatial movements, increasing significantly on event 5, before slowing down again on event 7. On event 9 the overall texture becomes contrastingly lighter: the metronome-driven sample is an arpeggio in the medium-high range of the piano, and the pianist plays sparse, isolated notes. The reverberation is also sent to the frequency shifter, the low frequency setting of which in effect provides amplitude modulation. At event 10 the electronics stop again, and the piano reintroduces repeated notes, culminating with a high F-sharp that provides the transition to the next subsection of the toccata.

You can use several features of Presentation 1 in the accompanying software to explore in more detail the elements described in this paragraph. The DSP graph view shows how the different modules are interconnected, while the Parameter Envelope view and the Parameter Panel attached to each module enable the examination of the parametric values of the relevant modules. Demonstration Video 3.10 shows how to access these interactive resources for section IA, and you are encouraged to use these for all subsections of Pluton *to complete the reading of the following paragraphs.* ▶

At the beginning of section IB (event 11), the repeated high F-sharp is captured into the first reverberation module and remains frozen as infinite reverberation through most of the subsection, until the overall electroacoustic part fades away before the final codetta. Concurrently, the continuous playback of a sample (numbered fifty-six in the Trevor module) holds the repeated high F-sharps introduced with the piano through the whole subsection. Both the infinite reverberation and the sampler are directed to the stage loudspeakers. The second reverberation unit is used to capture chords of the live piano (events 12, 14, 17, 20, and 24) and to pass the frozen harmony to the spatialization module, with varying rotation speeds and magnitudes. Additionally, the frequency shifter receives both infinite reverberations through most of the subsection (from events 12 to 25), introducing inharmonic sustained noises with varying frequencies, culminating with a strident whistling from events 18 to 21. At the fermata of event 25, all the electronic components slowly fade out, before the piano solo plays a two-measure codetta.

Section II: Antiphony

Following the intense and dynamic character of section I, the introduction to the antiphony contrasts in bringing sparser, quieter materials on the piano, initially heavily reverberated (event 1 of section IA). At event 3 the two gumbo oscillator modules appear with two sinusoidal chords going to the pitch shifter, which thickens their texture with a small amount of transposition, the stage loudspeakers, and the spatialization module. The oscillators are shaped by the spectral contents of the live piano, which plays a series of figures on its whole range and with contrasting dynamics; the MIDI velocities extracted from the performance affect the spectral spread of both Gumbo modules, as well as the frequency of the pitch shifter. At event 4 the oscillators disappear, and at event 5 the sampler plays a fortissimo reverberated sequence echoing the piano figure of event 4.

At event 6 the reverberation module, having received a signal from both the sampler sequence and the piano, is passed to the pitch shifter with a high amount of feedback, providing the "phasing" effect mentioned on the score. At event 7 a new toccata begins on the live piano and with the sample numbered fifty-eight played repeatedly; the notes played by the piano are recorded into the two Markov modules until event 9. From the F-sharp of the second figure of event 7, the contents of the first Markov matrix are used to play the sample numbered fifty-eight with different transpositions, resulting in an imitation game with the pianist's performance. From event 8 the Markov-driven sampler is fed into the reverberation module, and from event 9 the level of the sampler sent to both the stage output and the spatialization decreases, letting the Markov materials resonate through a long, slowly decaying reverberated sequence.

Section IID returns to a contemplative character, with Gumbo oscillators reappearing. The pitches of the first Gumbo module are updated by the piano notes from the beginning of the subsection (event 10 for gumbo1 and event 13 for gumbo2), and the oscillators start being heard, through the pitch shifter and the spatialization, at event 12. At event 14 the spectral shape of the oscillators is frozen with the "lpf" parameter set to 0; at event 15 the second Gumbo module reappears, with its pitches updated by the piano. Both oscillators are from then modulated by the pitch shifter (with randomized frequencies until event 18), the frequency shifter set with a sub-audio frequency, and the spatialization with slow circular motions. At event 19 the feedback of the pitch shifter goes up to its maximum value of 123, giving a characteristic slow phasing effect to the oscillators, adding some tension in preparation for the subsequent return of the Markov process, which reemerges at event 20. Technically, the Markov sequence had not been stopped since the end of section IIA: the amplitudes of the sampler toward the stage and quadraphonic loudspeakers had been turned down, but the Markov sequence had been silently feeding the reverberation with a high feedback; event 20 simply uncovers this invisible process by turning the output amplitude of the reverberation on again, leading to the following subsection.

The oscillators become less prominent in section IIE, while the Markov sequence continues its deployment. The two pianistic figures from event 24 are recorded into the Markov matrix as additional MIDI material; from event 25 each middle C triggers a recording on-the-fly of the sound of the piano, providing updated materials for the playback of the Markov chains. At event 26 the ambitus of the transpositions is reduced to zero, leading to a stuttering playback of the last figure at constant pitches; a quiet middle C concludes an ample piano sequence, lowering the intensity of the Markov production. A short figure starting again with a middle C enhances this density again; at event 29 the Gumbo oscillators come back into the foreground, are frozen through to event 31, before being shaped by the spectrum of the piano for the transition toward section IIF.

While the constant-transposition Markov process is still heard in the background, the final subsection of the antiphony starts with piano chords updating the pitch contents of the Gumbo oscillators; both the samples and the synthesis textures are spatialized with slow rotations. At event 8, the Markov ostinato decays, leaving room for a series of piano figures shaping the oscillators, passed through quick rotations of the spatializer at event 10. At event 11, the spatial rotations stop, and through event 16 the x and y positions and amplitudes of the spatialized oscillators are controlled by the piano velocities, giving a volatile character to the synthesis. At event 21, the oscillators are sent to the pitch shifter, the frequency of which is modulated with the Markov chain, providing a forceful phasing effect; the Markov process, not heard as audio with the sampler, is thus subjectively influencing the electronic production—it also controls the x and y positions of the spatializers until the end of event 22. At event 23 the Markov chain stops influencing anything; instead, the velocities of the piano start controlling the pitch shifter frequency. The Markov chain becomes directly audible again at event 24, where the sampler fades in to the stage loudspeakers and the spatialization. The ambitus for transpositions progressively increases from zero, and at event 27 the contents of the matrix is updated with chords, leading to what the composer calls a "progressive verticalization" of the Markov processes, which concludes the antiphony.[81]

> Demonstration Video 3.11 shows how to use Presentation 1 of the accompanying software to examine the behavior of the Markov process from its recording to its different modes of reemergence over section II, and Presentation 19, where Manoury explains his use of Markov chains as audible and inaudible processes. ▶

Section III: Sequences

The third section of *Pluton* is an open form: as its name implies, it is made of several mostly prewritten sequences; the pianist has the responsibility of ordering them according to certain constraints. The sequences are divided into three categories: nine recording sequences (labeled R1 to R9), five "Markovian sequences" (labeled A1 to A5),[82] and three "functional sequences" (labeled E, M, and S).[83] As indicated on the score, the recording sequences are sampled and recorded into the Trevor sampler, for subsequent playback by the two Markov engines. The MIDI information extracted from the Markovian sequences is recorded into and recombined by the Markov matrixes, which play the most recently recorded samples with transpositions.[84]

The functional sequences are all made of an opening note, a closing note, and a reservoir of notes that the pianist can play ad libitum, with free dynamics for E and M; each functional sequence has a specific behavior. In the E sequence (for *échelle*, "scale"), the dynamics affect the ambitus for the transpositions of the Markov playback: fortissimo (high velocity) sets the ambitus to its maximum value; pianissimo (low velocity) sets the ambitus to unisons on a transposition by a minor third above the original speed. In the M sequence (for *mixage*, "mixing"), the dynamics affect the balance between dry sound (fortissimo) and highly reverberant sound (pianissimo). The S sequence (for stop) has a reservoir of three notes, which must be played quietly: C-sharp stops the playback of the first Markov matrix, F stops the playback of the second matrix, A triggers the playback of both matrixes again.

Sequences from different categories must be interleaved to some extent; each of the A and R sequences must be played once and only once, while the functional sequences can be played any number of times in no predetermined order. The R sequences must be played in their given order, from 1 to 9. The A sequences can be played in any order; their very different melodico-rhythmic features lead to the generation of contrasting Markov sequences. The section must start with R1, and end with S before moving on toward the coda. For instance, the order of execution on the only commercially available recording of *Pluton* is as follows:[85]

R1 A3 A2 R2 A1 R3 E R4 R5 M R6 A4 A5 R7 R8 R9 S Coda[86]

In the score, Manoury provides another example of possible ordering:

R1 A2 A3 R2 R3 E A1 R4 R5 M S A4 R6 A5 R7 R8 R9 S Coda[87]

Through the section, the pitch shifter and the frequency shifter modulate very slightly the production of the Markov-driven samplers, according to several distinct interconnections.

Presentation 24 in the accompanying software gives access to the playback and processing of the sequences of section III. You can experiment with the different possible musical configurations by playing each available sequence in the order you wish, as shown in Demonstration Video 3.12. ▶

Section IV: Modulations

The fourth section of *Pluton* reintroduces the Gumbo oscillators and integrates them to the pianistic performance according to several distinct modalities. Section IVA starts with a synthetic chord from the gumbo1 module, followed at event 2 by a descending arpeggio generated with gumbo2 in skew mode. At event 3, simultaneously ascending and descending glissandi are heard from gumbo2 in slide mode, spectrally modulated by the piano trill; a second arpeggio is generated at event 4. Following this exposition of materials, event 5 dramatically introduces a drone that will last until the end of section IVB; this is obtained by reducing the "lpf" factor to zero, inhibiting the effect of the piano on the spectrum of the Gumbo oscillators. Additionally, a nonsinusoidal table is used, giving to the synthesis much richer harmonic contents.

The oscillators are passed to the spatializer, which rotates the sound in extremely large motions around the audience; the pitch shifter and frequency shifter also contribute to the modulation of the synthesis. From event 7 the second Gumbo module is activated, with sinusoidal contents, and provides a variety of gestures through to the rest of IVA. At event 12 long ascending and descending glissandi occur; at event 16 a series of piano chords act as gates, momentarily passing the signal of a long descending glissando.

While the first Gumbo drone continues, section IVB makes use of piano figures to fill the pitch contents of the second Gumbo module (at events 1, 3, and 5). These harmonies are then maintained with a return of repeated note sequences on the piano. At events 7 and 8 the whole electronic production is turned off, right before the following subsection.

After two arpeggiated synthetic chords (events 1 and 2), section IVC develops a large collection of glissandi with the gumbo1, gumbo2, and gumbo3 modules. These alternatively slide their current pitches to new harmonies from events 4 to 14, before the final chords are held with forceful repeated notes at the end of the subsection.

Section IVD introduces further synthetic chords with arpeggios or glissandi until event 10; from then, a sequence of chords that the performer is free to play with any dynamics from pianissimo to mezzo-forte shapes the oscillators, but also the speed of the spatialization, mapped to the piano velocities. Events 11 to 14 update progressively the Gumbo harmonies; from event 11 the velocities are also mapped to sub-audio frequencies of the frequency shifter, adding to the spatial rotations a permanently speed-changing amplitude modulation effect. The same mapping is held during a sequence of sparse notes, before the pianistic material becomes forceful again, anticipating the fifth section; the electronic part fades out at event 15.

Section V: Variations

After the virtuosic piano solo of section VA, the electronics reappear at event 2 in section VB with an infinite reverberation capturing the end of an anacrusis; this frozen sound is passed to the stage loudspeakers and to the spatialization with decelerating circular motions. At event 3 the piano figure is modulated with the pitch shifter and reverberated by both the second reverberation unit and the spatializer with a high distance factor. At event 4, a sequence played by the Trevor sampler is heard on the stage loudspeakers and in the surrounding reverberation. The piano chord of event 5 is captured into an infinite reverberation with the first module, again with decelerating rotations; at event 7 the last note of a piano figure is frozen by the second reverberation module and sent into the frequency shifter with a very high frequency.

Two sequences from the Trevor sampler follow; the second acts as a distant shadow of the first, as it is only sent into the spatialized reverberation. The circular motions are paused at event 8, and briefly reactivated before the electronics fade away at event 10, where the piano develops alone its repeated notes punctuated with chords. At event 11, the pitch shifter, reverberation units, and spatializer reappear in slow motion before fading out for the final piano gesture of the subsection at event 12.

Section VC starts with a piano figure passed into the pitch shifter with a long delay time and high feedback, reverberated within the spatializer. The section then alternates lively sequences of prerecorded samples (events 16, 18, 21, 23, 26) with quieter, more static piano interludes or short motifs, occasionally dry, modulated with the frequency shifter, or phased by the pitch shifter and reverberated. The last sample sequence (event 26) is concluded with constant retriggering from four asynchronous metronomes, recalling the technique used in section IA.

Throughout the eight events of section VD, the sound of the live piano is passed to the pitch shifter with specific upward transpositions indicated on the score and approximated with the frequency and window size of the module: minor thirds (events 1, 3, 5), major thirds (event 7), major sixths (events 2 and 6), minor tenths (event 4). From event 2 the spatializer operates slow rotations; the electronic transformations are completed by reverberation and, at event 4, amplitude modulation with the frequency shifter.

The pitch shifter processing of the piano continues over the first event of section VE, where a new toccata is transposed upward by a minor third. The high F-sharp of event 2 is captured and frozen by the second reverberation module. From event 3, the Trevor sampler records fragments of the live piano and plays them with metronomes with voice stealing deactivated, breaking the continuity of the polyrhythms; this principle is maintained through the whole subsection—depending on the events, the playback is regular or chaotic. Through the subsection, several phases of increasing and decreasing tension are achieved with different combinations and settings of the pitch shifter, the frequency shifter, the second reverberation unit, and the spatialization module, processing both the live piano and the samplers.

A low F frozen by the second reverberation module at event 44 of section VE is held through to the beginning of section VF, which starts with a dense, fortissimo piano sequence. At event 1 the infinite reverberation decays and the piano is dephased with the pitch shifter. At event 3 forceful chords from the piano are accompanied with the Trevor-machine function of the sampler, which plays short grains of a prerecorded sample corresponding to the piano measure of event 2, at various positions and with small onset increments, in effect operating a high ratio time-stretch. The sounds of the live piano are pitch-shifted; both the pitch shifter and the sampler are reverberated and modulated with the frequency shifter with randomized low frequencies, and the spatialization operates slow rotations. The time-stretched sample playback comes to an end before event 4.

At event 5, the Trevor-machine granulates a prerecorded sample corresponding to the first measure of event 4, while the piano plays sforzando chords and powerful trills, leading to the climax of the section, and arguably of the whole work. Through to event 15, the piano plays a series of sparser figures, colored with the pitch shifter and modulated with the frequency shifter. At event 16 the Trevor-machine function is reintroduced with a prerecorded sample corresponding to the first measure of event 15; the time-stretching operates with various ratios until event 24, where it decays again. At event 25 a G is played by the sampler with asynchronous metronomes; this is held through to the end of the piece. At event 29 the Trevor-machine function is triggered again; it generates a granular texture providing a background to the metronome-driven sample, spatialized with speed-varying rotations, and to the last piano figures. Finally, the time-stretched piano sample decays, leaving the single G alone, with no further intervention from the pianist.

Conclusions

Through the fifty minutes of *Pluton*, the longest work of the *Sonus ex Machina* cycle, the synthesis and processing techniques developed in the digital environment for the performance are used in a highly structured diversity of configurations, leading to a wide range of musical expressivity. Manoury took a significant step further following his first experiments on the interaction modes between instrumentalist and technology in *Jupiter*. In a paragraph titled "Form as a Function of Digital Instrumentation" in his analysis of *Jupiter*, Andrew May states that it is "possible to assess the large-scale form of *Jupiter* in terms of timbre by determining which instruments within the digital orchestra are used in each section."[88] This is certainly not as much the case in *Pluton*, where the processing modules (pitch shifter, frequency shifter, reverberation, spatialization) are ubiquitous and used with very different parameterizations and therefore sound outcomes.

If some subsections give prominence to a particular digital signal technique, such as the glissandi of oscillators in section IVC or the pitch shifter transpositions in section VD, most of the work implements the technological devices with configurations and interconnections serving higher-level musical ideas; for instance, frozen or slowly evolving harmonies are achieved by techniques as different as the metronome-driven samplers, the infinite reverberation, or the granular time-stretching of samples. The concept of virtual scores developed by Manoury at the time of the composition of *Pluton* is integrated with the music in a variety of ways, from the subtle changes of some parameters by the pianist's performance to the more spectacular Markov sequences, derived from the musical materials of the score but proliferating because of both randomness and performance features. This range of interactions provides the electroacoustic developments with the uncertainty and variability inherent to any kind of live music, a principle that has been guiding the composer through all his work with digital technologies.

4

Hildegard Westerkamp
Beneath the Forest Floor

Contexts for *Beneath the Forest Floor*

The World Soundscape Project and the evolution of soundscape composition

As noted in the Introduction, the diversity of creative and technical practices encountered in the study of works by nine composers of computer music embraces not only features that are unique to each context, but also in many instances merit further study in their own right as part of a wider perspective on the development of the medium over the years. Whereas a number of technical advances can be identified as particularly important in terms of the practical techniques used by composers associated with different composing perspectives and aesthetics, it should also be noted that a number of important synergies have emerged in the latter context in terms of shared experiences and creative thinking.

This characteristic strongly underpins Hildegard Westerkamp's distinctive contributions to the evolution of computer music, and the specific circumstances that led to this important focus of creative thinking merit close scrutiny. The inspiration for what is known as *soundscape composition* can be traced back to the late 1960s and a project led by R. Murray Schafer at Simon Fraser University, Vancouver. Known as the World Soundscape Project (WSP), this movement has over the years embraced a powerful and influential collective of educationalists, researchers, and composers.[1] Schafer was born in Sarnia, Ontario, receiving his initial education at a school in Toronto. His musical talents were evident from an early age, and in 1952 he was admitted to the University of Toronto, having completed a diploma at the Royal Conservatory of Music, Ontario. After completing his studies at Toronto, he moved first to Vienna in 1956 and then to London in 1958 to study privately with Peter Racine Fricker, both to improve his composing skills and develop his interests as a writer on music. In 1961 he returned to Canada, taking up an appointment as artist in residence at Memorial University, Newfoundland, in 1963, before joining the staff as a professor at the Center for Communication and the Arts at SFU in 1965. At this newly established university, the opportunities to investigate innovative areas of study were considerable, and Schafer soon took full advantage of this environment.

One of his first steps was to establish an electronic music studio in the basement of the SFU theater, only the third of its kind in Canada, following similar initiatives at the Universities of Toronto and McGill. Although the composing resources were relatively basic, by the end of the decade a number of works had been completed by Schafer, his students, and several visiting composers, including David Keane, Peter Huse, and Bruce Davis. It was, however, the nature of sound and its impact on the environment that were to become the primary focus of Schafer's personal research, explored in the first instance in the context of acoustic ecology. A primary concern with the effects of human-made sounds on the quality of life led him to concentrate on the characteristics of noise pollution, evidenced by the analysis of field recordings made at a number of key locations in Vancouver. Although these studies were revealing in an analytical context, this essentially negative approach to the issues arising became more a matter of record than a useful gateway to a better understanding of how such effects might be mitigated, a situation exacerbated by the general lack of enthusiasm shown by the students he engaged to assist in the recording project. Nonetheless, the publication of his findings in two educational pamphlets helped Schafer refocus his study of noise in a more positive context.[2]

His underlying concern at the time was to encourage students to study the nature of environmental sounds, especially those that were not of a natural origin. In due course this focus was expanded to embrace all the sounds of the world, this more inclusive perspective significantly enhancing the intrinsic value of the resulting recordings. A growing interest in their creative potential as composing materials during the early 1970s opened up new avenues of inquiry, but these early excursions into what became known as soundscape composition did not materially undermine his original quest to develop a better understanding of acoustic ecology, especially in the context of noise. A key element in this process concerns the art of listening, and how, in this context, to develop techniques of aural analysis that fully engaged with the associated sonic characteristics. The foundations for this wider perspective were laid in 1969 when Schafer proposed an initiative that would draw together students with shared interests in the characteristics of all aspects of environmental sound, embracing its scientific nature, its impact on society, and its creative potential as a resource for composing. With assistance of a grant from the Donner Canadian Foundation and subsequent support from both UNESCO and Canadian government sources, the World Soundscape Project was born in 1969. The publication of two further treatises by Schafer, *The New Soundscape* (1969) and *The Book of Noise* (1970), productively underpinned the launch of this important venture.[3]

The initial membership of the WSP under Schafer's leadership brought together a range of talents between 1969 and 1975, when he left SFU to pursue freelance interests, albeit still maintaining close contact with the continuing project. The first three years were essentially a formative phase, involving Huse and Davis, Howard Broomfield, Colin Miles, and Adam Woog. It was, however, the completion of this team by two further participants that was to prove axiomatic to the project: Barry Truax and Hildegard Westerkamp. Both were not only to have a significant influence on the early years of the World Soundscape Project, but also on its subsequent development after Schafer's departure. Although the contributions of Truax to the development of computer music have already been studied in Chapter 2 in the context of his pioneering work with the techniques of granular synthesis and the composition of *Riverrun* (1986), there is a further dimension to his work at SFU that is of material significance to the current chapter, as will become clear in due course.

Hildegard Westerkamp was born in Osnabrück, West Germany. She studied flute and piano at the Music Conservatory in Freiburg for two years, starting in 1966. In 1968 she emigrated to Canada and commenced music studies at the University of British Columbia, Vancouver, completing her undergraduate degree in 1972. Curiosity led her to attend concerts of electronic music, stimulating for the first time her interests in the creative possibilities of the medium:

They were putting on electronic tape concerts in a dark auditorium, and that was really unusual for me, I had just not heard anything like it. I kept going to those and I was really very fascinated by it, but really didn't know what to do with it. After my fourth year, the department offered a six week studio course and Barry Truax, who was a graduate student at the time, ran it, and I took it. I really wanted to take it because I thought that if I understand how the equipment works, maybe I will understand better what I've heard in those Monday concerts. Somehow I got closer to this strange soundmaking that was happening. It was all really haphazard, perhaps unconscious, almost dreamlike. I kept thinking, this is interesting.[4]

This initial contact with Truax at UBC was to prove fortuitous, not least in terms of stimulating a desire to engage directly with the techniques of electronic music. Indeed, the experience gained via this course led her to produce her first studio-based composition (subsequently withdrawn), based on simple manipulations of classical recordings, used in the context of a large-scale work for words and music. It was, however, a lecture she had attended given by Schafer, introducing her to the issues and concepts that were fundamental to the World Soundscape Project, that provided the key stimulus for her future career as a leading soundscape composer. These interactions between Westerkamp, Truax, and Schafer were to prove timely and productive, leading to her appointment as a research assistant for the WSP project at SFU. With the subsequent appointment of Truax in 1973, with a specific brief to work on the WSP, the project team was complete.

A unique and important legacy of the early years of WSP is an extensive library of field recordings that provides a fascinating record of the sounds of the environment. Whereas the sounds of nature are essentially timeless, for example the bubbling flow of water over stones in rivers and the sounds of birds and animals, those associated with the activities of humankind are often unique to the time of recording in history, and in many instances subsequently unrepeatable. A cogent example of the latter is a recording in the WSP library of a walk through a Vancouver shopping mall, where the background piped music that constantly emerges when moving from location to location strongly reflects a now very much dated soundscape. Starting with a series of recordings made in the immediate vicinity of Vancouver during 1972–1973, ranging from church bells and traffic sounds to animals at the zoo, a more extensive tour of Canada was carried out in 1973, followed by a tour of Europe in 1975, the latter consisting of an aural study of five villages, located in France, Germany, Italy, Scotland, and Sweden. A notable outcome of the Vancouver recordings was the release on vinyl of *The Vancouver Soundscape* in 1973, containing sound materials captured on the shoreline and in the harbor, along with signals and other distinctive sounds of the city.[5] Although the recording projects were directed by Schafer, significant credit is also due to the members of the recording team, variously Broomfield, Davis, and Huse, for their evident skills in the use of a Nagra analog tape recorder and a stereo pair of microphones to capture the individual soundscapes. The art of successfully capturing sounds in the environment is far from trivial, and the quality of this rich and varied library, even by today's technical standards, is remarkable.

The circumstances that led to the development of soundscape composition as part of the World Soundscape Project merit closer study at this point. In many respects the genre came about almost by accident, the result of increasing curiosity with the creative potential of looping back the processes of analysis and critical evaluation to explore the possibilities of resynthesis, developing new perspectives on the intrinsic characteristics of sounds thus captured from the environment. Truax has written extensively on the characteristics of this composing style. He wrote of this in 1986, at a time when the creative potential of soundscape composition had yet to be fully explored:

> Although the principal work of the WSP was to document and archive soundscapes, to describe and analyze them, and to promote increased public awareness of environmental sound through listening and critical thinking, a parallel stream of compositional activity also emerged that created, perhaps less intentionally, what I have called the genre of the "soundscape composition." Although in [Simon] Emmerson's terminology . . . soundscape composition may be defined in terms of "mimetic discourse" and "abstracted syntax," what also characterizes it most definitively is the presence of recognizable environmental sounds and contexts, the purpose being to invoke the listener's associations, memories, and imagination related to the soundscape.[6]
>
> The mandate to involve the listener in an essential part of the composition, namely to complete its network of meanings, grew naturally out of the pedagogical intent of the Project to foster soundscape awareness. At first, the simple exercise of "framing" environmental sound by taking it out of context (where often it is ignored) and directing the listener's attention to it in a publication or public presentation, meant that the compositional technique involved was minimal, involving only selection, transparent editing, and unobtrusive cross-fading. In retrospect this "neutral" use of the material established one end of the continuum occupied by soundscape compositions, namely those that are the closest to the original environment, or what might be called "found compositions."
>
> The aesthetic proposed by John Cage of treating any such material as music can be justified in that it emphasizes the listening process as being musical, not necessarily the inherent content. However, the WSP avoided proclaiming any such distinctions by first of all, not attributing these "compositions" to a single individual (instead, they were collectively authored by the group), and secondly, by emphasizing the educational rather than the possible aesthetic intent of the exercise.
>
> A subtle but important extension of this practice occurred with the "Entry to the Harbour" sequence from The Vancouver Soundscape recordings where, in order to simulate the experience of entering Vancouver harbour on a boat, past the various foghorns and buoys, it was necessary not only to compress the event in time, but also to mix together all of the separately recorded components, with appropriately engineered illusions of their approaching and receding. A recording of an actual boat trip would have been dominated by motor noise which would mask the desired sound signals and natural sounds. Of course, this abandoning of the ear as a navigational aid in favor of modern electronic instrumentation and visual orientation is indeed symptomatic of the modern experience that leads away from soundscape awareness, and historical examples drawn from aural history accounts with boat captains were reported in the written document. But the purpose of the

131

composition was to stimulate soundscape awareness by presenting a plausible, if simulated, aural experience.[7]

Schafer's role as director of the WSP was highly influential in shaping all aspects of its development during the early 1970s. However, apart from an early four-channel work, *Okeanos* (1971), exploring sounds and images of the sea, composed in collaboration with Bruce Davis and Brian Fawcett, his contributions to the evolution of soundscape composition were to remain largely those of a supportive nature.[8] Beyond the practicalities of documenting the growing library of environmental recordings, his personal interests became increasingly concerned with issues of aural analysis, public awareness, and critical listening. Issues of acoustic design feature strongly in his essay *The Music of the Environment* (1973), identifying and evaluating examples of both good and bad practice in this context, preparing the ground in turn for arguably his most significant text, *The Tuning of the World: Toward a Theory of Soundscape Design*, published in 1977, two years after he left SFU.[9]

New directions in the development of the World Soundscape Project

In 1975 Truax became director of the WSP. Then, in 1977, he made an important contribution to the literature of the WSP with the publication of his *Handbook for Acoustic Ecology*.[10] In the preface to this book, Schafer succinctly draws attention to the key objectives that underpinned the project from the outset, along with the progress being made in terms of drawing together the contributing disciplines in ways that facilitated a much deeper understanding of their interaction:

> The aim of the World Soundscape Project is to bring together research on the scientific, sociological and aesthetic aspects of the sonic environment. Right from the inception of the World Soundscape Project, we became aware that if we were to follow our plan of uniting the sciences and arts of sound, clear definitions of all terms relating to the subject would be necessary. In fact we looked forward to compiling the definitions as a means of instructing ourselves. It was not until Barry Truax took hold of the project, however, that it became possible to bring this ambition to completion.[11]

Truax's new role as director was to prove important in two key respects. First, he ensured that the core work of the project in terms of analyzing environmental sounds and developing public awareness of their significance was suitably sustained.[12] Second, the shared interests of Truax and Westerkamp in exploring the creative possibilities of soundscape composition secured its future as a distinctive and aurally engaging perspective on the possibilities of electronic and computer music.

Understanding the benchmarks that have become associated with this genre is an essential prerequisite for understanding the works themselves, and the critical thinking here has evolved significantly over the passage of time. Here again a considerable debt is owed to Truax for establishing key features that can be used as a useful aid to further study. One principle that he regards as paramount is as follows:

> The soundscape composition always keeps a clear degree of recognisability in its sounds, even if some of them are in fact heavily processed, in order that the listener's recognition of and associations with these sounds may be invoked. Or, to put it even more simply, it is always clear what the soundscape composition is "about," although with the absence of visual and other contextual cues, the composer may assist the listener with an explicit title and program notes. With highly clear and vivid sound materials, this information is probably unnecessary, but in other cases, a fair degree of ambiguity may exist in a soundscape recording and the listener may need to be oriented with an appropriate text. Where few if any of the environmental sounds used in a piece are recognizable, the listener will probably hear it as an abstract sound organization, not as a soundscape composition with real-world associations.[13]

These precepts are usefully developed by his identification of four key criteria. Although these naturally reflect a perspective personal to Truax and may not be universally shared, the scope and extent of their intersection with the creative work of Westerkamp at SFU provides a useful gateway to an understanding of her own stylistic engagement with the techniques of soundscape composition. For this reason, it is instructive to quote these criteria in full:

> **The first is the recognisability of the source material**. In the more documentary approaches, most of the material presented remains largely intact and generally recognisable. There are obviously limitations to this practice, one being that many sounds become ambiguous when listeners do not have a visual reference to the source, and another being that those listeners who lack personal experience of the particular environment or subject matter may relate to it differently, or possibly not at all. Both of these pitfalls suggest that compositional technique and expertise are required to base a work on sound material that can survive in an acousmatic (i.e. sound-only) presentation—sounds and soundscapes that create vivid imagery by themselves. A typical hard lesson of one's first attempts at field recording is that the product seldom conveys the environment as well as first-hand experience of it. The sound-effects person relies on simulations as being more psychologically "real" than actuality, and the soundscape composer relies on recording and sound design skills to do the same with real-world sounds. The cross-cultural problem may be equally tricky, but as with literature and other locally inspired art forms, the creator always hopes to suggest something more universal inherent within the specific material.

133

The second principle is that the listener's knowledge of context, together with associations and connotations, play a vital role in the reception of the work. Of course, this is true of all artworks, but in the case of the soundscape composition, it takes on a specific role, that of providing contextual meaning to the sounds heard. Although the composer may choose to have a "point of view" or "message" through the specific choice, juxtaposition and treatment of the material, to rely only on those intentions leads towards propaganda. Most soundscape compositions, I have observed, give the listener a generous role in their interpretation.

A third principle is that many or all aspects of the external context of the piece are allowed to shape its creation at every level from the micro aspect of the sound material, to its organisation and overall structure. This is perhaps the most challenging concept for the composer. To read their programme notes, one would think that every work has been "inspired" by some real world experience; composers cite everything from vacation encounters, to everyday family sounds, to media events, literature and philosophy as seminal to their work. However, most of the time, one can listen to the work satisfactorily with no hint of any of these sources of inspiration because, it seems, they are just that, relevant experiences which have acted as a catalyst for the composer, but the style and form of the piece can easily be related to previous practice.

Finally, the idealism of the soundscape composition reveals itself when it attempts to carry over its influence into daily life and the listener's perceptions. Instead of exploiting environmental sound material for its quasi musical qualities—and leaving the environment unchanged—the soundscape composition intends to change listeners' awareness of their environment (a goal of the original WSP group through their documentation of soundscapes). The composer may experience the change first. After working with environmental sounds in a concentrated manner in the studio, a curious phenomenon occurs if you hear similar sounds outside the studio—they appear to be a continuation of the piece! The audience's reactions may be more muted, but a clear bridge exists between the concert or radio experience and reality. It is difficult to imagine an abstract work having this kind of effect. Of course, something similar may occur when one listens to the piece again.[14]

Returning to the formative years of the genre during the early 1970s, Truax's comments on the "Entry to Vancouver Harbour" referenced earlier merit further consideration at this point. What amounts to a re-compilation of the original recordings was by no means an isolated example of what might be described as pre-compositional processes that were to prepare the ground for what was to follow. Truax also highlights the outcomes of two further developments in this context. Between the Canadian and the European tours, the WSP team prepared a series of ten one-hour programs for the Canadian Broadcasting Corporation (CBC), which although essentially a series of documentaries made more proactive use of such processes. In the first instance he refers to a documentary titled

Summer Solstice, in which two minutes of sound extracted from each hour in a twenty-four-hour period recorded near a monastery outside Vancouver are combined to create an artificially compressed documentary of the events thus captured within a fifty-minute time span. In the second he highlights an expansion of the recordings made in the early morning, titled *Dawn Chorus*, where the component events are juxtaposed and overlaid.[15]

A further key feature of these early manipulations of environmental sounds is that the team essentially regarded them as group compilations, with no specific attributions to the individuals concerned. This anonymity was subsequently to change, with individual authorship becoming increasingly attributed to further explorations of the creative possibilities of such materials. Three works composed as part of the 1974 CBC documentary project are identified as axiomatic in this context by Truax. The first, *Bells of Percé*, composed by Bruce Davis, combines fragments of bell and vocal sounds reflecting the church ministry and bells in the Gaspé region of Quebec. The second is a pair of works, *Play* and *Work*, that explore rhythmic and timbral manipulations of sounds associated with these human activities, also composed by Davis. The third work, *Soundscape Study*, was composed by Truax, using readily identifiable sounds drawn from the environment, such as bells, water sounds, ticking clocks, and footsteps, subject to transformations such as speed and density, thus extending beyond the natural sound environment to one that is clearly composed.[16]

Hildegard Westerkamp and her influences on soundscape composition

In 1976 Westerkamp composed *Whisper Study* in the electronic studio at SFU. The source materials consisted of a simple recording of her voice whispering a short sentence, "when there is no sound, hearing is most alert," plus the single word "silence."[17] Her engagement with these quiet sounds in a work concerned with exploring the subtleties of gently shaped manipulations of the individual words was very much influenced by the World Soundscape Project, specifically its mission to encourage people to listen critically to the sounds of the world. Here, the ability to concentrate solely on sounds entirely self-generated in the intimate environment of the electronic studio was to prove especially important to her. In a revealing interview with Andra McCartney conducted in 1993, a very real sense of her motivations as an aspiring composer can be gained, in turn providing important clues for an understanding of her subsequent works:

> As I was working more and more in the studio, I was in conversation with Barry Truax. I would watch him, and eventually I learned some of the classic tape techniques: tape delays, feedback, equalizing, and filtering. I began to do my first piece, which was *Whisper Study*. It was such an important and honest experience for me to do this piece. I had the sense that I was thoroughly getting into something that was me.

I wasn't cutting any corners. I had chosen to use very quiet material, whispering material, which forced me to be very careful in the studio with how I was technically reproducing the sounds without too much noise. I wanted it to be a quiet piece, and that approach forced me to be very, very careful. I couldn't fool myself. I wanted to work with silence, I was thinking a lot about silence, and I wanted the technology to be not audible. I really wasn't that conscious of what I thought about technology. I was just amazed at what it did. I came up with a piece that satisfied me completely. I just thought that is the best process I've ever experienced. And I've done it completely on my own. I had never composed a piece, but it felt like—this is it. I finished it, and then I played it to people, and people were responding very positively. Already with the soundscape context I felt that I had found something very important, because I was fascinated by the environmental sounds, and the meanings connected with them. But now there was another level of excitement, producing and doing something. Putting out.[18]

It would seem clear that at this time the notion of a specific genre of composition was still highly embryonic. Westerkamp confirms this in her contribution to a series of articles on soundscape composition, published in the journal *Organised Sound* in 2002:

The term soundscape composition did not exist when I started composing with environmental sounds in the mid-1970s. Through a variety of fortunate circumstances and because of what the 1970s were in Vancouver and Canada—artistically inspiring and moneys were available for adventurous and culturally, socially, politically progressive projects—I had discovered that environmental sounds were the perfect compositional "language" for me. I had learnt much while working with the World Soundscape Project at Simon Fraser University, about listening, about the properties of sound, about noise, the issues we face regarding the quality of the sound environment and much more. This in combination with learning to record and to work with analog technology in the sonic studio allowed me to speak with sound in a way I found irresistible. . . . In addition, the start-up of Vancouver Co-operative Radio gave us the—at that time rare—opportunity to broadcast our work. It was a place where cultural exploration and political activism could meet. It was from within this exciting context of ecological concern for the soundscape and the availability of an alternate media outlet that my compositional work—now often called soundscape composition—emerged. And it came as a surprise to me, as I had never thought of composing nor of broadcasting as a professional choice in my life.[19]

The title of this article, "Linking Soundscape Composition and Acoustic Ecology," goes straight to the heart of her compositional philosophy, which involves a proactive engagement with both perspectives. Of particular significance here are her evident skills in terms of selecting and capturing sounds in the environment, and the strategies she adopted in making the associated recordings, both for further critical study and also compositional purposes.

A notable example of her acute sense of judgement in terms of choosing both the time and place of such recordings, but also the actual techniques of sound capture via a pair of microphones, is her personal contribution to the *Soundscape Vancouver '96* project, consisting of a track of the sounds of boats celebrating the New Year in 1988. This recording is, for all intents and purposes, unedited, thus reproducing an entirely natural experience captured with remarkable acuity.

Westerkamp's reference to Vancouver Co-operative Radio highlights an association that was materially to influence her subsequent development as a soundscape composer. While working with Schafer on the original field recordings produced for the WSP, she developed further his concept of "soundwalking," an activity that was to become of paramount importance to her. Essentially this is a development of the techniques employed when making field recordings in the environment, where sounds are not only captured from static locations but also as a result of walking from one location to another. What becomes especially striking in the latter context is the greatly enhanced sense of listening when all visual references to the trajectory of such movement are entirely absent. Westerkamp's personal engagement with this compositional environment dates back several years before her project with Co-op Radio, to a time when she had yet to discover the techniques of recording in this creative context. Her early compositional ideas were thus based purely on live listening experiences, using her imagination to stimulate a type of inner composition, based on the ear alone. In 1974 she contributed an article of the same name to the WSP, setting out the criteria to be applied in such a formative activity, supported by a critical commentary on such a walk around Queen Elizabeth Park.[20] In providing a context for the different approaches that may be taken to such an activity, she provides an embryonic perspective on the possibilities of using such an experience as the basis of a composition:

Soundwalk Composition

The main purpose of this] kind of soundwalk is . . . aesthetic rather than practical.

Go out and listen. Choose an acoustic environment which in your opinion sets a good base for your environmental compositions. In the same way in which architects acquaint themselves with the landscape into which they want to integrate the shape of a house, so we must get to know the main characteristics of the soundscape into which we want to immerse our own sounds. What kinds of rhythms does it contain, what kinds of pitches, how many continuous sounds, how many and what kinds of discrete sounds, etc. Which sounds can you produce that add to the quality of the environmental music? Create a dialogue and thereby lift the environmental sounds out of their context into the context of your composition, and in turn make your sounds a natural part of the music around you. Is it possible?[21]

A notable feature of the resulting radio "soundwalks" is the addition of spoken comments to guide the listener in terms of the contexts associated with

137

138

these individual recordings, in the absence of any visual clues to their associated environments.

The possibilities of communicating with a wide audience via community radio led Westerkamp to produce a number of programs highlighting the arts and culture, including a series of weekly programs on "soundwalking" in 1978 and 1979, using her own recordings of Vancouver and its environs. In 1978 she composed *Fantasie for Horns I*, for four-channel tape, based on the sounds of horns as experienced in the natural environment. Her sources ranged from boat horns and factory hooters to train and fog horns. In this case most of the sounds were taken from the WSP library, supplemented with a few additional recordings she made herself. She notes:

> Listening to the various horns in the collection was fascinating because of the way their sounds were shaped and modulated by the surrounding landscape. Some horns would echo only once, others many times, their sounds slowly fading into the distance. One foghorn had an echo that was an octave lower than the actual sound, another was an octave higher. A trainhorn's echo was half a tone lower as the train approached, but the same pitch as it passed. Each horn acquires its unique sound from the landscape it inhabits. This strong interaction between these sounds and their environment gave the inspiration to work with this material. Horn sounds are interesting for another reason—they rise above any ambience, even that of large cities. They are soundmarks that give a place its character and give us, often subliminally, a "sense of place."[22]

The pitched characteristic of these sounds becomes a key component in the resulting musical argument, considering both the altered characteristics of the resulting echoes thus generated and the characteristics of sounds moving toward the recordist and then away again, the so-called Doppler effect. This was also the first of her works to attract the attention of the wider composing community as a result of the award of the status of honorable mention at the International Competition for Electroacoustic Music in Bourges in 1979.[23] A second version of the work, *Fantasie for Horns II*, with an additional part for acoustic horn, was completed the same year.

In 1979 Westerkamp received a commission to compose an installation work for the Western Front Gallery, Vancouver, as part of the Music from the New Wilderness Festival, held in 1980. The work opened up a whole new dimension to her creative writing in terms of soundscapes, one that was to prove highly influential in later works, including the piece selected for special study in this chapter, *Beneath the Forest Floor* (1992), composed twelve years later. *Cordillera* combined the voice of Norbert Ruebsaat, reading a collective of seventeen short poems from his book of the same name, with sounds drawn from the wilderness, in this case a range of mountains extending from Tierra del Fuego to Alaska. Both the content of the poems and the accompanying soundscapes reflect the geographical and acoustical characteristics of the associated regions.

In the early 1980s Westerkamp's industry gathered pace, driven both by her concerns for the impact of environmental sounds on the quality of life and her desire to cultivate a deeper understanding of their intrinsic characteristics via the creativity of soundscape composition. Whereas the sounds of the wilderness were a source of much that could be considered of beauty and pleasure, many of the sounds resulting from human actions result in opposite perceptions. In so doing she returned very directly to Schafer's concerns in terms of the negative impact of noise. Impressed by her "soundwalking" programs produced for community radio, the Hornby Collection, CBC, commissioned her to compose a piece on the impact of aircraft noise. A shortened version of the resulting work, *Under the Flightpath*, was broadcast in January 1981; it is an essay on the repetitive and intrusive sounds of airplanes taxiing, taking off, and landing, integrated with the comments of those living near the airport and under the flight path. The original inspiration for the piece dated back to 1978 and the development of a citizen's group to prevent the construction of a third runway for the Vancouver International Airport. Here the intersection of acoustic ecology, creativity, and societal impact is powerfully evident, adding further momentum to the significance of the continuing World Soundscape Project.

A second commission came from *Two New Hours*, CBC Radio. *A Walk Through the City*, first broadcast in April 1981, provided an opportunity to engage with an enhanced repertory of environmental sounds, creating a perspective that is both engaging and thought-provoking. Once again use is made both of sound materials drawn from the WSP tape library and additional recordings of her own, based in turn on a Ruebsaat poem of the same name. Westerkamp notes:

> It takes the listener into a specific urban location—Vancouver B.C.'s Skid Row area—with its sounds and languages. Traffic, carhorns, brakes, sirens, aircraft, construction, pinball machines, the throb of trains, human voices, a poem, are its "musical instruments." These sounds are used partly as they occur in reality and partly as sound objects altered in the studio. A continuous flux is created between the real and imaginary soundscapes, between recognizable and transformed places, between reality and composition.[24]

Her interest in combining the sounds of acoustic instruments with an accompanying soundscape, first explored in *Fantasie for Horns I*, was explored further in *Streetmusic*, a sound document completed in 1982. Here the soundscape is almost entirely unprocessed, based on the sound world associated with a street musician and subject to simple editing and minimal mixing/cross fading.[25] She notes:

> *Streetmusic* is a sound document which celebrates the beauty and diversity of Vancouver's street music scene. . . . [It] occurs on three levels. There is the music itself, which the musicians produce, and passers-by listen to; there is the interaction

and the chit-chat, the verbal exchange between the performers and the street audience; and there is the street itself, with its noises and intrusions, its randomness and ambience-creating a context for and, occasionally, a musical counterpoint to the acoustic event being played out.[26]

As in the case of *Fantasie for Horns I*, the original version of *Streetmusic* was a complete prerecorded soundtrack, composed in this instance as a sound document for Co-op Radio. The inclusion of a live horn part for *Fantasie for Horns II* may have acted as the stimulus for a second concert version of *Streetmusic*, using a shorter version of the soundtrack and a part for a live musician to improvise to it.

Her next work, *Cool Drool*, composed in 1983, was designed from the outset as a concert work for voice and two-channel tape. It is a satire, about the use of music in commercial and industrial work environments, tracing the development from the Muzak Corporation's background music market to a new, so-called foreground music market, produced by an expanding number of leased music companies. Although today Westerkamp regards this piece as a slightly dated sound essay,[27] it is nonetheless of interest as a historical commentary on society in the early 1980s, foreshadowing the ever-increasing presence of music that by now is colonizing all corners of public and private life spheres. The impact of Muzak was to become a major preoccupation for her during the 1980s, and a critical study of its characteristics is to be found in her master's thesis, completed at SFU in January 1987.[28]

Starting in 1984, Westerkamp broadened her horizons still further to embrace film soundtracks. There are strong affinities between the now well-established techniques of sound design in films and the characteristics of soundscape composition, thus blurring more traditional distinctions between sound and music in this context. At the same time, her interests in the sounds of the wilderness were developed a stage further with a three-week trip with other artists to explore the sounds of the area known as the Zone of Silence in the north-central Mexican desert, in December 1984 and January 1985. This led to a series of recorded soundscapes, in due course developed as a sound installation at the Museum of Quebec, Quebec City, December 1985 to January 1986, once again working in collaboration with Ruebsaat.

A number of freestanding works were to follow, including *Cricket Voice*, completed in 1987, and a trilogy comprising *Desertwind* for spoken voice and tape, *Meditation* for improvising voices and tape, and *The Truth is Acoustic* for clay vase, sopranino recorder, voice, and tape, which premiered at the 1988 Sound Symposium in St. John's, Newfoundland. At times the transformations employed on the source sounds and the complexities of their combination take the listener close to the limits of recognizability discussed earlier in the context of Truax's definitions of soundscape composition. This is especially so in the case of *Desertwind*. However, the inclusion of a spoken part in each work ensures a secure and convincing gateway to this extended sound world.

A notable feature of Westerkamp's soundscape compositions is not only the diversity of perspectives she embraces, but also her ability to develop these components essentially in parallel. Two further works composed during her Zone of Silence project are a case in point. *His Master's Voice* (1985) is "a collage of the 'macho voice' as it appears in all walks of life: on the street, in the media (AM/FM radio), in the political and religious realms, in the contexts of popular culture and of high culture."[29] This intentionally negative perspective on sounds she regards as intrusive and objectionable, as in the case of Muzak, contrasts markedly in scope and nature with *Harbour Symphony* (1986), a work commissioned for the opening of the Canada Pavilion at Expo '86. Whereas the sounds of Vancouver Harbour, in particular those associated with the yearly New Year's events, were clearly an important inspiration for the new work, the scale of the commission was altogether of a different order. Moreover, the harbor soundscape that forms the basis of the piece was a performed event, involving almost 150 boats, large and small, assembled near Canada Place in Vancouver Harbour, sounding their horns in a precomposed manner. A second *Harbour Symphony*, albeit on a much reduced scale, was composed in 1988 using the sounds of six boat horns in the harbor of St. John's, Newfoundland, for a series of daily noon performances at the Newfoundland Symposium.

Westerkamp left Simon Fraser University in 1990, giving up her post teaching acoustic communication in partnership with Truax to concentrate more fully on her work with soundscape composition and acoustic ecology. Before leaving she completed a further series of works, including *Kits Beach Soundwalk* (1989). The inspiration for this piece was her earlier work with Vancouver Co-operative Radio, now to be revisited and extended in compositional terms. Kits Beach, the colloquial name for Kitsilano Beach, is located toward the center of Vancouver, and during the daytime subject to the noises of a bustling city. Late in the evening these intrusions are far less evident, which allowed her to capture the gentle ripple of water sounds, including the delicate sounds of barnacles eating. Her enduring interest with breath sounds, which provided the basis of *Whisper Study* (1975), also resurfaced at this time with *Breathing Room* and *Breathing Room 2*, both completed in 1990. A third work, *Breathing Room 3—A Self Portrait*, was completed in 1991. Her program note for *Breathing Room* provides a useful insight into her creative thinking in this context:

> Music as breath-like nourishment. Breathing as nourishing musical space. The breath—my breath—is heard throughout the three minutes. All sorts of musical/acoustic things happen as I breathe in and out. Each breath makes its own, unique statement, creates a specific place in time. Meanwhile the heart beats on, propelling time from one breath to the next.[30]

The breath sounds are self-generated, signaling the start of a major and lasting engagement both with human breath sounds and also those occurring elsewhere in nature. *Breathing Room 2*, for two-channel tape, sound sculpture, tuned bottles, and audience, is an adaptation of *Desertwind*, combining the sounds of wind in the desert with extensions thereof created by blowing across the top of tuned bottles, and breath-like sounds created through movements of the sound sculpture. *Breathing Room 3* for spoken voice and two-channel tape is a personal reflection on her achievements to date as she reached the age of forty-five. As both a complement and a contrast to this group of pieces, Westerkamp composed *Moments of Laughter* in 1988, based on the sounds of her daughter Sonja from birth, including recordings made by Sonja herself from the age of four onward. *The Deep Blue Sea* (1989), for two-channel tape and spoken word, combines the sounds of wind chimes and church bells with a text by Brian Shein, read by Ruebsaat.

Her next work, *École Polytechnique*, is scored for eight church bells, mixed choir, bass clarinet, trumpet, percussion, and two channel tape, commissioned in 1990 by Montréal Musiques Actuelles/New Music America. This is an especially powerful piece, recalling the shooting of fourteen women at the college on December 6, 1989. The tape sounds, drawn from broadcast reports at the time, contextualize and underpin the harrowing aural perspective generated by the contributing performers.

In 1991 Westerkamp started *The Soundscape Newsletter*. This publication brought thoughts and ideas together from sound ecologists and soundscape composers, thus establishing the foundations for the World Forum for Acoustic Ecology (WFAE), established in 1993 at The Tuning of the World: The First International Conference on Acoustic Ecology, cohosted by the Banff Centre, Alberta, and the University of Calgary.[31] Now free from the constraints of regular university teaching, Westerkamp could finally concentrate fully on both her critical and creative work in the context of acoustic ecology and soundscape composition. The stage was thus set for the composition of *Beneath the Forest Floor* (1992), commissioned by CBC Radio for David Jaeger's *Two New Hours* program and realized in the company's all-digital Advanced Recording Facility in Toronto.

Inside *Beneath the Forest Floor*

Premiered on May 17, 1992, on *Two New Hours*, *Beneath the Forest Floor* is a seventeen-minute work for stereo tape, entirely composed with materials derived from recordings made in British Columbia. Although Hildegard Westerkamp explored—both literally and musically—environments from several locations of the Canadian province, the forest evoked in the title and through the musical narration is that of the Carmanah Valley, in the southern part of Vancouver Island. The composer presents it in her program notes:

This old-growth rainforest contains some of the tallest known Sitka spruce in the world and cedar trees that are well over one thousand years old. Its stillness is enormous, punctuated only occasionally by the sounds of small songbirds, ravens and jays, squirrels, flies and mosquitoes. Although the Carmanah Creek is a constant acoustic presence it never disturbs the peace. Its sound moves in and out of the forest silence as the trail meanders in and out of clearings near the creek.[32]

Westerkamp describes her intention of sharing with the listeners her experience of the forest, but also of stimulating a willingness to experience it themselves:

A few days in the Carmanah creates deep inner peace—transmitted, surely, by the trees who have been standing in the same place for hundreds of years. *Beneath The Forest Floor* is attempting to provide a space in time for the experience of such peace. Better still, it hopes to encourage listeners to visit a place like the Carmanah, half of which has already been destroyed by clear-cut logging. Aside from experiencing its huge stillness a visit will also transmit a very real knowledge of what is lost if these forests disappear: not only the trees but also an inner space that they transmit to us—a sense of balance and focus, of new energy and life. The inner forest, the forest in us.[33]

Such an intention is actually a musical equivalent to the preservation activities held in this area, nowadays known as the Carmanah Walbran Provincial Park, as the composer recalls in our interviews with her:

By the time I got to go into that area, the logging had been stopped. And the second part of [the area] had been declared a park. And that was the work of the then called Western Canada Wilderness Committee—it is now called the Wilderness Committee—a very creative environmental organization that decided that they wanted to build trails into this forest, so that people who had never been in old-growth forests, and would not know what was lost, would actually be able to go in there, and get to know what an old-growth forest really is like, what it feels like. . . . So it was really a matter of giving access to the wilderness, to especially people from the city, to get to know these places. Because the issue of not knowing what we are losing is huge. Which happens, of course, in Canada a lot, because people that are in cities are really not in touch with what the meaning of wilderness is, of what these places feel like. And therefore they also really do not understand the relationship that First Nations have with wilderness, who know really well what it is like, how to live with it, how to survive in it.[34]

You can watch videos of our interviews with Hildegard Westerkamp in the accompanying software, which contains several presentations where the composer discusses different aspects of her creative process and aesthetic orientations. Demonstration Video 4.1 shows how to access these resources with Presentation

143

2 of the accompanying software, where Westerkamp presents the contexts from which she started composing Beneath the Forest Floor. ▶

With both the will to explore the West Canadian primary forests and the opportunity to work with high-quality recordings to be later used in the brand new facilities of CBC Radio, Westerkamp decided to go and experience these areas, where the materials for *Beneath the Forest Floor* were chosen.

Recording as part of the creative process

Field recordings are central to Westerkamp's repertoire, and the active listening engaged with the aural capture of a particular location is of capital importance to her creative process:

> I made the recordings, and then you have the experience of being there. You are doing your own listening while you are recording, you are experiencing the environment, you are experiencing specific situations, and you bring that with you, with the recorded sounds, into the studio. And that, to me, is the most significant and pleasurable aspect of working with environmental sounds. Because I am recording them myself, I am not bringing a recording. I am bringing a whole lot of experience with it: the air of the place, the enormous quiet, which you do not pick up on a microphone, the majesty of the place, the majesty of the trees, the river that had its own majesty, the intimate quiet places in the forest. You feel the geology, the geography. All that becomes a very significant part of making decisions in the studio.[35]

For *Beneath the Forest Floor*, the composer decided to rent a high-quality stereo electret microphone, the Sony ECM-MS5, which "had a very wide range, so it would actually reach out quite far into the landscape":[36]

> With that kind of environmental recording, you want a microphone like that, because it gives you distance and depth. And I was really, really happy with that choice, when I got a very sensitive microphone, picking up all sorts of details, both from the distance, and from close-up, reaching further than my own ear.[37]

Once on site, the microphone was used as a listening instrument, enabling the composer to focus her attention on very specific sonic details of the environment. Discussing the third section of the work, largely dedicated to water sounds, she describes some of her recording activity as highly dynamic and engaged:

> When I record water, I really love to move the microphone along flowing water. I love to explore the architecture of a river, or a stream, or a creek, because it determines what the water sound will be like. If it goes through rocks, if it hits a leaf, if it hits the sides, that all determines what the water is going to sound like. And I like to zero the microphone into those details. Many of my recordings will have the general river

sound, and then it zeroes in onto specific flows. I like to move it that way, monitoring it on headphones, I could do it for hours![38]

In the composer's typical working pattern, recording is systematically followed by a rigorous documentation:

> I probably spent about three or four days in the [Carmanah Valley] forest making recordings, walking only for a few hours every time. . . . Then the listening back, and making notes, takes a lot of time. . . . [Documenting is part of the creative process], because I would comment, and I would already begin to think about . . . [I would] mark this and say, this I want to explore.[39]

Westerkamp's archive for *Beneath the Forest Floor* thus contains, for all relevant sound files, indications on their contents and recording location (for instance, "Carmanah raven, set of 3 calls + 1 single call");[40] but also, occasional notes for later use (such as "could be combined with creek I8 47′00″ also has high bird twitter").[41]

Field recording locations in British Columbia

Following her recording sessions in the Carmanah Valley, Hildegard Westerkamp got additional field materials from several other locations in British Columbia. Two of these are also on Vancouver Island: Cowichan Lake, located only several kilometers northeast of the Carmanah Valley, and a place named "Romeo's" after a person met during the trip in the Cowichan Valley. Some atmospheres were recorded on Galiano Island, immediately adjacent to Vancouver Island in the Strait of Georgia, and at Lighthouse Park in West Vancouver. Finally, Westerkamp herself did not record the entire set of environmental sequences eventually used in *Beneath the Forest Floor*—she also used the sound of ravens and a Steller's jay on Haida Gwaii (formerly called the Queen Charlotte Islands), recorded by Norbert Ruebsaat.

Presentation 4 of the accompanying software, "Locations of field recordings," exposes a range of field recordings made in these different areas of British Columbia. You can listen to the recordings from the composer's archive and familiarize yourself with the sound of these different environments and the materials used for the composition of Beneath the Forest Floor. *Demonstration Video 4.2 shows how to operate these interactive resources.* ▶

The raw materials of *Beneath the Forest Floor*

If Westerkamp used intensively the resources of CBC Radio to process her audio sources, as discussed in more detail shortly, the contents of the raw recordings lend themselves to a first categorization. Throughout the composition of the work, she used several large excerpts of field recordings as such;

145

that is, with no particular focus on one of their components. For instance, the file named "ID47_squirrel4_ambience_LighthousePark.wav" in the first of her archive folders contains prominently seagulls and a squirrel, but also a very rich variety of bird calls and twitters, as well as the hiss of the nearby Pacific Ocean in the background.[42] Two short excerpts of this field recording from Lighthouse Park can be heard in the opening section of *Beneath the Forest Floor*. In the first excerpt, the seagulls are the principal component, while the squirrel dominates in the second, but in both cases the excerpts convey the environment as a whole. Likewise, the recording of the creek heard continuously through the third section of the piece also contains many bird twitters, and the composer did not try to isolate the water from the twitters, or vice versa; rather, she used the entire sonic environment for inclusion in the musical work.

In many other instances, however, Westerkamp focused on a particular element of the recorded environment, using precise editing, gating, and equalizing for isolation purposes. This was the case, for example, with the winter wren chirpings, isolated from another field recording at Lighthouse Park. The captured environment is never heard as such in the final work—only the sound of the winter wren is heard, close to its original form or digitally processed, in the opening and ending sections.

The specific elements from the raw field recordings, as considered in the creative process of *Beneath the Forest Floor*, can be categorized as follows:

- **Several ravens** from different recording locations appear through the entire work. The most emblematic was recorded on a parking lot of the Carmanah Valley; it can be heard in its original form and under different transpositions, as detailed later in this analysis. Another adult raven, contrasting in timbre with that of the Carmanah Valley, is the one provided by Ruebsaat as recorded on Haida Gwaii. Another recording from Haida Gwaii contains various ravens, including babies, which can only be heard after a variety of downwards transpositions. Finally, a raven was recorded on Galiano Island, but it does not seem to have been used for the composition of the work.
- **Other birds** include a Steller's jay recorded on Galiano Island, a thrush from the Carmanah Valley, the previously mentioned winter wren from Lighthouse Park, and an unidentified bird named "Phuit bird" by the composer after its high-pitched, fast upwards glissandoing call.[43] Seagulls also appear in the previously mentioned recording at Lighthouse Park.
- **Flies and mosquitoes** were extracted from various recordings and can be heard up to the beginning of the third section of the piece.

- The only nonflying animals of this categorization are **squirrels**. A first squirrel was recorded at Romeo's on Vancouver Island; the second one is part of the rich fauna of Lighthouse Park, which also includes the prominent seagulls.[44]
- **Tree sounds** can be heard, both in the creaking trees sequences, and with tree trunks hitting each other.
- **Water** materials were derived from recordings of different locations of Carmanah Creek.
- Finally, the only non-natural element heard in the piece is a **chainsaw**, which serves as a sonic metaphor for the logging of the Carmanah forest.

You can use Presentation 1 of the accompanying software, "Interactive structural chart," to look at the successive steps of editing or transformation applied to the original recordings up to the final premixes of Beneath the Forest Floor. *The chart uses a color code facilitating the identification of materials according to their categories, and all materials can be listened to. Presentation 15, "Paradigmatic analysis of the work," provides a repartition of these categories through the chronology of the work, and again each visual item can be played. You can watch Demonstration Video 4.3 to see how to operate these resources, and you are encouraged to explore them further.* ▶

Digitally processing the environmental sources

As Westerkamp recalls, the conditions of the commission from CBC Radio implied an exclusive use of its new studio resources, and the anticipation of working with digital tools influenced the entire compositional project:

> [Jaeger] explicitly said, "I want you to compose [the piece] in our brand new digital facility in Toronto," and that was in 1990 I think. And that then caused me to make decisions about what I wanted to record, what I wanted the piece to be about. And knowing that the digital domain was "cleaner" than the analog domain, in terms of dubbing, and processing, and making many layers of copies in the studio, I thought, well, this is my opportunity to go in a quiet place in the world, in Western Canada, and make as high-quality recordings as possible in that environment, and then I will come with these very clean recordings and work exclusively in that studio. He said, "do not do anything before at home."[45]

With technical assistance from Rod Crocker and Joanne Anka in Toronto, the composer experimented extensively with a variety of different processes, and many of the final components of *Beneath the Forest Floor* are the result of multiple stages of digital transformations.

Isolating sounds from their original environment: Equalizing and gating

After short excerpts are selected from the original recordings, some processing can be applied to emphasize a specific component, such as a bird call, by isolating it from the rest of the environment to a certain extent. For instance, four thrush calls are heard in an excerpt of a field recording near the Carmanah River.[46] In this excerpt, the river flows loudly and has a strong and constant presence. In another file produced from this excerpt, gating has been applied in such a way that the intervals between each thrush call are silent; the river can now only be heard at the same time as the bird calls. This gated sound file was the basis for all the subsequent transformations applied to the thrush calls.[47]

In the case of the winter wren, a drastic equalization, only retaining the treble part of the spectrum to which the twitter belongs, was applied to the already mentioned ambience recorded at Lighthouse Park. Some subsequent gating was used to remove a discrete but constant hiss in the unfiltered area, remaining from the original atmosphere. Interestingly, both the gated and the ungated versions were assembled in the file that served as the source for further transformations; a careful listening enables the detection of the dry and processed areas.[48] Indeed, the composer favors both approaches, that of retaining the ambience of the environment, and that of extracting sound objects in the Schaefferian sense:

> Of course, you have river sounds in many of the recordings, you have wind, you have air. So that quiet in the wilderness is not without sound, there is always an ambience. And you also want to retain that level of silence in your piece. In some cases, I gated the sounds that I made, in order to get rid of even that ambience, because I just wanted to get the clarity of the sounds, and gating does it to an extent. You still have, say in the bird song, you still have a little bit of that silence . . . the moment that makes the sound, you still hear the ambience, but it gets masked to an extent. So it can be as clear a "studio recording," an "object" as possible. I love the process of the sound object idea of Pierre Schaeffer.[49]

Presentation 7 in the accompanying software, "Gating," enables you to experiment with this process. A menu provides specific examples from the archive of Beneath the Forest Floor, *and you can explore this process and its parameters further by loading any file from the archive, or your own sounds. The interactive structural map of Presentation 1 enables you to explore the genealogies leading from raw recordings to isolated sound objects in the context of the overall compositional process, as shown in Demonstration Video 4.4.*

Reversing and looping

Reversing a sound file by playing it backward was experimented with by Westerkamp in two documented instances: a fourteen-second sequence including flies, and a one-minute ambience where mosquitoes dominate. The latter was also transposed upward.[50] As with many of the composer's archive files resulting from the exploration of the CBC Radio resources, none of these were eventually used in the piece.

> You can use Presentation 8 in the accompanying software to experiment with backward playback. And again, Presentation 1 shows the path leading from the original recordings to their transformations; a menu enables you to highlight those sounds of the archive that were not included in the final work. Demonstration Video 4.5 shows how to operate these features. ▶

Westerkamp looped several of her materials, either unprocessed or already transformed. The opening sound of the piece, used as a deep, bass ostinato through to the entire first section and returning in the ending section to conclude the piece, is derived from the downward transposition of the adult raven recorded on the Carmanah Valley parking lot, an excerpt of which was subsequently looped *ad libitum*. Before selecting this particular material, the composer tried different looping strategies motivated by the idea of a drum:

> When I brought [the Carmanah raven recording] into the studio, I slowed that one down. And because it is close up to the microphone, and its graininess . . . each grain had an attack sound like a drum. . . . And it had an envelope that started quiet, and a crescendo, and then back. . . . And [each call] had a slightly different envelope and crescendo. And I ended up using three of those, slowed down, in the piece, and they became an instrument. They were my punctuation, percussive instrument. . . . Once I had slowed it down, making the association with the First Nations' drum, I thought, well, let us make it into a drum. It was not concrete enough to me. And that failed completely, we spent hours trying to make it sound like a nice Indian drum, and all it did, it sounded mechanical . . . that sounded electronic. So I gave that up, and returned to the original slowed-down sound, that has this wonderful envelope.[51]

Other loops, heard in the third and fourth sections of *Beneath the Forest Floor*, were made from the recordings of a trickle in the forest. The looping process is reminiscent of the cyclic, mechanical movement of water wheels:

> [In the third section,] you hear little, what I call "water wheels," little loops of water dripping sounds, coming in and out of that ambience [of Carmanah Creek]. And that came from a recording I made of just a little trickle in the forest, trickling from

underneath tree roots, onto a pathway. And it was literally just, kind of individual drops, coming down. . . . So I cut out little sections of that and made loops out of them. As a child, I was obsessed with trying to build water wheels, and it reminded me of that.[52]

Demonstration Video 4.6 shows you how to use Presentation 1 in the accompanying software to locate looped sounds, including some of the eventually withdrawn trials with the transposed raven, and further materials produced with this technique. ▶

Extending materials over time with delay and reverberation

A stereo delay was tried on some of the materials found in the archive, such as tree trunks with a very short delay time (approximately 35 milliseconds), leading from "ID05_treetrunk_resonant_gated.wav" to "ID07_treetrunk_delay.wav" in folder 2. A transposed version of the Carmanah raven was also delayed with a much larger time interval (about 1,250 milliseconds).[53] As can be heard particularly clearly in this latter example, the delayed signal is symmetric to the original signal in the stereo field: the signal from the left channel is delayed to the right channel, and conversely. No feedback was used.[54] Both the delayed tree trunks and the delayed raven were trials, and their resulting files were not explored further or included in the premixes of the piece. On the contrary, two of the three water wheels heard in the second half of the piece were produced from a looped recording subsequently processed with the delay, emphasizing what Westerkamp calls the "minuscule aspects of the sound."[55]

The extension of materials over time was also made using reverberation. This processing was applied to relatively few sound files, including a sloweddown version of the squirrel recorded at Romeo's, the chainsaw, and a transposed version of the thrush. Reverberation was not considered as a post-processing effect, but rather as a means of composing musical variation; for these three categories, the sounds can be heard in both their dry and reverberated forms in *Beneath the Forest Floor*. Besides, in the case of the thrush, the reverberated sound file (folder 4, "ID21_thrush_III.63_reverb.wav") was itself explored with further transpositions downward, three of which were then merged, eventually leading to the large texture heard through the final section.[56]

You can explore these processes in the accompanying software, with Presentation 9, "Stereo delay," and Presentation 10, "Reverberation," with examples from the composer's archive; you can also use Presentation 1 to explore the corresponding genealogies of sound transformations, as Demonstration Video 4.7 shows. ▶

The Doppler effect

Westerkamp used a hardware sampler at the CBC to apply a Doppler effect, involving synchronized panning and frequency modulations, to short excerpts of Carmanah Creek, and of calls of the Steller's jay recorded on Galiano Island:[57]

> I did not know [the sampler] that well, but the technician [Rod Crocker] who worked with me really knew it well, and he made suggestions, that is where we got, I think, that whole Doppler effect thing from, and other things. So he guided me a little bit through some of the potential processing set I could do in that.[58]

The Doppler effect led to a series of short figures characterized by a fast left-to-right movement, with Carmanah Creek in the opening section, with the Steller's jay in the second section, and with both these materials toward the end of the transition between the second and third sections.

Transposing and harmonizing

While the previously presented digital processes were used relatively sparingly, transposition by means of playback speed variation is certainly the most significant transformation used by Westerkamp for the composition of *Beneath the Forest Floor*: apart from the creaking trees, all the categories of sounds found in the composer's archive were subjected to transpositions, generally downward. As she affirms, the hardware interface of the AudioFile digital audio workstation by AMS Neve favored her exploration of this particular process:

> There were certain techniques that [the CBC] studio provided that I would not get anywhere else. For example, and I really explored this, there was this knob, which reminded me of a knob that we had in the analogue studio at SFU, which allowed for tape recorders to be slowed down . . . and you could have this fluid glissando experience, by having this big knob, slowing down the tape recorder, and then speeding it up again. There was a similar knob like that, in the [CBC] studio. . . . When we played back some sounds, and somehow it was connected to the playback system, I could do exactly the same thing. . . . You will hear [in my archive files] a few examples where I am slowing down, I think it is a squirrel, and I try to find a particular pitch, and you can hear me moving that knob. There is a kind of glissando sound in there, which I never used, until I get to the pitch that I wanted.[59]

Indeed, if many of the archive files retained the trace of experimentation with several pitches, the sounds edited for inclusion in the piece have, in almost all cases, a constant transposition factor. The one notable exception is the file "ID54_winter wren_peeps_var.speeds.wav" in folder 1, where the composer can be heard continuously turning the transposition knob, transforming the winter wren twitters into a randomly sounding sequence of high tones with thin spectral contents. This file was mixed along with the continuous flow of the Carmanah water in the third section, and is barely perceptible among the rest of the highly entropic texture.

The available range of transposition factors was very large. Many of the sounds result from a use of drastic speed variation factors; the file "ID63_winter wren peeps_var.speed0.01.wav" in folder 1 is six octaves lower than its source, the winter wren twitters.[60] The emblematic bass raven ostinato of the piece[61] is the result of a transposition of the original Carmanah raven by forty-four semitones down,[62] itself transposed further down by eight semitones,[63] making a cumulated transposition by four octaves and a major third. In most cases, many speed factors were tried; in particular, the four-note melody of the thrush led to twenty recorded transposed files.

In addition to speed transposition and subsequent mixing, the use of a pitch shifter, where the original duration is preserved, led to several harmonized sounds. In folder 2, "ID77_phuitbird_ID54open5th_pitchchange_Lexicon. wav" is derived from the already processed "ID54_phuitbird0.12_reverb.wav," pitch-shifted a fifth downward and merged with itself; the file "ID19_winter wren_fr.I.59_ed.var.speed0.07.wav," a transposed winter wren, was similarly harmonized in fifths, major thirds, and so-called tritones (in effect, intervals of six semitones and a half).

> In the accompanying software, Presentation 11, "Transposition with speed variation," and Presentation 12, "Harmonization," enable you to investigate these processes, with sounds from the composer's archive or your own, and you can use Presentation 1 to see how resulting files were mixed to create complex harmonies, as introduced in Demonstration Video 4.8. ▶

Westerkamp's approach to pitch is essentially intuitive, and she does not try to elaborate any particular harmonic system:[64]

> [My choice of pitches] is very intuitive. If there is a kind of chordal structure, I just do what I like. And, of course, sometimes I become very conscious of that, because that is where certainly the compositional preferences, as a composer, come through, of certain harmonic structures. I have never analyzed them. . . . I had to do it when I created my . . . third piece, Fantasie for Horns . . . and writing the score forced me to actually analyze the pitch structures, and I found it really difficult and really tedious. So, no, when I do this kind of electroacoustic work, I just go purely by taste, and what I like.[65]

More generally, the composer's approach to processing sounds is exploratory, as assessed with the numerous unused trials found in her archive; she also mentions a systematic approach, which is also apparent in the genealogy of her materials, with several series of files resulting from the same processing of a given file, with different parametric settings:

> The structure [of Beneath the Forest Floor] emerged as I was quite sort of systematically going through the sound set I thought would be interesting to process. And

see what happens. What comes out if I slow down a sound. What comes out when I speed it up, what comes out if I filter it, reverb, whatever. Simple, simple processing things.[66]

Assembling the processed sound files into premixes

As with the processes themselves, assembling the consequent materials into the premixes of *Beneath the Forest Floor* followed an exploratory approach, and several section alternatives, eventually withdrawn, can be found in Hildegard Westerkamp's archive. For instance, the file "ID03_rough first mix_section1. wav" is very similar to the premix actually used, "ID06_probably final mix_section1.wav";[67] both have the exact same structure, with the bass ostinato from the Carmanah raven all along, and sound objects from various environments punctuating the music. However, the electronic-sounding thread, generated from several transpositions of the winter wren twitters and appearing at 0′57″, remains relatively sparse in the alternative unused premix, while it densifies progressively in the actual premix, and in turn in the final work.

For the third section, five alternative premixes can be found in the archive folder 4. The first three—"ID16_premix_water section.wav," "ID17_premix_water section_busy.wav," and "ID18_premix_water section_less busy," all lasting 4′13″—have a similar structure, with the constant Carmanah River flow heard in the premix actually used,[68] and the sound of a truck, emerging at the end of the second minute and culminating at 2′57″, not found in any other mix. Several other elements punctuate these sequences: in all of them, the ravens and jay recorded on Haida Gwaii, as well as the unprocessed thrush calls; in the latter two, accelerated tree trunk sounds, a transposed and denser version of the thrush melody, the quickly and dynamically transposed winter wren giving a babbling effect, and polyphonies obtained by transposed calls of baby ravens. In the two other alternative premixes, "ID19_premix water section_w.o.creek. wav" and "ID20_premix_water section_w.otreetrunk.wav," a water flow can be heard, although much less prominently, along with the baby raven sequences, the babbling winter wren, and both the nontransposed and transposed versions of the thrush melody. The "ID19" file additionally contains the accelerated tree trunk sounds. Many of these elements can be found in the premix used for the final piece, but with a very different balance; the dry and wet thrush calls and the creek itself dominate the atmosphere of the section, and the other materials are much more discrete than in the alternative premixes. The premix actually used also introduces the massive texture derived from the harmonized reverberated thrush calls, announcing the transition into the final section:

We had [at the CBC] a mixer that was already automated, so we could set levels and readjust them, and things in the final mix. Those were all totally new to me, and were delightful, because they allowed a kind of precision that I really like, especially in terms of levels between the various tracks, and so, the various layers of sounds, you can do a huge amount with volume control, which is another aspect that I work a lot with. The subtleties of volume control, the subtleties of fades, I get very picky.[69]

Between the section premixes and the final work, Westerkamp added many additional elements, except for the opening. In section 2, the chainsaw was added to the section premix, as well as tree trunks, a slowed-down squirrel sound, and some of the general environment recorded on Galiano Island. In section 3, a mosquito, several water wheels, additional baby ravens, winter wrens, and additional thrush calls were added to the section premix "ID04_mix_water section_ending_peeps etcwav.wav" of folder 5. For section 4, the composer added winter wren calls, transposed baby ravens, one water wheel, and the emblematic transposed Carmanah raven to the premix "ID06_submix_ending-no peeps etc.wav," also located in folder 5. In our studio discussions on this final section, starting with the addition of the water wheel, Westerkamp explains:

That was like a real afterthought, at the end. You will see that I have a mix of the last section where neither the water nor the birds are in it, nor the raven either. And I think what happened was that I ended up putting the raven at the very end, as a kind of ending, and then I felt that, in that section, you can get beautifully lost in the musical thing, but you can also get lost perceptually, sort of a bit too far away. And I always like it when there is change. And when you can wake up the listener out of the reverie, also! And so that is when I decided to put these water wheels . . . in, just as a kind of echo from what we heard before. And the same with the little bird [the winter wren]. Because that is the smallest bird sound I had, among the processed ones, I thought the irony between that sort of larger, almost electronic kind of musical world, to put that little bird in the front, gave a lovely sense of dimensions, huge dimensions and space. So those things really happen at the very end of composing. They just came as, kind of, final ideas.[70]

You can use Presentation 1 of the accompanying software to listen to alternative premixes, and highlight the files from which the premixes and sections were assembled, as presented in Demonstration Video 4.9. ▶

The environmental materials through the structure of *Beneath the Forest Floor*
Section 1: Opening
The opening section of Hildegard Westerkamp's *Beneath the Forest Floor*, from 0′00″ to 3′53″, is characterized by the permanence of the deep bass ostinato derived from the recording of an adult raven in the Carmanah Valley.[71] Several short environmental sounds, mostly close to their original recorded form, punctuate this ostinato at regular intervals. The first of these is actually the

raven itself, with two calls appearing between 0′26″ and 0′30″. As Duhautpas, Freychet, and Solomos remark in their analysis, "the normal speed raven is heard several times in the piece, but it is impossible for the ear to link it to the transformed sound."[72] Nevertheless, the connection of the ostinato with the raven is particularly significant to the composer, as she explains in the context of her aesthetic intentions and creative process. The raven had been recorded by chance:

> I had a variety of . . . raven recordings. . . . And then I got, as we were leaving the forest . . . and we were getting ready to leave, and pack up . . . I hear a raven approach from the forest, and I very quickly put my microphone back in there, and I am literally standing beside the car, like this, with my microphone, and the raven flies right over, about . . . five meters above it. And it was calling . . . this kind of very grainy, beautiful sound. And it had this reverberance that was different from the forest reverberance . . . not as diffused as in the forest. It had this parking lot reverberance, ironically. It gave me the main sound of the piece![73]

Later, the composer specifies how this accidental recording impacted her consideration of the raven in the compositional project:

> The association with the Indian drum, coming from a raven, was just incredibly fascinating to me. Because the raven in Indian mythology on the West Coast is a trickster. And . . . the way it appeared, the last minute in the parking lot, that is trickster behavior! . . . It just gave me this idea that, well, we are here in this old-growth forest, this is the land that the First Nations lived in when it was still intact. That is what it was, that is where the totem poles came from; those trees, those Sitka trees that we saw there. And it gave me a general sense that the piece could perhaps try to replicate the idea of totem, in the acoustic sense. Make it an aural totem.[74]

After the presentation of the Carmanah raven, the section exposes successively the following elements: the Carmanah Creek, with a slow left-to-right Doppler effect; the raven again; the seagulls and squirrel from Lighthouse Park; creaking trees from the Carmanah forest, prefiguring the second section; a quicker Doppler effect applied to the creek; the Phuit bird; the Steller's jay of Galiano Island; winter wren twitters and rustling wings; the squirrel of Romeo's; the Phuit bird again, together with a fly; a longer excerpt of the river (between 2′34″ and 2′56″), superimposed from 2′48″ with the adult raven from Haida Gwaii; a fly again; the seagulls and squirrel; and a slow Doppler effect on the creek. The opening section thus has a role of exposition in the classical sense: apart from the thrush, the mosquitoes, the tree trunks, and the chainsaw, all the categories of recorded environmental sounds contributing to the work are presented in these first four minutes. All the recording locations are also represented, with the exception of Cowichan Lake.

155

In addition to the bass ostinato, another electronic thread appears at 0'57"—that, already mentioned, produced with a variety of transpositions of the winter wren. This thread slowly amplifies through to the rest of the section, before fading away shortly after the last occurrence of the Carmanah River. In the notes on her creative process, Westerkamp states that the first section

> is meant as a sonic journey into these forest places, all of which have, in a subtle way, a different soundscape along with different vegetation and animal life. The "drumbeat" of the slowed-down raven gives this section its rhythmical pace. The chord that gradually becomes audible in the background, is a foreshadowing of the musical treatment of the songbirds in the last section of the piece.[75]

You can use the paradigmatic chart of Presentation 15 in the accompanying software to investigate the repartition of materials through the chronology of Beneath the Forest Floor. *Categories can be displayed according to material types, or to degrees of processing, highlighting the predominance of raw recognizable sources in section 1. Demonstration Video 4.10 introduces you to these interactive features, and you are encouraged to use these as you read the text on the following sections of the work.* ▶

After the winter wren harmonies have faded away, only the totem ostinato remains, continuing through a transition (3'53" to 4'44") toward the second section. At 3'55", a transposed call of the Carmanah raven, 44 semitones below the original, appears. It is then repeated, superimposed with another transposition (37 semitones below the original), and the introduction of the chainsaw. The two transpositions are repeated, along with a new one (30 semitones below); finally, along with persistent occurrences of the chainsaw, this arpeggio of fifths from raven calls is repeated twice, finally joined by the original raven again, in a form of interpolation between the aural totem and its own origin from the Carmanah environment.

Section 2: Storm

As the opening totem ostinato disappears, the second section (4'44" to 7'35") is introduced with a door-like creaking tree, opening a long sequence made of three mixed atmospheres named "creaking trees" by the composer and recorded in the Carmanah forest on a stormy day, at Cowichan Lake, and at Romeo's—the three different recording locations of Vancouver Island. To this mix are added tree trunk sounds, sparingly punctuating the agitated atmosphere through the duration of the section. Along with this stormy vegetal soundscape, several animals appear; unlike in the opening, most of them are transformed, sometimes to a point where they are not recognizable as such. A fly heard on three occasions, and eleven variations of a Doppler figure based on the Steller's jay of Galiano Island, are perceptually relatable to their sources, presented in the

overture. Other animals are transposed, making them more difficult to identify: ravens from Haida Gwaii and other occurrences of Steller's jays—both
from Galiano and Haida Gwaii—are transposed downward; the squirrel from
Lighthouse park is sped up. Finally, the scream of the squirrel from Romeo's is
transposed downward to such an extent (by five octaves in most cases, by four
octaves in two occurrences) that it provides an abstract, mysterious figure:

> I had developed enough of the sounds, and processed enough of the sounds, that
> then I could eventually bring in the slowed down [bird song] sounds underneath,
> gradually, the more abstracted sounds, the musical undertone, really, of the piece.[76]

In addition to these materials from the animal and vegetal wildlife, the
chainsaw emerges several times; for the composer, the only non-natural element of the piece is key to the particular dramaturgy of the section:

> The second section spends time with the dark side of the forest, forest as a myth-
> ical place full of powerful natural forces and potential dangers. Acoustically this
> expresses itself through the use of storm sounds with creaking trees and slowed
> down animal sounds (mostly squirrel and jay). The chainsaw appears in opposition
> to these sounds as a modern-day "monster" fighting with the "forest giants." I see
> it as a mythical confrontation between the ancient forces of the forest and the de-
> structive forces of modern-day economic "progress."[77]

At 7′05″, the slowed down iterative Steller's jay becomes gradually more
prominent, and the last occurrence of the chainsaw disappears with a spectacular downward glissando, marking the end of the Storm section; subsequently,
the slowed-down squirrel figure followed with the Doppler-processed Steller's
jay act as a doorway between the dense and chaotic battle of elements and a
quiet, two-minute long transition toward the Water section.

The iconic slowed-down squirrel reappears twice, at 7′35″ and 7′51″; at
8′03″, a downward transposition of the Carmanah raven accompanies the introduction of a new material: the harmonized Phuit bird, slowly and quietly
glissandoing upward in several iterations through the entire transition. The
raven punctuates this thread, both in its original and transposed forms; at
8′43″, the Doppler figure made with the Carmanah Creek reintroduces the
water element, unheard since the end of the first section, into the piece; the
original Phuit bird environment also reappears, superimposed with its own
slowed down, harmonized version. At 9′10″, the Doppler Steller's jay figure is
immediately followed with its Carmanah Creek equivalent; at 9′15″, this latter
Doppler figure is then repeated, opening the third section.

Section 3: Water

The Water section is primarily characterized by the continuous flow of the
Carmanah River, initially occupying the entire listening space. Many other elements are added to this environment: at the beginning, a mosquito and two

occurrences of the nontransposed raven recorded at Haida Gwaii contrast clearly with the water flow. The only previously unheard bird is also introduced: the thrush's four-note melodic call distinctly accompanies the creek through the entire third section and beyond. Other materials are more difficult to perceive, as they tend to be masked by the river. Almost imperceptibly, the quick dynamic speed variations operated by Westerkamp on the winter wren twitters are present in the background. The polyphonies of transposed baby raven calls can be heard from the second occurrence of the Haida Gwaii adult raven, at 9′50″. Finally, several loops made from water materials complete the main creek flow. The file named "ID50_creek loop_eq.wav" in folder 2 can be heard through most of the section, and three different versions of the previously mentioned water wheels appear in several instances on top of the creek materials. The composer explains her intention to compose acoustic ambiguity by merging such a variety of sonic elements:

> The third section spends time at the creek and attempts to lead the listener into the rich microcosm of creek-water timbres and rhythms. Individual water melodies and rhythms are extracted and looped. They fade in and out of the general creek ambience. This section is exploring creek water as an acoustic presence within which the listener can get lost in his or her own acoustic imagination; where it is never clear whether the sounds that one hears are real or an acoustic illusion.[78]

As the water loops become more prominent, the thrush calls are developed from 10′25″ with a reverberated version of the nontransposed melody. At 11′20″, a large texture, obtained from three mixed transpositions of this reverberated file, extends this development. Progressively, this abstract texture takes over the listening space, until the water element finally fades away.

Section 4: Ending

While the thrush-derived abstract texture keeps floating, the fourth and last section starts at 13′41″ with a re-exposition of the totemic transposed raven call, here only heard in a single instance. The baby ravens reappear with their lowest transposition, contrasting with the abstract texture by providing a perceptually percussive material. Other abstract elements include previously unheard chords obtained by a harmonization of winter wren calls, appearing at 14′38″, and the harmonized Phuit bird glissandi, as introduced in the transition between the Storm and the Water sections, complete the overall texture from 15′28″.

In addition to this combination of abstract materials, the transposed and reverberated but recognizable thrush melody can be heard through the entire Ending section; one of the water wheels reappears three times—here detached from any other water-based environment. After the original thrush calls disappear completely at 14′16″, the only unprocessed source sound left in the ending of the piece is the winter wren. Westerkamp explains:

[T]his tiny peep appears purposely in the foreground of the grander musical chords in this section as I was fascinated by the enormous difference in proportion between the smallness of this little sound and its (and other bird calls') slowed-down versions. The peep's deep inner beauty, its purity and clarity are revealed when the sound is slowed down.[79]

At 16′55″, as the last occurrence of the water wheel fades away from the overall texture, the totem transposed raven is reintroduced, announcing the end of piece: the abstract sound world of the ending section disappears, giving way to the initial and emblematic sound of *Beneath the Forest Floor*.

Conclusions

Willing to experience and record old-growth forests and other environments in British Columbia, and challenged by the opportunity to work with new digital resources at CBC Radio in Toronto, Hildegard Westerkamp assembled a large and diverse reservoir of audio sources to compose *Beneath the Forest Floor*. By focusing on specific elements of her recordings as well as considering entire soundscapes as musical material, her experimentations over a variety of digital processes helped her identify and exploit the sonic potential of these sources. Very rich faunas, creaking trees, rivers, and water trickles can be recognized as such; one non-natural element—the electromechanical chainsaw—symbolizes the issue of logging, involving the Carmanah forest prior to Westerkamp's exploration.

The processing of these materials led to a variety of abstract materials, which cannot be linked aurally to their natural origins; but the composer, through her creative process, integrated together the identifiable environmental sounds with the processed melodies, rhythms, and textures. As she explains, the articulation between these two poles is of utter significance in her artistic practice:

I was interested in reconnecting the abstracted sound with the original. So *Beneath the Forest Floor* starts like that. I mean, it shows the whole philosophy of soundscape composition. It starts with a sound object, with the slowed-down raven sound, and then, after two or three times, you hear the actual raven. And that, to me, is the essence of how I work. I like to connect the beauty of what comes out of a sound . . . by that kind of processing of a sound object approach. It highlights the beauty of a sound, it makes you conscious of the inner ingredients of the sound.[80]

This approach to the recorded sound can serve as a metaphor for Westerkamp's broader compositional process and its grounding into her experience of the Western Canadian soundscapes. The journey through *Beneath the Forest Floor* indeed connects the listener with the environments it originates from, by accounting musically for the variety of the wildlife, the violence of storms and human-driven destructions, acoustic ambiguities and illusions, and the majesty of the old-growth forest.

Westerkamp's contributions to the evolution of the musical repertory of computer music are significant in a number of respects. First, as a pioneer of soundscape composition, she has expanded our knowledge and understanding of the world of naturally generated sounds as a rich and varied source of musical materials beyond the boundaries of our human experience in contexts that have proved deeply revealing. In turn, her creativity has proved highly influential on those who have subsequently engaged with the world of sounds that reflect and represent the characteristics of the environment that influence and shape the world that we inhabit. Perhaps most significantly, her work has stimulated the art of listening to the underlying characteristics that determine the nature and significance of what we hear in everyday life.

Francis Dhomont
Phonurgie

Contexts for *Phonurgie*

Background and early career

Francis Dhomont's long-standing association with the Groupe de Recherches Musicales (GRM) in Paris has resulted in a repertory of electroacoustic works that has been shaped and influenced by the shared but individually distinctive aesthetics of the many leading composers who have worked with GRM over the years, including Luc Ferrari, François Bayle, Bernard Parmegiani, Denis Smalley, and Daniel Teruggi, to name but a few.[1] The resulting legacy of works makes an important contribution to the repertory, advancing perspectives that are arguably different from those produced by composers working at IRCAM and elsewhere. Born in Paris in 1926, Dhomont's early education during the 1940s led to an early appreciation of the creative arts, leading to private studies with Ginette Waldmeier, Charles Koechlin, and Nadia Boulanger, and the launch of his career as a composer, working at first with conventional instruments.

His curiosity with the possibilities of electronic means of sound production was stimulated by a chance encounter with a Webster Dictaphone recorder in 1947, brought back from America by the uncle of a friend. He realized that the recording medium, a magnetized wire, could be used to manipulate recorded sounds, and started to explore the creative possibilities of this resource, initially unaware of the similar pioneering experiments being carried out by Pierre Schaeffer just a few miles away. The very first broadcast of Schaeffer's initial studies in this new composing genre in a concert titled *Concert de bruits* on October 5, 1948, was thus to prove both a revelation and a stimulus for him, though it would seem that no direct contact was made with Schaeffer and his associates at this time.[2]

In 1951 Dhomont relocated to Provence in the South of France, where he had an early opportunity to experiment with a tape recorder when preparing materials for a workshop on contemporary music for local teachers. This recording medium was altogether more versatile than that used by the Dictaphone, and he became aware of the possibilities of editing sound material with a razor blade and splicing tape, and also of manipulating the playback speed of recordings by physically interfering with the drive capstan. He also discovered it was possible to overlay materials by recording new material over a previous recording while physically restraining contact of the tape with the erase head.[3] Further work with the possibilities of music technology were then put to one side as he concentrated on acoustic composing. Unfortunately, his aspirations in the latter context fell short of his expectations, and by 1956 he had almost completely changed his direction career-wise to become a wood craftsman.

By the early 1960s Dhomont's latent curiosity with manipulating recorded sounds led him to revisit his earlier interests, and in 1963 he established a private studio in Les Baux-de-Provence, based on a small collection of domestic tape recorders. Unfortunately, their technical limitations inhibited his investigations for a time, a situation that was materially improved a few years later when he was able to acquire a couple of secondhand professional recorders.[4] Interestingly, he discovered it was possible to vary the speed of the capstan incrementally by replacing the conventional step-based speed regulator with a cone-shaped drive system, anticipating a time when such changes could be achieved electronically.[5] Although his creative achievements at this time were little more than experiments, his knowledge and understanding of the medium continued to develop, embracing the publication of Schaeffer's discourse *Traité des objets musicaux* in 1966 and a series of broadcasts of electroacoustic works written by members and associates of GRM, first established in 1958 and by the mid-1960s well established as the leading center for electroacoustic music in France.[6]

Dhomont completed his first electroacoustic work, *Cité du dedans,* in 1972, quickly followed by *Assemblages,* composed in the same year, the latter being a stereo work reflecting the sculptures of Michel Anasse and designed to accompany an exhibition of his work. Three years were to elapse before his next piece, *Syntagmes* (1975), premiered in Saint-Rémy-de-Provence, Bouches-du-Rhône. The latter piece is notable for being an early engagement with the use of processed sound fragments to reflect extra-musical concepts, in this case the phonemes of speech. Inspiration for the techniques employed in this piece owes much to the outcomes of his attendance at a training course at GRM in 1973–1974.

Although the non-urban environment of Provence offered many advantages, the area was necessarily far removed in a geographic context from the primary centers of creative activity, which were located for the most part in major cities. As a result, opportunities for public engagement were relatively few and far between. The nearest city, Marseille, provided a possible locus for the exchange of ideas via the Centre National de la Recherche Scientifique (CNRS), which had established a regional laboratory for scientific research. However, CNRS had yet to embrace the medium of electroacoustic music.[7] Undeterred, he set about attracting support for a contemporary music festival in Provence, named Musiques Multiples and first staged in 1975. Although the primary focus was acoustic music, he invited François Bayle from GRM to present a concert of electroacoustic works, marking the start of a long and productive friendship. This encounter convinced him of the necessity to return to Paris, where he also met Michel Chion for the first time and established the foundations of what was to prove a long and fruitful association with GRM.

It was at this point that Dhomont decided to embark on a full-time career as an electroacoustic composer, and he returned to Provence to continue the development of his private studio. His growing reputation was given a significant boost in 1976 with a performance of *Syntagmes* at the Bourges International Electroacoustic Competition, where it received an honorable mention. In 1978, following an invitation by Marthe Forget, a Canadian soprano and music teacher, he visited the Faculty of Music at the University of Montreal, bringing him into direct contact with the burgeoning electroacoustic music community in French-speaking Quebec. Although this initial residency was limited to just a few months, interrupted by a return to France to continue his contributions to the now well-established contemporary music festival in Provence, the ground had usefully been prepared for a more substantial, long-term association with developments in Canada that was soon to follow. His subsequent appointment by the dean Henri Favre as a member of the faculty led him to relocate to Montreal in 1980, albeit traveling back to Europe periodically to work at GRM. Although he retired from the university in 1996, he remained in Quebec until 2004, when he returned to Avignon.

Dhomont's influence on the evolution of electroacoustic music is substantial, not least for what he personally achieved in terms of a creative axis linking GRM with Montreal, stimulating the joint exploration of aesthetics that have their roots in the pioneering work of Pierre Schaeffer. His association with both institutions brought him into close contact with several Canadian electroacoustic composers who had previously worked at GRM. These included Marcelle Deschênes, Yves Daoust and Philippe Ménard. The fostering of these institutional links can be traced back to 1959, when Gilles Tremblay crossed the Atlantic to work with Pierre Schaeffer in Paris.[8] An important key to understanding the technical and musical characteristics of Dhomont's electroacoustic works is thus the development of GRM itself, and it is for this reason that close attention is paid to its evolution.

163

Musique concrète and the birth of Groupe de Recherches Musicales (GRM)

In 1932 Pierre Schaeffer was appointed as a technical apprentice with the national broadcasting institution Radiodiffusion française (RDF), developing professional skills in sound mixing and recording. During the German occupation of France he collaborated with the theater director Jacques Copeau with a view to establishing a training academy for sound design, otherwise known as radiophonics or radiophonic art. This initiative led to the construction of a small experimental studio, known as the Studio d'Essai in late 1942. Although his remit was primarily to provide engineering support, his creative interests led to a joint project with Claude Arrieu in 1943–1944, producing a series of one-hour programs combining spoken drama with acoustically generated sound material.[9] These wartime experiences proved to be a major stimulus for his growing interests in sound design, and in 1948 the RDF, soon to be renamed Radiodiffusion-Télévision Française (RTF), agreed to establish a Club d'Essai de la Radiodiffusion, with Schaeffer as director.

The early development of what became widely known as *musique concrète* is an area of study in its own right, beyond the immediate scope of this study, but some key features of this formative period need to be considered here in the context of the subsequent development of GRM.[10] The first phase of this trajectory, from 1948 until the early 1960s, has been described as the "mechanical phase," given its high dependency on the physical characteristics of the machinery used.[11] This consisted not only of conventional broadcasting equipment such as microphones, mixers, and recorders, but also a number of specially engineered devices designed by Schaeffer and his associates. As previously noted, the functional characteristics of the technologies used by electronic composers provide important clues to the scope and nature of the creative processes explored in their works. The *techné*, or the art of translating creative ideas into practical realities, is especially significant in terms of acquiring a well-informed understanding of how GRM came into being and how these early experiences were to influence and shape subsequent developments in the institution, embracing in due course the extended possibilities of digital signal processing.

Musique concrète was born in an era that predated the commercial tape recorder, Dhomont's early encounter with a wire-based recorder notwithstanding. Prior to 1951 the recording facilities available to Schaeffer were limited to direct disk cutting lathes, comprising shellac-coated disks and an associated stylus used to imprint an acoustic groove in response to an applied signal, much in the manner used at the time to manufacture 78-rpm records. Whereas the resulting recording could be played back in a number of ways, including speeding up, slowing down, and/or reversing the direction of travel of the turntable, the only way the content could be changed was by looping one revolution of the groove at a predetermined point. Such technical conditions materially influenced the compositional process and provide a striking early example of the importance of understanding the functional characteristics of the resources actually used to create specific works.

In 1949 Schaeffer was joined by the composer Pierre Henry, and, together with technical support from a gifted engineer, Jacques Poullin, this team began to explore further the possibilities of manipulating sound materials in a studio environment, using an audio mixing unit to envelope sound objects and overlay recordings to build up sound montages. A material breakthrough occurred in 1951 with the introduction of magnetic tape recorders to replace the aging disk cutters.[12] Significant improvements in audio fidelity, and the ability to edit recordings directly using a razor blade and splicing tape, radically transformed the working environment for composers of *musique concrète*. The year 1951 also marked a major step forward in terms of institutional recognition and support with the establishment in October of the Groupe de Recherche de Musique Concrète à la Radiodiffusion-Télévision Française (GRMC).

In technical terms, the most notable achievement of this development phase was the design and construction of a set of tape-based signal processors.[13] The first of these, known as the Morphophone, consisted of a continuous tape loop system with ten adjustable playback heads, the latter providing successive reiterations of the recorded signal that could be blended to produce a pulsing type of reverberation. Carefully controlled feedback of these signals to the record head allowed these effects to be extended in time. The other two systems, known as Phonogènes, played tape loops at different speeds. One machine, known as the Phonogène chromatique, created tempered pitch transpositions via a set of selectable drive capstans of different sizes, controlled via a twelve-note keyboard, with a two-position motor speed switch extending the functional range of the keys to two octaves. The other machine, known as the Phonogène à transposition continue (or Phonogène à coulisse), offered a continuously variable playback speed range regulated by a lever that directly controlled the speed of a single capstan, from zero to maximum.

Although by the mid-1950s several manufacturers were producing stereo tape recorders, GRMC continued to work with the standard mono recorders routinely supplied by the RTF. An early desire for multitrack facilities, however, led to the engineering of a specially designed three-track recorder in 1952, known as the Magnétophone tripiste, consisting of a platform of three mono tape drives stacked vertically, each equipped with a mono tape head assembly with individual supply and take-up spools. Although such an arrangement could not achieve the exact synchronization possible when recording multiple tracks on a single tape, the arrangements served the interest of the early pioneers well. By this point a number of composers were becoming acquainted with the possibilities of the studio and the growing ethos that was to become a distinctive feature of the works subsequently to be associated with GRM. Early encounters with the resources available at the Club d'Essai by composers such as Pierre Boulez, Olivier Messiaen, and Karlheinz Stockhausen were to be

165

followed by more extended associations that were to prove influential in the evolution of the institution, including François Bayle, Michel Chion, Luc Ferrari, Ivo Malec, Guy Reibel, Bernard Parmegiani, Michel Philippot, Alain Savouret, and Iannis Xenakis.

Pierre Henry was to play an increasingly important role in shaping technical and musical developments as the decade progressed, prompted in the first instance by an extended period of absence on the part of Schaeffer, from 1953 to 1957, to pursue other duties on behalf of RTF. On Schaeffer's return it became clear that the time had come for a significant upscaling of the work of GRMC. The RTF had itself been subject to an expansionist agenda, and the climate was thus favorable for such a development. Schaeffer, with the support of his colleagues, renamed GRMC as the Groupe de Recherches Musicales (GRM) in 1958, and set about lobbying RTF seeking to establish a unit within the organization that would embrace both GRM and related areas of research interests.

At the end of 1959 a Service de la Recherche was established, with GRM as a major subdivision, the others units being the Groupe de Recherches Image (GRI), the Groupe de Recherches Technologiques (GRT), and the Groupe d'Études Critiques (GET), the last being concerned with the societal implications of broadcasting. Although the individual areas of responsibility were clearly delineated, collaboration was strongly encouraged where mutual interests could be identified. In the case of GRM the desire to develop more advanced technologies to advance its creative objectives soon fostered a strong relationship with GRT, notably with Francis Coupigny, the director of this division. This association signaled the start of the next phase of GRM's development, known as the "electronic phase," covering a period that extended from 1960 to the early 1970s.

The early 1960s is associated with several changes in the management of the GRM. Although Schaeffer remained the official director until 1965, day-to-day management passed to a succession of people, starting in 1960 with Michel Philippot, followed by Luc Ferrari, who discharged these responsibilities from 1961 to 1963. Between 1964 and 1966, management was delegated on an alternating basis to Bernard Baschet and François Vercken, pending the appointment of François Bayle as Schaeffer's successor in 1966, a position he held until 1997. One consequence of this delegation of responsibilities between 1960 and 1966 was the stimulus given to an underlying debate as to the future direction of GRM. Perspectives on both the future aesthetics of the medium and the technologies to be used were already expanding beyond concepts allied exclusively with natural sound sources and electromechanical signal processing technologies. Indeed, the seeds of a more electronic approach to signal processing had already been sown as early as 1952 through the use of filters to modify the feedback characteristics of sounds recycled via the Morphophone, and by the end of the decade interest in such devices was growing.

It is instructive at this point to take a closer look at the creative imperatives that were becoming central to the work of GRM. Fundamental to these are the descriptors that are often attached to works that subscribe to the GRM ethos. One in particular has achieved particular prominence, that of acousmatic music, primarily concerned with the intrinsic characteristics of sounds that one hears without being able to identify their origins, thus trading on the relationships that may be developed between the known and the unknown in terms of composing with materials drawn from the natural sound world. Over the years the true meaning of this term has been the subject of some debate. Whereas the term *musique concrète* became synonymous with Schaeffer's pioneering work, and indeed was retained as a key descriptor by advocates and associates of GRM for many years, it lacked a certain depth and any sense of gateway to a more refined perspective. He indeed was to reflect on this drawback in his earlier treatise *À la recherche d'une musique concrète*, published in 1952, although he was uncertain at the time how best to resolve this question.[14] A solution was to emerge a few years later when he became aware of the useful parallels to be drawn between our perception of abstract painting and the way we perceive sound materials outside their natural context. Following a suggestion from the poet Jérôme Peignot, he then adopted the concept embraced by the Greek word *acousma*, meaning to describe the object of hearing.[15] The study of Dhomont's *Phonurgie* that follows provides a cogent exemplar of the acousmatic tradition of composing that has been so central to the evolving aesthetics of GRM.[16]

In 1963 a third and final version of the Phonogène was built, the Phonogène universel. This is an especially interesting development, since on the one hand it looked backward in time to its earlier electromechanical relatives, and on the other, albeit in a fairly rudimentary manner, it looked forward to the digital era of sampling. The underlying technology dates back even further to a commercial product known as the Springer machine or Tempophon, dating from the late 1950s. Designed as a speech processor, this device used a rotating array of four playback heads mounted on the circumference of a large head capstan, one quadrant of which engaged with a tape transport, driven in turn by a normal drive wheel. If the head capstan remains stationary, then the content of the passing tape is reproduced normally by the tape head in most immediate contact. Changing the speed of the drive capstan proportionally changes the pitch and speed of the recorded material in exactly the same manner as that associated with the Phonogène à transposition continue. If, however, the head capstan is rotated in either direction, the recorded sound material is sampled by each of the playback heads in turn, thus making it possible to uncouple this otherwise fixed relationship and vary pitch and duration independently. Early access to such a versatile technique was to prove a significant stimulus for composers at GRM at a time when the enhanced possibilities of digital signal processing had yet to be encountered.[17]

The 1960s are associated with a series of technical developments at GRM that in some respects might appear counterintuitive. The invention of the transistor in the late 1950s paved the way for a new era in electronics, leading in turn to the integrated circuit and a design revolution that was to transform the world of audio engineering. Thus, the previously somewhat piecemeal development of studios using individual items of equipment was materially transformed with the introduction of the commercial voltage-controlled synthesizer in the mid-1960s, providing a fully integrated system for the production of electronically produced music.

Viewed simply as alternatives to conventional instruments, it would seem at first sight that these systems had very little to offer GRM. It was recognized, however, that the signal processing facilities were of material interest, accessibility being significantly enhanced by the modular design of these synthesizers, allowing an extended range of possibilities for working with externally generated sound material. GRM not only acquired a Moog synthesizer, it also designed and built a synthesizer entirely to its own specifications, calling upon the skills of Francis Coupigny and his associates in GRT. The versatility of the Coupigny synthesizer was further enhanced by integrating this facility with a custom-designed mixing desk, known as the Studio 54 mixing desk after the name assigned to the room by what had now been renamed the Office de Radiodiffusion-Télévision Française (ORTF).[18]

Whereas the Coupigny synthesizer embraced the standard synthesis and signal processing facilities of its commercial counterparts, subtle but important enhancements were made both to the facilities for external audio communications and to the design of the control surface. In the former context an array of input and output audio connections were hard-wired to a twenty-four-track mixer, which in turn acted as a conduit to the array of studio recorders and tape-based signal processors such as the Morphophone and the Phonogènes. In the latter context the services of a conventional music keyboard were deliberately dispensed with, thus placing a particular emphasis on the scope and nature of the programmable functions that were used to vary the component device parameters with respect to time. A further notable design feature was the use of a pin matrix board system for interconnection between both audio and control signals.[19]

In terms of the individual modules, the repertory of synthesis and signal processing functions were generally typical of a conventional synthesizer, embracing, for example, oscillators that could be used for additive synthesis; modulators; a noise generator; high-pass, low-pass, band-pass, and resonating filters; and a variety of envelope generators that could be used as amplitude and/or frequency function generators. It was the sophistication and versatility of these generators, however, that transformed the GRM synthesizer into a powerful composing facility. Although Coupigny began work on the synthesizer in 1960, thus predating the commercial voltage control revolution by a number of years, a working prototype was not completed until 1966, the year in which the Moog synthesizer was purchased, and it was a further three years before the final, definitive version was installed in Studio 54. Bernard Parmegiani completed the first work to be composed using the new synthesizer, *L'œil écoute* (1969–1970), marking the start of a period of extensive use of these facilities by GRM composers that was to peak toward the end of the 1970s.[20]

During the early 1970s, the future of the ORTF became the focus of increasing debate in a world increasingly populated by commercial radio and television stations, and in 1975 it was relaunched as Radio France. This had material consequences for its various departments, not least the research divisions. Fortunately, Schaeffer was able to secure an assured future for GRM as part of the Institut National de l'Audiovisuel (INA), now with an enhanced role to secure a lasting legacy of French electroacoustic music, both in terms of creating and managing an archive of documents and recordings and in the proactive dissemination of such materials through writings and CDs, using the label INA-GRM. This was an astute and highly beneficial development, not least in terms of seeking to preserve and enhance its status in the face of the competition now being faced from IRCAM, as these objectives were further reinforced by its physical relocation to the main building of Radio France (Maison de la Radio).[21]

These major changes, also coinciding with Schaeffer's retirement as director of GRM and the appointment of Bayle as his successor, marked a watershed in the processes of transition from analog to digital technologies. By this point the third phase of development, concerned with the possibilities of using computers, had progressed from uncertain foundations at the start of the decade to an area of significant importance within GRM. Prior to 1970, interest in the pioneering work of Max Mathews and his associates at Bell Telephone Laboratories had been very limited, not least on the part of Schaeffer, who initially was hostile to such a prospect. A major area of concern was the entirely deterministic approach associated with these early developments. In his view this was totally alien to the philosophy underpinning the work of GRM, where naturally generated sound materials were directly manipulated and intuitively processed by the composer. Computer music, composed remotely via large scale mainframe computers using predetermined synthesis instructions, could not be further removed from the intimate working environment of the traditional analog studio.

New directions for GRM: From analog to digital

Differences of perspective, however, were starting to appear in such a sharply polarized view of the scope and nature of acousmatic music. In terms of exploring synthetic means of sound production, composers such as Pierre Henry had made occasional use of electronic oscillators for a number of years,

169

in his case starting with his *Haut voltage*, composed in 1956, and with the introduction of the Moog and Coupigny synthesizers attitudes were to change materially in this regard, leading in due course to works such as *L'expérience acoustique* by François Bayle (1972), *Triptyque électroacoustique* by Guy Reibel (1973–1974), and *De Natura Sonorum* by Bernard Parmegiani (1974–1975), all of which make significant use of electronically generated sounds.[22]

For Schaeffer the most compelling reasons for finally taking an interest in computers arose during the late 1960s, when he became aware of a rather different working environment associated with what was to prove a transitional phase of "hybrid" synthesis, where via a combination of smaller dedicated computers used to control analog studio-based resources it became possible to integrate the most attractive features of both technologies.[23]

Matters came to a head for GRM in 1970 at a conference on "Music and Technology" organized by UNESCO in Stockholm that brought together key people from both sides of the equation, including Schaeffer. He had previously cultivated an interest in the work of Knut Wiggen, the primary architect and director of the EMS studio in Stockholm, leading to the EMS 1 system, based upon a PDP-15 computer and a modular studio system combining both analog and digital devices. Significantly the system operated in real time, and this opportunity directly to experience the new facility was highly influential. Other leading practitioners present at the conference responsible for the development of similar hybrid systems included Peter Zinovieff and Max Mathews. It was agreed that the time had come for GRM to start to engage with a digital agenda, a further motivation being the announcement that IRCAM was to be established under the direction of Pierre Boulez, and that it was possible that this rival institution would from the outset take an all-digital approach to research and development, a prediction that was to prove entirely correct.

For his part Schaeffer entered into a partnership with Wiggen to develop a hybrid system for GRM, drawing upon key features associated with EMS. Without the substantial funding associated with the development of the Stockholm studio, the project was necessarily of more modest proportions. Perhaps crucially, the project had to pursue concepts central to Schaeffer's theoretical writings on the subject, a requirement that created its own challenges, and indeed was embedded in its name, SYNTOM (*SYNthèse Traité des Objets Musicaux*). Sadly, the project failed, primarily for two reasons. First, GRM did not have direct access to a suitable computer, and second, the initial reactions of many composers at GRM were less than favorable. However, the seeds had been sown for an alternative approach to composing electroacoustic music that was eventually to bear rich fruit, based initially on exploring the potential of Music V as the starting point for developing digital signal processing algorithms tailored to GRM's requirements.

In this context GRM was fortunate to acquire the support of Jean-Claude Risset during the early 1970s. As noted in Chapter 1, Risset, along with

Chowning, made significant contributions to the development of the Music N suite of programs at Bell Labs during the 1960s, and on return to his native France at the end of the decade he installed a version of Music V at the Faculty of Orsay, using a Hewlett-Packard computer located in the engineering department (1970–1971).[24] In 1975 he joined IRCAM as head of the computer department, a post he held until 1979 when he returned to Marseille as director of the Laboratoire de Mécanique et d'Acoustique (LMA) at CNRS. Notwithstanding this career trajectory that included four years at IRCAM, he fostered and sustained a close association with GRM, and indeed subsequently used its signal processing resources to compose *Sud* (1985).

The birth of SYTER

Bernard Durr and Pierre-Alain Jaffrennou led the original team of researchers set up after the Stockholm conference alongside the SYNTOM project to investigate the possibilities of implementing Music V, succeeded in 1974 by Bénédict Mailliard and Jean-François Allouis, albeit with further contributions from Durr. Risset had also attended the 1970 Stockholm conference, and was thus well aware of the challenges to be faced by GRM in implementing Music V. Crucially, it did not have a computer, and the only possibility was occasional access to an IBM 360, otherwise used by the ORTF to process accounts. Further, there were no facilities for converting the resulting digital sound files to an analog format. Here Risset came to the rescue, offering access to his own conversion facilities. These, however, were located in the South of France, resulting in further delays while copies of the digital files recorded on magnetic tape were sent for conversion and the audio results returned as conventional recordings. Although these conditions were little better than those endured by Max Mathews and his associates in the late 1950s and early 1960s, the team at GRM was sufficiently encouraged to start the development of signal processing algorithms based on the library of functions provided by Music V.

This project, however, was soon to have a companion. With the move to INA in 1975, the former association with GRT had ceased and it became clear that future initiatives would have to be developed entirely in-house. Furthermore, it was becoming increasingly important that GRM's identity and standing as an institution at the forefront of developments in electroacoustic music was not to be undermined by the competition forthcoming from IRCAM. It was these considerations that gave rise to a project that was to become of the utmost significance both for the institution and, in due course, for the wider composing community. Known as SYTER (originally SYnthèse en TEmps Réel, then subsequently SYstème en TEmps Réel), this real-time digital system became a key resource for GRM composers, including Dhomont, leading directly to the suite of signal processing software known as GRM Tools, used by many composers to the present day.

The original brief for the SYTER project, produced late in 1975, reads as follows:

This project includes:

– The development of a prototype for digital sound synthesis in real time using a model inspired by MUSIC V.
– The development of suitable hardware and software for composers.
– The development of control panels that are fully accessible for performers.[25]

The first prototype, SYTER I, was completed in 1976. It consisted of a wire-wrapped board based on a Motorola 68000 processor with a simple keypad and specially constructed joystick interface, registering and generating voltage control functions for analog synthesizer modules. Instructions had to be written in hexadecimal machine code, and the system was thus difficult to program, but for its time it was remarkably versatile, providing a performance control environment way beyond that associated with a commercial digital sequencer. SYTER I was first demonstrated in public at a GRM concert in March 1977, when it was used in the realization of *Cristal* by François Bayle.[26]

This exposure established a convincing proof of concept, but it was clear that there were some material shortcomings. Although the joystick provided a useful real time control facility, it was evident that the composer/performer interface needed to be significantly improved. Furthermore, it was already clear that such a hybrid approach combining digital control technology with analog synthesis devices had major limitations. Nonetheless, the success of *Crystal* inspired the GRM director to create a research group of three students drawn from the Paris Conservatoire specifically to explore the creative potential of digital technology as a means of controlling real-time composing and performing. The GRM+ Trio, comprising Denis Dufour, Laurent Cuniot, and Yann Geslin, was to provide a significant stimulus for SYTER-based initiatives, especially during the all-important years of its further development.

In a technical context it was clear that an all-digital approach was required, and Allouis was only too aware of the significance of important developments just down the road at IRCAM.[27] Work on SYTER II had already started by the time SYTER I had been demonstrated in public, and this second prototype was partially operational by 1978. This version also used a Motorola 68000 processor for basic program management and input/output communications, along with a networked array of AMD 2901 bit slice processors for high-speed signal processing.[28] Although there was clearly still a long way to go before the true potential of an all-digital real-time signal processing environment could thus be achieved, the results were promising.[29]

One major hurdle remained to be overcome. As was to prove the case for the other specialist digital signal processing systems of the time, such as the DMX 1000 and the IRCAM 4n series, culminating in the 4X, a host computer was required to configure and control these systems, extending in scope to a well-designed control surface for composers and performers.[30] In this context the needs of the SYTER project were essentially no different from those of the Music V team. The solution for both materialized in 1978 with the acquisition of a dedicated PDP-11/60 computer, physically located in GRM. This was installed in Studio 123 as part of a comprehensively equipped mixing and recording system. Although the Music V–based developments were necessarily to remain non–real time, the enhanced working environment proved attractive to many GRM composers, and the project, renamed Studio 123, also became an important studio facility, leading to further improvements and refinements to the associated array of software resources.

SYTER also was to materially benefit from direct access to this computer, and by 1982 SYTER II had been completed. A report published in September by Allouis and his research associate Jean-Yves Bernier provides useful insights into the imperatives that were influencing and shaping the project:

> The main purpose of the SYTER project is to provide electroacoustic musicians with new tools for sound manipulation in real time, using the digital technology. As "concrete" approach to electroacoustic music is a rather practical and empirical one, a special benefit is expected from real time interaction and audition.

> Specific design goals may be related to this particular musical environment:

> Capability of treating and transforming natural recorded sounds with good audio quality; this feature looks to us more important than the synthesis performances.

> Special attention paid to manipulation of continuously varying command parameters. The musicians whom we work with may sometimes use notes, are dealing often with discrete events, but they do have a particular interest in evolving phenomena.

> Of course, we have to consider more common constraints: costs, obviously, and also ease of programming and size, keeping in mind a later possible realization for live performance (actual system is mainly intended for studio use).[31]

The last observation is especially interesting, making it clear that the ability to interact with the system in real time was first and foremost to be seen in a studio context at this time.

By this stage the processing capabilities of the hardware had been usefully enhanced to embrace an expanded memory for holding resident processing functions and direct access to a 160-megabyte disk for storing and retrieving sound files. Major improvements had also been made to the processor architecture in terms of streamlining the flow of instructions and data. The software, however, was still relatively primitive, requiring extensive use of assembler level coding to write programs, and only limited facilities were available to control the system when it was working in real time. Again, the observations of the authors provide a useful perspective on the direction of travel:

First: we want to solve the problem of generating a program for two tightly coupled machines (the synthesizer and the controlling computer).

Second: we want a higher-level user interface, hiding the technical constraints as far as they are not musically meaningful.

Third: we want better control and feedback on the performance, with sophisticated edit capabilities.[32]

A high-resolution graphics interface had yet to be added to the system, and the facilities for control other than a standard alphanumeric keyboard were restricted to a flatbed digital tablet and stylus and/or a joystick controller.[33] The graphics-based personal computer revolution that was materially to inform phase four of developments at GRM was not yet even on the horizon. Pressure was thus mounting to find a more immediate resolution for this drawback.

Work started in 1982 on the design of SYTER III. By this stage it was becoming evident that the PDP-11/60 was inhibiting further development in more ways than one. It had become clear, for example, that in order to preserve fidelity when executing digital signal processing functions involving significant changes of amplitude, the internal sample data resolution of SYTER needed to be increased from sixteen to twenty-four bits, with corresponding increases in the amount of memory available for such tasks. Unfortunately, the 11/60 used an older PDP-11 machine architecture ill-suited to the increased memory management requirements. Secondly, there were further major technical problems to be overcome in the context of developing a high-performance interactive graphics interface. Thirdly, there was no prospect of achieving the goal of a portable synthesizer. It thus became a matter of priority to seek an alternative, more suitable host computer, notwithstanding the implications of having to re-engineer key aspects of SYTER itself.

Toward the end of 1983 Allouis contacted Digitone with a view to acquiring a significantly improved audio interface, capable of providing high quality stereo analog-to-digital input and four channel digital-to-analog output facilities. Digitone had previously been contracted to provide custom-designed components for the Coupigny synthesizer, and this new order led to further discussions with a view to producing a commercial version of SYTER. Interest in acquiring such a facility was forthcoming from other quarters, notably the Conservatoire National de Région de Marseille, and this goal became a key design objective for SYTER III.

The purchase of a PDP-11/23 microcomputer was a major step forward in terms of providing a more suitable computing environment.[34] However, despite being physically very much smaller than the PDP-11/60, the PDP-11/23 was still too large to be regarded as truly portable. A satisfactory solution presented itself with the subsequent release of the even smaller PDP-11/73, physically little larger than SYTER itself.[35] Development of the interactive graphics-based control facility was still to prove problematic, however, the key issue being how best to reconcile a significant and unavoidable trade-off between operational versatility and the speed of interactive response when SYTER's functions are manipulated in real time.

The engineer concerned, Jean-Yves Bernier, would ideally have wished to develop a fully integrated programming environment, mindful of the possibilities being opened up by the new generation of high performance workstations that were becoming available from other manufacturers, based on Unix. This option, however, was not open to him, and instead he developed a library of extensible functions specifically for the 11/23 and 11/73 computing environments, leaving open the possibility of developing these tools further as and when more powerful computing resources became available.[36] The first version of the graphics-based programming system known as SYG (SYstème Graphique), was completed in 1984, facilitating the official launch of SYTER III. In terms of the political benefits for GRM in the face of increasing competition from other quarters, this was most timely, since it facilitated its public debut in the form of a performance of *Pli de perversion* by Denis Dufour at the 1984 International Computer Music Conference, hosted by IRCAM.

The reaction of composers at GRM was very positive. In terms of the resources provided for signal processing, Allouis had successfully blended an initial repertory of tools designed specifically for SYTER with key elements of the algorithms developed for Studio 123, now able to operate substantially in real time. By this stage discussions with Digitone concerning the production of a commercial version of SYTER were also well advanced. Further improvements to the SYG software and additions to the data storage facilities and communications, notably facilities for MIDI control and industry standard digital interfaces (AES and SMPTE) thus led to the production prototype. The basic configuration of the system is shown in Figure 5.1.

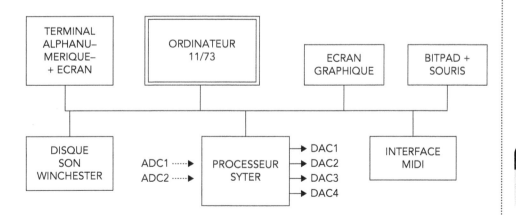

FIGURE 5.1

Basic configuration of the SYTER environment.[37]

Seven commercial systems were built for the market, with a further two destined for GRM, and by 1987 all had been sold, including a system acquired by Jean-Claude Risset for CNRS de Luminy à Marseille. The signal processing

175

facilities provided by Version 5 of SYG, bundled with the commercial version of SYTER, were extensive, with the twenty core functions providing tools such as harmonizers, random shuffling, delay lines, real-time sound reversal, an eight-band equalizer, resonant filters, additive and frequency modulation oscillators, and tools for freezing sounds, reverberation, speed variation, and ring modulation.[38]

By this stage, however, it was becoming clear that the long-term future of custom-designed hardware signal processors such as SYTER was increasingly open to doubt, given the rapid advances in the design and performance of conventional microprocessors. This debate was brought into focus by the departure of Allouis in 1987 to take up the position of director of science at IRCAM. The future of Studio 123 also had to be considered following the departure of Mailliard that same year. The PDP-11/60 was also reaching the end of its useful life and was withdrawn in 1990, forcing those still wishing to use the non-real-time features of the studio to seek an alternative host computer for the associated software.

The appointment of Hugues Vinet as successor to Allouis led to a strategy that secured the future direction of GRM on both counts. As an immediate priority, further work was carried out on SYTER to fix the remaining software bugs, resulting in SYG 6. Introduced in 1989, the enhancements including an expansion of the library of algorithms from twenty to twenty-four primary functions.[39] Secondly, a new research program was initiated, exploring the enhanced possibilities arising from the launch of the Apple Macintosh II in 1987. It is interesting to note that at a time when other leading institutions such as Stanford and IRCAM were still deeply engaged in developing a new generation of specialist high-performance digital signal processing systems, GRM chose to engage directly with the emerging personal computer revolution as its fourth phase of development, confident that this would ultimately be the way forward. By the time the technology had fully come of age, the unique resources provided for composers at GRM had seamlessly evolved from the old to the new.

An important first step in this process was establishing the best possible method of linking SYTER to a Macintosh. Whereas facilities already existed for communicating MIDI, none were available for other types of digital data. This was solved by adding an Ethernet port to SYTER, opening up a wealth of possibilities in this context. The issue then was how best to make use of the Macintosh, not least its sophisticated WIMPS (Windows, Icons, Mouse, Pointers, Systems) graphics environment. One possibility would have been to develop a new version of SYTER, hosted by a Macintosh instead of an 11/73 system. In 1992 a proposal for "SYTER nouvelle génération" was put forward by Vinet, but sadly the financing necessary for it could not be secured and the project was finally abandoned in 1993. With his departure in 1994, also for IRCAM, interest in developing SYTER any further all but disappeared within

GRM. Undeterred, Digilog, a newly established research division of Digitone, developed a new commercial version, "Genesis," in 1998, but this lacked the advanced graphics capabilities that were by then a standard feature of personal computers, not least the Macintosh, and at the end of 1999 SYTER was finally retired.[40]

Back in 1988 Vinet had realized that the long-term future of the signal processing facilities provided by SYTER lay in developing a version that could run entirely in software on a personal computer, in the first instance a Macintosh. Whereas even the fastest version of this computer then available could only execute a very small repertory of simple audio processing algorithms in real time, a solution to this limitation presented itself with the launch of the Sound Designer system by Digidesign in 1989.[41] This system consisted of two components, a plug-in Sound Accelerator card based on a 56001 processor, specially developed for digital signal processing by Motorola, and Sound Designer, a software package that allowed a Macintosh to operate as an audio recording and editing system. It occurred to Vinet that such a resource might be sufficiently powerful to run at least some of the SYTER algorithms in real time. Accordingly, he set about the task.

The result was the first version of the previously mentioned GRM Tools. One consideration that proved helpful in maximizing the possibilities here was that whereas systems such as SYTER were still significantly faster in terms of processing speed, they were constrained by the very limited amount of memory that could be used. The architecture of processors such as the 68000 series used for the Macintosh allowed fast access to a significantly larger memory space, and by making strategic changes to the way some time-critical functions were executed, significant compensation for a lower overall processing speed could be achieved. The prototype for GRM Tools was completed in 1991. Known as the DSP Station, the system offered a selection of ten algorithms derived from the SYTER SYG library, supported by a simple mouse-driven graphics interface.[42] By the end of 1992 the first commercial version, 1.0, had been completed and was ready for release early in 1993. However, the introduction of a significantly improved Sound Accelerator card from Digidesign (Version II), offering a larger memory and improved I/O facilities, made it abundantly clear that further work should be undertaken to improve the performance of GRM Tools before the product was fully marketed.

The revised version (1.5) was launched in 1994 and offered the following algorithms, all operating in real time:

additive synthesis (**Addsynth**)
accumulated delays (**Delay Accum**)
equalizer with 23, 14, or 8 filters with linear phase (**Equal23/
    Equal14/Equal8**)
comb filtering (**Comb Filters**)

177

variable filtering (**Band Pass**)

harmonization and re-injectable delays (**Pitch Accum**)

random oscillator-controlled transposition algorithm (**Pitch Random**)

ring modulator (**Gate Ring**)

random micro-splicing (**Shuffling**)

sampling rate conversion and speed variation (**Freq Conversion**)

time freezing (**Time Freezing**)

time compression/expansion (**Time-Stretching**)

two-dimensional movement in space through a Doppler effect (**Doppler**)[43]

In several cases the algorithms could be manipulated to produce a range of functions, including the various options offered by the equalizer. In the case of the time compression/expansion algorithm, it was also possible to introduce pitch transposition without changing the duration. The band-pass filter could also be programmed to produce high-pass, low-pass, and band-reject characteristics, with control in each case over the cut-off frequency and the gradient of attenuation.

Its release, however, coincided with another significant technical development. In 1991 Digidesign had introduced the first version of Pro Tools, an up-market hybrid hardware/software facility for sound editing. This in turn fueled the development of the now ubiquitous "plug-ins," providing software modules that can be inserted in a variety of real-time digital audio processing systems. Emmanuel Favreau recognized the significance of plug-ins for GRM Tools, and in 1994 he started work on a plug-in version of the software. Digidesign also realized the value of such a resource and agreed to bundle GRM Tools with Pro Tools under license, starting with Pro Tools 4.0 early in 1996. By 1998 material improvements had been made to the performance of GRM Tools, and the rest, as it may be said, is history.

Dhomont, Quebec, and GRM

It is with this technical chronology in mind that it is now possible to consider the significance of Dhomont's extensive association with the evolution of GRM, in particular the circumstances that led to the composition in 1998 of *Phonurgie*, the central focus of study in this chapter. Having moved from France to Canada in 1980, he became a significant influence on the development of French Canadian electroacoustic music, developing powerful synergies between what may be described as the Quebec school of composition and shared interests with those working at GRM. Whereas the groundbreaking technologies being developed in the latter context could only be experienced firsthand, involving extensive periods of working back in France, he was able to develop methods of composing, especially in later years, that took full advantage of both polarities,

178

creating extensive libraries of recorded materials generated at GRM to be subsequently worked on in Canada.[44]

Dhomont's first Quebec work, *Sous le regard d'un soleil noir*, was realized primarily in the studios of the Faculty of Music, University of Montreal, during 1980–1981. This powerful electronic poem, based on the writings of Ronald D. Laing, engages deeply with the inner struggles of a troubled individual, progressing slowly but inexorably toward a state of insanity. Significantly, while composing the piece he received a commission from INA-GRM, which he used to realize the sixth section, *Citadelle intérieure*, at GRM. The work was performed at the 11th Bourges International Festival of Experimental Music in 1981, achieving first prize in the Electroacoustic Program Music category. The work was a major success, further securing his position as a leading international electroacoustic music composer. Subsequently it was extensively reworked, and the new version premiered in the Grand Auditorium de la Maison de Radio France in 1983.[45] His next work, *Points de fuite*, realized in his personal studio in 1981–1982, was to provide a particular stimulus for other Quebec-based composers pursuing the possibilities of acousmatic music. Here the interrelationships between processed sounds and their acoustic origins are powerfully explored as the basis of musical argument playing on the creative potential of musical metaphors.[46]

Following very much in the French acousmatic tradition, Dhomont was to explore extensively the engagement of close listening with the processes of aural recognition. For example, *Chiaroscuro* (1987), a commission from Événements du neuf, challenges the ear by creating ambiguities through interpolating sounds that are immediately recognizable either directly or by inference with those that are transformed to the point of near or complete ambiguity.[47] His composing style and evolving musical perspective, however, was to engage with territory that embraced a highly individual approach to electroacoustic composition, powerfully reflected in the work chosen for detailed study here, *Phonurgie*, composed using the resources of GRM and his personal studio in Montreal.

A final homage to *musique concrète* within Dhomont's *Cycle du son*

Phonurgie is the final work of the larger *Cycle du son*, comprising *Objets retrouvés* (1996), *AvatArsSon* (1998), *Novars* (1989), and *Phonurgie* (1998). This nonchronological order respects a progression that reflects the composer's intention for the whole cycle: a celebration of "sound ([as] a major discovery of the twentieth century) and music concrète" and "a fiftieth-anniversary homage to the inventiveness of Pierre Schaeffer, who created an upheaval in the world of music that had no precedent."[48] The first piece of the cycle, *Objets retrouvés*, composed for Bourges, is described by the composer as a paraphrase of the first movement of Schaeffer's *Étude aux objets*, "Objets exposés." The second piece,

AvatArsSon, can be seen as a tribute to the pioneers of music for fixed media, including, although not exclusively, aural references to the early GRM composers.[49] *Novars*, written before the conception of the cycle as such, establishes a link between two new forms of art: the Ars Nova of medieval times and the twentieth century *musique concrète*. Dhomont recalls its origins as follows:

> GRM, on the occasion of the forty years of *musique concrète*, commissioned me for a piece. I wanted to pay tribute to Schaeffer, the father of *musique concrète*, and to *musique concrète* itself. I called this *Novars*, which is a pun on Ars Nova, because I was considering that Schaeffer was in a way the Philippe de Vitry of our times, that is, the inventor of a new music. And Guillaume de Machaut, from whom I borrowed something in *Novars*, was the equivalent of today's Pierre Henry.[50]

Although *Novars* was completed in his Montreal studio, substantial components of the work were created at GRM during a series of visits dating from the mid-1980s.[51] The studio records indeed note that he was proactively working on possible materials as early as 1986.[52] In revisiting the formative years of *musique concrète*, it thus seeks parallels with the early development of Ars Nova in the fourteenth century, combining quotations from Machaut's *Messe de Nostre Dame* (1364) with material drawn from Schaeffer's *Étude aux objets* (1959) and references to Pierre Henry's *Variations pour une porte et un soupir* (1963).[53] According to the progression of the cycle, *Phonurgie* is the most emancipated of the four works from references to *musique concrète*: "the allusions to the origins melt away before the original propositions; filiation is not renounced, but here the child, finally grown, reveals its identity."[54] By the time he came to compose the piece, Dhomont was very much looking to the future in terms of his now highly developed compositional style. Commissioned by Deutscher Akademischer Austauschdienst (DAAD), the work was premiered on September 25, 1998, as part of the Inventionen '98 festival in Berlin. Although there are references to earlier works, not least *Novars*, the musical language is very much more personal and highly distinctive.

Inside *Phonurgie*

After *Stria, Riverrun, Pluton*, and *Beneath the Forest Floor*, Francis Dhomont's *Phonurgie* is the first work examined in the chronology of the case studies to make use of a large variety of material types as sources for the composition. Such a heterogeneity also characterizes the hardware and software environments used to transform these sources and integrate them into the final work, and reflects the composer's general creative method and resulting aesthetics.[55]

From a poietic perspective, Dhomont's approach consists in generating and accumulating musical materials over years, constituting a vast and diverse library from which he can then, for a specific composition, select sounds that may fit his immediate needs in terms of color and morphology, and process those further to experiment with their possible integration into his work. In general, the composer's approach to technology is essentially pragmatic. Unlike Chowning or Truax, he does not pursue the development of new technologies that would be required by his artistic needs; he rather explores the resources that are available to him in his studio or in places he visits, and, as he expresses in our interviews, does not speculate on how technological limitations could be overcome:

> I never feel limited by technology. Generally, I only ask of technology what it can give me, and I only imagine things that are feasible. Excepted when, as I did at the very beginning, with tape recorders and somewhat prehistoric machines, I was fiddling with all this so that it returned what I wanted. But [nowadays] I do not feel a lack of technical means—it is quite the opposite: I find we have a very large number of technical tools, and that I use a very small part of it all, maybe 2 percent of what exists on the market, with which I find we can do so many works. . . . If I find in software something that I get interested in, then I work with it, I try to make the most of it—indeed this has always been my approach: when I am invited to a studio where there are tools that I don't have, I don't take over all the tools of the studio, but a couple of them, that I don't have at home, and that can be interesting to me, from which I feel I can get something interesting and valuable.[56]

You can use the accompanying software to watch videos of our interviews with Francis Dhomont, where he evokes several aspects of his creative process on Phonurgie and beyond. Demonstration Video 5.1 presents this feature and shows an excerpt of Presentation 18 with the composer expanding on his general approach to technology as introduced above. ▶

On the esthesic side, the heterogeneity of sources and processes leads to a work that is shaped around audibly distinctive sections, some of them being agitated and dense in terms of occurrences of sound objects, others being more static, slowly evolving, and dominantly textural.

The very opening sound of *Phonurgie* acts both as a landmark within the work and as a signature for the whole cycle: it has the same quick-attack/long-resonance morphology as the opening sound of Schaeffer's *Étude aux objets*, and such a morphology characterizes the initial sound objects of the three other works of the cycle. This landmark inherits directly from the global genealogical approach to Pierre Schaeffer's materials, and can be seen as symbolic to Dhomont's referential creative approach. Indeed, the opening sound of *Phonurgie* finds its direct origin in the beginning of the first work of the cycle, *Objets retrouvés*, which is musically the closest to Schaeffer's *Étude*. The introduction to *Objets retrouvés* comprises several successive sound objects that are simple transformations that add a characteristic color to objects extracted from Schaeffer's *Étude*.[57] In turn, extracting the fifth object of *Objets retrouvés* and transposing it upward by a factor of 1.165 (equivalent to a transposition of about 2.64 semitones) results in the opening sound of *Phonurgie*.

> Presentation 4 in the accompanying software allows you to compare these materials and manipulate sound transposition. It demonstrates the genealogy from Schaeffer's Étude aux objets to the opening sound of Phonurgie via Dhomont's Objets retrouvés. A menu highlights correspondences between Schaeffer's original objects and Dhomont's processed objects, and a number box gives access to the transposition of the sound objects of Objets retrouvés. Demonstration Video 5.2 shows this process in action. ▶

The materials of *Phonurgie*

As is typical of Dhomont's practice, *Phonurgie* contains a wide range of sound materials. The sound objects or sequences that appear in the final Pro Tools session of the work belong to the twenty categories below, as defined, named, and described by the composer.[58] These categories are themselves grouped into three main types: principal elements, secondary elements, and punctuating elements:[59]

Principal elements:

– Boul1	Rhythmic figure
– Boul2	Grain texture
– Crot	Treble figures (crotales processed with SYTER)
– Mach	Iterative thread (brassage of Machaut's *Messe*)
– Martel	Iterative thread (brassage of guitar)
– Sch1	Reminder of *Novars* (processed objects from *Étude aux objets*)
– Stél	Series of figures
– Sté4	Swarming thread
– T1	Granular thread (bass + treble)

Secondary elements:

– AKS iter	Iteration / allure (serves as linking agent)
– Porte	Percussion
– Porte SY	Percussion of same type as Turbo (SYTER process)
– Punch	Accentuated thread (counterpoint element)
– Syn1070	Flux (Materiology from Synclavier)
– Turbo	Percussion (elements generated with TurboSynth)

Punctuating elements:

- Ailes   Hapax (iconic image)
- Cloch   Treble tight allure (marker for beginning/end)
- Elém.LdS   Hapax (punctuation)
- Novars   Reminder of *Novars* (connexion)
- Sch0   Short citation/reference to *Étude aux objets*

You can explore these categories and materials in Presentation 1 of the accompanying software, which represents Phonurgie *and its constitutive sound objects and sequences. Menus in the presentation inspector enable you to highlight the objects according to their main and secondary categories. Playback features enable you to listen to the work as a whole or to individual sound objects. Demonstration Video 5.3 shows how to operate these features.* ▶

As can be seen from Dhomont's brief descriptions, these materials tend to be categorized according to their sonic properties rather than their actual means of production. However, the categories are consistent with the sources and processes used. For instance, the nine clips of the "Crot" category are all extracted from the same sequence generated from crotales processed with a gentle SYTER brassage, a process described below in further detail; the eleven clips of the "Boul1" category all come from sequences resulting from various degrees of processing applied to recorded petanque balls, the sonic quality of which can easily be identified aurally, even when the material has been subject to advanced processing.

The sound sources

The sound materials as heard in the final work are grouped by Dhomont according to description-based categories that can be linked to terminology inherited from Schaeffer's typologies (such as threads, allures, textures, figures).[60] Alternatively, the sources from which they have been elaborated can be divided into five main categories: synthesis, sampling of preexisting works, indoor object recordings, instrumental recordings, and field recordings.

Synthesis

Typical of the acousmatic tradition, as discussed above, synthesis techniques are not excluded, but neither are they predominant in the generation of the materials used in *Phonurgie*. Four sound objects from two categories were obtained primarily by means of synthesis: three "AKS iter" objects, generated from an EMS Synthi AKS synthesizer, can be heard in the opening and final sections of the work; one four-minute long "Syn1070" sequence, generated from a NEDco Synclavier, emerges in the second section and fades away in the fourth section.

You can listen to the materials mentioned here by exploring them in the context of the piece by referring again to Presentation 1 of the accompanying software. The menu in the presentation inspector enables you to highlight categories such as "AKS iter" or "Syn1070," or any of the categories described below. Demonstration Video 5.4 shows how to explore these materials in the structure of the piece. ▶

Sampling of preexisting works

In addition to the already mentioned opening sound, several materials of *Phonurgie* come from sampled excerpts of preexisting works. As for *Novars*, the first section of Schaeffer's *Étude aux objets*, "Objets exposés," and the *Kyrie* of Machaut's *Messe de Nostre Dame* are the two major sources of sampled materials. Excerpts from *Étude aux objets* are the source of the "Sch1" category, which includes the opening sound and many of its variations, as well as longer sequences, and appear throughout the whole work. "Sch0" is the unprocessed third object from Schaeffer's *Objets exposés*. The "Mach" category includes two concatenated sequences, appearing in the fourth section of *Phonurgie*, resulting from the brassage of the first seconds of the Kyrie of Machaut's *Messe*. The "Crot" objects come from a sequence of crotales based on the recording of an acousmatic work of unknown origin. The "LdS" object relates to Dhomont's own *Lettre de Sarajevo* (1996), although it does not seem to be a direct sample from the final work, and it is not clear whether it was an object that served as a source for this earlier composition.

Indoor object recordings

A common feature of Dhomont's practice is to record sequences by playing with various physical objects and processing them for use in later works. In *Phonurgie*, the "Boul1" and "Boul2" categories were derived from the petanque balls, "Cloch" is a recording of a bell with a small amount of transformation, "Porte," "Porte SY," and "Turbo" come from recordings of a creaking door, echoing Pierre Henry's *Variations pour une porte et un soupir* (1963), but also Dhomont's own *Sous le regard d'un soleil noir* (1979–1981).

Instrumental recordings

Only one category of material comes from an instrumental recording in *Phonurgie*: "Mart" is a long sequence of sounds produced by a classical guitar, processed with a brassage, and used as a counterpoint to the Machaut brassage in the fourth section of the work. This material was recorded with guitarist Arturo Parra, who also played for other acousmatic composers in Montreal, such as Robert Normandeau, Gilles Gobeil, or Stéphane Roy.[61] Dhomont simply asked Parra to play sequences, with vague instructions regarding playing modes but no strong specification or conventional notation. Materials from this recording session were also used, much more predominantly, in Dhomont's *En cuerdas* (1998), premiered only a few months before *Phonurgie*.[62]

Field recordings

Dhomont is a keen field recordist, and he captures sounds of the environment with microphones of various properties and qualities. He describes the process in the video interviews in the accompanying software:

> Generally, I make these recordings when the sound I hear interests me. That is, if the sound is beautiful, or has a particular interest, then I try to capture it. Of course, I sometimes make field recordings with a precise goal in mind. If I need a sound that has a specific property, I try to create it from some material that I already have or that I go and get. . . . These two approaches coexist. But indeed, in my sound library, there are many sounds that I have recorded because I considered them interesting.[63]

In *Phonurgie*, only one field recording is directly evident as such: used as a punctuation of the climax of section 2, "Ailes" is the recording of pigeons flying in a cage at Denis Dufour's house in southern France, with little subsequent processing. This source was also used in Dhomont's *Forêt profonde* (1994–1996). However, the origins of another sound used in *Phonurgie*, also derived from field recordings, are not recognizable by the listener: the "T1" category contains four large threads, principally heard in section 2, as well as more discretely in the final section, which were entirely derived from the sound of roadworks, recorded in Montreal in the mid-nineties, and then heavily processed digitally.

Presentation 8 of the accompanying software is an excerpt showing Francis Dhomont discussing his practice as field recordist, and Presentation 9 gives access to the field recordings of Montreal roadworks and some of the successive transformations (filtering, transposition) leading to one of the "T1" threads. Demonstration Video 5.5 shows how to explore these interactive resources. ▶

Processing the sound sources

Most of Francis Dhomont's sources go through several stages of processing. As mentioned for the opening sound of *Phonurgie*, some of these processes are made with specific dedicated hardware devices (e.g., his Lexicon digital reverberation units) or software environments (e.g., Studio 123, SYTER), while others could have been achieved in both the analog or the digital domain, and with any generic-purpose computer environment.[64]

185

Basic transformations

As can be heard in the work, some of the processes applied to the sound objects are, in essence, simple. For instance, one object of the "Boul2" category and one object of the "Cloch" category are simply reversed: after the exposition of the opening sound, the "Cloch" bell is heard backward and immediately forward; this characteristic figure is also used with a "Boul2" object before the conclusion of the work. Simple pitch transposition is also occasionally used, such as with two successive "Sch1" objects in the final section of the work.

> You can experiment with these simple transformations (file reversal, pitch transposition) from the mentioned sources in Presentation 6 of the accompanying software. You can also use Presentation 1 to locate the mentioned sounds in the structure of the work. Demonstration Video 5.6 guides you through these resources. ▶

Complex transformations

The basic transformations are clearly audible when listening to *Phonurgie* as a whole. However, most of the transformations leading to the sound objects constituting the final mix are more complex, and they make it difficult for the listener to recognize the particular types of sources mentioned above.[65] Brassage is an example of such a complex process: the source is sliced in fragments of varying durations, and these fragments are enveloped and rearranged in time, with a control over density and pitch transposition. This process typically preserves the color of the original sound, but breaks its morphology, leading to different degrees of recognition between the input and output signals.[66] In *Phonurgie*, brassage was predominantly used for two threads that appear in the fourth section, from two different sources: Machaut's *Messe de Nostre Dame*, and the acoustic guitar material played by Arturo Parra.

> Presentation 7 of the accompanying software shows the application of brassage to these two sources. You can play the original sources, play the result as heard in Phonurgie, and experiment with the process itself, as shown in Demonstration Video 5.7. ▶

The composer's documentation notes indicate that the "Martel" category, in effect the guitar material, used the BRASSALQD instrument of SYTER.[67] This instrument was also used for the "Crot" category, sampled from crotales found in an unknown work, along with SYTER's speed variation, noted "varvit" in the composer's documentation.

The processes used for the opening sound of *Phonurgie*, from Schaeffer's *Étude aux objets*, and also heard in Dhomont's *Objets retrouvés*, also transform a source in a complex way, keeping some of its morphology, but drastically changing its color. The composer recalls:

> I still have these Lexicon PCM 60 and PCM 70 in my home studio. I used these devices a lot at some point, I am almost sure I used those for *Objets retrouvés*, there are some phase effects. These machines were very efficient and of good quality. By plugging one into the other, I was able to make transformations that played with the phasing. There was a phase effect on the reverberation. I was applying phasing to the reverb, I think, which provided a very particular characteristic. It was a way of coloring the sound. I also used this technique a lot for *Chiaroscuro* [1987], for processing aircraft sounds.[68]

Successive sound transformations

Most of the sounds heard in Francis Dhomont's works are the result of several iterations of sound transformations, sometimes spread across vast periods of time. The "T1" category, already mentioned, comprises dense, large, and strongly harmonic material that characterizes the second section of *Phonurgie*. From its initial source, a noisy field recording of roadworks, this important texture was obtained by the following transformations: first, a coloring through a bank of resonating filters gave the recording its abstract harmony.[69] Then, this colored intermediary step was pitch shifted downward by a factor of 0.38 (equivalent to a transposition of about 16.75 semitones), and also time-stretched, along with further possible processes such as reverberation.[70]

> *Presentation 9 of the accompanying software again shows some of the stages leading from the initial field recording to one of Phonurgie's "T1" sound files, as shown in Demonstration Video 5.8.* ▶

Building reservoirs of sound materials

One important characteristic of Francis Dhomont's creative process is the long-term accumulation of large reservoirs of sound materials. For instance, brassages of Machaut's *Messe de Nostre Dame*, heard in different forms both in *Novars* and *Phonurgie*, are only a small subset of the composer's experimentations with this specific source. His archive includes many sequences generated from the Kyrie and exploiting different parameters for brassage and other processes, such as resonant filters. The two materials labeled "Ball" in *Phonurgie*, "Boul1" and "Boul2," come from a similar source—a sequence recorded by playing with a metallic ball in contact with a surface. "Boul1" has a distinctive coloration, obtained by applying comb filters (the PEIGNE instrument of SYTER) along with speed variation, while the "Boul2" material has the same inharmonic content, although it is the result of several other sequences generated with different instruments of SYTER, including ETIR4[71] or ACCHAR, which delays and transposes a signal four times.[72] The "Syn1070" central sequence of *Phonurgie* is itself a concatenation of several materials generated from a common source, recorded with a Synclavier, with different processes such as comb filters, speed variation, harmonization, or accumulations.

> Presentation 11 in the accompanying software shows the process of generating materials from these three sources. You can listen to excerpts from the composer's archive, as presented in Demonstration Video 5.9. ⊙

188

Improvising with sounds and processes: *Séquences-jeu*

Central to Dhomont's generation of large amounts of sound material is the notion of *séquence-jeu*, an expression coined by Guy Reibel for pedagogic purposes and commonly used in the field of acousmatic music. As Denis Dufour and Thomas Brando specify:

> [T]he notion of *séquence-jeu* was developed from 1975 by Guy Reibel within the framework of his teaching of electroacoustic music at the national conservatoire of Paris, in order to escape composing by editing sound objects or mixing threads, and to reintroduce the instrumental gesture.[73]

Dhomont himself is keen on playing in an improvisatory fashion with particular materials and sound transformations, a creative process largely facilitated by the rise of real-time software environments such as SYTER. In our interviews, the composer recalls the contrast between the deferred time of Music V in GRM's Studio 123 on the one hand and a real-time approach on the other:

> Studio 123 was very powerful. It had been fitted with Music V and enabled you to create very original sounds, but there were calculations at that time—calculations were very long before you could get the result. Sometimes you had to come back the next day to get the result. But it enabled you to create really interesting sounds, very detailed and particular. The problem was that sometimes it was taking time before you find the right programming. But when you were making sounds with the Studio 123 system, then, ideally you would directly go and work your sounds with SYTER, which had real-time access, enabling you to work in real time, almost by improvising. At least in my case, I worked a lot improvising. So there were these two aspects: very methodic, calculated, proactive things, and a way to exploit this that was more intuitive.[74]

In fact, Schaeffer's *Étude aux objets* again was the source for such *séquences-jeu* with GRM's real-time processor, and excerpts from several sessions following this principle, dated from June and July 1988, can be heard both in *Novars* and in *Phonurgie*. These sessions were documented by the composer, as shown in Figure 5.2.

189

This document shows various source sounds ("TRAIN1," "SCH1," "SCH4") used with different instruments of SYTER (ACCHAR, PEIGNE, HAR7, RINGST, REVGLISS), and occasionally specifies the explored parameters, as in the case of the use of ACCHAR with "TRAIN1" (dry/wet balance, transposition ratios, direct/harmonized mix for the reinjection, delay times). Speed variation of the source sound is also often mentioned ("varvit"). As noted in the document, several excerpts from these *séquences-jeu* were used for the composition of *Novars*. Another fragment, found on another tape dated from the same period, and generated from the first objects of Schaeffer's *Étude* processed with speed variation and comb filters in SYTER, was used in *Phonurgie* and can be heard distinctly in the second half of section 1.

Presentation 12 in the accompanying software includes excerpts from these sources, and enables you to play with Schaeffer's objects through comb filters and harmonizers, along with speed variation. Demonstration Video 5.10 guides you through these processes and indicates the material of Phonurgie derived from these séquences-jeu generated with SYTER. ▶

Exploring empirically software environments and SYTER

In spite of his skills in building analog machines for musical creation, Francis Dhomont has no fascination for technology, and considers it from a very pragmatic standpoint: as a set of tools enabling him to explore the expressive potential of sound and to generate musical materials:

> As far as I am concerned, the problem is not at all that we have lost something with digital technologies, I don't think. I think that from the standpoint of composition, we have gained a lot, particularly in precision: you can do much more precise things, much more organized, too, so you can control your work more. Of course, you can lose a bit of spontaneity, but it is up to the composer to do what is needed not to lose it. For instance, at GRM, I worked a lot by improvising, as with an instrument. That is, instead of playing with the strings of a double-bass, I was playing with sliders, in real time, and this was allowing me to make very lively things. And it also allowed me to compose very precise works, with an organization that had no randomness, when that was what I wished. So yes, I think that with digital we gained a lot. On condition that you do not let yourself become overwhelmed by, should I say, the taste of the digital achievement. When I see, for instance, young composers who change their systems all the time, even before they know the one that they started practicing with, I think that they waste time because they are constantly studying, but they do not go deep into things. You'd better have one or several pieces of software that you know well and use originally, rather than to constantly upgrade to the next software and do what everybody does at the same time.[76]

Occasionally, Dhomont explores devices succinctly, as is the case of TurboSynth, a non-real-time modular synthesizer software developed by Digidesign in the 1990s. The composer recalls: "I knew of it without really using it. I had given it a try, and I kept a couple of sounds that I had found interesting."[77] Used with a door recording as source, these sounds make the "Turbo" category, heard in the first and final sections of *Phonurgie*.

However, as noted above, Dhomont tends to spend large amounts of time experimenting with particular systems, as is the case with SYTER. Beyond *Phonurgie*, the composer's archive documents a use of the following instruments of GRM's real-time system: ACCHAR, a set of four harmonizers with delay lines and feedback; ACCHARNEW, a variation of ACCHAR; BRASSALQD, the already mentioned quadraphonic brassage; ETIR4, a time-stretcher; HAR7ST, a set of seven parallel harmonizers; PEIGNE, a set of comb filters; PEIGNECL, a MIDI-controllable version of PEIGNE; REVGLISS, a reverberation with glissandi over the reverberated sound; and RINGST, a simple ring modulator. The composer often generated materials by interacting with the two main types of screens of SYTER: the sliders screens and the interpolations screen. For each instrument, the user can modify parameter values by manipulating up to sixteen vertical sliders[78] on two different screens. For example, the ACCHAR instrument has the following parameters, all modifiable in real-time with individual sliders: input level, feedback amount, direct/harmonized balance for reinjection, global delay time, and, for each of the four harmonizers, a transposition ratio and a delay time coefficients.[79] Two adjacent sliders can be coupled into a two-dimensional slider, allowing for the control of two parameters at once.[80] On the other hand, the interpolation screen enables the user to memorize all the parameter values of an instrument and to represent different presets in the form of balls on a two-dimensional grid. Entering the "play" mode of the interpolation screen, the user can then drag the cursor between the balls to interpolate between the presets, modifying all or some of the parameter values.[81] Daniel Teruggi specifies the context of the development of this important interpolation feature:

> The ergonomic model for building SYTER was that of the traditional studio. The sliders screen was a virtual mixing desk upon which other parameters than dynamics could be controlled. The problem was that, on a [physical] desk several parameters can be controlled at once with one or two hands. When SYTER was considered for a real-time live situation, as was the case for Denis Dufour's work *Pli de perversion* at the ICMC in 1984, Dufour's first remark was to wonder how to control several parameters simultaneously and, most of all, how to memorize configurations.[82] The analog practice, made of dials to set manually and of approximations in settings, had been experienced for too long as a handicap by people like Denis Dufour. It was only fair that the first thing to expect from a digital system was precision and memory. This qualitative jump in the approach of the digital tool has been fundamental in the evolution of SYTER. Until then, SYTER was considered as a tool similar to those of the analog studio with some improvements. From this awareness raised around precision and memorization, a true gap was being established between studio practices and new control possibilities. Jean-François Allouis perceived this gap immediately and developed a screen enabling enabling the placement of objects ["*boules*"] containing the memorization of the parameter values. But in introducing the possibility of interpolating between these fixed states, he brought a whole new dimension to the control of parameters. In this new dimension, a virtual space of evolution was configured from the *boules*. . . . The user learns to "circulate" within a space in which several paths are possible, with very different results. This mathematically simple "invention" represented by the interpolation screen was one of the greatest novelties that SYTER brought to the work upon sound.[83]

Presentation 14 in the accompanying software is an emulation of the SYTER environment. You can load some sounds used by Francis Dhomont or any other sound file, choose an instrument, and explore those either from the slider screens or by making your own presets and interpolate between them. Demonstration Video 5.11 guides you through the use of this emulation. ▶

Concerned to avoid any aural effect that would be too idiomatic of a given musical tool, Dhomont willingly uses his environments by hijacking particular functions. For example, the ETIR4 instrument of SYTER was only designed to work normally on mono files: as indicated in the reference manual, "if the [source] sound file is stereo, the sound is read one octave lower."[84] But the composer often used this latter possibility:

> I used ETIR4 a lot, it transformed the sound in time, and I could do very interesting things. But I used it in stereo, which was not a feature at all. It was not right to do so. In mono, it was generating very interesting materials, which conformed to what the designer had wanted. But I had found that when I was using it in stereo, it provided even more interesting results, and I almost always used it like this.[85]

The speed variation used by Dhomont, already mentioned here as "varvit," is another example of unconventional practice of SYTER.[86] Often, the composer modified the playback speed of an input sound jointly with the loaded instrument—a process that can, for instance, be heard and seen in the aforementioned *séquences-jeu* from Schaeffer's objects. But here again, doing so was not a conventional use of the environment, and is in fact explicitly discouraged in the reference manual:

> The speed variation [accessible in the input screen[87]] makes it possible to play a sound file with different speeds, or in reverse, to facilitate the detection of fragments. You need to watch the distortions that happen with low transpositions (for good speed variations, it is advised to use the VAR instrument).[88]

Dhomont had been told that using the speed variation of the input screen jointly with a SYTER instrument was not recommended, but found that using this function, only designed for exploration purposes, with an expressive and musical goal, enabled him to generate lots of exploitable materials.

Editing the materials into the final mix

During the assembling stage of sound materials into the final mix of the piece, Dhomont does not seem to use much transformation, although some amplitude envelopes are used in the Pro Tools session. The materials are mostly heard as they have been designed through the prior stages of sound exploration. But an important work of editing takes place, and many sequences result from the slicing and rearranging of those materials. For example, the nine clips of the "Crot" material all come from a one-minute sequence from which shorter fragments have been extracted and located in different sections of *Phonurgie*. The exact same material can therefore be heard in different contexts. Likewise, the "Martel" sequence is in fact a repetition, the same excerpt played twice, with only minor editing variations. The source track for this material contains an audible click, which was excluded during the editing process.

In Presentation 1 of the accompanying software, you can explore the editing process leading to all the materials of **Phonurgie,** *using the "Source track panel" available from the presentation inspector. This displays the source track for any explored sound object, and represents the different occurrences of a given fragment across the musical work. Demonstration Video 5.12 shows how to operate this feature.* ▶

Dhomont's editing process, therefore, introduces much redundancy into the musical organization of his work, which will now be explored further in the context of the shaping of *Phonurgie*.

The structure of *Phonurgie*

Francis Dhomont considers the form of *Phonurgie* as four major sections, plus an interface between the second and third parts.

You can refer to Presentation 1 of the accompanying software, in which the header displays the sections and transitions, as discussed below.[89]

As described by the composer, the first section, from the beginning of the work to 3′32″, "recalls the spirit of *Novars*," and exposes many elements of the whole composition. Its "general character is energetic, and the writing is articulated."[90] The second section overlaps by fourteen seconds with the first one. Starting from 3′18″ and ending at 6′59″, its style "contrasts with that of the preceding section," is "very plastic," and "gives more importance to threads." The "climax at 4′43″ [is] followed with an iconic image (flapping wings) and its imitating echo with 'Crot' . . . and then with a slow decay adorned with a few figures."[91] The interface, starting at 6′59″ and ending at 7′25″, is a "preparation of the third section. It is constituted with elements already present in the previous sections, and a new element, "Sté4," which continues into the next section."[92] The third section, from 7′25″ to 10′00″, is

> a period of flurry, very animated in particular with two new elements: "Mach" the variation of a brassage much present in *Novars*, and "Martel," other brassage of a guitar sequence. Several developments of "Crot" contribute to the composition of a very dynamic and agitated counterpoint. "Punch," a thread punctuated with accents, discretely completes the overloaded harmony of this section.[93]

The fourth section overlaps by thirty-one seconds with the third one, starting at 9′29″ and lasting to the end of *Phonurgie* at 12′29″. It includes

> the return and variations of the "Boul2," "Boul1," "Turbo," "Sch1," and "Cloch" elements of section 1; of "T1" of section 2; "Crot" of sections 2 and 3. The very characteristic rhythmic figure "Boul1," as well as the "AKS iter" and "Sch1" elements, remind unequivocally of the beginning of the work, but avoid repetition by introducing many variations. Besides, the concluding object "Cloch" is a variation of that of the

beginning (at 0′11″); these two very identifiable morphologies are only heard at the boundaries of the piece, and constitute a sort of input/output or frame.[94]

Presentation 16 of the accompanying software provides a paradigmatic analysis of Phonurgie. *You can visualize the different categories of materials, arranged across the vertical axis representing the chronology of the piece. The objects are numbered according to their variation within a given category. Each object can be played by clicking on the paradigmatic chart. Demonstration Video 5.13 shows how to operate this interactive explorer, and you can refer to it while reading the following analytical considerations.* ▶

As noted by the composer, the first section of *Phonurgie* exposes many of the materials present through the whole piece: out of the twenty categories defined by Dhomont, eleven are introduced in the first section.[95] A short, thirty-six-second introduction presents four materials. The beginning of the piece is a strong punctuation ("Sch1"), reminiscent of Schaeffer's objects and Dhomont's own *Cycle du son* including *Novars*. While this opening sound decays, a granular inharmonic texture from the "Boul2" material emerges; shortly after, the first "Boul1" object provides an accelerating and decaying pulsation, while the "Cloch" reversed bell fades in. This leads to a second punctuation (0′36″) built from a variation of the first "Sch1" object, along with the "Cloch" bell played forward and a discrete door element ("Turbo").

This punctuation marks the end of the introductory passage, and sets in motion the first continuous thread of *Phonurgie*: the "Punch" material, which acts as a background binding agent for the other objects in most of the remaining of the first section. In addition to further materials from the "Sch1," "Boul1," and "Turbo" categories, other objects appear and contribute to the dynamic articulation of the section: another door element ("Porte"), two punctuating objects (the "Elem. LdS" sound and "Sch0," the literal quotation of Schaeffer's *Étude*), and the *séquence-jeu* from Schaeffer's objects ("Sch1' ").[96] The synthetic "AKS iter" pulsation completes "Punch" in linking objects together. At 2′28″, a new appearance of the noisy granular "Boul2" material announces the conclusion of the first section: the general character gets quieter and the density of events decreases slowly. The "Punch" thread fades away and, after a new door motif ("Porte SY") followed by a brief repetition of the AKS pulsation, the listener is only left with objects from the "Sch1' " sequence and the tail of the "Boul2" material.

The second section starts fading immediately after the last gesture of the "Sch1' " sequence at 3′18″. While the "Boul2" material is still decaying, the first of three layers of the "T1" thread emerges. Initially thin and discrete, this harmonic texture gets progressively more agitated, loud, and dense. At 4′08″

a characteristic whistling appears and contributes to the massive aspect of the thread. At 4′30″, when the "T1" material has reached its maximal volume, a climax is introduced by a fast crescendo on a new synthetic material generated with the Synclavier ("Syn1070"), and immediately followed with the clearly identifiable recording of flapping wings ("Ailes" at 4′47″), which acts as a climax for the second section, but also for the overall piece.

While the massive texture starts decreasing, the wings are echoed with the introduction of two new harmonically colored categories, having an artificially flapping aspect: "Crot" (4′59″) and "Sté1" (5′17″). At this point, the "T1" texture and its characteristic harmony become quieter, and the thread is maintained by the "Syn1070" element. The articulation of a variety of punctuating sound objects, as a principle presented in the first section and suspended from the beginning of the second section to its climax, is restored: first reintroduced with the "Ailes," "Crot," and "Sté1" materials, with the combination of "T1" and "Syn1070" now acting as a background thread, as could be "Punch" earlier, it is reinforced by the reiteration, at 5′30″, of the "Boul2" category and, at 5′45″, of a "Sch1" object. A bell, categorized as "Novars" by the composer, also punctuates the decaying side of the section (6′04″). After a second variation on the "Sch1" object, the section reaches its end with another whistling from the "Syn1070" material, along with the ending of the "T1" thread and a continued "Boul2" in-harmonic granulated texture.

While the Synclavier variations continue, the interface between sections 2 and 3 is introduced with a new thread category: "Sté4" is colored and described by Dhomont as "swarming." A reminiscence of the "Sch1'" sequence emerges briefly, followed by a return of short fragments from the granular "Boul2," followed with "Crot" and the flapping "Sté1."

Among the "Sté4," "Syn1070," and "Crot" materials, the beginning of the third section is signaled by the appearance of a new material: the guitar brassage of "Martel" (7′27″), immediately followed by another new granular thread: "Mach," a material familiar to the listener in the context of the *Cycle du son*. A short "Boul2" fragment can be heard in the background as these two new materials appear. The chaotic agitation of this section, obtained with the accumulation of the two threads "Martel" and "Mach" with a third one made with a blending of "Sté4" and "Crot," is completed by two successive smoother descending glissandi obtained with the "Syn1070" material. At 8′30″, the "Crot" material stops and the "Syn1070" category disappears. It is replaced by a discrete return of the "Punch" thread, already heard in section 1. At 8′53″, while the overall agitation continues, the "Crot" material reappears, in effect replacing the "Sté4" thread. The "Mach" thread varies in density and harmony and fades away at 9′29″, marking the beginning of the transition toward the last section of *Phonurgie*.

Immediately after the end of the "Mach" thread, the "Boul2" material emerges in a form heard at the very beginning of the whole work, announcing the beginning of the fourth and final section. While "Punch" is still present, "Martel" and "Crot" both disappear at 10′00″, in effect finishing the preceding section, and the reversed colored "Ball1" object emerges distinctly from the "Punch" and "Boul2" textures. Another variation of "Ball1" appears, in a form heard twice in the first section, and is followed with an "AKS iter" signal. The association of the three materials "AKS iter," "Ball1," and "Punch" unequivocally remind one of the spirit of the initial section, soon confirmed by a dramatic punctuation with a "Sch1" object and a "Turbo" fragment (10′33″), which also terminates the "Punch" thread. In the absence of any background thread, for the first time since the beginning of section 2, "Crot" and "Boul2" then reappear, soon followed with two successive "Sch1" objects. After a discrete re-emergence of a "T1" thread along with the "Crot" materials, a "Boul1" object (11′53″) introduces the final punctuation, marked at 12′04″ with another combination of "Sch1" and "Turbo," and only followed with the "Cloch" bell heard in the introduction to the piece, now decaying toward the end of the work.

In Presentation 16 of the accompanying software, you can order the categories according to three main modes: "chronological" (the default), "punctuating to continuous," where punctuating objects are toward the left and continuous threads are toward the right, and "referential," where sounds that clearly refer to Schaeffer, Dhomont, or specific objects are toward the left, and abstract sounds are toward the right. Demonstration Video 5.14 shows how to access these different visualizations, which you can refer to while reading the following text. ▶

In many regards, Francis Dhomont's *Phonurgie* contains factors of symmetry. As is apparent from the chronological description of the work presented above, the overall form has two sections, 1 and 4, that give an important role to punctuating and articulated sound objects, while the two central sections, 2 and 3, as well as the interface between them, include predominantly continuous threads and textures.

You can use the "punctuating to continuous" visualization of Presentation 16 in the accompanying software to observe this.

Section 1 introduces a variety of punctuating objects that have no strong internal development or continuity: the "Sch0" and "Sch1" references to Schaeffer, the "Cloch" bell, the door elements ("Turbo," "Porte," and "Porte SY"). Such objects are rarer in section 2: the pigeon wings ("Ailes"), two instances of "Sch1," and the "Novars" element. They are absent from the third section, which is almost entirely textural and made of long, continuous sequences, but reappear in the final section, although in a sparser way than in section 1 ("Sch1," "Turbo," and finally "Cloch"). On the other hand, after the discrete "Punch" thread, section 2 introduces the predominance of continuous textures, with "T1," soon to be completed with "Syn1070," and "Crot," which appears in a fragmented form but develops rapidly as a more sustained material. This predominance of continuity is even stronger in section 3, before the articulation of punctuating objects dramatically reappears in the final section.

Some more localized symmetries appear in *Phonurgie*. The variations of the "Sch1" object, exposed in four occurrences noted 1, 2, 3, 4 in section 1, are then represented in reversed and extended order across section 2 (4, then 3) and the final section (3 again, two successive pitch-shifted variations of 2, and finally 1). The "Punch" material acts as a background material in the first section, and reappears as such toward the end of the piece. Finally, the above mentioned reversal technique obviously serves as a mirroring element, for the "Cloch" figure heard at the beginning of the work and the second half of it as the final sound, and for the "Boul1" figure at the beginning of section 4, the second half of which was already heard in the first seconds of section 1.

Another global distinction for the sounds of *Phonurgie* is that between strongly referential elements and abstract materials.

> You can use the "referential" visualization of Presentation 16 in the accompanying software to consider this distinction.

In section 1, many direct references to Schaeffer can be heard: the "Sch0" direct quotation from *Étude aux objets*, and the "Sch1" transformations. The door elements ("Turbo," "Porte," "Porte SY") recall Pierre Henry's *Variations pour une porte et un soupir*, but also Dhomont's own *Sous le regard d'un soleil noir* and *Novars*. Such references are omnipresent at the beginning of the work, and become rarer in sections 2 and 3—the third section is, however, dominated by the "Mach" material, which is a strong reference to *Novars*. The transformed Schaeffer objects and the door material reappear in the final section, although again more sparsely than in section 1.

Conclusions

In light of the composer's own comment on *Phonurgie* as the most emancipated work of the *Cycle du son* in terms of the filiation to *musique concrète*,[97] the distinctions between, on the one hand, punctuating objects and large continuous threads and, on the other hand, referential elements and abstract materials shed light on a movement starting from the world of Pierre Schaeffer and the music he invented using a more generic and abstract approach to the recorded sound: that of acousmatic music, in which the references to the sources are not abandoned, but are not exclusive anymore, enabling the exploration of sound to encompass an unlimited range of musical expressivity. In these ways, the *Cycle du Son* and particularly *Phonurgie* are emblematic of Francis Dhomont's creative approach to technology: a relentless exploration of what any resource can offer to generate sound materials of all kinds, and the elaboration of a personal language in which paying homage to those who paved the way seems to permanently inspire and reinforce the desire for sound exploration.

A number of interesting comparisons and associations can be made between the creative aesthetics of Dhomont and those of the other composers who are the subject of individual case studies in the current context. His strong association with the work of GRM and its technologies and composing traditions both complement and contrast with the achievements of Manoury. In the former context both composers are bound by perspectives that embrace many features in common, closely aligned to concepts that are strongly associated with French traditions of composing electronic and computer music, extending back to the work of pioneers such as Pierre Schaeffer in the former context and Jean-Claude Risset in the latter. At the same time, their roles as creative practitioners with no direct involvement in the design of the resources used to achieve their objectives was materially to shape their studio experiences, not least in composing the works selected for detailed study in each case. Looking from the other end of the telescope, it is also instructive to study the evolution of the technologies developed at IRCAM and GRM and the associated motivations for so doing. Despite being geographically just a short distance apart, these studios were essentially competitors, and individuality in both contexts was to prove a key distinguishing characteristic.[98]

Trevor Wishart
Imago

199

Contexts for *Imago*

The Composers Desktop Project

Trevor Wishart, like John Chowning and Barry Truax, has played a major role in the evolution of computer music, embracing both the composition of important additions to the musical repertory and the development of the technologies used in their production. Although his initial engagement with the medium was limited to the creative possibilities of analog equipment, his interest in computers was stimulated at an early stage in his composing career, leading to his participation in an important UK-based initiative, the Composers Desktop Project, or CDP, launched in 1986. This venture was established by a group of composers and programmers associated with the University of York: Martin Atkins, Andrew Bentley, Archer Endrich, Rajmil Fischman, David Malham, Richard Orton, and Trevor Wishart.[1]

The primary motivation for this collective lay in the lack of dedicated computing facilities within the United Kingdom for the production of digitally generated music. Although by the early 1980s the electronic studios at the Universities of Durham and York had acquired dedicated PDP-11/23 minicomputers for such purposes, no UK music department could match the extensive mainframe resources available at institutions such as IRCAM, Stanford, and MIT. Given their shared interests in the Music N family of programs pioneered by Max Mathews, the group pooled its creative and technical expertise with a view to developing an affordable desktop-based system offering the resources necessary to explore the creative possibilities of computer music.[2] Such an objective was ambitious. Although by the mid-1980s technology had developed to the point where microprocessors could be used to control the operation of hardware synthesis and signal processing devices, the challenges to be met in terms of meeting the processing demands of software-based techniques of sound production in such a context were far greater, by several orders of magnitude.

The introduction of the IBM PC in 1981 and the Apple Macintosh in 1984 laid important foundations for the personal computer revolution that was to follow, but the CDP concluded that neither of these computing environments was yet adequate for their purposes. Instead they initially chose the Atari 520 ST, launched in 1985, one major advantage being the availability of 512 kilobytes of programmable memory.[3] Further attractions included the simplicity and accessibility of the operating system and the comprehensive range of data communication ports that were provided, including facilities for MIDI. In engineering terms, the biggest challenge lay in the design of a facility for the input and output of digital audio. Conveniently, the computer was equipped with a bidirectional parallel ROM port with direct access to the internal microprocessor, and in terms of an external bulk audio data storage facility, the Sony PCM recorder offered an attractive possibility. Designed as a free-standing digital tape recorder, the device also provided direct access to high-quality digital-to-analog and analog-to-digital audio converters.[4] However, missing from this arrangement was a suitable converter that could translate parallel computer data into a serial format for the PCM, and vice versa. Dave Malham accordingly designed the SoundSTreamer, a hardware interface with an internal memory facility to buffer the flow of data between the devices.

In terms of audio fidelity, the PCM recorder dictated a standard format of stereo sixteen-bit resolution at a sampling rate of 44.1 kHz, although provision was made in the CDP software both for working with a mono resolution and the lower (half) sampling rate of 22.05 kHz. In terms of the programming environment, the most crucial consideration was the availability of a C compiler for the Atari, thus making it possible to compile and run music software written in this increasingly popular computer language.

As noted in Chapter 1, the first C-based version of the Music N series of programs was Cmusic, an expanded version of Music V, written by Richard Moore and Gareth Loy at CARL, the Computer Audio Research Laboratory at the University of California, San Diego (UCSD). Although the program was initially restricted to CARL, a publicly available version was produced in 1985. This development was extremely timely for the founding members of the CDP, an added attraction being its functional similarity to the version of Music V that had been developed at IRCAM, and by mid-1987 a suitably modified version had been implemented on the Atari ST.[5]

The greatest drawback for users was the lack of processing power, resulting in delays perhaps amounting to several hours while individual synthesis tasks were executed, and the resulting digital audio data accumulated using the Sony PCM recorder. However, the ability of CDP members to run the software on their own dedicated machines at home at any time of day or night was a material compensation.[6] Had the venture started a year later, consideration might have been given from the outset to Csound, developed by Barry Vercoe at MIT from his earlier Music 11 program, originally written in native assembler code for PDP computers and released to the wider community in 1986. Indeed, by the end of the decade it was becoming clear that Csound would soon eclipse Cmusic, and the CDP supplemented and subsequently replaced its initial adaption of Cmusic with one based on Csound.

Although the porting of these programs to the CDP provided a flexible and comprehensive set of computer music tools for the user community, they also provided the foundation for a more versatile composing environment that was in due course to embrace a comprehensive suite of programs written by members of the CDP, starting with applications such as Groucho, a set of signal processing routines written by Andrew Bentley, a graphical interface for additive synthesis developed by Richard Orton; Midigrid, a MIDI device controller developed by Dave Malham; and, of particular significance in the current context, a suite of spectral manipulation programs, developed by Trevor Wishart. During the 1990s further contributions to the expanding repertory of CDP software focused attention on an increasingly important consideration: how best to combine these components within an environment that would allow composers to retain flexibility of choice and at the same time be able to explore the processing opportunities in ways that were coherent and also, where appropriate, suitably interconnected. Rajmil Fischman had produced the initial graphic desktop environment for the launch of the CDP, but it soon became clear that simply extending it to embrace new applications would not be sustainable in the long term. What was required was a radical rethink of how best to design a composing interface, and it was also in this context that Trevor Wishart was to play a major and significant role, resulting in the development of Sound Loom, which provides the primary synthesis and control environment for the CDP to the present day.

An important feature of the CDP is its ethos from the outset based on the notion of a collective of individuals, working independently of any institution. Although in due course some important external links were cultivated, such as a three-year association with the Partnership for Advanced Computing Technologies (PACT) at the University of Bristol, following a move from York to Bristol in 1996, and a start-up grant of £20,000 awarded in 1988 by the Gulbenkian Foundation, its activities have essentially been self-funded. Thus, an overriding objective from the outset has been affordability. Although today the availability of powerful personal computers capable of meeting the requirements of the medium ensures that such a consideration is no longer a material issue, this was most certainly not the case back in the late 1980s, which makes the achievements of the collective all the more remarkable. It is against this background that the early career of Trevor Wishart can now be considered in more detail, specifically in the context of the developments that led to the composition of *Imago*.

The following account draws upon a comprehensive repertory of information that Wishart has provided over the course of his career as both a software designer and a composer, and the inquiring reader is directed to three publications that provide a detailed perspective on his pioneering work over the years.[7] The first is *On Sonic Art*, first published in 1985 and written during a residency at Queen's University, Kingston, Ontario.[8] It presents a thorough account of his compositional experiences and the associated aesthetics that shaped and influenced his creativity from the start of his career up until the mid-1980s. A second, revised and updated version, edited by Simon Emmerson, was published in 1994.[9] The second is *Audible Design*, published in 1994.[10] It includes a comprehensive introduction to the technical precepts that informed the development of Wishart's software up to the mid-1990s, in turn establishing the key features of Sound Loom, released to members of the CDP in 2001 and used for the first time by Wishart for the composition of *Imago* (2002).[11] Finally, *Sound Composition*, published in 2012, describes the key musical and technical features in each of his works composed up to the early 2010s, including *Imago*.[12]

Wishart's initial explorations of the medium took place in an era still dominated by the reel-to-reel tape recorder, used as both as a recording device and a sound processing facility in its own right. At this time tape-based techniques of editing and mixing sounds, including pitch transposition by changing the capstan speed and playing recordings in reverse, were extensively employed by electronic composers, working with both synthesized and acoustically generated materials. Wishart chose to concentrate on the creative possibilities of naturally produced sounds, his early works, culminating in *Red Bird* (1973–1977), being concerned with the transformation of associative sounds in a free-ranging compositional environment:

> I crystallized the idea of using sounds in a mythological way. So instead of saying "this is the sound of something," I thought "this is a sound of something which probably represents something else, and I can work with it in a mythical world of sound transformation." *Red Bird* distils that idea and develops it as far as it would go, from my point of view.[13]

Although the musical outcomes of such an approach strongly underpinned an aesthetic that was subject to no material constraints or boundaries in terms of the scope and nature of the sound worlds thus embraced, Wishart came to realize that such concepts of sonic art could be productively reinforced and expanded in a more precise manner. His objectives thus turned increasingly to the possibilities of using sound transformation as the basis of formal ideas, a journey embracing an expanding and increasingly sophisticated repertory of processing techniques, progressing in turn from an analog environment to the expanded possibilities of digital signal processing.

The possibilities of manipulating vocal sounds, inspired by the techniques employed in creating *Red Bird*, became a major preoccupation during the late 1970s, leading to the composition of *Anticredos* (1980), for six amplified voices. An important technique explored in this work, preparing the ground for a methodology used extensively in the composition of *Imago*, was that of deconstructing a short sound event and then subjecting the resulting fragments to a series of structured transformations. Here the word "Credos" provides the material for the entire piece using two classes of vocal transformations: (1) continuous transformations, where a sustained sound begins with certain characteristics and ends with different characteristics, and (2) textures of discrete sounds in which the constituents gradually change in quality, or where the balance of constituents of different quality gradually changes.[14] As in the case of *Red Bird*, the processing techniques employed were still entirely analog, in this instance generated live by the vocalists, with the resulting sound streams being diffused spatially via a four-channel diffusion system, requiring three performers to control the associated panning joysticks.

Anna's Magic Garden (1982) concentrates on two primary sound sources explored for their symbolic associations, those of a child's voice, and those of birdsong. Here the transformations take on a subtle dimension in terms of bridging the continuum between the known and the unknown. In many respects the work occupies a transitional status between the sound world of *Anticredos* and that of the major suite of voice-based works that was to follow, the *Vox Cycle*. The ideas and techniques that underpin these six works were already coming into focus during the late 1970s, fueled to no small extent by the recognition that the computer could provide an important gateway to their further exploration. Access to suitable resources prior to the CDP, however, presented a significant challenge. The primary technologies associated with the early *Vox* pieces thus remained those of extended vocal techniques, live processing, and prerecorded tape components working in an analog domain. Whereas digital technologies were coming available in the context of commercial processing devices, and Wishart was able to use a digital harmonizer in *Vox 2* (1984) and also generate sync tracks for *Vox 3* (1986) using the Cmusic version of Music V installed on a PDP-11/23 computer in the Department of Music, University of York, the level of versatility and sophistication he required in this context was not yet available anywhere in the UK.

The only institution in Europe that could provide a suitable gateway to such resources was IRCAM, and access to its facilities became an important imperative. Following an application first submitted in 1979, Wishart was accepted for an induction course in 1981, pursuing a project specifically designed to explore the possibilities of manipulating vocal sounds using computer-based signal processing techniques. Here he came into contact with the technique of linear predictive coding (LPC), and although the course only lasted six weeks, he was able to start material work on some preliminary sketches. Unfortunately, as noted in Chapter 3 (Manoury), the DEC PDP-10 mainframe computer he used for these investigations was almost immediately replaced by a DEC VAX-11/780 computer, leading to the development of an entirely new repertory of signal processing software. These changes delayed further work at IRCAM, and it was not until 1985 that circumstances facilitated his return to conduct further and more substantial investigations into the possibilities of processing voice-generated material, now working as a visiting composer.

During this second visit he encountered the phase vocoder, originally introduced to IRCAM by James Moorer, following pioneering work on the technique carried out at the Center for Computer Research in Music and Acoustics (CCRMA), Stanford University, during the late 1970s.[15] At the time only limited interest was being shown in the technique by other IRCAM composers.[16] However, with assistance from Mark Dolson, who had worked on refining the technique at CARL,[17] Wishart developed a series of advanced phase vocoding algorithms that he subsequently used to compose *Vox 5* (1986).[18] Although his sound sources, as before, consisted entirely of analog recordings, in this instance based on extended articulations of self-generated vocal fragments, all the signal processing for this entirely electroacoustic piece was carried out in the digital domain. On his return from IRCAM the prototype version of the CDP system was nearing completion, and Wishart was thus soon able to continue his work developing phase vocoding algorithms locally, leading in turn to the start of the Sound Loom project. Key features of his phase vocoding and associated signal processing techniques subsequently used in *Imago* will be returned to in due course.

The pioneering work of the CDP was soon overtaken by events, as the technology of the Apple Macintosh became increasingly superior to that of the Atari toward the end of the decade with the release of the Macintosh II in 1987, precipitating the demise of the company as a computer manufacturer during the early 1990s. The CDP project, however, was to continue and prosper following a change of direction in terms of its host computer, and by 1994 the software had been rewritten for Microsoft MS-DOS, leading to a Windows-based version, first for Windows XP and then subsequently Windows 7. At first sight the choice of the PC computer might appear a little puzzling, given the competing attractions of the Macintosh II. Affordability, however, was a major consideration, and the significantly higher cost of the Macintosh in the UK and elsewhere in Europe was a material reason for the choice of the Windows environment, further stimulated by the availability of low-cost music quality sound cards for PCs, providing attractive low cost alternatives to the SoundSTreamer. Cross-platform capability was finally achieved early in the 2000s, following the release of the desktop version of the Macintosh OS X operating system that resolved some key compatibility issues, and in 2014 the CDP system became available free of charge as shareware for all. Readers are thus able to augment their study of the characteristics of *Imago* using the analysis tools that accompany this project with firsthand experience of original software, downloaded directly from the CDP website.[19]

The development of Sound Loom as a composing resource

Before studying the key characteristics of *Imago*, it is instructive to look more closely at Wishart's compositional techniques, both in terms of their influence on the creative process and the development of Sound Loom, the resource used to realize his objectives. A particularly striking feature of his approach is the rejection of a fully interactive real-time mode of composing such as that pioneered by Barry Truax. Whereas during the early years of the CDP the associated processing delays rendered such an approach impracticable, the steady improvements in computing power progressively reduced such constraints to the point where such a mode of working could be seriously considered.[20] Wishart, however, has chosen to remain one step removed from such an immediate environment, engaging instead with the processes of incremental aggregation, where the outcome of each processing task is evaluated and accepted or rejected before progressing to the next one. The following extract from *Audible Design* provides a useful perspective on his approach:

> In many studio situations in which I have worked, in order to produce some subtly time-varying modification of a sound texture or process, I had to provide to a program a file listing the values some parameter will take and the times at which it will reach those values (a *breakpoint table*). I then ran the program and subsequently heard the result. If I didn't like this result, I had to modify the values in the table and run the program again, and so on. It is clearly simpler and more efficacious, when first exploring any time-varying process and its effect on a particular sound, to move a fader, turn a knob, bow a string, blow down a tube (etc.) and hear the result of this physical action as I make it. I can then adjust my physical actions to satisfy my aural experience—I can explore intuitively, without going through any conscious explanatory control process.
>
> In this way I can learn intuitively, through performance, what is "right" or "wrong" for me in this new situation without necessarily having any conscious explicit knowledge of how I made this decision. The power of the computer both to generate and provide control over the whole sound universe does not require that I explicitly know where to travel.[21]

The importance to him of this method of composing is further reinforced in an interview with Wishart published in *Digimag Magazine*:

> Offline and real-time work are different both from a programming and from a musical perspective. The principal thing you don't have to deal with in offline work, is getting the processing done in a specific time. The program must be efficient and fast, and understand timing issues. Offline all this is simply irrelevant. Offline also, you can take your time to produce a sound-result e.g. a process might consult the entire sound and make some decisions about what to do, run a 2nd process, and on the basis of this run a third and so on. As machines get faster and programmers get cleverer (and if composers are happy for sounds to be processed off-line and re-injected into the system later) then you can probably get round most of these problems. . . . Working offline you can work with the unique characteristics of a particular sound—it may be a multi-phonic you managed to generate in an improvising session but is not simply "reproducible" at will, or it may be the recording of a transient event, or a specific individual, that cannot be reproduced at will in a performance.[22]

Interestingly, a gap of more than fifteen years separates these two statements, the latter dating from 2009. In another interview, published in the same year, he observed:

> The way I work falls into three main stages. The first stage is the idea itself. To start a piece, I need to link together a set of sounds (it could be just one sound, as in *Imago*, or over 8,000 sounds, as in *Globalalia*) and some general overarching idea (in these cases, respectively, surprising metamorphosis, and the universality of the sounds of human discourse).[23] This is often the hardest part of composing for me. It's not so much a problem to work with sounds, and to make successful or even spectacular sound events. The main problem is why start on a piece at all?
>
> The second stage is to transform the sounds. With pieces like *Tongues of Fire* and *Imago*, I subject the source material to transformation using all the tools in the CDP armory. From these transformations, I select the most interesting or potentially useful sounds, and then I transform those sounds further. In this way, I build up a tree of related sounds. A sound may be "useful," for example, if a harmonic (pitched) sound comes to be strongly inharmonic, or a strongly attacked sound loses those attack characteristics. This means that it will develop in some completely new direction when further transformations are applied. (It's like modulating to some distant key in traditional pitch space.) Some sounds also need to be retained because they establish an audible link between (say) a harmonic and an inharmonic variant. These linking sounds are important in the structure of the piece to ensure the sonic coherence of the materials. Some of these materials will become long enough (e.g., via time-stretching, or creating textures of many individual events, or "zig-zag," or "drunken-walk reading") to become the basis of musical phrases in their own right. Combining these with other events, I'll work up materials into phrase-length structures.

The third stage is to determine the structure of the piece. Eventually, I will make some phrases that are particularly striking and select these as the nodal events of the entire piece to be placed at particular points in time in the whole structure. This also implies that the sounds from which they evolve can be placed somewhere in that structure to prepare for the nodal events, or to act as memories of them (perhaps codas). As this process continues, the options for placing further materials become more and more restricted until the large-scale form of the piece almost "crystallizes out." It's at this stage that materials that seemed ideal when they were first made get trimmed, occasionally 'extended, or entirely rejected, because of the surrounding context. I want to end up with a formal structure that has the feeling (as I'm listening to it) of some kind of musical "necessity" in the way it moves from one section to the next.[24]

The direct references to *Imago* provide some useful clues as to the way in which he set about the task of constructing an entire work from just a single source sound, the clink of two whiskey glasses, and the methods employed are studied in the documentation that accompanies the analysis section of this study.[25] By way of an introduction to a more detailed study of the key features of the work, it is instructive first to consider further the implications of this method of working, both in terms of the associated methodology and the scope and nature of the tools that were available for its composition.

A primary consideration here is the step-by-step process of generating materials, where the result of each process is evaluated, accepted, or rejected, or rerun with different parameter settings, before proceeding to the next step. The authors were granted access to the complete library of source materials for *Imago*, thus providing a valuable insight into their evolution. Indeed, the method of working reveals further clues as to compositional process, since each of these component sounds were routinely saved to disk with an associated date and time stamp. Although this forensic insight does not extend to those synthesis results that were rejected, in many instances the output of each stage in a sequence of processing tasks was also output to disk, providing further clues as to the way in which Wishart approaches the art and practice of composition.

It has already been noted that the CDP evolved as a collective. In recognizing Wishart's key role in its evolution, not least in terms of the development of Sound Loom, the associated repertory of sound processing and sound management resources draws upon contributions made at various stages by other people, not only the pioneers listed above, but also subsequent contributors such as Richard Dobson.[26] The centrality of his role in thus combining his own pioneering work in areas such as phase vocoding with that of others, however, must not be underestimated. It is one matter to gather together a repertory of contributing resources. It is quite another to combine them in a coherent and suitably integrated manner within an all-embracing composing environment. Thus, for example, the audio mixing facilities within Sound Loom are based on

207

a text-based system originally developed by Andrew Bentley, but now enhanced with a graphics-based control environment. It also has to be recognized that whereas some processing tools are genuinely groundbreaking in terms of what they do, others will explore new horizons in terms of how existing techniques may be explored in novel ways. The facilities for filtering within Sound Loom are a case in point in the latter context. Whereas they are almost entirely based on tried and tested methodologies that are well known to electronic composers, it is the ways in which the associated control environment has been implemented that makes the use of these resources particularly distinctive.

While the evolution of Sound Loom has continued to the present day, almost all of its key features were in place by the end of the 1990s. Thus, a comparison of the version used to compose *Imago* in 2002 with the current version reveals no changes of a substantive nature, but more those of refinement in terms of the ways in which the various underlying algorithms may be used.

It is important to understand that Sound Loom is first and foremost a graphic user interface, bringing together a repertory of signal processing algorithms within a fully integrated composing environment that can essentially be approached from two perspectives. The first treats the associated software essentially as a toolbox for the generation of processed materials, creating recordings that are subsequently transferred to a conventional commercial digital mixing environment such as Pro Tools or Logic. The second approach, that adopted by Wishart, is to complete the production of works entirely within Sound Loom, using its own integral mixing facilities, the advantage being that migration between the two stages of composition can in effect be seamless. The description of the toolbox that follows is concerned in the first instance with the resources available for the generation of the materials used in *Imago*. The gateway to understanding how these materials were then combined to produce the work is provided via the accompanying analysis of the acoustic results, and of the associated models of the processes actually used to achieve key sections of the piece.

The descriptions in *Audible Design* differ slightly in perspective from those provided in later interviews and more recently on Wishart's website, in that the latter reflect more clearly the processes of grouping and interlinking in Sound Loom. However, the information provided via these various sources is essentially one and the same, and the following summary of the key concepts discussed in *Audible Design* usefully prepares the ground for the subsequent study of *Imago*. The early chapters of the book consider the nature of sound, notably the differences between the time domain and the frequency domain, spectral and harmonic conceptions of pitch, and by extraction the notion of timbre, in each instance related to specific techniques of acoustic manipulation. Attention then turns to specific processing characteristics, starting with the onset of sounds and how these might be altered, the techniques available to modify their continuation, and, most significantly, the micromanagement of sounds via the use of grain streams.

More general but equally important concepts of composing are then discussed, starting with the role of sequences using techniques such as splicing and shuffling, and continuing with concepts of time in perceptual contexts, in particular the significance of event density and the control of energy in terms of enveloping the constituent sound materials. The next chapter deals with the possibilities of time-stretching, a technique used extensively in many of Wishart's compositions. The penultimate chapter deals with another characteristic of Sound Loom that is of particular significance in the context of Wishart's compositional processes, that of interpolation. His definition of the term provides important clues as to ways in which he interrogates and manipulates his materials:

> Any perceptually effective compositional process applied to a sound will produce a different sound. However, if the process is sufficiently radical . . . we will produce a sound which we recognize as being of a different type. . . . We can, by using a similar compositional process create a whole set of sounds, whose properties are intermediate between those of the source and those of the goal. We will describe this mediation by progressive steps as *static interpolation*. Alternatively, provided our sound is sufficiently long, we may gradually apply a compositional process changing the value of various parameters through time, e.g. we may gradually spectrally stretch the harmonic spectrum of an instrumental tone until we reach through a continuous process, a complex and inharmonic sound. Or we may gradually add vibrato . . . so that it eventually involves such extreme and rapid swings of pitch that the original percept is swallowed up by the process. In these cases we have a process of *dynamic interpolation* taking place through the application of a continuously time-varying process.[27]

Examples of both methods of working are evident in the development of the material for *Imago*. The final chapter of *Audible Design* deals with Wishart's concepts of form, thus viewing electroacoustic music from a higher-level perspective, notably the relationship between the low-level generative processes that are currently being studied and the ways in which these components are ordered and combined to develop a coherent and convincing musical argument. Here the importance of interpolation as a structural function receives further attention, providing further clues as to the evolutionary strategies he uses to create his works.

It has already been noted that the primary catalyst for his subsequent contributions to the CDP was the discovery of the possibilities of the phase vocoder, otherwise known as PVOC. The origins of this processing technique can be traced back to an analog device developed at Bell Telephone Laboratories, New Jersey, shortly after World War II. This comprised two distinct but interlinked components. The first was an analyzer that measured the energy levels of applied sounds measured over the entire audio spectrum via a bank of band-pass filters, connected in parallel. The resolution of this real-time spectral analysis was a function of the number and associated frequency spacing of the filters, typically three per octave. The resulting amplitude levels could simply be displayed as an array using a two-dimensional graphics screen. Alternatively, these amplitude functions could be applied essentially in a reverse direction to control the output levels of equivalent filters in a matching filter bank, now used in the normal way simply as a sound processor.

This device was conceived simply as an artificial talking device, but its value as a resource for composing electronic music led to the manufacture of a number of commercial derivatives.[28] One popular technique, often referred to as cross-synthesis, typically involves superimposing the analyses of speech-generated sounds on pitched music materials, such as the sounds produced by a string quartet, thus creating superimposed and recognizable vocal textures. It was, however, with the transition to the digital domain and the work of pioneers such as Moorer and Dolson that the technique finally achieved its full potential. Wishart's personal contribution to its development was to prove especially significant, not least in terms of the ways in which the associated techniques were applied to create an extensive and versatile repertory of vocoder-based resources within Sound Loom.

Two groups of frequency-domain processing functions were developed in the first instance: (1) those associated with techniques that stretch the audio spectrum as a function of time, and (2) those concerned with morphing between two different sounds by spectral modification. Whereas, with just a few application-specific modifications, the analysis stages of the functions were based on traditional vocoding principles, the distinctive characteristics of each function were determined by variations in the ways in which the resulting analysis data may be applied, extending in many instances to a further stage of intermediate processing before the final resynthesis stage. The following extract from an article by Wishart on the composition of *Vox 5* provides a useful insight into the early development of the associated techniques:

> The phase vocoder (PV) effectively divides the source sound into a number of channels that are equally spaced through the range of frequencies. In each channel it stores the amplitude of the signal component, and its frequency (usually known as "phase" in this context). It is now possible to manipulate these analysis data. For example, to shift a spectral component in channel n up one octave, we need to move the amplitude and phase in this channel into channel 2n (which is centered around twice the frequency) and also multiply the phase by two. (Phase corresponds to frequency, so an octave shift means multiplying frequency by two.) It is possible to devise programs that will systematically transform the complete spectrum generating a second analysis-data file, which can then be resynthesized using the phase vocoder synthesis option. These transformations can be time-dependent (the spectral

shifting can follow an envelope, or read a value-time function to ascertain its value at any particular time).[29]

These investigations laid the foundations for his repertory of techniques known individually as "instruments." These extend from more basic implementations of the phase vocoder to embrace an expanded spectrum of signal processing techniques engaging with both the frequency and the time domains. These can be classified under three primary headings: waveset manipulation, grain manipulation, and sound shredding. Wishart describes these as follows:

> **Waveset distortion**: I defined a waveset as the signal between any pair of zero-crossings. With a simple sine-wave the waveset corresponds to the waveform. But even with a harmonic tone with very strong partials, the waveform may cross the zero more than twice in a complete cycle. In this case the wavesets are shorter than the waveform. A whole suite of procedures was developed to manipulate wavesets. I have used three at prominent moments in compositions.
>
> The first of these involves replacing each waveset with a standard-shape waveform (e.g. a sinewave). This produces a very pronounced spectral transformation of the source, but one where the zero-crossings of the result are exactly aligned with those of the source. It is thus possible to use a simple mixing procedure (another CDP process, **Inbetweening**, does this) to produce a sequence of sounds intermediate between the source and the new sound.
>
> The second, **waveset averaging**, involves extracting the shape of each waveset, and then averaging this shape over a group of N adjacent wavesets. Again, this produces an extreme modification of the source (usually a relatively harsh sound and often a transformation so distant from the source that little audible connection is apparent!).
>
> Finally, **waveset repetition** generates unusual pitch artefacts in complex signals. In particular, any small fragment of a noise signal, if repeated a number of times, generates a tiny pitch artefact.[30]

Wishart's experiences working at IRCAM were supplemented by a period of study at Groupe de Recherches Musicales (GRM), which was to prove highly influential in terms of expanding his knowledge of sound processing techniques, not least in the context of time-stretching.[31] This led to a useful solution to removing the undesirable artifacts that occur when stretching a sound that contains a sharp attack or series of attacks, whereby the stretching is only applied to the body and decay of each sound event. Two possible solutions were explored in this context. The first was technically relatively straightforward:

> **Time-variable time-stretching** procedures were also implemented, more general than those existing in the CARL Phase Vocoder implementation itself. These are important if one wishes to preserve the attack characteristics of a sound while time-stretching the sound (as a whole) by a large factor.[32]

The second solution is more sophisticated, with the capacity to process multiple attack transients within a sound:

> To deal with these [problems] a number of **Grain manipulation** instruments were developed. These instruments extract the (loudness) envelope of the sound by gating it. Using this envelope the source can be fragmented into attacked elements and these elements repositioned in time (or in pitch or both) in the output sound. (The process can also track the overall amplitude of the source and adjusts the gate level for the grains correspondingly).[33]

Changing the ordering of these fragments provided further processing options. For example, it is possible to create the illusion of a sound being played backward, while maintaining the original identity of transients that would otherwise be extensively modified if a recording was simply played in reverse. The descriptions of two of these instruments illustrate the power and versatility of these processing facilities:

> The **Iteration** instrument allows a signal to be looped, but imposes (user-controlled) random pitch, amplitude and timing fluctuations on the repeated elements. Using Iteration the sound generated from the single flap can be extremely natural (but, of course, more distant transformations are also possible). Various instruments allow scrambling of a sound through simple editing and rejoining of the edited segments. In particular, in **Sound Shredding**, I cut up a sound (at random time-points) into a number of separate segments, shuffles [sic] these segments, and reassembles [sic] them to the exact duration of the original. The *resulting* sound is then cut up again, differently, and the reassembly repeated.[34]

The family of instruments associated with his techniques of spectral modification is of particular interest, given their scope and versatility, and extensive use was made of them in the composition of *Imago*. Indeed, the concept of morphing between two different sounds, which at the most basic level can be viewed simply as interpolation, takes on a much expanded perspective in the context of the possibilities of sound transformation:

> In the first phase of development (post 1986), many spectral transformations were implemented in the Atari environment. These included **spectral morphing** and various types of **spectral shifting** and **spectral stretching**, from a linear shift (adding a fixed value to all frequency data, thus e.g. making a harmonic spectrum become inharmonic), through a multiplication (preserving harmonic relations between data, but transposing the pitch—but with the ability to split the spectrum at a given frequency, and hence produce doubly-pitched output sounds) to differential multiplication of the data.[35]

The resulting library of processing resources is extensive, including for example the following techniques:

Spectral cleaning was developed using a comparative method—part of the spectrum deemed to be (mainly) noise (and, in some options, part of the spectrum deemed to be clear signal) being compared with the rest of the signal and appropriate subtractions of data or other modifications made. From a musical point of view, the most innovative early new developments were **spectral banding**, a rather complicated "filter," which enabled the spectrum to be divided into bands, and various simple amplitude-varying (and in fact frequency-shifting) processes to be applied to the bands, **spectral tracing** and **spectral blurring**.

Spectral tracing simply retains the N [filter analysis] channels with the loudest (highest amplitude) data on a *window-by-window basis*. The small number of PVOC channels selected by the process will vary from window to window. Individual partials will drop out, or suddenly appear, in this elect set. As a result, the output sound will present complex weaving melodies produced by the preserved partials as they enter (or leave) the elect set.

Spectral blurring is an analogous process in the time dimension. The change in frequency information over time is averaged—in fact, the frequency and amplitude data in the channels is sampled at each Nth window, and the frequency and amplitude data for intervening channels *generated* by simple interpolation. This leads to a blurring or "washing out" of the spectral clarity of the source.

Arpeggiation of the spectrum (a procedure inspired by vocal synthesis examples used by Steve McAdams at IRCAM to demonstrate aural streaming) was produced by "drawing" a low frequency simple waveform onto the spectrum. This oscillator rises and falls between two limit values—values of frequency in the original spectrum—specified by the user. Where this waveform crosses the spectral windows, the channel (or surrounding group of channels, or all the channels above, or all those below) is amplified. **Spectral plucking** was introduced to add further amplitude emphasis (and an element of time-decay of the emphasized data) to the selected channels. A number of other processes (such as **spectral freezing** and sustaining of the spectrum at particular moments, and **spectral interleaving**, timewise, the spectra from different sources) were implemented in this early phase.[36]

Although, as already noted, these techniques were subsequently modified and refined, the essential principles are retained in the instruments provided by Sound Loom. These later refinements included **Tune spectrum**, which works by selecting channel data lying close to the partials of a specified set of pitches, and moving the frequency of that data to (or toward) the desired partial frequency, and **Choose partials**, which works by selecting channels that contain frequencies close to those of a specified set of partial frequencies. Wishart also implemented PVOC versions of conventional filters, including various types of **low-pass**, **high-pass**, **band-pass**, **notch**, and **graphic EQ spectral filters**, together with a **chorusing** procedure, which he notes was suggested by Steve McAdams's work introducing jitter into the partials data.

213

A key feature of spectral modification is the ability to engage in pitch tracking. Over the years a number of techniques have been developed to implement this, some more successful than others. Matters become especially complicated if the sounds contain inharmonic partials and/or multiple pitches:

> After discussions with Miller Puckette about his work on tracking the pitch produced by instrumentalists performing in real time, procedures to **extract the pitch** of PVOC data were finally developed into a useful form, and instruments to correct the data, to transform the pitch data (**quantise, shift, vibrato, approximate, or randomise the pitch**, and **exaggerate, invert or smooth the pitch contour**), and **apply the pitch to other sounds**, were developed.[37] At the same time, the **extraction of formants** from the PVOC data was implemented satisfactorily for the first time within the CDP environment. This enabled the **inner glissando** procedure to be developed. Here, the process retains the time-varying spectral envelope (the formant envelope) of the sound, but replaces the signal itself by an endlessly glissandoing Shepard Tone signal.[38]

One feature of Wishart's compositional technique is the micromanaging of segmented sounds, for example the processes of **grain manipulation** discussed above. In a more general context he provided facilities for

> [s]huffling the sequence of windows, and **weaving** a specified path (including possible repetitions and omissions) through the windows were implemented at an earlier stage. A **"drunken-walk"** through the analysis windows was suggested by Miller Puckette's work in MAX.[39]

In addition to the above, he introduced a third group of instruments that enhanced the functional characteristics of signal processing techniques developed by others, both internal and external to the CDP. Some of these instruments drew significantly on what he classifies as **granular synthesis** procedures, which he notes were developed at an early stage of the CDP. There are parallels to be drawn here with the work of Barry Truax, although the methodology is somewhat different. Readers will need to experiment with the software tools that have been made available via the project in both cases to fully understand the nature and significance of these differences. Wishart's implementations are known as **texture-generation** instruments:

> Texture Generation was (and is) able to use an arbitrarily large number of input sounds, to generate a stream of events where all the following parameters can themselves vary through time:
> - the average time between event repetitions (the density of events) *or* the specification of a sequence of event times
> - the scatter (or randomisation) of event timings (which means the instrument can generate anything from dance-music-like regularity to complete arhythmicity)

- a quantisation grid for times (or none)
- a specification of which range of input sounds are to be used
- the range and range-limits of pitch-transposition of the events
- the range and range-limits of event amplitudes
- the range and range-limits of durations of the individual events in the texture
- the spatial centre of the texture on the stereo stage, and its motion
- the spatial bandwidth of the texture on the stereo stage.

  A neutral texture is generated from independent events over a transposition range without regard to tuning, tempering etc. However, the texture can also be generated . . .

- over a harmonic field (not necessarily tempered) which can itself change through time
- clustered into groups of events of specified or random pitch-shape
- formed from a line with arbitrary or specified decorating patterns (which themselves have properties with independent parameters of their own).[40]

Perhaps the most significant external influence in this context was that of GRM, in particular the techniques known collectively as *brassage*. The basic principle here is very simple, involving the ability to segment sounds into small fragments of time and then change their ordering, and indeed an example of this technique has already been discussed in the context of **grain manipulation**. GRM, however, had developed an extensive repertory of brassage-based tools, and Wishart was able to use these as the starting point for a series of unique instruments, also available in the Sound Loom library. He notes:

> The G.R.M. have divided **brassage** into a series of sub-categories based on musical outcomes (based on many years of musical experience), providing the user with control of parameters over a musically meaningful range for each resulting tool. I admire this approach and accept that it is much more accessible to the user who is a computer *user* rather than a programmer. However, compositionally I often find it interesting to explore the areas where a process pushes against its limits and falls over into another area of perception. E.g. if the size of grains used in a time-stretching brassage routine (as used in the *harmonizer*) exceeds a certain threshold we begin to hear the resulting sound as a rapid collage of elements rather than as a simple timestretch. Hence the CDP brassage routine offers **timestretch, pitch-shift, granulation** and **source-scrambling** as independent modes, but also allows access to *all* the parameters of the brassage process at the same time.

- timestretch or compression and its range
- segment density and its range
- segment size
- segment transposition and its range
- segment amplitude and its range
- segment splice-length
- segment spatial position

- segment spatial scatter and its range
- segment timing randomisation
- segment search-range in the source

where every parameter can also be varied in time. The process can also be applied to more than one input sound.[41]

One final group of instruments to be considered here is concerned specifically with manipulating the amplitude of selected sounds:

Envelope extraction and superimposition (written by Richard Orton) and **envelope manipulation** (which I developed from Richard's programs) were some of the earliest processes to be developed in the CDP. These allow the envelope to be extracted at different resolutions (e.g. a tremolo sound which crescendos has a small-scale, rapidly-varying loudness envelope defining the tremolo, and a large scale overall envelope defining the crescendo. These can be extracted separately using a different window-size for the envelope extraction). The envelope can then be changed (**envelope warping**—normalise, limit, compress, exaggerate, corrugate etc.), and applied to the original, or a different sound. However, we can also **envelope replace**, where the new envelope replaces (rather being superimposed over) the envelope of the processed sound. In this case we force the original sound to have a flat level throughout (treating in a special way points in the sound where the envelope approaches zero), then apply the new envelope to the flattened sound.[42]

Inside *Imago*

Imago is a substantial work, lasting over twenty-five minutes, derived from a single brief recorded source sound, the sound of two whiskey glasses clinking, borrowed by Trevor Wishart in homage from Jonty Harrison's . . . *et ainsi de suite.* . . . The musical material for the work is developed using a variety of processing techniques to create a wide range of different sounds and textures from the one source. Whereas in John Chowning's *Stria* and Barry Truax's *Riverrun* whole sections are produced by large-scale processes shaped in advance (*Stria*) or in real-time (*Riverrun*) by the composer, in *Imago* each event is individually crafted before being assembled into larger passages. As already noted, Wishart's software, Sound Loom, does not run in real time. It comprises a wide collection of different processes, each of which can be applied to a source sound file in order to produce a new output sound file.

Although multiple processes can be programmed to operate in one pass by working in batch mode, Wishart's normal approach is to try out each process individually, listening to the outcome before applying further processing. The sounds used in the final work are often the result of multiple processes applied sequentially. This way of working also means that a processed sound may subsequently be used as the basis for several different strands of further processing. As the whole work derives from a single source sound, the overall process of generating the work can thus be conceived of as a tree branching out in many different directions. The compositional structure itself then is the result of bringing these many varied but related sounds together into a work in which different sections are characterized by a variety of sounds often coming from different branches of the tree. The sounds resulting from such multiple processing vary greatly both in character and type, from single short sounds, like the source sound itself, to longer, sustained sounds, to extended granular textures and melodico-rhythmic sequences.

From a single source to a variety of processed sound files

At the time of composing *Imago*, Wishart started keeping the sound files produced with Sound Loom in a systematic way. The materials studied in this analysis come from the composer's archive, which comprises 1,210 sound files and 244 text files, generated between April 17 and October 22, 2002, and organized in thirty-eight main folders.[43] This is particularly useful from a musicological poïetic perspective: in many instances, the process having led from one sound to another can be retrieved with intermediary sound files; occasionally, the text files provide the parameters of the processes concerned.[44]

> *Presentation 19 in the accompanying software is a chart displaying all of Wishart's archive, in chronological order. Each sound file can be played, and each text file can be viewed, and the objects' colors represent the folders in which the composer saved them. This can be used as a first introduction to the multiple iterations within the composer's creative process. Demonstration Video 6.1 shows how to use this interactive resource.* ▶

On day one of creation (April 17), two sound files appear in Wishart's archive: "ttball.wav," the source sound extracted from Harrison's piece, and its mono version, "ttballm.wav."[45] On day three (April 23),[46] thirty-seven different sound files were generated, showing a large variety of experimentations with the source sound: basic editing ("ttballf.wav"), simple looping ("ttloop.wav"), basic transpositions ("ttdn15.wav"), short melodico-rhythmic developments ("falltolo.wav"), large iterations with random pitches within a harmonic field ("diatonic.wav"). On that same day, some of these processed sound files are themselves "recycled" into further developments;[47] for instance, "gamtex.wav" is a massive texture generated from many iterations of "falltolo.wav"; a text file named "making_octpulse.txt" shows that the massive synthetic "opls.wav" was generated by coloring the highly noisy "str60tex_wejdn3.wav" with a bank of filters.

In some other periods, Wishart adopted a more systematic approach and focused on one particular process to generate many variations around a unique idea. On day ten of creation (May 3), he created several occurrences of distorted versions of the source sound, using waveset distortion. On days fifty-three and fifty-four (July 22 and 23), he developed many chords by stacking a sustained version of the source sound, transposing them, and assigning them envelopes. On day fifty-seven (July 26), the composer generated a number of time-stretched and transposed variations of the source glass sound; on the following day (July 27), he assembled those into larger phrases.

Demonstration Video 6.2 shows the use of Presentation 19 with a focus on the above-mentioned days of creation and sound categories. ▶

Successive Sound Loom processes

If the whiskey glass source sound can clearly be heard in its original form across the whole piece, much of the material constituting *Imago* is the result of several iterations of different processes, leading to sound objects or processes that are aurally very distant from the source. For instance, the composer created "ttballf_sust.wav" by spectrally freezing the original sound, leading to a thirty-second crystalline sustain. This was in turn harmonized as nineteen chords ("belholda_b0.wav" to "belholda_b18.wav"), by stacking the sustained sound with two or three of its own transpositions downward, with ratios in semitones.[48] Each of the chords was then transposed one octave down and given a decaying amplitude envelope ("belholda_b0_dn8_e.wav" to "belholda_b18_dn8_e.wav), and then assembled in several larger sequences, such as "chordusphras1.wav," making the pebbles heard in the first Sparse section presented below along with the large-scale structure of the work.

Presentation 1 in the accompanying software is an interactive structural map on which you can follow some of the paths leading from the source sound, at the bottom, to the eight final premixes of the work, at the top. You can also use Presentation 7 ("Time-stretching processes"), Presentation 11 ("Stacking processes"), and Presentation 6 ("Transposition processes") to experiment with simulations of the processes discussed above (freezing, stacking, and transposing, respectively). Finally, Presentation 5 is a video excerpt in which Trevor Wishart demonstrates his use of Sound Loom to transform a source iteratively. Demonstration Video 6.3 introduces these interactive resources by showing each step of the succession of processes leading to the pebbles in the Sparse section. ▶

Much of the material making the Gamelan section of *Imago* was generated in the early stages of the overall compositional process. On day two of creation (April 23), an even sharper version of the original source sound was edited ("ttballe.wav"), and then transposed with speed variation two octaves and four octaves lower ("ttdn15.wav" and "ttdn31.wav"). Each of these transpositions was then stacked with the untransposed "ttballe.wav" ("octo1.wav" and "octo2.wav"). The first of these two short stacked sounds was then iterated with a specific rhythmic and melodic profile, leading to a first germ of the gamelan material ("gamelor_prequel.wav").

The second short stacked sound was transposed further, one octave and two octaves down ("octo2dn8.wav" and "octo2dn15.wav"). The one-octave transposition was used as a second gamelan melodico-rhythmic motif ("gamelor_prequel_xtra2.wav"), while the two-octave one was used as the basis for five brief descending iterations ("descender.wav" to "descender5.wav"). A stack of the larger iterations, "gamelmor.wav," was assembled from "gamelor_prequel.wav" and "gamelor_prequel_xtra2.wav," played at original speed and accelerated; the first four "descender" objects were then added, leading to a now complex polyphony: "gameld_noend.wav." The following step, "gameld.wav," is one of the most prominent features of the Gamelan section (discussed below); as the file names make explicit, it is made of a concatenation of "gameld_noend.wav" and "gameld_endbit.wav," a high-factor time-stretching of "octo1.wav."

In a parallel path, "ttballe.wav" was iterated into a brief and quick motif: "falltolo.wav." As mentioned above in the discussion on the early days' experimentations for *Imago*, this motif was used to generate the massive texture "gamtex.wav," and its shorter equivalent "gam.wav." This short version was then transposed two, four, and eight octaves higher ("gam-2.wav," "gam-4.wav," "gam-8.wav") and two and four octaves lower ("gam-h.wav" and "gam-q.wav"). The upward transpositions were directly integrated into the final Gamelan section premix, but were also stacked along with the downward ones into more complex and massive textures (the similar "gamtex2.wav" and "gamtex3.wav"). In turn, "gamtex3.wav" was stacked with its own transpositions a fourth above and a fifth and an octave below, leading to a further variation ("gamtex4.wav").[49]

219

Demonstration Video 6.4 shows Presentation 1 to illustrate the path leading to the Gamelan section, as well as how to use Presentation 6 ("Transposition processes"), Presentation 12 ("Iteration processes"), Presentation 7 ("Time-Stretching processes"), and Presentation 11 ("Stacking processes") to experiment with the different transformations used by Wishart in this instance. ▶

Assembling the work

Ultimately, *Imago* was assembled by mixing individual sound files together. The mixing process took place over several levels: for instance, the Opening premix was constituted with three sound files ("op_phras1.wav," "opening_phras2e_a.wav," and "alarmjoin.wav"); the first two are themselves the result of a mixing for which a mix file exists in Wishart's archive.[50] Thirteen files make up the first phrase, and twenty-five make up the second; some are themselves mixes with associated mix files, and so on.

Eight top-level premix sound files were assembled into *Imago*. They were all finalized in the latest stages of the overall creative process, between August 21 and September 13.[51] However, "gamelphrase_edited.wav" is the result of minor edits on a file resulting from a mix that actually took place earlier: "gamelphrase.wav" was generated on June 23 from materials created across three periods: April 23–24, May 22–27, and June 21–23. On the other hand, the direct components of the Ending premix were created in the very last days of creation (September 9–13); the files located in the "ending" folder of the archive were all generated from September 7, indicating Wishart's focus on writing the final section at the very end of his compositional path for this work.

> You can use Presentation 4 in the accompanying software to investigate the waveforms for different levels of mixes in Imago. The interactive map of Presentation 1 also features a visualization option displaying the sound files according to their date of creation. Demonstration Video 6.5 shows how to operate these resources. ▶

As indicated in a "readme.txt" text file located in the "finished" folder, the final mix from the eight top-level premixes was then processed with an overall amplitude envelope, completed with two short reverberated extensions; following this, four short fragments (up to seven seconds) were excised from the resulting file, leading to the definitive work. In the following paragraphs, the Opening and the Gamelan section are scrutinized in more detail, before a presentation of the large-scale structure of *Imago*.

The Opening of *Imago*

Trevor Wishart has himself written at some length about *Imago* in his book *Sound Composition*, including a detailed account of the Opening section of the work.[52] The following analysis aims to complement his composer's perspective, making use of the accompanying software to illustrate the discussed aspects of this section.

Imago begins with the original source sound, the clinking whiskey glasses. It comprises a sequence of short events gradually developing this source sound in different ways. From a technical perspective, the listener is introduced to some of the key transformational processes that will be employed in the work, one step at a time, illustrating a range of techniques that are developed further and expanded upon later. From a musical perspective, the passage introduces a number of sounds and gestures that will play an important part in the often larger, more continuous textures appearing in later sections. Musically, this passage can also be heard as presenting a lesson in classic motivic development, a single "note" developing into a phrase that in turn develops into a whole section. This almost didactic approach, both musically and technically, relates to the composer's account of how the work came about as a result of a challenge from a friend:

> I played [this friend of mine] a little bit of one of my pieces, and he said "I simply can't follow electroacoustic music, I can't hear any structure, or anything." And I was really puzzled by this, because he was really a musician, with a very good ear, he could understand musical structure, he was a very good listener. And so I thought this was a sort of challenge, and in this piece [*Imago*] I decided I would make a piece where the sonic structure was absolutely clear and explicit.[53]

> You can listen to the composer's account on the origins and overall compositional process of his work in more detail by watching the full interview in Presentation 2 of the accompanying software. Demonstration Video 6.6 shows a larger excerpt on the origins of Imago. ▶

Wishart's file archive shows that the first phrase of the Opening of the work is a mix of thirteen sound files or musical events. Figure 6.1 is the mix file for this phrase as formatted in the archive, with the addition of event numbers from 1 to 13. The file name is followed by the start time in seconds and further data (number of channels, amplitude, spatial positioning) for the mixing process.

The names Wishart gives to the component sound files sometimes give some indication of the processes by which they were derived and of their interconnection. For instance, "ttbtwice.wav" derives from the original source sound "ttballmf.wav" played twice. The labels were, however, originally intended only for the composer's own use, and their precise meaning is often

```
1.   ttballmf.wav 0.0 1 1 C
2.   ttbtwice.wav 6.0 1 1 C
3.   a1aaaa_upam.wav 11.73 1 1.33 C
4.   ttballf_cop.wav 26.0 2 1
5.   ttbtwice_cop.wav 30.2 1 1 C
6.   a3msemp.wav 34.37 2 1.4
7.   ttballf_cop2.wav 41.2 2 1
8.   ttbtwice_cop2.wav 45.7 1 1 C
9.   startercextr.wav 50.13 2 1
10.  from_tbr.wav 55.43 2 1
11.  ttbtwice_cop4.wav 60.7 1 1 C
12.  chromwej_a.wav 65.7 2 1
13.  tt_to_airnu.wav 73.7 2 1
```

FIGURE 6.1

Mix file for the opening phrase of *Imago*.[54]

obscure. By listening, sometimes aided by indications given in the filenames, the thirteen events in this opening passage can be grouped into five categories (A to E) according to their technical derivation and their musical characteristics:

A: Three of the events, 1, 4, and 7, are the original source sound underlying the whole work.

B: The simplest processing of this sound results in a gesture in which this source sound is played twice in quick succession. This gesture occurs four times in the opening phrase: events 2, 5, 8 and 11. It is the only one of the five categories that is entirely invariant, and as such it might be heard as an anchor point for the passage.

C: A slightly more complex transformation, which involves successive transposed repetitions of the source sound following a pitch contour. Different versions of this occur as events 3, 6, 9, and 10. The first of these, event 3, follows a rising contour, an anacrusis leading back to the original pitch of the source. Event 6 follows a more complex shape, rising then falling, slowing, and decaying as it does so and moving across the stereo space. Event 9 is again a rising anacrusis but rapidly accelerating and leading to a decaying resonance. This resonance is terminated by event 10, a close variation of the initial anacrusis in event 3.

In our reading of the work, the fourth recurrence of motif B marks the end of the initial exposition of material. Although incorporated into the "op_phras1.wav" mix file, the two events which follow, D and E, mark the start of a new phase of development, exceeding the simple transformations of the opening and beginning to evolve toward more elaborate transformations. As will be described later in the overview of the structure of the work, they represent, in our reading, the start of the first development phase of the work.

D, event 12, anticipates material that will feature strongly in some later sections of the work, which is there labeled "gamelan" by the composer.[55] It is a fast sequence of repetitions of the original short source sound following a pattern of pitches randomly picked from a chromatic scale, within a growing range.

This leads directly into **E**, event 13, which comprises a mix of four sound files. The main sound file is a process in which fast repetitions of the original source at the same pitch fade in and out, leading to a noisy resonance derived through granulation and time-stretching and ending with time-stretched granulation of the source in reverse (creating an effect like playing an attack/decay morphology backward), followed by a resonance. This final gesture prefigures the "gong"-like sounds in the following passage, but is more immediately echoed by the three other sound files more quietly in the mix. Figure 6.2 summarizes the sequence and distribution of the first thirteen events.

FIGURE 6.2

Distribution pattern for the thirteen events of the first phrase of the Opening of *Imago*.[56]

A B C A' B C' A' B C" C"' B D E

Within this sequence the following distribution pattern can be found:

A	B	C		
A'	B	C'		
A'	B	C"		
		C"'		
	B		D	E

Presentation 14 in the accompanying software includes the above pattern as an interactive explorer, where you can click on each category to hear the corresponding sound. You can also use Presentation 4 to explore these files in their mixing context, as shown in Demonstration Video 6.7. ▶

Technically, the opening phrase is developing from the original source sound through a succession of progressively more elaborate transformations. Musically, the listener is being introduced to a range of different types of musical events that will become important as the work progresses. The foundations of the work are here established, firmly rooted in the original source, emphasized by frequent return to it, but gradually opening out into new musical territory.

The mix file for the second submix of the Opening, "opening_phras2e_a.wav," comprises twenty-five events, some of which are themselves premixed from component files. These continue the development from the end of the previous submix toward more and more complex processing of the original source sound and toward the creation of longer, more sustained musical excursions. Figure 6.3, based on the composer's mix file for the phrase, distributes the sound files into different categories.

This chart is also presented in an interactive version in Presentation 14. And as for the first phrase, you are encouraged to use Presentation 4 to explore these files in their mixing context.

The mix begins with a series of variations on motif C from the first phrase (event 1 of this second phrase begins in very similar fashion to event 6 of phrase 1). Each of the first fourteen events of this section involves repeated iterations shaped by different variations in acceleration/deceleration and rising/falling pitch contour. In some cases, the iterations accelerate to the point where they merge into continuous timbres, and some transformations also incorporate significant timbral modifications. Some of the gestures are pseudo-palindromic, returning more or less to where they began, whereas others are clearly directional, moving toward a goal. Sometimes this goal is a gong-like sound with a long resonance. Three such gong sounds articulate the earlier parts of this phrase, and the gong returns once more during the dense "bird" passage that follows (see below). These gestures, all interrelated variations of one another, are juxtaposed, often overlapping, to create a lively dialogue.

The next development in this passage is toward bird-like sounds. In events 15–20, by slightly extending the duration of the iterations and adding pitch variation to them, a twittering effect is generated. At first simply a further decoration of the iterative motif, the twittering birds rapidly take charge of the musical texture. Event 18, a long gesture, almost one minute in duration, develops into a complex flocking of birds, which then transforms into a noisy texture, itself underpinned by a gong sound and a reverse resonance (events 21–22), before descending and dissolving into fragments which in turn transform back once more into more percussive sounds.

Out of this complex mix of mainly percussive sounds, a regular steady set of seven impulses emerges (event 24, itself a submix). This leads immediately to a return of the rising iterations (event 25), a gesture first heard in event 3 of the first phrase of the Opening. In fact, it is the version presented as event 10 of the first opening phrase that is here repeated literally, and indeed the same sound

Event	Gong	Iterative	Bird-like	Percussive
1	cadence_anticip_poss			
2		xxx_x		
3		zzz1		
4		rrr		
5		rrpup		
6		www		
7	cadmorph1long			
8		wmwshort		
9		uuu		
10		yyyshort		
11		startercextrup		
12	cadmorph2longa			
13		wmw		
14		wmwe		
15			tosqk	
16			bird1	
17			bird2up	
18			birdtex5_pre	
19			bdnu1_a	
20			bdnu0_a	
21	bba			
22	[cadchord-ext]			
23				clink_prephras
24				chimephras1_1b_up
25				wchime_phras_temp
Cadence		[cadential passage-based on rising iterative gesture]		

FIGURE 6.3

Structure of the second phrase of the opening of *Imago*.[57]

file is repeated again three more times articulating the passage that follows. Although this is by no means a precise recapitulation, there is a sense here of return to the initial source as the starting point for new developments.

The second occurrence of this rising gesture has a fluctuating reverberant tail added to it, which acts as the precursor for a "rolling" sound that then develops and intensifies in a series of clearly defined stages, each articulated by a strong attack. This is interrupted abruptly by a short cadence leading to the following section, comprising three more radical intensifications of the rolling texture, the third of which descends and dissolves into silence. However, as is often the case in this work, the end of one section does not necessarily mean a general pause: before the final texture of the Opening premix has faded, a new section is taking over from it and the music continues without break.

The Gamelan section

The Gamelan section appears toward the end of *Imago* and illustrates the more complex and continuous textures that often occur after the Opening. This section of the work (from 20′13″ to 21′47″) is dominated by the gamelan material. Although sonically more complex than the Opening, this section again comprises a mix of sound files, each representing the result of processes applied to the source sound. And again, the mix file from the composer's archive provides a useful starting point for examining the structure of the passage, as introduced with Figure 6.4, derived from the original mix file.

The section is in two parts, each underpinned, respectively, by the sound files "gamelda.wav" and "gameldv.wav." These files, like event 12 of the first opening phrase of the work, comprise fast successions of transposition of the slightly transformed original source sound, following algorithmically determined pitch sequences. A short silence at 20′58″ separates the two parts. In each large phrase, superposed over these two files, is a variety of other material that enriches and varies the texture.

The italics in Figure 6.4 highlights a repeating pattern of material between the two parts. The relative timings indicated in the figure between the start times of successive files shows that it is not just the order of events that is repeated, but often also their timing. In the second phrase, "longbel6a.wav" and "longbel6.wav" have been added over this pattern.

Indexes from values 1 to 32 indicate the order of appearance in the original mix file. Relative times show durations separating consecutive events in the groups represented in italics. Fonts (normal, italics, bold, bold italics) highlight groupings of files.

The indentation in Figure 6.4 aligns the file names with five paradigms of material, labelled A to E plus their derivatives, that can be defined as follows:

A: "gamel": this is the rapid gamelan material already discussed.
As indicated in the above paragraph on successive Sound Loom

A	B	B2	B3	C	D	D2	E	E2	Start (abs)	Start (rel)
Paradigms										
PHRASE 1										
1 GAMELDA									0.00	
	2 gam-2								0.48	
					13 chromwejaccel.wav				0.95	
	3 gam								2.48	
	4 gam-4								5.48	
		5 gamtex4							8.48	*0.0*
		6 gamtex3							17.48	*9.0*
						14 wejacclstakrise			20	*2.52*
			7 gam-2up2s_str						29.00	*9.0*
			8 gam-2up4s_str						31.381	*2.381*
						15 wejacclstakrise_b			31.4	*0.019*
		9 gamtex2							31.90	*0.5*
						16 wejacclstakrise_a			41.7	*9.8*
				10 descender5					42.2	*0.5*
11 gam-8e_str									44.45	
PHRASE 2										
12 GAMELDV									47.321	
							17 risernue3		48 2	
					24 chromwejaccel_cop				48.27	
		32 gamup_up9.wav							54.634	
		18 gamtex4_cop							55.7	*0.0*
								[30 longbel6a]	63	
		19 gamtex3_cop							64.8	*9.1*
						25 wejacclstakrise_cop			67.32	*2.52*
			20 gam-2up2s_str_cop						76.32	*9.0*
			21 gam-2up4s_str_cop						78.701	*2.381*
						26 wejacclstakrise_b_cop			78.72	*0.019*
		22 gamtex2_cop							79.22	*0.5*
								[31 longbel6]	87	
						27 wejacclstakrise_a_cop			89.02	*9.8*
				22 descender5_cop					89.52	*0.5*
			29 gamup						90.5	
28 gam-8e_str_cop									91.77	

FIGURE 6.4

Paradigmatic representation of the mix file for the Gamelan section.[58]

226

processes, it is constituted with different gamelan passages counterpointing each other in pitch and rhythm.

B: "gam": a metallic granular texture with a crescendo followed by a diminuendo. Different files vary in length but retain the same focal pitch class.

B2: "gamtex": closely related to B but without the crescendo, starting from a sudden attack followed by a granular decaying texture.

B3: "gam2up": similar in morphology to B but transposed up.

Taken together, B, B2, and B3 play an important role in articulating the section, standing out from the more frenetic material with their longer durations and attacks and resonances. They are reminiscent of and function similarly to the various gong-like sounds elsewhere in the work.

C: "descender5": a repeated sound falling in pitch.

D: "chromwejaccel": a very rapid repetition of the original source sound, widening in pitch range and increasing in speed with events merging into a texture toward the end. This is a close relative of the "chromwej_a.wav" sound found in the opening phrase.

D2: "wejacclstakrise": taking up where D finishes, a rapid granular texture.

E: "risernue": a texture growing out of an initial gong-like attack.

E2: "longbel": a massive texture following another gong-like attack.

> *Presentation 15 in the accompanying software includes an interactive version of the paradigmatic chart in Figure 6.4. And again, you can also use Presentation 4 to explore these files in their mixing context. Demonstration Video 6.8.* ▶

The combination of these different layers results in a rich and complex texture, bursting with manic energy. Nonetheless, there is a clear structure underlying the music both temporally and texturally. And, by default, because of the way that the whole work is derived from one source sound, all the material is related. This analysis also shows different groups of family relationships emerging within the transformed material, taking on different functions within the section. Although a more dense and continuous texture, this section is constructed according to the same basic principles as the opening of the work: the processing of the original source sound to create a range of sounds, followed by the combining of the resulting sound files to form larger-scale phrases and sections.

The large-scale structure of *Imago*

The overall form is complex and rich in detail, often with many different variants of the source sound overlapping. The division of the work into sections is at times, by the very nature of the work, ambiguous, with passages overlapping, elisions, and fluid transitions. What follows therefore is just one possible reading. Many of the metaphoric labels for different sonorities and gestures are those used by the composer as labels in his diffusion score and/or in labeling component sound files.[59]

1. Opening: Exposition (0′0″–1′04″).[60] As discussed in detail above, the Opening section of the work is in the form of an exposition, a presentation of the source sound, and some of the basic transformations of this sound. These form the basis for further transformations later in the work or reappear later in more or less the same form as points of reference in the musical structure.

This initial exposition is followed by a series of three more extended developments in which more complex transformational processes are applied and a wider range of timbres and textures result, deviating further from the original source sound.

2a. Development Phase 1 (1′04″–3′49″). The first of these developments begins with rapid repetitions of the source sound varying in pitch and leading to "spectral transforms" of the source. Resonant gong sounds punctuate these developments, which intensify into a dense noisy texture of birds before reducing to impulses. The texture fragments before the rising iteration gesture from section 1 reappears. It recurs punctuating a short development of "rolling ball" sounds, which is abruptly interrupted by what Wishart calls "alarm" sounds which terminate this development.

2b. Development Phase 2 (3′49″–5′41″). The next phase of development features iterative textures once again, along with sustained pitch clusters reminiscent of the "shō." Again, the texture intensifies punctuated by a series of glissandi (as if played on a piano or marimba). This development is interrupted by a short passage introducing two distinct textures that will later be of greater significance in the work. They are preceded and followed by an accelerating repeating gesture. The first of these textures is what Wishart refers to as the "funny gamelan" (5′23″–5′32″), a precursor of the longer Gamelan section analyzed above). This is followed by an even briefer introduction to another significant texture later in the work, the "machine" (5′32″–5′35″), with its incessant robotic pulses.

2c. Development Phase 3 (5′41″–7′15″). Following this interruption, the development of materials continues with a third phase featuring time-stretching techniques and, partly as a result of these, becomes increasingly reverberant. The sense of distance resulting from this reverberance together with a series of descending glissandi lend to this passage a sense of closure, signaling the end of this phase of the work.

3. Sparse 1 (7′15″–9′40″). The end of the development phases is followed by the first of four Sparse sections that punctuate the central portion of the work. Each comprises a series of attacks (four in this case) interrupting otherwise quiet, sparse textures. In the first and last of these sparse sections, the intervening textures comprise irregular attacks varying in duration and pitch. Wishart describes them as "wood." Their resonant quality might also recall pebbles being dropped into a pond, with the resulting ripples. After the fourth attack the pebbles cease and are replaced by short gestures, largely transformed versions of materials from the opening section. Although initially still sparse, these begin to build the momentum to lead out of this section into something more dynamic.

4. Machine 1 (9′40″–10′20″). What follows is a more extended version of the manic machine texture (5′32″–5′35″). The density, intense energy, and accelerating pace of this material contrast dramatically with the preceding section. As it accelerates and threatens to spiral out of control it is cut off by another brief occurrence of the gamelan texture.

5. Sparse 2 (10′20″–11′32″). The gamelan material leads into the second of the Sparse sections. The sharp attack/resonances are in this case interspersed with more active material, including "warbling" sounds and "insect-like" material. These gradually become more active leading to the development of the next section.

6. Storm (11′32″–14′15″). This section gradually builds with variants of the various core motifs of the work, often in a form that is quite noise-based, produced using time-contraction, over a simmering underlying texture.[61] The composer refers to this as "the sea" and it is as if a storm is brewing, and a sequence of large crescendos/diminuendos, at first increasing in intensity before fading, create a powerful trajectory perhaps reminiscent of the thunder storm in the composer's *Vox 5*.

In Presentation 16, "Discussions around excerpts of Imago," Wishart presents the sea material in more detail, as shown in Demonstration Video 6.9. ▶

7. Sparse 3 (14′15″–15′51″). As the storm subsides another Sparse section begins. This version combines the warbling textures of Sparse 2 with the pebbles of Sparse 1, but without the prominent attack/resonances of the other Sparse sections. As the section proceeds motifs from elsewhere in the work, including the Gamelan section and from the Opening, begin to emerge.

8. Machine 2 (15′51″–16′27″). These lead eventually to a return of the "Manic machine" texture. Its incessant energy and drive persist until cut off by a resonant attack.

9. Sparse 4 (16′27″–17′40″). The gong attack triggers the final Sparse section. This is almost identical to the first of these sections, with the pebbles in the intervening passages between loud attack/resonances.

10. Explosions (17′40″–20′13″). In the following section attacks also feature, but triggering more frenetic outbursts of activity, a variation of the manic machine material. This energy leads to the first of two deep resonant gongs. The resonance from these gongs underpins the rest of the section, over which other textures build and then dissolve. These use time-varying filters to create voice-like sounds referred to as the "oracle" by Wishart (2012, p. 110). Eventually, a recurrence of the rising gesture from section 1 triggers the start of an upward glissando in the gong resonance, disappearing as it does so.

11. Gamelan (20′13″–21′47″). After a brief pause, the most extended version of the gamelan materials begins. This was examined in detail above. It is a sustained rhythmic passage in two parts, which then ends abruptly.

12. Machine 3 (21′47″–23′30″). Three variations of the rising motif lead into a section in which the manic machine materials reappears but in a fragmented and disrupted form. Repeated attempts to kick-start the machine fail, and the "machine dies"[62] and the texture dissolves.

13. Coda (23′30″–25′40″). The coda begins with motifs from the Opening. A gong sound triggers a resonance, which together with other materials from the work, including the voice-like "oracle," creates a texture that spins and shudders, eventually glissandoing upward, slowing as it does so and disappearing out of hearing.

You can use Presentation 17 in the accompanying software to access an interactive paradigmatic chart representing the sections described above, as shown in Demonstration Video 6.10. ⊙

Conclusions

From the above analysis of passages from *Imago* and the examination of Wishart's working methods and use of technology, it will be clear that this composer's approach to composing with technology is significantly different from some of the other composers we have considered. Wishart's Sound Loom software is not designed to operate in real time, and he does not therefore perform the sounds as they are being generated. Nor is Sound Loom designed to operate as a single unified process generating results to be used in the composition in a single pass. Rather, individual operations are performed and auditioned before subsequent processing is applied.

Building blocks for the eventual composition are often developed in stages and assembled, sometimes through several stage of mixing, once the initial stages of sound design have been completed. Algorithms are sometimes used to generate materials (e.g., in the Gamelan section), but these passages are component parts of larger textures, and algorithms do not shape the overall structure of the music. More like the working approach of Francis Dhomont, Wishart develops individual sounds or textures, carefully crafting each one in turn, before assembling them into the finished work. However, like Chowning and Truax, there is an intense unity to the approach, one that comes in this case not from using a single synthesis or processing method but from using a single source sound. In extending this single source into a substantial work, Wishart's approach, as demonstrated most clearly in the opening section of the work, shows similarities with classical motivic development. But here the motivic workings extend beyond melodic and rhythmic patterns to the complex timbral transformations and textures afforded by the processing software.

Nonetheless, the recurrence of motifs, be they brief sounds or phrases or complex textural passages, plays an essential role in the formal structure of this music. This is not music of large-scale processes slowly evolving, but instead about musical characters emerging, interacting, developing, and recurring.

Of particular significance, both from a historical and a present-day perspective, is the groundbreaking potential of Wishart's system for composers working with computer music resources now readily available to individuals composing within an environment that is entirely self-contained in the context of home computing. Whereas today such facilities can be regarded as far from exceptional, the circumstances associated with the development of systems such as Sound Loom deserve close study and further consideration. The proliferation of commercial resources for composing computer music in recent years is both encouraging and also challenging for those who wish to select and profitably engage with their creative possibilities. The above detailed study of a particularly significant pioneering system provides important insights into the techniques that may be explored in determining the true potential of such resources as the basis for composing new works for the ever-expanding repertory.

Jonathan Harvey
Fourth String Quartet

233

Contexts for the *Fourth String Quartet*

First steps exploring the possibilities of electronic and computer music

Jonathan Harvey's musical repertory embraces compositions that are scored for conventional acoustic resources, as well as fixed media works realized entirely by electronic means. In between these two polarities he has composed a number of works that combine acoustic and electronic resources, including the *Fourth String Quartet* that is the central focus of this chapter. He occupies a position as one of the most notable modern British composers, his untimely death in 2012 bringing to an end a distinguished career that has materially enhanced our understanding of the possibilities of computer technology in terms of music composition and performance. Harvey, like Philippe Manoury, has been closely associated with developments at IRCAM, and the earlier discussion of *Pluton* in Chapter 3 provides useful background for the current study.[1] However, there are a number of features concerning Harvey's engagement with these advanced resources that require detailed consideration in their own right.

In studying the characteristics of Harvey's use of electronics in music, it is useful to start with the formative stages of his musical training. As a chorister at St Michael's College, Tenbury Wells, UK, during the late 1940s, he became directly immersed in the English choral genre of church music, gaining an early fascination with the functions of both texture and harmony in this deeply expressive medium. Undergraduate studies in music at St. John's College,

Cambridge, followed by postgraduate study at the University of Glasgow, led to a PhD in music, completed in 1964. Although this was an entirely text-based critique, his engagement with the concepts that underpin a composer's creative inspiration established important aesthetic foundations for his subsequent career as a composer, already being strongly cultivated through private lessons with Erwin Stein and Hans Keller.[2] In the same year he was appointed lecturer in music at the University of Southampton, a post held until 1977, when he was appointed professor of music at the University of Sussex.

Harvey had become acquainted with the music of Karlheinz Stockhausen during his studies at Glasgow, bringing him into contact with the pioneering electronic works of this German composer, including *Gesang der Jünglinge* (1955–1956) and *Kontakte* (1959–1960).[3] His interest in Stockhausen's aesthetics and techniques of acoustic and electronic composition stimulated his own interests in the creative possibilities of the electronic medium during the 1960s.[4] Although no suitable resources were yet available to him in an institutional context, he was able, via personal contacts, to gain access to some simple electronic devices for group experimentation:

> There were some of us who were very keen on improvisation and even in those days in the sixties we were using electronics—in the late sixties anyway and early seventies—and I remember we would improvise for two whole days; except for the break for a night's sleep. Such changing of consciousness was very powerful.[5]

Harvey first came into direct contact with computer music following the award of a Harkness fellowship for study at Princeton University in 1969–1970. As noted in Chapter 1, the 1960s was an important formative era for the development of Music N synthesis programs, not only at Bell Labs and Stanford but also Princeton, starting with the installation of Music IV on an IBM 7094 computer in 1963. By the end of the decade the revised Princeton version of this program, Music IVBF, had greatly improved the intelligibility of the software to prospective composers, and Harvey took a keen interest in exploring its creative possibilities. His desire for a fellowship to study at Princeton had been motivated by the opportunity to study serial techniques of music composition with leading members of the music faculty, notably Milton Babbitt, and this extension of his studies beyond the domain of purely instrumental techniques to embrace computer-based techniques of sound synthesis was a fortuitous development.

Although he completed a short computer-generated study, *Time-Points* (1970), during his residency, the scope and nature of the musical and practical challenges he encountered were significant, and he subsequently withdrew the work. Central to his initial concerns was the nature of the creative relationships that could be productively forged between materials of a purely acoustic nature and those that are generated synthetically. His early deliberations on these key considerations were to prove crucial for his subsequent resolution of these challenges, which were for him of an intensely aesthetic nature. His journey in this regard was predicated on exploring the potential of mediation between these perceptual polarities, proceeding in one direction from the natural to the synthetic by means of incremental signal processing, and in the other direction by means of synthesis techniques that progressively embrace the characteristics of acoustic sounds.[6] Although these early conjectures were subsequently to be materially expanded and refined, the underlying principles were to remain essentially the same.

A more positive engagement with the medium, establishing the foundations for further exploration of these emerging principles, was to result from a visit by Harvey to the Elektronmusikstudion (EMS), Stockholm, in 1972 as a participant in an international workshop studying the creative possibilities of the recently installed EMS computer music system, the hardware synthesis facilities consisting of a custom-designed bank of audio oscillators and signal processors, controlled in turn by a PDP-15 computer.[7]

The issue uppermost in Harvey's mind at the time was the ways in which serially based compositional principles could be mapped to the complexities of sound synthesis, most especially in the context of manipulating timbre.[8] The hardware synthesis facilities at Stockholm were linked to a physical console interface that displayed the corresponding control settings via a series of on/off binary lights. These settings could be manipulated directly using a metal brush to change the binary parameter values via surface-mounted split metal contacts, and sequences of events programmed step by step using an associated digital control tape. Although the latter facility allowed the resulting sounds to be auditioned directly and was useful for the initial exploration of ideas, it proved altogether too time-consuming for use as a composition tool, hence the development of EMS 1 as a software-based facility for programming the system via the PDP-15.[9] Despite the continuing requirement to work in an essentially non-real-time environment, reminiscent of the conditions associated with Music IVBF, Harvey's generally positive experiences working with the Stockholm system convinced him that the computer held the ultimate key to investigating his emerging compositional ideas in this context.

There were, nonetheless, some significant practical hurdles to be overcome before his intentions could be fully realized. During the 1970s the opportunities for composers to engage with electronic and computer music were still relatively limited, no more so than in the United Kingdom. Although the British Broadcasting Corporation (BBC) established a radiophonic workshop in 1958, providing technical facilities comparable to those provided by leading European studios, access to the workshop was all but denied to the wider composing community, except in the case of a handful of BBC commissions. The initiative in the UK thus passed to university-based studios, starting in the late 1960s with the establishment of an electronic music studio at Goldsmiths College, London, followed by studios at the Universities of York, Durham, and Cardiff.[10] During the 1970s further university studios were established within the UK, but the lack of a major national initiative was a material constraint.

One notable exception to this situation was the MUSYS system developed during the late 1960s by Peter Zinovieff in his private London studio, consisting of two small PDP-8 computers controlling an array of custom-designed synthesis devices in a manner not dissimilar to that developed for the Stockholm studio. This venture led to the establishment of EMS (London), a commercial manufacturing company producing a range of voltage-controlled synthesizers, starting with the VCS 3 in 1969. Jonathan Harvey attended an inaugural course on MUSYS in 1970, but for reasons that are not entirely clear he did not pursue the opportunities for further work opened up by this UK Arts Council–funded initiative. The lack of suitable studio resources at the University of Southampton was thus to prove a major drawback for Harvey's further work with the electronic medium at this time.

Fortunately, a solution emerged from discussions with Keith Winter, a co-participant, during the 1972 EMS workshop. Winter was responsible for establishing the electronic studio at Cardiff in 1970, using a grant secured from the Leverhulme Foundation. Unlike other pioneering university studios in the UK, the Cardiff studio was situated in the Department of Physics, rather than the Department of Music, and such an environment facilitated ready access to supporting technical resources. Moreover, Winter had advanced skills both as an electronic engineer and a musician, and was thus well placed to stimulate research and development in areas directly relevant to Harvey's aspirations. The early synthesis and signal processing facilities at Cardiff were entirely analog, but Winter and his associates were keen to develop computer-based control facilities at the earliest opportunity.[11] Establishing a direct connection between the studio and the university mainframe computer was considered but ultimately rejected on practical grounds. Instead, attention turned to the possibility of developing a custom-designed control system based on the emerging possibilities of microprocessors. Although it was to take a number of years before the outcomes of these pioneering investigations fully materialized, viable digital control facilities were established by the mid-1970s, and by the end of the decade this unique hybrid synthesis system was starting to achieve its true potential.

The key resource for the synthesis component of this system consisted of a Synthi 100, the commercial flagship voltage-controlled synthesizer designed by David Cockerell for EMS (London) in 1971. Although originally supplied with just a simple digital sequencer, Zinovieff's intention was to develop a fully programmable computer control interface for the synthesizer. This project, however, was never completed.[12] The decision by Cardiff to develop its own computer-based control system was thus to prove especially significant, and although Harvey was not able to enjoy the full benefits of the results before moving on to work at IRCAM, his direct engagement with these important technical advances during the formative years was to prove invaluable for his future exploration of the possibilities of computer music.

The Cardiff control system was based on a Texas Instruments 990/4 microcomputer using a TMS 9900 processor and an associated custom-designed hardware interface for the Synthi 100, allowing sounds to be generated in real time by the latter using a maximum of four independently controlled voices.[13] Although not finally completed until 1980, the primary control program Sequemuse was specifically designed to allow composers to use composing algorithms to generate event sequences, and in this context offered many features in common with those provided by EMS 1 at Stockholm.[14] Although the memory of the computer was small, just 12K of sixteen-bit words, and the control data storage facilities were limited to a pair of digital tape cassettes, the versatility of the hardware control interface and the associated software materially compensated for these drawbacks. A notable feature of the programming environment was the ability to adopt a "top-down" hierarchical approach to the specification and manipulation of sound events, in this context reflecting the similar approach taken in the design of Truax's early POD programs, developed at the Institute of Sonology in Utrecht during the early 1970s.[15]

Harvey's association with the Cardiff studio led to the composition of a trilogy of works involving the use of electronics with live instruments: *Inner Light 1* (1973), *Inner Light 2* (1977), and *Inner Light 3* (1975). Although the former element was limited primarily to prerecorded tape tracks, these initial encounters with the possibilities of combining acoustic and electronic components in such a context were to prove significant for his subsequent engagement with the creative possibilities of computer music, using more sophisticated technical resources.[16] As noted in the preface to the score, the tape part for *Inner Light 1* was realized at the studios of Swedish Radio and University College Cardiff, the former association reflecting the fruits of his work during the 1972 EMS conference. The choice of orchestral instruments, seven in total, provide a rich and varied palette of acoustic sounds, ranging from piccolo and bass clarinet to string trio, piano (organ), and percussion. Pamela Alcorn's critique on Harvey's electronic music prior to 1992 in her PhD thesis provides a revealing perspective on this initial journey toward an expanded compositional aesthetic:

> *Inner Light (1)*, (1973), for seven instruments and tape, sets up a continuum between instrumental timbre and structural harmony. The harmonic "spaces" of the work are created in approximation to the analyzed spectra of the instruments in the group. The basic twelve-note row . . . is established in the first section of the work: noise sounds gradually change into simulated cello sounds in the tape part on low C, the real cello's first note . . . and all eleven remaining pitches are subsequently introduced in this way, the tape always giving the cue for the real instrument to enter on its associated note. . . . The upper partials of each simulated sound

on the tape are then increased in volume until they are heard as a chord: it is this chord which is used as a harmonic framework for the music which follows. . . . Thus, timbre "flowers" into harmony, and the harmonic "spaces" from which new sets are drawn. Each note of the row is further linked to a rhythmic figure, so that the instruments finally become characterized on four related levels: timbre, harmony, derived pitch material and rhythm. Instrumental timbre is used as an integrating medium through which the interrelationships of different musical parameters can be explored.[17]

Alcorn's perspective demonstrates the centrality of the analysis of the timbres of the instruments in the ensemble to the compositional process, in turn providing the basis for the development of the different harmonic fields that provide a key characteristic of the musical argument. In this instance the tape components were composed using a simple stereo playback format. However, as will be seen in due course, more sophisticated spatial techniques were to become a primary preoccupation for Harvey, not least in terms of the potential of multiple speaker configurations, and an important first step was taken in this context in the composition of *Inner Light 3*, a piece for large orchestra and quadraphonic tape commissioned by the BBC, completed in 1975 and first performed in March 1976 by the BBC Symphony Orchestra.

The tape tracks in this case were composed entirely in the Cardiff studio, the rare availability of suitable if not potentially more sophisticated resources at the BBC Radiophonic Workshop notwithstanding. It is clear from the program note written by Harvey for the work that the primary consideration in compositional terms was the use of the tape component to facilitate transformations between one instrumental timbre and another, taking advantage of the possibilities of four-channel surround sound:

The piece constantly strives to expand [the] tempo, enticed on by the tape. One of the tape's other roles is to transform one instrument's waveform into another's, often in the course of a journey round the concert hall. For instance, a trumpet sound leaves the orchestra, changes progressively into a clarinet in mid-flight, so to speak, and returns to the stage area where the orchestral clarinet takes it up. The spatial engulfment of quadraphony and the dreamlike reverberation of orchestral events are, together with the alpha wave treatment, further aspects of the "superhuman" role of the tape. There is nothing new in regarding the mechanical as superhuman; everyone in Western tradition who has ever thought of the organ as a bearer of sacred meaning, or in the East of the gong in such a light has done the same.[18]

Inner Light 2, completed in 1977, is essentially an intermediate work in terms of scope and proportions, using a chamber orchestra plus voices with a three-track tape part, again created in the Cardiff studio. The interest here in exploring the possibilities of manipulating vocal formants added a further dimension to Harvey's experience with electronic signal processing, in this case providing a means of mediation between instrumental and vocal sounds.

The IRCAM dimension

By the end of the decade Harvey's growing international reputation as an instrumental composer with particular interests in the possibilities of electronic music had attracted the attention of Pierre Boulez, leading to the award of an IRCAM commission for the realization of a new work. Not only was this development extremely timely from a personal point of view, it was to result in the composition of a work of material significance, regarded by many as one of the key landmark works in the emerging repertory: *Mortuos Plango, Vivos Voco* (1980). This piece, composed with technical assistance from Stanley Haynes, is a fixed media work lasting approximately nine minutes. Furthermore, it is the first of Harvey's works to be produced entirely in a digital domain.

A particular constraint for Harvey in terms of both this and subsequent works realized at IRCAM was the time available to work with the advanced resources thus placed at his disposal, even in the context of a funded commission. The contrast here with the working conditions for a composer such as Truax, using resources he had personally developed at Simon Fraser University, is thus of some significance. Although the increasing accessibility of such technologies in the current century has materially overcome such barriers to creativity, it is still the case that sophisticated techniques such as multichannel audio spatialization require access to facilities that are not readily available in a domestic environment. The practical challenges thus to be faced by Harvey in this context, even with the invaluable technical support provided by Haynes, were significant. However, his former experiences with computer-based systems at Stanford, Stockholm, and Cardiff, coupled with his highly structured approach to musical composition in both acoustic and electroacoustic domains, provided useful preparation for what lay ahead. His initial account of these experiences, published shortly after the completion of the work, provides a useful insight into the scope and nature of his clearly focused objectives, as the following extracts from a personal article succinctly demonstrate:

> *Mortuos Plango, Vivos Voco* for eight-track tape was commissioned by the Centre George Pompidou in Paris and was realized at the Institut de Recherche et Coordination Acoustique/Musique (IRCAM) with technical assistance from Stanley Haynes. It is a very personal piece in that the two sound sources are the voice of my son and that of the great tenor bell at Winchester Cathedral, England. I have written much music for the choir there, in which my son was a treble chorister, and have often listened to the choir practicing against a background of the distant tolling of this enormous black bell. The text for the voice is the text written on the bell: Horas Avolantes Numero, Mortuos Plango: Vivos ad Preces Voco (I count the fleeing hours,

239

I lament the dead: the living I call to prayer). In the piece the dead voice of the bell is contrasted against the living voice of the boy.[19]

Harvey continues with the following more detailed description of the processes used:

Analysis of the Bell

The spectrum of the bell was analyzed with the fast Fourier transform (FFT) program at IRCAM, part of the interactive sound analysis package imported from Stanford University. The analysis commenced 1/2 sec after the initiation of the sound. The spectrum is shown in musical notation [see Figure 7.1].

FIGURE 7.1

Bell Spectrum, as presented in Harvey's article.[20]

This typical moment, when the spectrum was at its fullest, forms the structural basis of *Mortuos Plango, Vivos Voco*. I added to the analyzed spectrum one of the most, to me, supernatural attributes of this extraordinary sound, a clearly audible, slow-decaying partial at 347 Hz with a beating component in it. It is a resultant of the various F harmonic series partials that can be clearly seen in the spectrum (5, [6], 7, 9, 11, 13, 17, etc.) beside the C-related partials. Such "unanalyzable" secondary strike notes are quite common in bells.

The synthesis and mixing work was done with the IRCAM version of Music V (Mathews 1969). . . . I first synthesized the bell spectrum shown in Fig. 1. Then, using Music V (IRCAM) I could give the partials any envelope I chose, for instance I could turn the bell inside out by making the low partials, which normally decay slowly, decay quickly. The normally fast-decaying high partials could be made to decay slowly or even reach crescendo over varying durations. Modulations from one bell transposition to another were achieved by sine-tone glissandi. . . . Thus subsidiary "bell-tonics" are set up in hierarchies analogous to (but distinct from) the traditional western tonal system. . . . The straight digitized recording of the Winchester bell in various transpositions was read by the computer in different ways.

The sound file reading modules in the IRCAM version of Music V are able to read files forward or backward, with the option of continuously varying the speed. Often a rapidly oscillating forward/backward reading was made that gave a decre-scendo/crescendo of high partials as the attack was left or approached. Rhythmic patterns of great subtlety were easy to devise, sometimes in interplay with pro-grammed spatial movement. Elsewhere the partials of the bell, or selections from them, were individually distributed around the eight speakers, giving the listener the curious sensation of being inside the bell.

Recordings were made of the boy (1) chanting the Latin text on one partial-note, (2) singing all the phonemes of the text separately, and (3) singing a short melody based entirely on the spectrum pitches. I was able also to simulate these sounds using the singing synthesis program Chant developed by Gerald Bennett and Xavier Rodet, though getting the degree of random fluctuation and rudimentary vibrato right for the pure treble voice was a problem at first.[21] I often disguised the beginning of the synthetic transformations with a "real" voice fragment. In another technique, recordings of vowels sung by the boy were digitized. The digitized files were then read by the sound-input modules, looped, and given pitch and amplitude contours analogous to those applied to the sinusoidal components in the synthetic bell spectra.

The boy's synthetic voice sang on the bell partials instead of sine tones, and modulations as described previously were effected. Bell-like envelopes were given to some of these "bell sounds composed of boy's voice." Transformations were also applied to the spectra of the boy's vowels, which could be made into pitch and amplitude glissandi to the nearest bell equivalents in a bell spectrum. Such a file could again be read backward and forward, giving rapid oscillations of "boyness" with "bellness" in varied rhythms.[22]

His references to Music V and Chant reflect the state of computer developments at IRCAM during the early years up to 1980. Both of these programs were non–real time, requiring the synthesis instructions and associated data to be specified in advance before submitting these tasks to the PDP-10 mainframe computer. His reasons for choosing these resources rather than exploring the new generation of real-time resources being developed at IRCAM such as the 4X synthesizer are illuminating as to his thinking at this time:

Other systems available there are the Yamaha frequency modulation synthesis system and the 4X real-time digital signal processor. Both of these are well designed to suit a composer's needs: they will produce ready-formed sounds without the composer having to think precisely about every detail, and the intuitive element which a performer brings to his music can be directly applied by the composer. . . . By comparison, the programs which I used require the composer to be precise about every aspect of the sound, to fix exact quantities for every parameter. Because of this using them is a very slow process and doubtless future production at IRCAM will concentrate on the Yamaha and 4X systems; but IRCAM is an institute for research and . . . the slower and perhaps more demanding systems enhance our understanding in very profound ways. This has not always been fully recognized and needs emphasizing.[23]

This overriding concern with method and precision was to be sustained in the composition of all Harvey's subsequent works involving the use of computer techniques, including, as will be seen in due course, the *Fourth String Quartet*. His views on the superior merits of a non-real-time working environment in this context, however, were soon to be modified, as with steady advances in the power and sophistication of computer-based resources for synthesis and signal processing, it was to become clear to him that a productive continuum could be established between the sophistication and intricacy of composing algorithms and their realization in a real-time environment.

The steady evolution of his concepts of timbral composition now became integrated with the possibilities of spatialization first explored in the earlier *Inner Light* pieces. Whereas listeners have usually been limited to stereo-only copies of *Mortuos Plango, Vivos Voco*, those fortunate to have heard the original eight-channel version or the intermediate four-channel version developed for concert hall performances will be aware of the scope and extent of his engagement with the possibilities thus afforded. In this case the technique first used in *Inner Light* 3, whereby the transformations of sounds take place in auditory space well away from the associated acoustic instruments, is subtly and powerfully extended. The polarities are the naturalness and immediacy of the sounds of the boy's voice, contrasting with the deep mystery of the resonances of the bell, the processes of mediation and transformation providing the kernel of the underlying musical argument.[24]

Two years after completing this work, Harvey returned to IRCAM to complete a second commission, *Bhakti* (1982). This work, for fifteen instruments and four-channel tape, builds on ideas emerging from earlier pieces in terms of blending acoustic and synthetic materials, in particular the continuum that can be created by mediating between the melodic characteristics of instrumental sounds and the subtleties of the underlying spectral components that collectively determine their nature. Here this continuum is extended to combine materials that originate from different instruments to create events that morph between two sources in terms of their attack and resonance characteristics, such as harp and piano, or tubular bell and vibraphone. Different spectral components are manipulated to create new, dynamically changing timbres, and it is in this context that use is made occasionally of entirely synthetic spectra. For the most part, however, the source materials are derived from studio-based acoustic recordings.

Harvey's direct access to IRCAM resources in this instance was limited to a period of just two months, and even with technical support from three assistants, Denis Lorrain, Stanley Haynes, and Jean-Baptiste Barrière, his musical objectives had thus to be especially constrained in scope and extent. However, in limiting the use of computer processing to techniques that concentrated on strongly focused but subtle transformations of his sources, he was able to produce an expanded sound world that strongly encourages the listener to focus on the inner detail of the resulting aural perspective:

Because a tape playing back and instruments playing live are so fundamentally different from an aesthetic, social and spiritual point of view, this difference should be contradicted by having the two as similar as possible in terms of sound and structure: the *same* sounds and structures from an *opposing* aesthetic, social and spiritual sphere. . . . For the composer, some of the best moments *of Bhakti* are when the instruments double the tape, playing almost exactly the same sounds.[25]

The subtlety of the transformations thus achieved was in turn significantly dependent on the quality of the source recordings. Each of the instruments was recorded separately, concentrating in the first instance on single notes lasting up to ten seconds or more in duration. In the final mixing process, developing further a technique used in *Mortuos Plango, Vivos Voco*,

[sounds] were recorded on 16 track tape, sometimes modified with analog devices (filters, reverberator, etc.), together with additional sounds produced directly by analog means (modifications or expansions of some Music V results, or sounds taken or expanded from other instrumental sources), and ultimately mixed down "by hand" into the final quadraphonic result. This unconstrained and heterogeneous approach proved to be efficient, and made possible the completion of the tape in the allotted time: the simplest and most immediate means were always used to achieve specific musical goals.[26]

This account is especially interesting insofar it specifically cites the use of analog as well as digital signal processing techniques, again a practical expedient to overcome the significant time overheads of relying exclusively on Music V–based signal processing. It also hints strongly at a change in perspective to allow for a more immediate engagement with the possibilities of digital signal processing and thus the potential of live interaction between acoustic and synthetic resources. The live dimension will be studied further in the subsequent discussion of the *Fourth String Quartet*.[27]

His next work to embrace acoustic and synthetic materials, *Nachtlied* (1984), for solo voice and piano, uses a prerecorded tape part. In this instance the electronic materials were generated using a Fairlight CMI digital synthesizer, the processed sound material being subsequently edited and mixed in a conventional recording studio. Pamela Alcorn notes:

"Nachtlied" is one of the best examples of Harvey's instrumental approach to the use of tape. By far the largest part of the material used in preparing the tape involves piano or vocal simulation, with clearly defined melodic lines and polyphonic writing in places. . . . Very rarely does the range of pitches in the tape part extend beyond the natural compass of the piano or voice, and the timbral or technical extensions which do take place serve to integrate the two sound worlds of voice and piano rather than adding a new dimension to each individually.[28]

243

In the absence of bespoke resources such as those available at IRCAM, it is understandable why Harvey should engage with the possibilities of commercial synthesizers. The Fairlight, along with its rival the Synclavier, heralded a major design revolution that was materially to transform the development of computer music from the late 1970s onward.[29] Whereas the Synclavier was based on a bank of synthetic timbre generators, the Fairlight sampled acoustically generated sounds, hence its particular interest to Harvey. Both synthesizers, however, were very expensive, and sales were thus limited for the most part to successful popular musicians and a handful of commercial studios. Fortunately, the BBC Radiophonic Workshop acquired a Fairlight I in 1980, and Harvey was able to negotiate sufficient access to generate a useful repertory of source materials for *Nachtlied*, based on sampled instrumental sounds. However, the quality of processed sounds produced by the early Fairlight left much to be desired, and in the context of Harvey's environment of carefully crafted timbres the resulting deficiencies in quality are at times all too evident.[30]

The year 1984 also saw his first material engagement with the use of live electronics in combination with acoustic instruments, with the composition of *Gong Ring* for chamber ensemble and electronics and *Ricercare una Melodia* for trumpet and electronics, the latter subsequently adapted for a number of different solo instruments. In the case of *Gong Ring* the live processing requires a single ring modulator, whereas the original specification for the *Ricercare* relied on a tape delay system. These early experiences prepared the ground for his next major work, *Madonna of Winter and Spring*, composed in 1986. This large work for orchestra and live electronics was commissioned by the BBC for the 1986 Henry Wood Promenade Concerts, London. Although there was no formal connection with IRCAM in the production of this work, the award of a third IRCAM commission in 1985 for *Ritual Melodies* and the start of some preparatory investigations for this with his assigned assistant, Jan Vandenheede, provided a useful gateway to technical advice on how to select and configure the resources he required for the live electronics component in *Madonna*.

A key decision here was to rely primarily on commercial devices that could be readily hired for the purpose. The generosity of two suppliers, Syco Systems and Yamaha-Kemble, made it possible for Harvey to install much of the associated equipment on loan in his own house, and thus spend significant time exploring its functional characteristics *in situ*. Further help was forthcoming from the BBC Radiophonic Workshop in terms of creating sophisticated reverberation effects to enhance the spatial characteristics of the sound materials when subsequently diffused in the concert hall. The technical requirements are as follows:

- Yamaha DX1 FM synthesizer with TX816 voice bank extension;
- E-mu Emulator II sampling synthesizer;

- Ring modulator and associated microphones to process piano, harp, and vibraphone sounds;
- Individual microphones specifically to capture and amplify sounds from the cor anglais, clarinet (1), horn (1), and trumpet (1);
- A diffusion system consisting of a sound mixer for the above, linked to two quadraphonic loudspeaker systems, one mounted high in the auditorium, the other mounted low.

Both the keyboard synthesizers were equipped with foot pedals and operated by a single performer. Although the Emulator relied on eight-bit samples and used a relatively low sampling rate of 27 kHz, the special coding algorithm it employed facilitated a much higher quality of sound than that produced by the Fairlight. Moreover, the significantly expanded maximum sample length of 17.6 seconds allowed Harvey to craft extensive soundscapes of processed sound. The individual sound sources and the associated synthesizer voice settings are stored on three Emulator II disks, augmented by a custom-designed bank of FM sounds for the DX1 synthesizer, similarly stored on a plug-in Yamaha cartridge. The configuration and operation of the sound diffusion system is also of significance in terms of his emerging ideas of sound spatialization, not only to achieve clarity and purpose in the context of mediation between acoustic and synthetic materials, but also musical concepts specific to this expanded environment.

A clear sense of his direction of travel at this time in terms of combining instrumental and live electronic resources can be gained from his following observations on the composition processes explored in *Madonna*, published in 1986:

Music has two dimensions. One is its perceived physical sensuous quality, which we usually perceive as a well-known source, e.g. violins, muted trumpet, etc. The other is its constructed quality wherein we string together our percepts in the mind and make shapes, melodies, forms. It has often been my aim to make their borderlines ambiguous, for instance by having acoustic structure perceived as form itself rather than as articulating form. One reason for diffusing sound is that it's a step in the direction of making more ambiguous the physical source of the sound. It no longer issues from player X with the grey hair and moustache or player Y with red hair and glasses. It becomes disguised, as in theatre, it moves about the ceiling, it inhabits the cornices and arches. One is "peopling" a building with imaginary musical beings, invisible spirits: one might imagine them as Tiepolo did in his ceiling and mural paintings or one might allow the music alone to engender them. And when the sounds are sufficiently transformed or purely electronic, the removal from the easy, unambiguous picture of instrument and player is complete, and we are encouraged as listeners to be more attentive to the actual role of physical percept and its interface with structured form. Everything is called into question.[31]

245

Another article, written thirteen years later, provides a further perspective on this important trajectory:

> *Madonna of Winter and Spring* (1986) is for full orchestra with three synthesizers, ring modulation, amplification of certain instruments, octophonic live panning and reverberation which selects certain moments and freezes them while the orchestra continues. The reverberation, for instance, clearly takes in an instrumental datum and extends it in time in a way which is contradictory of the orchestral world, yet at one with it in that there is no point at which reverb and orchestra could be prized apart. Time is arrested, physically unplayable sound is heard (another world). Near the end the conductor is requested to lose all sense of time, the timeless world takes over, and the passage can last a very long "time." Electronics heal the suffering/rejoking instruments with their detachment and expansiveness. They contain within themselves the traces of passion yet forgive the crime. In my piece the weariness of "Winter" is deepened to lifeless melancholia and death, the energy of "Spring" is brightened to the radiance of spiritual ethereality. The dangerous extremes can be redemptively lived through in a transferred form.[32]

The next work for acoustic and electronic resources, *From Silence*, was composed in 1988. This cantata, based on four mystical texts, was composed at MIT during a year's residency and is scored for soprano, chamber ensemble, tape, and live electronics. The tape part is limited to short introductions to each of the four main sections of the work, the first being especially significant to the overall aesthetic. Harvey observes:

> It starts from silence, with tape. For a long time, the sound is almost indistinguishable from silence (or hall ambience). . . . The sense of inaudible, invisible presence within this "zero-sound" is carried over into the live electronics; they bridge the span from this on the one side into quasi-instrumental physicality at the other extreme, connecting invisible presence with physical presence.[33]

The live electronics are generated using the following devices:

- Yamaha DX1 FM keyboard synthesizer with TX816 voice bank extension
- Akai S900 sampler
- Yamaha KX88 keyboard for the above
- Yamaha SPX90 effects unit (x2)
- Apple Macintosh computer

Harvey's exploration of the possibilities of live electronics at this time took place in parallel with his research at IRCAM in preparation for his third commission, *Ritual Melodies*, completed in 1990. In many respects the composing environment for this quadraphonic work could not have been more different. Quite apart from the fundamental distinction that it was, like *Mortuos Plango, Vivos Voco*, an entirely studio-based work, the scope and nature of the synthesis techniques employed required the extensive use of non-real-time computation, with delays once again extending to several hours if not occasionally overnight.

Harvey was to benefit greatly from the continuing technical assistance provided by Vandenheede. The forensic scale and depth of the processing techniques underpinning Harvey's investigations required sophisticated resources, leading to the use of Formes. Developed by Xavier Rodet and Pierre Cointe, this program provided an advanced facility for the composition and scheduling of processes in an object-oriented environment using the programming language Lisp.[34] Formes was inspired by the programming challenges faced in using Chant as an advanced synthesis tool, extending beyond its original purpose as a vocal synthesis facility to embrace a much larger repertory of musical sounds, including those with instrumental characteristics.[35] In 1985 IRCAM initiated a research program using these resources to model the characteristics of both Western and non-Western instrumental sounds, the associated processes of analysis and resynthesis opening up the possibilities of creating hybrid virtual instruments. The VAX 780 computer was used to host the Formes preprocessing computations, linked to an FPS 100 floating-point array processor hosting the Chant-based synthesis stage.[36]

Given Harvey's growing interest in the spectral characteristics of instrumental sounds and the possibilities of creatively manipulating the associated timbres in a digital environment, this resource was especially useful for the composition of *Ritual Melodies*. His choice of sonic models was influenced by the gestural characteristics of the instruments chosen for the purpose. These consisted of the Vietnamese koto, Indian oboe, Japanese shakuhachi, and Tibetan temple bell, augmented by the sounds modeling of Tibetan monks and Western plainchant. Particular attention was paid to the possibilities of creating hybrid virtual instruments. Vandenheede describes these processes as follows:

> The essence of the hybridisation procedure used in the piece is as follows: The models contain three types of components: sinusoids, FOFs (Formes d'Onde Formantiques) and filters (2nd order bandpass filters). At the start of each note of a melody that interpolates, a mapping is established between the components of the two models in question. If two components of the same category fall into the same frequency-region that is determined by an adjustable threshold, they are paired, i.e. interpolation takes places. The other components fade in and fade out. A mapping is produced at every note, because some models have formants on the partials and thus the formants are dependent on the fundamental (shakuhachi, oboe), others have not (the koto and the plainchant, abstraction is made from the usual CHANT-adjustments according to the fundamental in the case of the plainchant). The pitch behavior is interpolated at the same time as the timbral interpolation.[37]

The construction of these sound models involved intricate crafting, in many instances combining different synthesis techniques:

The koto, for instance, used formant synthesis mostly, with a little additive synthesis at the attack. The shakuhachi by contrast demanded two levels of formants, one to make the partials and one for their spectral envelope, plus an independent "effort" system of noise filtering which can be increased as the breathier lower notes are played. The temple bell was made from pure additive synthesis, as precise control is needed over its evolution in time and its vibrating partials.[38]

In terms of the composing environment, the sophistication of the processes implemented using the VAX-780/FPS-100 system came at a considerable practical cost. Vandenheede notes that each of the constituent melodies took up to an hour of processing time to synthesize, necessitating a return to the world of overnight batch processing and innumerable recompilations with suitably adjusted parameters.[39]

During the 1990s Harvey continued to compose extensively, both for purely acoustic instruments and for various combinations of acoustic and electronic resources, with an increasing emphasis on live processing techniques. In terms of preparing the ground for his *Fourth String Quartet*, his continuing association with IRCAM during the intervening years is of particular interest, marked by a succession of visits to further his experimental work with state-of-the-art computer music techniques. A further dimension to his association with these pioneering developments was his appointment, following an invitation from John Chowning, to Stanford University as professor of composition in 1995, a post he held until 2000. This appointment brought him into direct contact with staff and students at the Center for Computer Research in Music and Acoustics (CCRMA), and these experiences greatly enhanced his understanding of the possibilities of state-of-the-art resources at first hand.

In terms of the equipment used for works using live electronics, however, he continued to rely almost exclusively on commercial hardware-based resources throughout the 1990s, not least for the purely practical reason that accessibility to such devices was a critical consideration in terms of securing concert performances worldwide. A summary of the technical requirements for different pieces composed during the 1990s reveals the extent of this continuing engagement. For example, *Soleil Noir/Chitra* (1995), for mixed chamber ensemble and electronics, requires both a Yamaha SY77 synthesizer and two Eventide H3000 harmonizers. *Ashes Dance Back* (1997), for choir and electronics, and *Wheel of Emptiness* (1977), for chamber ensemble and electronics, use E-mu E-64 samplers, and *White as Jasmine* (1999), for soprano and large orchestra, also requires a SY77. However, by the end of the decade, it was becoming clear that the long-term availability of such equipment, each item offering a unique set of electronic resources, could no longer be guaranteed. As personal computers became progressively more powerful, attention was increasingly turning toward the possibility of entirely software-based facilities for digital synthesis and signal processing, in due course comprehensively embracing live applications. As a consequence, the manufacture of many of these pioneering devices, including those listed above, was progressively discontinued.

The problems thus faced today in performing such works dating from the 1980s and 1990s, not only by Harvey but also several other composers who have similarly engaged with such now obsolete technologies, are materially significant. The only solution in many instances lies in designing software using programs such as Max to simulate the functional characteristics of the original devices. Whereas in cases such as the design of a software-based alternative to the tape delay system required for Harvey's *Ricercare una Melodia*, the challenges to be met here are relatively straightforward, this is not the case for works such as *Madonna of Winter and Spring*. However, the importance and lasting significance of works such as this for future performances has provided a major stimulus for such tasks to be undertaken. Solutions were to emerge during the following decade with the introduction of custom-designed "plug-ins" for desktop, and subsequently laptop editing and sequencing programs,[40] but the task of converting Harvey's sample data, in the first instance often stored on device-specific media, was to prove a considerable challenge.[41] A key milestone in a journey that was finally to take Harvey into a computer-based environment that was to secure direct sustainability for his later compositions occurred in 1994 when he composed *Advaya* for cello, keyboard, and electronics.

True to form, the latter component was originally conceived for an Akai S1000 sampler and Yamaha SPX-100 (or alternatively SPX-1000) effects unit, combined with a twin CD-based system for the playback of sound files. The work, however, was an IRCAM commission, and for the first performance the latter component was transferred to the IRCAM Signal Processing Workstation (ISPW), thus bringing Harvey into direct contact with developments associated with the live signal processing research team at the institution.[42] Cort Lippe, as in the case of Philippe Manoury, provided significant technical support for Harvey in this context, and his significant contributions to developments at IRCAM are discussed in the following chapter. Although the ISPW was itself to suffer the same fate as its commercial counterparts, the seeds had been sown for the development of Max, opening the gateway to the powerful suite of signal processing software that is widely used today.

By the mid-1990s it was possible for Harvey to start exploring the potential of the ISPW-based Max/FTS and subsequently the purely software-based program then known as Max/MSP for himself at IRCAM, including the characteristics of the associated spatialization program Spat, made compatible with Max/MSP toward the end of the decade.[43] The stage was thus finally set in the technical context for the composition of the signal-processing components of his *Fourth String Quartet*, to which attention is now turned.

249

Inside the *Fourth String Quartet*

Inspiration and structure[44]

The *Fourth String Quartet*, like many of Jonathan Harvey's works, combines cutting-edge technical innovation in its use of real-time electronics with a deep engagement with spiritual issues. These two aspects are not independent but are closely interrelated, as this analysis will show. In examining the *Fourth Quartet* it is not meaningful to consider the different aspects totally independently. The acoustic writing for string quartet, the electronic transformation of sounds, and the aesthetic and spiritual dimensions are all interconnected and interwoven.

Buddhist ideas and practice play a key role in much of Harvey's music, and here they play a significant role in the overall shaping of the work. The form of the work reflects ideas about reincarnation, of life cycles, and of in-between states. A term used in Harvey's sketches but not found in the score is *bardo* (see Figure 7.2).

Bardo is a Tibetan word used in some branches of Buddhism to refer to an intermediate state, an in-between, liminal place, between two incarnations. It is a time of transition leading to rebirth. It plays an important role in Harvey's conception of the form of the *Fourth Quartet*. As the sketch of Figure 7.2 shows, Harvey planned the structure of the work as a series of five cycles, each preceded by a bardo passage. These passages are to represent "ghostly noise, no 'flesh': blown by winds of Karma."[45] Descriptive and spiritual concerns, even at this stage, are closely linked to the musical and the technical:

> [R]hythms are Karma—the form of emptiness at first only in SPAT, later in tailpiece bowing rhythm or circular bowing rhythms, then in spectral harmonics (unstable and unclear) alternating.[46]

"SPAT" designates the software developed at IRCAM for sound spatialization,[47] which plays an important role in the work, as detailed later; from the work's early stage of planning, the technical (use of Spat), the musical (for instance, bowing techniques), and the spiritual (ideas about Karma) go hand in hand.

Another significant influence on the formation of this work was Gaston Bachelard's essay *L'air et les songes*[48] (*Air and Dreams*), a book Harvey was reading while working on the *Fourth Quartet* at IRCAM. The composer described the influence of this book in his article "The Genesis of Quartet No. 4."[49] The subtitle to Bachelard's book is *An Essay on the Imagination of Movement*. He refers to "ascensional imagination,"[50] "sumptuous radiance,"[51] and "profound heights,"[52] and he says that "aerial being is pure being."[53] Such expressions relate to the compositional thinking on spatialization in the quartet: of movement of sound through the air, of sounds apparently without substance on the edge of existence, almost inaudible, shimmering.

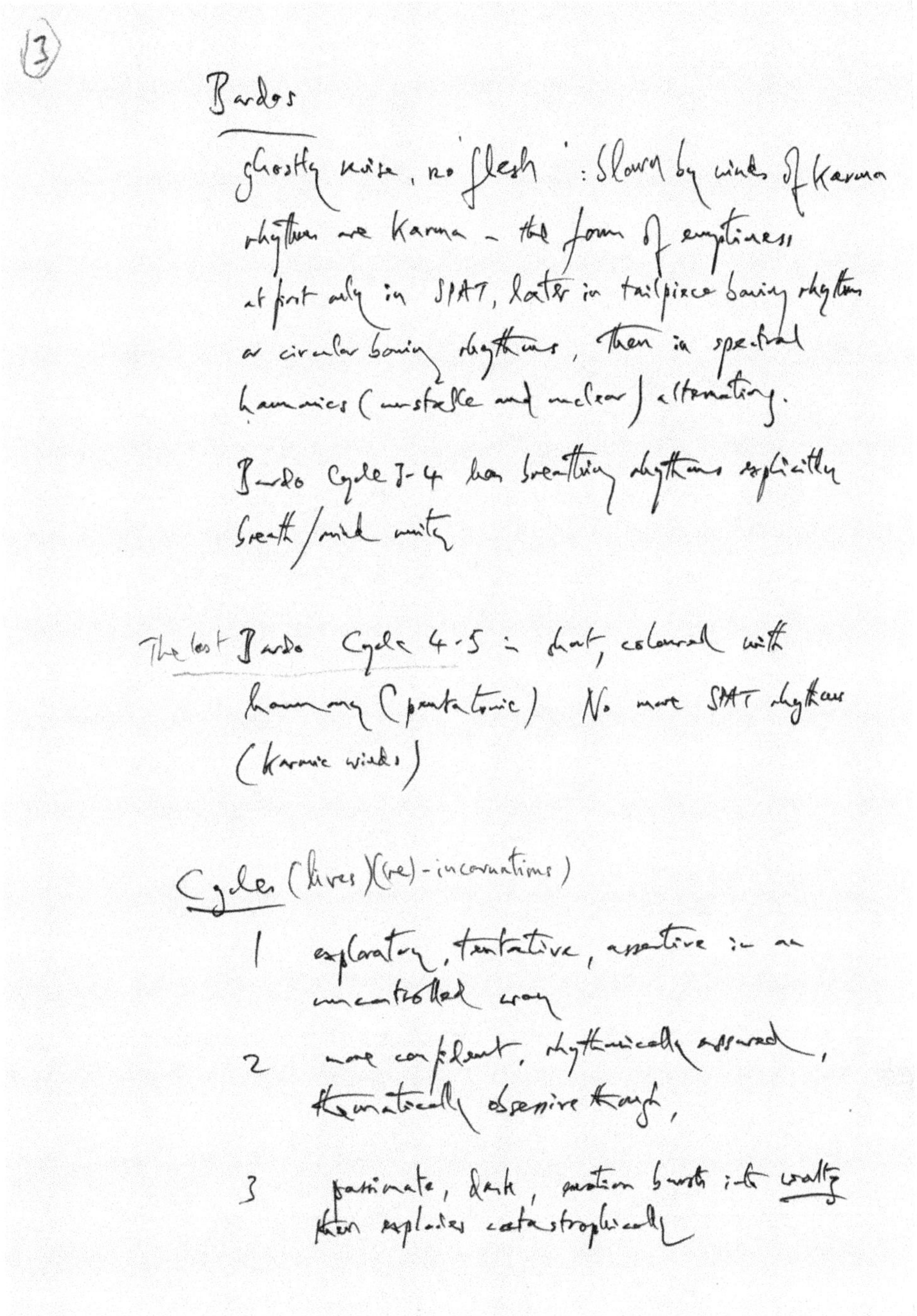

(3)

Bardos

"ghostly noise, no flesh": blown by winds of Karma
rhythms are Karma — the form of emptiness
at first only in SPAT, later in tailpiece bowing rhythm
or circular bowing rhythms, then in spectral
harmonics (on-staffel and nuclear) alternating.

Bardo Cycle 3-4 has breathing rhythms explicitly
breath/mind unity

The last Bardo Cycle 4-5 is short, coloured with
harmony (pentatonic) No more SPAT rhythms
(Karmic winds)

Cycles (lives)(re)-incarnations)

1   exploratory, tentative, assertive in an
    uncontrolled way

2   more confident, rhythmically assured,
    thematically discursive though,

3   passionate, dark, emotion bursts into waltz
    then explodes catastrophically

251

FIGURE 7.2

Sketch by Jonathan Harvey with preliminary notes on the composition of the *Fourth String Quartet*. Reproduced by kind permission from the Jonathan Harvey Collection, Paul Sacher Foundation, Basel.

Another of the composer's sketches shows an early plan for the unfolding of the work through the five cycles (see Figure 7.3). Although the detail of this changed as the piece developed, the eventual goal of arriving at the "pure mind" remains central to the work. This sketch also shows other important aspects of the work beginning to take shape, such as the looping of sounds and layering of textures.

In outline, the final form of the work is as follows: five cycles are each preceded by a bardo passage.[54] Each bardo section introduces and leads

FIGURE 7.3

Sketch by Jonathan Harvey, including the global structure of the *Quartet* in five cycles. Reproduced by kind permission from the Jonathan Harvey Collection, Paul Sacher Foundation, Basel.

seamlessly into the cycle that follows. They are less clearly defined in terms of musical material with the sound coming from nothing, growing out of silence, with a strong element of noise and the harmonic, rhythmic, thematic ideas slowly emerging out of this "ghostly" state.

As the work progresses, the cycles, the reincarnations, become purer, with each new life a development, a movement toward pure land, pure mind.[55] The bardo sections, being a liminal state between lives, tend to become shorter, although this not a simple linear progression; the final one, preceding cycle 5, is very brief, almost nonexistent. This is perhaps because they represent a stage of purification, and this is less important toward the end as the reincarnations themselves become purer.

Acoustic compositional techniques
Melodic cycles

Cycles and repeating loops play a key role in this work. We have already seen the link with Buddhist ideas of reincarnation and the way that recurring and transforming cycles are at the heart of the structure of the work. Melodic cycles are central to the development of pitch material in this work. Interlocking melodies play an important role in other works by Harvey, such as *Ritual Melodies*. Here, six melodies are employed, as shown in the composer's sketch in Figure 7.4.

The original melodies, six distinct melodic characters, appear labeled A to F on alternate staves on the manuscript. They have been deliberately constructed so that successive melodies do not overlap at the same point in time. For example, melody A comprises two fragments separated by a rest; melody B dovetails with this, sounding at the point of this rest and after the end of melody A. It is therefore possible to merge any two successive melodies to form a new hybrid melody. The resulting hybrid melodies are shown on the alternate staves as AB, BC, CD, EF. When the process reaches melody F, it can repeat, returning to melody A by means of a hybrid AF melody as shown in the final stave of the sketch, continuing the melodic cycle.

In order to become familiar with this process in practice, you can use Presentation 3 in the accompanying software, which provides examples of the individual melodies as they appear in the work and some of the combinations. First, you can play an example of each of the melodies in turn taken from cycle 2, where they first fully appear, while they are still forming in cycle 1. Then, you can play an example from cycle 2 of some of the interlocking melodies (e.g., AB, BC, CD). Next, various examples of how the melodies are varied using melody A as the basis are available. They show how melody A emerges from its point of origin in cycle 1 to become a fully formed melodic idea in cycle 2, and how it appears in a rapid pentatonic variation in cycle 4, as a slow motion variation in cycle 5, and then in imitation between

FIGURE 7.4

Sketch by Jonathan Harvey, showing six melodies labeled A to F, and their combinations. Reproduced by kind permission from the Jonathan Harvey Collection, Paul Sacher Foundation, Basel.

> the viola and violins. Finally, there is an example of one of the other melodies being transformed: melody F, in its original form and as a version transformed into a slow-motion variation with added decorations in cycle 3. Demonstration Video 7.1 introduces this software resource and illustrates it in action. ▶

These melodies, their interaction and variations, underpin the musical material played by the quartet. Not only do such cyclic processes reflect the larger-scale structure of the work, they also appear in the electronic processing of sounds as will be seen later.

Rhythms

Figure 7.5, taken from Harvey's sketches, shows four rhythms derived from the cyclic melodies—respectively from melodies B, F, D, and E.

These rhythms feature in the work independently of the melodies themselves in a number of ways. Another sketch shows Harvey listing possible uses for the rhythms, including "Rhythms of 4tet," "Rhythm of looped buffer," "Rhythm . . . of frozen segment," and "Rhythms of Spat loops" (Figure 7.6). As already noted, Spat is the IRCAM spatialization software, and an example of the rhythms in relation to spatial movement can be found at the very beginning of the work. The first page of the score shows, beneath the string parts, rhythm 2

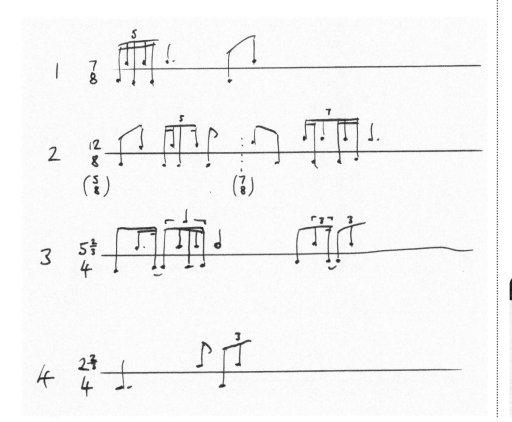

FIGURE 7.5

Sketch by Jonathan Harvey showing the four fundamental rhythms of the *Fourth Quartet*. Reproduced by kind permission from the Jonathan Harvey Collection, Paul Sacher Foundation, Basel.

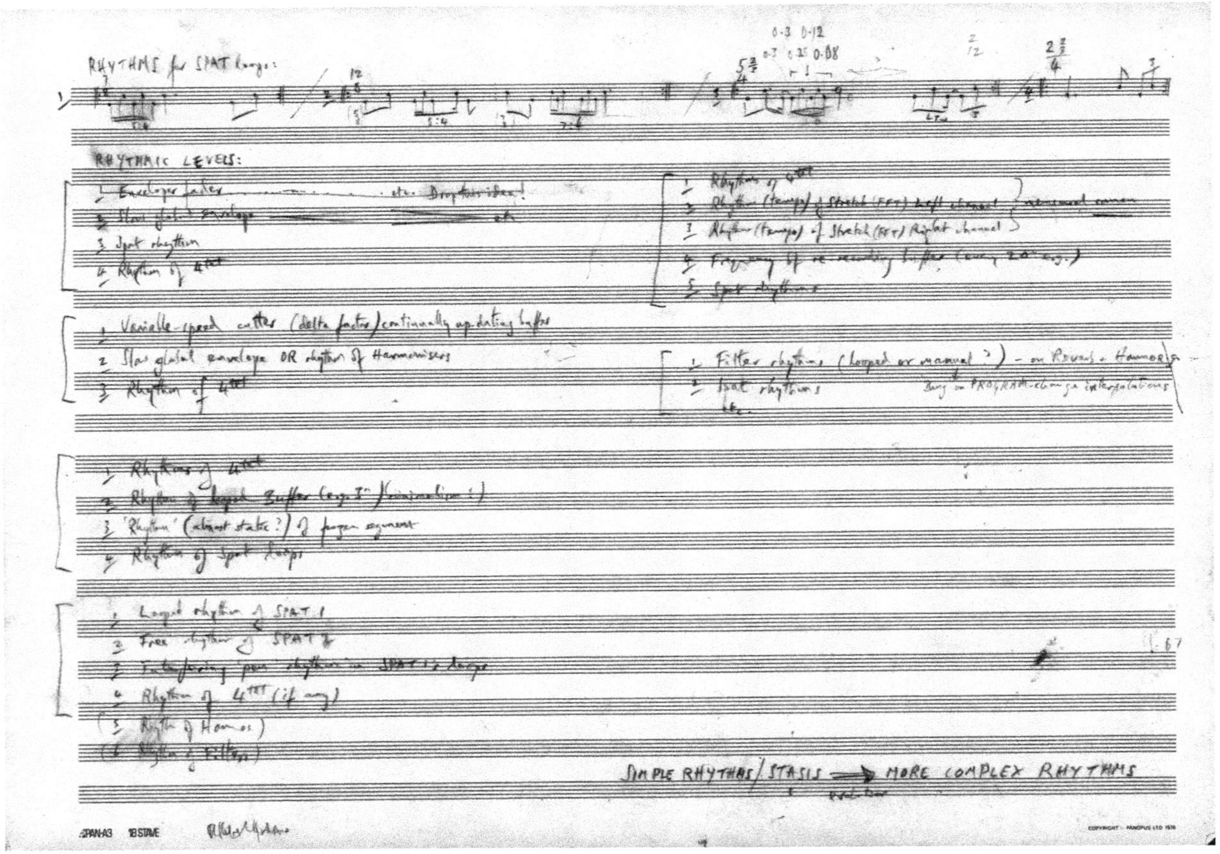

FIGURE 7.6

Sketch by Jonathan Harvey, showing possible applications of the four fundamental rhythms. Reproduced by kind permission from the Jonathan Harvey Collection, Paul Sacher Foundation, Basel.

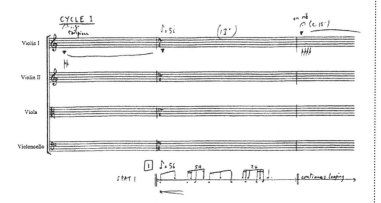

annotated on a stave labeled "SPAT 1"[56] and marked "continuous looping" (see Figure 7.7). As we will see later, there are various modes of spatial movement employed in the *Fourth Quartet*. Here, the movement of the sound between the different loudspeakers is performed rhythmically using rhythm 2 in a looped, cyclic pattern.

There is very little sound in the system to be spatialized at this point: it is almost silent, just the faint sound of violin 1 bowing the instrument's tailpiece. Such subliminal sound, almost imperceptible, immaterial noise moving in space, evokes Bachelard's "imagination of movement" and "aerial being." It creates a sense of the embryonic, of musical material being formed. Although the sounds are barely audible and lack clear form and shape, hidden within them are the seeds of the new cycle, the new life emerging, in this case in the form of a rhythm. Here, we see an example of the way the technical (computerized spatialization), the musical (rhythm), and the spiritual (the idea of bardo) are closely linked.

Electroacoustic techniques

Alongside the acoustic techniques, and fully integrated with them, is a range of electroacoustic techniques: the computer plays a full and essential part in this music. The digital processes almost exclusively involve the processing of sounds played live by the quartet and transformed immediately or after being stored temporarily in buffers.[57] The processes, each of which is presented in more detail below, are buffering and looping, time-stretching and spectral transformations with phase vocoding, granulation, reverberation, filtering, harmonizing, and spatialization.

Presentation 1 of the accompanying software, "Interactive structural map," provides an overview of these processes and how they are used in the course of the whole work. In this presentation, lines show the routes taken by sounds captured by microphones on each of the string instruments to one or more processes, in parallel or in succession, before being distributed to the loudspeakers by one of the two

> Spatializer units.[58] The setup is dynamic, with different processes and combinations being activated at different times in the work. You can bypass individual processes by clicking on them in the display in order to hear and understand their contribution to the overall sonority. In Presentation 2, "Composing and exploring technology," Gilbert Nouno, Jonathan Harvey's musical assistant for the Fourth Quartet, discusses the process of their collaboration and exploration of different techniques. Demonstration Video 7.2 shows how you can use these resources and explore them further. ▶

The sections that follow examine in more detail each of the different electroacoustic processes used in the *Fourth Quartet*. Further consideration will then be given to how the processes are combined over the course of the work.

Loop buffers

Since most of the sounds in the *Fourth Quartet* are derived from the live performance by the string players, the use of buffering provides an essential means of enriching the texture by delaying and transforming the performed sounds. The sounds from each of the performers are independently picked up by microphones and can be temporarily stored in buffers in the Max environment that runs the real-time electroacoustic part of the piece. For Jonathan Harvey, the process of recording has an important aesthetic function:

> All one's actions have consequences and they follow "like the shadow of a body," inseparably and invariably. Using electronics meant often that sounds the quartet played were recorded, stored in the computer, and then played back in transformed form later as a consequence of that earlier action.[59]

Several processes in the real-time environment make use of recordings of relatively large sequences of audio, and two modules named "loop buffers" are entirely dedicated to the purpose of recording and subsequent playback.[60] Both modules can receive and record audio from the four string instruments independently. The first loop buffer can send its playback to the first harmonizer (at the end of cycle 4), and the two spatializers (in cycles 2, 3, and 4); the playback of the second loop buffer can be directed to the first harmonizer and to the second spatializer (in cycle 2).

In the Max environment used for the *Fourth Quartet*, the duration of the recordings made by the loop buffers is variable, and cannot exceed a value defined as "loop length" which affects both recording and playback. This loop length can itself be changed dynamically—it varies between a minimum of three seconds and a maximum of five seconds for the first loop buffer, and is constant at 3,200 milliseconds for the second unit.

In several instances, the recording is triggered for the duration of the loop length; subsequently, the module simply plays the recorded contents as a simple, continuous loop. This electronic looping reflects the looping of melodic motifs described above, and also the cyclical nature of the overall structure of the work and the underlying ideas of life cycles. But the contents of the loop buffers can also be altered on a more microscopic scale. As the composer explains,

> Untreated recordings into the buffer of the quartet's sound are made on the fly with triggering. What happens after that could be determined in different ways. Either this recording loops unchanged, or new recordings are placed over it. If these new recordings are very short, perhaps only one per cent of the length of the original recording, then it would take at least a hundred new triggerings to obliterate completely the original recording.[61]

Such short recordings are named "bursts" in the software environment of the *Quartet*. They are automatically triggered at regular intervals; both that interval and the burst duration are varied through the piece. For example, in cycle 2, when the automated burst recording starts for the first loop buffer at event 11, recordings last one second and are triggered every four seconds; at event 12, these two values are changed drastically and recordings are then made every 50 milliseconds, and the duration of recordings is 27 milliseconds. Still in cycle 2, at event 16, the input levels for the second loop buffer, and then for the first loop buffer, are turned down; this implies that the bursts record silence:

> These recordings are of very small duration, so only gradually punch holes in the passage which was recorded in the buffer, causing its evaporation into particles and finally silence.[62]

Presentation 4 in the accompanying software, "Loop buffers," allows you to experiment with this process using sounds from the Fourth Quartet *or others sources. You can also use Presentation 1 for more detailed scrutiny on how the loop buffers behave through the chronology of the work, by looking at their parameter panels and envelopes showing the evolution of the relevant values. Demonstration Video 7.3 illustrates these resources and shows how to explore them further.* ▶

Phase vocoders

The *Fourth Quartet* uses two phase vocoder modules. Unlike the other processes used in the work, which transform sounds in the time domain, phase vocoding operates in the frequency domain. Sounds are first analyzed by means of a fast Fourier transform (FFT). The resulting magnitude and phase data are then recorded and processed before the modified sound is resynthesized using an Inverse FFT. The two phase vocoder modules are only active during cycle 3. Both send their sound to the first spatializer through the entire cycle, and to the first harmonizer at the end of the cycle. The first unit receives sounds from the two violins while the second unit processes the viola and the cello.

An important function of phase vocoders in the *Fourth Quartet* is that of time-stretching, but the modules also operate spectral distortion:

> If one uses a recorded buffer and loops it with an increasing stretch one can hear the passage become more and more reverberated, slowed down and stretched out. This can be combined with frequency shift, which changes the spectrum in a complex distortion, or with spectral inversion, which changes the amplitude of the partials from loud to soft and soft to loud. This latter gives a kind of ring modulation effect which reminded me of Stockhausen's *Telemusik*. That group of techniques was rather complex, and was probably best used with simple, melodic sorts of line.[63]

As with the loop buffers, recording works with a given loop length, which varies between one and three seconds for both units. Unlike the loop buffers, however, recording can either be made on the fly—one recording triggered for the duration of the loop—or itself looped, constantly renewing the entire contents of the module memory, as is the case, for both modules, from events 1 to 12 and from events 15 to 16 of cycle 3. The recording of short bursts is also implemented; it can be automated in the same way as with loop buffers (briefly at event 14), but most of the time it is up to the fifth performer, operating the computer, to manually trigger recording bursts to renew sporadically the contents of the buffer from the interface for the live performance of the electroacoustic part.[64]

According to the successive events of cycle 3, the time-stretching factor can vary from one to ten with the first phase vocoder module; with the second module, the factor can be negative, in effect reversing and time-stretching the contents of the buffer. The spectral distortion evoked above by Harvey is obtained by shifting the FFT frequency bins. The spectral inversion computes, for each successive FFT frame, the maximum magnitude of all frequency bins, from which the magnitude is then subtracted if above a certain threshold.

> Presentation 5 in the accompanying software, "Phase vocoders," enables you to play with these features and hear the effects of the different parameters, and you can investigate the two phase vocoder modules in the context of cycle 3 using Presentation 1, as shown in Demonstration Video 7.4. ▶

Granulation

There are two different types of granulation modules in the Max environment for the performance of Harvey's *Fourth String Quartet*. The first and most prominent type is a Brownian granulator, which has two instances.[65] This first type of granulation also involves the recording of the instrumentalists' sounds into buffers. Here, the playback of sounds stored in the granulator's internal buffer involves different types of grain-based processes.[66] As with the loop buffers and phase vocoders, a loop length is defined for the recordings; however, each unit has two buffers, and a "record and swap" command enables the environment to change the recording buffer and gradually start extracting grains from the newly selected buffer. Recording can be made on the fly, again by recording just the duration of one loop, and recording bursts are implemented as well—in this type of granulation, this process can be automated for the first Brownian granulator, but only triggered manually for the second one. The composer presents the wide range of possible sonic outcomes of the process:

> One of the most far-reaching treatments was that of granulation. This entails recording what the quartet play and either storing it as a buffer of a few seconds' duration or continuously rerecording the buffer so that after a little delay the treatment of what the quartet has just played will come out, like a following distorted echo. If a buffer is stored statically without renewal for a fair amount of time the granulator will read and cut the recording into tiny grains of sound (which can be shaped in any way one likes, to give different timbres and qualities) and these grains are read off the buffer at different points in the recorded few seconds of music. The reading-position can be fairly static, always in the same place, or can move along the stored sound slowly, so that very gradually the resultant sound colour changes as different pitches and timbres are addressed. One can change the position of reading this stored passage in the buffer either quickly or slowly. In fact, one can make the position change by jumps with great volatility and mobility. . . . The quality here is of frenetic activity, a bit like Berio at his most active, or often in a rather delicate vein like Mendelssohn's fairy music, for example.[67]

Through the *Fourth String Quartet*, the length of the grains extracted from the buffers might vary from very short—around 30 milliseconds—to significantly longer—around 400 milliseconds. More generally, four parameters are subject to Brownian movements: the triggering speed, the position in the buffer, the grain length or duration, and a transposition factor. Each of these parameters are randomly varied away from their current value—these Brownian motions are controlled with a basis or central value, a range within which the values can be set, and a mobility factor which rules the maximum size of jumps between two successive values. If mobility is null, the parameter will have a constant value; if it is maximal, the parameter will evolve in a very entropic way. A low mobility typically allows for a shimmering effect. For instance, in cycle 1 the second Brownian granulator has a mobility of 8 percent for the grain position in the buffer; this, along with a low mobility of the other parameters, leads to a quite static texture, but just volatile enough not to sound frozen. Additionally, the grains are processed through bandpass filters, for which starting and ending values are controllable for the center frequency, the gain, and the resonance.

As the resonance grows higher, the effect of the filter is more perceptible, and important differences between the start and end values of the center frequency lead to a quick swiping effect.

The two Brownian granulators can receive sounds from the four string instruments; the first granulator sends its output toward the second spatializer in cycle 1, both spatializers at the end of cycle 2, and the first spatializer in cycle 4. The second Brownian granulator only appears in cycle 1 and can send its output toward the reverberation module and the second spatializer.

The second granulator type is a multichannel granulator, developed on the basis of Nathan Wolek's granular toolkit, and is used only at the very end of the fifth cycle to complete discretely the high-pitched final lines and punctuated tremolos of the quartet.[68] This six-channel granulator does not process the live sounds, but extracts grains from a prerecorded sound file; it sends its grains directly to the six loudspeakers, and an auxiliary output is also directed to the second spatializer.

You can investigate both types of granulator in Presentation 6 of the accompanying software, "Granulation." Presentation 7, "Granulation within the String Quartet," is a video interview of Gilbert Nouno focusing on this particular treatment. And again, Presentation 1 enables you to investigate these processes in the context of the musical work. Demonstration Video 7.5 guides you through all these interactive resources. ⏵

Reverberation and biquad filters

Although reverberation is present in the spatializer units used through the entire work, an independent module of reverberation is used, in tandem with a biquad filter unit, in the second half of cycle 1.[69] The reverberation unit takes the grains of the second Brownian granulator and sustains them with an infinite reverberation, periodically renewed by an automated process that varies the input level of the module. This sustained texture is then processed by a bank of five parallel biquad filters configured in bandpass mode. These contribute to give an ethereal quality to the texture, with center frequencies between 1,000 and 4,800 Hz and high resonances; these parameters, along with the filter gains, are subjected to Brownian motions in the same way as the parameters of the granulators described in the previous section. Ultimately, the output of the filter module is directed toward the first spatializer.

You can use Presentation 8, "Reverberation," and Presentation 9, "Biquad filters," to experiment with these processes yourself; and you can use Presentation 1 to investigate them in the second half of cycle 1, as shown in Demonstration Video 7.6. ⏵

Harmonizers

Four harmonizer units are used in the *Fourth Quartet*. Harmonizers, as the name implies, may be used to add specific harmonic content to the music or to thicken the texture. For the most part, only the first of the four harmonizers is used. At the end of cycle 1, from event 10, all four string instruments are processed by this same unit. Likewise, in cycle 2, the first harmonizer is used to process either just the first violin or all four instruments. At the end of this cycle, it processes the output of the second loop buffer module, harmonizing the sounds already delayed by this unit. At the end of cycle 3, it is used to process the sounds output by both phase vocoder units, further enriching the already spectrally transformed sounds. It is only in cycle 5 that all four harmonizers come into action, and at the end of the work all four are used together, each harmonizing a different member of the quartet, and then in different combinations. The output of the harmonizers is always sent to one of the two spatializer units, or both. Each harmonizer has six transposing lines, and Jonathan Harvey gives the following account of the effect of different harmonizations as experienced during the compositional process:

> Set to semitones, the resultant clustered sound was quite spectacular when mirroring changes of timbre like a transformation to *sul ponticello*. This was because the whole chord would change timbre in an extravagant and striking way. Quarter-tones on the other hand gave a more elemental, "less musical" effect more like nature; water and wind came to mind. This is the fascinating point at which music approaches close to nature, which is such an important topic in music of today and in a lot of my music too. The "natural" world displaces the "cultural" world of instruments. Eighth-tone clusters with the harmonizers sound almost like a big vibrato and have a chorusing effect, which again is quite distinctive from other musical purposes.[70]

> You can experiment with this process in Presentation 10 of the accompanying software, "Harmonizers," and observe the four units, their connections, and their transposition amounts through the Fourth String Quartet using Presentation 1. Additionally, Presentation 11, "The use of techniques through the Quartet cycles," is a video in which Gilbert Nouno discusses the various processes presented so far, and how they are used across the work. Demonstration Video 7.7 introduces you to these resources. ▶

Spatialization

Spatialization plays a fundamental part in the *Fourth String Quartet*. As noted earlier, almost all the electroacoustic sounds in the work go finally to one or the other of the two Spatializer units[71] to be distributed, statically or dynamically, in the loudspeakers. In a conversation with Nicolas Donin,[72] Jonathan Harvey discusses the importance of the immersive nature of the experience with the six or eight loudspeakers used in performance surrounding the audience on the horizontal plane:

> If you just see musicians on a stage, in the distance, as is the case normally, you tend to have a sense of *self* and *other*, of *them* and *us*. They're different, and there is a kind of wall between us—however involved we are in the performance. In the case of speakers placed all around the auditorium, however, there is sometimes a different and rather profound psychological change. It becomes a way of living the music, or swimming in the sea of music, or moving as body in a quite different way.[73]

The movement of sound in space is a significant part of the musical structure. The sounds that are spatialized, like all the sounds in the work, derive from the performance of the quartet players, and another highly significant aspect of the spatialization is that the quartet becomes transformed and disembodied as it flies around the space, freed from the normal restrictions of its physical reality. It takes on an aerial quality.

The six or eight loudspeakers are placed surrounding the audience.[74] Each of the four string players can be independently transformed by the software; the resulting sounds can be distributed around the space in a number of different ways. Two different Spat units are used so that two different spatial movements can be performed simultaneously in counterpoint. Movement can be controlled manually, by pen, or hand gesture on a tablet; it can also be driven by a variety of preprogrammed processes, as presented in more detail now.[75]

On top of the standard distribution of IRCAM's Spat, a higher-level positioning set of controls was implemented in the Max patch for the *Fourth String Quartet*. A new spatial position in the two-dimensional space surrounding the audience can be defined in azimuth and distance coordinates; these values can be varied using Brownian parameters, as with the granulators and the biquad filters described earlier. Besides, new positions are calculated with a central symmetry parameter, which enables successive positions to be shifted by 180 degrees. A duration parameter, in milliseconds, defines the time taken from the current position to the new position. The trajectory from a point to another can be linear or circular; in this latter case, the distance from the center is constant, and it is possible to decide whether to use the shortest or longest arc of the circle between the origin and the destination. Finally, rotations can be activated, with their speed also subject to Brownian deviation; in this case, the azimuths are incremented accordingly. The triggering of new spatial positions is often controlled with one of the four fundamental rhythmic patterns of the *Quartet*, as seen in Figure 7.4 above. When active, a pattern is looped and can have its tempo varied. A time multiplying parameter is implemented so that the time taken to go from one position to another is proportional to the duration of the rhythmic event. For instance, with a tempo of 60 beats per minute, a quarter note lasts one second. If the time multiplier is set to 25 percent, the trajectory goes from the current position to the new one in 250 milliseconds; the position then remains constant for 750 milliseconds before the next note triggers a new position, and so on. The composer recalls the genesis of this modality of control:

> In order to make the spatialization something more than just a cosmetic addition, I gave the rhythmic movements in space a thematic structure. The sounds would go from one part of the room to another, constantly changing position, going more or less through the center. . . . And this they would do at a certain speed of travel, either travelling rapidly at the beginning of the unit of time and then staying a little, or travelling throughout the unit of time and not staying at all (one could adjust all such parameters). It was also possible to rotate the sounds. . . . Four rhythms were composed . . . and they were usually looped. The repetitive structural rhythm was by no means intolerable, in fact in the experiments forty or fifty repetitions of the loop as a counterpoint and background to the musical arguments of the quartet was completely acceptable, indeed very interesting; a polyphony of movement was set up which was completely absorbing.[76]

Another high-level modality of controlling spatialization in the *Quartet* is the implementation of very fast movements, at play with the second Spat unit in cycle 5. Harvey refers to this as "stroboscopic," with the impression being created that the sound is moving so fast that, paradoxically, it almost seems stationary, shimmering. The sounds rotate around the audience at speeds varying between 13.83 and 16.5 cycles per second—this is an effect that has rarely been used, although Stockhausen's late electronic work *Cosmic Pulses* is another example of very rapid cycling movement. This use of spatialization to create a shimmering, ethereal sound world again reflects the interrelation of the technical and the spiritual, coming at a point in the work where the reincarnated life cycles are approaching "pure mind:"[77]

> The speed varies slightly to re-attain the sense of slow rotation, although, like the wheel in an early film, in fact the rotation is very fast, but the illusion is of slowly turning. The static dots seem to be everywhere, like an illuminated mist.[78]

Overall, the control of space in the *Quartet* is subtle and includes the rhythm of the movement, the speed of a pattern, and other features, such as whether movement is continuously flowing or pauses each time it arrives at a specific location. Just as with other aspects of the music, Harvey plans out the spatial dimension in his sketches. It is something that is given detailed attention and is thoroughly integrated into the conception of the music, not merely a decoration added as an afterthought. Figure 7.8 shows one of the composer's sketches for the spatialization. It is labeled "SPAT tempi" and shows the changes in speed of movement of the two different Spat units. As the annotations show, one is controlling the movement of the second violin and viola, and the other that of the first violin and cello.

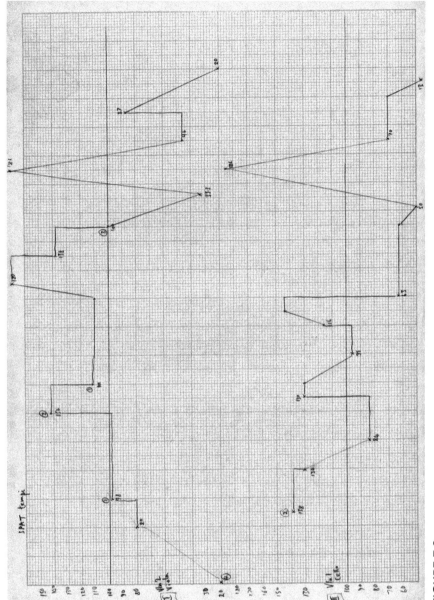

FIGURE 7.8

Sketch by Jonathan Harvey, showing evolutions of tempi for the spatialization movements. Reproduced by kind permission from the Jonathan Harvey Collection, Paul Sacher Foundation, Basel.

> *Presentation 12 of the accompanying software, "Spatialization," allows you to engage with the different parameters and control modes at play in the* Fourth String Quartet. *Demonstration Video 7.8 shows how to familiarize yourself with the positioning parameters manually, before having them controlled with rhythmic patterns, and to engage with the fast Spat movements as implemented in cycle 5.* ▶

Performing the electroacoustic part of the *Fourth String Quartet*

In a work such as the *Fourth String Quartet*, the realization of the live electronics is an essential part of any performance. Of the three pieces for instrumentalists and live electronics studied in this book, the *Quartet* is the only one that involves a performer dedicated to actually playing the electroacoustic part.[79] One common aspect of the implementation of the real-time software across these three musical works is the definition of a number of events, notated at specific locations on the score with Arabic numbers. In the *Quartet*, the implementation in Max, for each of these events, is a number of commands stored in "qlist" objects—one per cycle—and controlling the relevant digital modules and their interconnections when appropriate. Unlike the case of *Pluton*, no score following is involved: the triggering of each event is done by the electroacoustic performer by simply pressing the space bar of the computer keyboard. In our interviews with Harvey's collaborators at IRCAM, Arshia Cont discusses the distinction between these two approaches:

> [There is a] contrast between [Harvey's *Quartet*] and [Manoury's] *Pluton*. . . . I would say that in a dense piece, in a very dense piece like [Boulez's] *Anthèmes 2*, for example, or *Pluton*, having a score follower that works actually enables [you] to musically interpret the piece. Because otherwise, you have so many discrete actions, and the synchronicity is so important. Here [with the *Fourth String Quartet*], if you come a little bit late . . . synchronicity is not a huge issue throughout the piece. But in Boulez and Manoury, it is a huge issue. You end up just trying to be synchronous. But having a score follower that is musically acceptable allows you to actually perform the piece, because at the end of the day, you need to mix colors.[80]

Performing the electroacoustic part of the *Quartet* involves triggering new configurations of the software at specified points in the score, but also using controllers to shape continuous gestures, for example in relation to the movement of sounds in space. The way in which this is performed and the creation of means to achieve this using software and hardware are a vital part of the way in which technology interacts with creativity in such a work. The development of techniques and devices for real-time performance featured in the works of Jonathan Harvey over the years became increasingly sophisticated and refined, in part as a result of technological advances, in part as a result of the composer's own promptings. As Gilbert Nouno recalls:

> Jonathan has always been interested in the devices. Also, for *Bird Concerto with Pianosong* [2001], we had lots of fun driving the bird in space with two joysticks. . . . He really liked to have these kinds of devices. He was really happy when, one day, I brought the Wacom tablet to do the movement in space, and then later when we had [the Lemur and the iPad].[81]

The live interface used for the performance of the *Fourth String Quartet* gives access to several controllers. Through the chronology of the work, the qlist events activate and deactivate them dynamically, and often automate their values; when the controllers are active, the performer can use them to set the values manually, sometimes interfering with the automated processes. A set of vertical faders enable the performer to set the levels of the individual digital modules. This is not just about adjusting the overall balance: the performer is required to be active. For instance, in cycle 2, the loop buffers are automatically activated, but their output levels remain at a very low, inaudible level if the performer does not take action. Likewise, in cycle 3, the level of the two phase vocoders needs to be actively increased from a default minimal value between event 2 and the second half of event 13. In addition to the control of the levels of the individual modules, a "main" fader controls the level of the global output of the software environment, a "direct" fader controls the amount of sound sent from the four string players to the two Spat units, and two faders control the distance between the listener and the sound of each spatializer.

A pair of two-dimensional surfaces—one for each Spat unit—display the automated positions of the spatialized sounds and, when active, enable the performer to position the sound in space manually. In some instances, a surface is mapped to other events: for example, in the second half of cycle 1, the production of the first Brownian granulator is not directed anywhere; it is only by touching the second Spat surface that it is sent to the second spatializer. At the beginning of cycle 4, acting on this surface also impacts the second spatializer's acoustic attributes, such as the room presence or the reverberation time.

Finally, keystrokes or buttons on the tablet enable the performer to manually trigger the recording bursts mentioned earlier for the phase vocoders (in cycle 3, from event 13) and the second Brownian granulator (in cycle 1, from event 7); this enables the performer to, as required by the composer, renew part of the contents of the module's internal buffer and therefore update its outcome with the most recent production of the quartet. All these possibilities of control of the electroacoustic part, along with the corresponding indications on the score, require a permanent engagement of the performer, who is entirely considered as such in the *Fourth String Quartet*, as Nouno assesses:

You cannot just run [the patch] by going through the cues, you really have to be active, to listen. In the hall, it is even more perceptible, that you can hear the very light differences of sounds, with the reverb, with the space. . . . Even if it is . . . a touchscreen, you can feel some very musical good moments, feeling the sound moving exactly when you want it to move. . . . It is not only the balance, it is really something you can play with, like composing the space with the electronics.[82]

You can watch Gilbert Nouno demonstrating the live interface in Presentation 11 of the accompanying software, and Arshia Cont discussing it in Presentation 16. Presentation 17, "Approaches to real-time electronics at IRCAM," and Presentation 18, "Performing works with live electronics," contain further accounts of matters related to performance in computer music. And you can use Presentation 1 to play with our implementation of the live interface for the Fourth String Quartet, *as explained in Demonstration Video 7.9.* ▶

Summary of the integration of acoustic writing and electronics

In discussing the various electroacoustic techniques, their use at different points in the work has sometimes been noted. It is by no means the case that all the processes are used all the time. Indeed, while there is no simple pattern, it can be observed that certain processes feature predominantly in certain cycles, contributing to their characterization. In cycle 1, initially only the spatializers are used. Later, the Brownian granulators are added, with the addition of reverberation and biquad filtering, and finally, the first harmonizer enters. In cycle 2, it is primarily the harmonizer that is used at first, and later the loop buffers, too, and the first Brownian granulator. Cycle 3 features mainly the phase vocoders initially, their output later being processed by the first harmonizer, while the first loop buffer reappears at the end of the cycle. Cycle 4 features the first Brownian granulator and the first loop buffer. Cycle 5 is characterized by the use of all four harmonizers. Each cycle, therefore, is characterized by different processes, and tends toward more complex processing as it progresses. The processing works in conjunction with the instrumental techniques to realize the aesthetic and spiritual concerns of the composer.

Conclusions

Jonathan Harvey's *Fourth String Quartet* is a work that combines sophisticated writing for traditional musical instruments with advanced technological processes. From a technological perspective, a number of features stand out, including the integration of live instrumental performance with electronic processing of these sounds; the live control (by a fifth performer) of the electronic transformations; and the use of multichannel spatialization not only to project sounds around the auditorium, but also to change the relationship between acoustic and electroacoustic sounds by dematerializing the quartet.

Unlike several of the composers represented in this book, Harvey was not, and would not have claimed to be, a technical expert. Over the years, he worked closely with a number of musicians and technical assistants who did have such expertise, in particular, though not exclusively, through his long association with IRCAM. This enabled him to bring his creative imagination into dialogue with many of the latest technical developments of the time in a succession of groundbreaking works. He was able to bring his musical imagination to bear on the technical innovations presented to him. This creative partnership of musical and technical expertise demonstrates one very important model for the production of computer music. We have therefore incorporated extensive interviews with Harvey's assistant for this work, Gilbert Nouno, and others he worked with at IRCAM, as part of this study.

Also, unlike some of the composers in this book who are perhaps known primarily as electroacoustic composers, Harvey did not work exclusively with new technology and had a well-established reputation as a composer of many works that are purely instrumental or vocal. He was equally innovative and inventive in his use of these resources often, including using extended instrumental techniques. In the *Fourth Quartet*, Harvey's skill and inventiveness in both instrumental and electroacoustic writing come together. It is perhaps interesting to examine how Harvey's creative use of technology compares to that of composers more exclusively working with technology, and also instructive to compare how Harvey's creativity manifests itself both in works that are purely acoustic and those that are mixed or purely electroacoustic. Although the means vary, there is a strong consistency in Harvey's compositional and aesthetic approach. What matters is not the means of sound generation but his approach to the shaping the sounds. One important aspect of this is his deep concern for the spiritual, which shapes Harvey's work throughout his career and, as has been shown, shapes the *Fourth Quartet* on many levels.

The *Fourth Quartet* is therefore a striking example of how compositional and technical creativity can be successfully combined through collaborative working, of how acoustic and electroacoustic compositional activity can contribute to a composer's vision, and how aesthetic and spiritual concerns can be fully integrated with innovative technical means of production.

Cort Lippe
Music for Tuba and Computer

Contexts for *Music for Tuba and Computer*

Early exploration of the possibilities of computer music

Cort Lippe's achievements as a computer music composer and software developer add a further perspective on the specific contributions made by those who have directly engaged with advancing the underlying technology as an integral part of the creative process, notably, in the current context, John Chowning, Barry Truax, and Trevor Wishart. At the same time, a further important connection can be made with the development of real-time signal processing facilities at IRCAM, allowing interesting parallels to be drawn with the creative work of Philippe Manoury, notably his compositions for the 4X that are considered in Chapter 3. In the same way that Truax was to engage with important developments in Europe, Lippe was to make a similar journey a decade later. A personal account of his early experiences with the electroacoustic medium provides a useful background perspective on the significant contributions he made to electroacoustic music at a number of European institutions, most especially IRCAM.[1]

As an undergraduate student in Florida during the early 1970s, Lippe encountered the world of analog synthesizers and tape recorders, and at a summer school held in 1974 at Colgate University, he came into contact for the first time with the possibilities of computer music via Music 10, the version of Music V developed for the PDP-10 mainframe computer by John Chowning and James Moorer at Stanford University.[2] Although he was unable to implement either program back in Florida, he was able to access a PDP-8 mini-computer in the psychology department, equipped with a digital to analog converter. Thus, he was able to carry out some initial experiments on imported acoustic sounds, albeit limited at this time to the processes of analysis rather than resynthesis.

An important step forward came in 1976 when he transferred to the University of South Florida to study with Larry Austin, who had recently established an electronic music studio for computer music at SYCOM (Systems Complex for the Recording and Performing Arts), supported by a dedicated PDP-11 computer. Unfortunately, the PDP offered only a very basic configuration of facilities, with limited memory and no hard disk facility, requiring the extensive use of paper tape for data storage. The primary use of the computer was as a control device for conventional analog synthesizers, but Lippe was nonetheless able to develop some experimental programs that used the computer directly as a means of sound production, including both an envelope follower and a harmonizer. His growing interest in computer music led him to look further afield for more powerful facilities and like Truax before him the Institute of Sonology in Utrecht was to prove the destination of choice.[3]

By the time Lippe started work at the Institute of Sonology in 1980, a number of composers had explored the synthesis possibilities of the PDP-15/20, and in a practical context he took a particular interest in the work of Paul Berg, notably his development of composing programs for real-time digital synthesis. He started work on a series of automated sound programs (ASPs) using algorithmic procedures to generate data streams that could be sonically realized and shaped via tendency masks, thus employing techniques similar to those used by Truax for POD. Having developed a suite of twenty-two programs, it became clear to him that a number of features provided the basis for developing an extended syntax for a language-based compiler developed by Paul Berg, known as PILE.[4] Lippe's project, completed in 1982, took this line of investigation a stage further, developing his own software *ab initio* to compose a series of algorithmically-based works. In order to minimize processing delays, like Truax he thus had to use the low level macro assembler code of the PDP-15 for time-critical synthesis functions and a FORTRAN compiler to write the associated control program.[5] The overall flow diagram of this two-stage program is shown in Figure 8.1.

Known as 8110 K, the project resulted in a suite of four experimental works, *Tapewalk I, Tapewalk II, T'Which,* and *Saamba.* In essence Lippe's

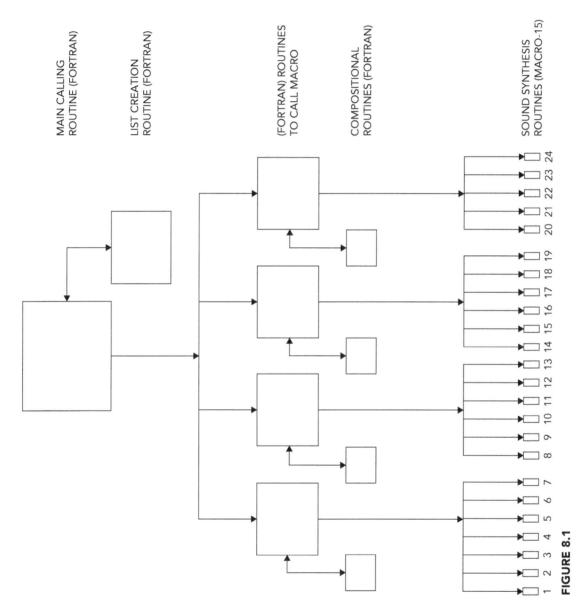

MAIN CALLING
ROUTINE (FORTRAN)

LIST CREATION
ROUTINE (FORTRAN)

(FORTRAN) ROUTINES
TO CALL MACRO

COMPOSITIONAL
ROUTINES (FORTRAN)

SOUND SYNTHESIS
ROUTINES (MACRO-15)

1 2 3 4 5 6 7   8 9 10 11 12 13   14 15 16 17 18 19   20 21 22 23 24

FIGURE 8.1

Project 8110 K flow diagram.[6]

research took him back to the very roots of stochastic methods of composing as originally proposed and explored by Xenakis.[7] The following extracts from his project report provide a useful insight into his methods of working:

> Concerning sound synthesis, 23 routines are used to achieve a diversity of timbres, spatial relationships, and a number of sounding voices. . . . In conjunction with some of the output routines, waveforms can be operated on by 18 routines which act to sort, reorder, replace, and transform the individual samples of the waveforms while sounding to add further diversity to the timbral possibilities.
>
> There are 17 stored lists used for a variety of purposes: (1) waveforms, (2) envelopes, (3) modulators on a timbral, rhythmic, or pitch level (i.e. in the defining of duration/rhythm; pitch/fundamental frequency; glissandi; distortion modulation; location modulation; frequency modulation; and amplitude modulation). The 17 lists can be recalculated rapidly in real-time to allow for the use of different list sizes and scale factorings.
>
> Many of the ideas and processes involved on the lower level of composition (sound synthesis) intersect and parallel compositional procedures of a higher level. This is an important characteristic of my work which involves the establishment of connections among higher and lower levels of composition and music. My attitude of diversity in regard to timbre is reflected in a variety of routines pertaining to the compositional level. As an overview the following ideas are developed:
>
> 1) stochastic (probabilistic) choices, Markov chaining, random weighting (Brownian, etc.);
>
> 2) tendencies (both stochastic and composer detailed), masking of variable ranges to produce directional tendencies (i.e. movement from pitched sound to noise across various modulations of timbre during an event sequence);
>
> 3) algorithms (i.e. exponential functions, etc.) to control various parameters and structures;
>
> 4) sorting, reordering, and replacing routines to act on sound event strings syntactically (i.e. sorting of a group of sound events having random pitch ordering into a directional pitch sequence);
>
> 5) transformations of sequences of sound events with various tied and/or untied relationships among parameters.[8]

From composing software to real-time synthesis: The road to IRCAM

Lippe's interest in stochastics led him to transfer from the Institute of Sonology to the Center for the Study of Mathematics and Automation in Music (CEMAMu) in Paris in late 1982, thus enabling him to explore the UPIC system developed by the director, Iannis Xenakis. A notable feature of this system was the emphasis placed on exploring the creative possibilities of a specially designed interactive interface, which even at this early stage was exploring the characteristics of touchscreen technologies. However the computer used for sound synthesis and signal processing at the time, a Solar 16-65 minicomputer, was not sufficiently powerful for real-time modes of operation, resulting in delays at each stage when externally generated sound material was input to the system and then subject to the application of graphical control commands.[9] Nonetheless, the experience thus gained with the control interface was to prove useful for Lippe's subsequent works, notably *Music for Bass Clarinet and Tape* (1986). This was composed at CEMAMu using UPIC in response to a commission from the Dutch Ministry of Culture for the 1986 International Computer Music Conference (ICMC), hosted by the Royal Conservatory in The Hague, and written for the bass clarinetist Harry Sparnaay.

The work is very different from his earlier experimental works, developing a subtle and engaging dialogue between the prerecorded tape part and live performer that establishes a distinctive and very personal environment for an aesthetic that was to shape and materially influence the works that followed. In the program note for the work, Lippe gives this description of it:

> Sound material for the tape was limited to approximate the confines one normally associates with individual acoustic instruments in order to create a somewhat equal relationship between the electronics and the bass clarinet. Although contrasts and similarities between the tape and the clarinet are evident, musically a kind of intimacy was sought—not unlike our present-day "sense" of intimacy with machines in general. There are five major sections in the work. The opening section is a dialogue between the instrument and tape, and is followed by a section in which the tape part dominates. This, in turn, gives way to a bass clarinet solo, while in the fourth section the tape part is dominated by the clarinet. In the final section the instrument and tape are again somewhat equal—reminiscent of the opening section.[10]

The year 1986 was to prove a key milestone in Lippe's development as a composer and researcher. From an early stage in his career he had cultivated a keen interest in the possibilities of composing computer music in a completely interactive environment, long before such aspirations became a practical proposition, except in some very limited circumstances. During his years of study in Europe, the development of real-time synthesis and signal processing software for the 4X at IRCAM had progressed to the point where such modes of working were indeed viable, providing a powerful incentive for him to seek access to this resource. Following preliminary investigations carried out informally late at night, he secured a formal transfer from CEMAMu to IRCAM. Although initially he had the status of a visiting composer, his contributions to the 4X project led in due course to a contract as a technical assistant. As already noted in Chapter 3, the 1980s were associated with significant technical and musical developments at IRCAM, and Lippe's arrival was thus particularly timely, both in terms of his skills as a programmer and his personal development as a composer.

One characteristic of this evolutionary phase in the development of real-time computer music that is worth further consideration at this point is the range of different processes and procedures that were thus embraced. At one end of the spectrum of possibilities, the primary consideration is the ability to control specific sound production processes interactively, the intention usually being to edit and combine the results of these tasks via intermediate recording and editing processes either to create a free-standing studio composition or the components of a hybrid work for an instrument(s) and tape. At the other end of the spectrum, the computer is required to perform as a live synthesizer and signal processor, essentially creating works in real time. All manner of composing and performing techniques can be explored between these two polarities.

In many respects the middle ground here presents the most engaging spectrum of musical possibilities for further study, especially when circumstances conspire to bring composers together, as is the case with Lippe and Manoury at IRCAM. Lippe was indeed to make a notable contribution to the sustainability of Manoury's *Pluton*, working as an assistant to Miller Puckette on a project to reconfigure the live computer part for use with the IRCAM Musical Workstation in 1991.[11] He was exceptionally well placed to address this particular programming challenge, having worked as a technical assistant for the original 4X version of the piece, and he also produced a detailed technical report on its composition.[12] Although Lippe's work at IRCAM is perhaps better known for his contributions to the evolution of the Workstation, the significance of his hands-on engagement with software enhancements for its predecessor should not be underestimated.[13] The following remarks usefully encapsulate his activities in this context:

> I originally started using the 4X at IRCAM to realize a piece, and I continued with certain threads of ideas I had experimented with at both SYCOM and the Institute of Sonology. I used the 4X for six years, writing 4X micro-code, C programs, and Max interfaces for a variety of projects. I composed three pieces with the 4X, but like my previous real-time works, the final results were either tape or tape and instrument pieces, due to the lack of portability of the 4X.[14]

The last sentence is especially interesting in that, notwithstanding the real-time capabilities of the 4X, such a material practical obstacle to performances of his works other than at IRCAM militated for a pragmatic decision to continue working with fixed tape media for some considerable time. In terms of the resources used for preparing the tape parts, however, he was to explore the real-time possibilities of the system with considerable industry.

It is helpful at this point to return to the repertory of software for the 4X considered by way of background to the earlier discussion of Manoury's pioneering works at IRCAM in Chapter 3. It will be recalled that of all the possibilities being opened up by researchers at IRCAM, it was Puckette's Max that was to prove key to the production of these works, and the same holds true for the resulting portfolio of compositions written by Lippe, both at IRCAM and also subsequently following his return to the United States in 1994. In programming terms, it was the development of Puckette's Patcher programming language that established the basis of Max as it is known today, in the first instance used to control MIDI-based objects in real time via a graphics-based user interface. Once again Lippe was to make a useful contribution to the development of the language, including an application that allowed the spatialization of the sounds of amplified instruments over multiple loudspeakers in live performance.[15] He was also instrumental in persuading Puckette to develop "help" windows for the user interface to assist the composer.[16]

In terms of Lippe's creative work during this period, the first of his three 4X-based works, *Music for Harp and Tape* (1989), was commissioned by Masumi Nagasawa and premiered at the Ueno Cultural Center, Tokyo, in March 1990. The work was also awarded first prize at the 19th Annual Electronic Music Competition, Bourges, 1991. The following extract from the program note usefully locates this output in the context of his work with the 4X and Max, and also highlights the specific processing techniques he employed to create the tape part:

> The tape part was created at IRCAM, Paris using the control program *Max* developed by Miller Puckette, whose technical advice made this piece possible) along with signal processing and control software written by the composer and Puckette for the 4X real-time digital signal processor; and the digital mix of the final tape part was made with the valuable assistance of the sound engineer Xavier Bordelais. The piece is divided into four main sections. Tremolos at registral extremes define the first section. The second section uses a repeated sforzando chord in the highest register to separate gestures exploring descending major and minor seconds. Muted chords becoming arpeggios characterize the third section, and the use of two clearly separated layers and extended techniques make up the fourth section.
>
> The tape part is composed entirely of digitally transformed and processed harp sounds taken from the composed instrumental part. The computer system tracked parameters of the harp, such as pitch, amplitude, continuous pitch change, rests, articulation, tempi, etc., and used this information to continuously control and/or influence digital synthesis algorithms running in real-time on the 4X. Time stretching, granular sampling, and other more standard signal processing such as harmonizing, frequency shifting, phasing, spatialization, etc., were employed. The instrument/machine relationship is entirely symbiotic—the instrument and tape are equals in the musical dialogue. At times one part may dominate, but in the overall formal structure, a duo is implicit.[17]

To return to the earlier explanation of the reasons why Lippe felt it necessary to create prerecorded tapes for his 4X works, it is nonetheless evident from a closer study of these works that the ability to work interactively with the 4X in real time during the compositional stage greatly enhanced the degree of craftsmanship he could exercise from such an immediately "hands on" working environment, not least in terms of achieving such a productive sense of integration and interaction in performance between the live harp and its prerecorded partner.

His second 4X work, *Music for Guitar and Tape* (1990), was commissioned by Carlos Molinaro and premiered in Paris in 1991 at UNESCO. This composition shares many of the musical characteristics associated with the previous work, but the differences in the sonic qualities of the acoustic instruments used in each piece provide fertile ground for exploring features that are unique to each. In the latter context the expressive possibilities of the guitar, notably in the context of articulating melodic content, are productively captured and extended using the available repertory of digital signal processing routines. What is especially interesting here, as noted in the above commentary, was the decision to use event-tracking software in the manner described for *Music for Harp and Tape* simultaneously using this information to control digital synthesis algorithms running in real time on the 4X.

The IRCAM Musical Workstation and Max

A further incentive for this engagement with score-following techniques was the completion of the prototype IRCAM Musical Workstation (IMW) in the same year and his clear grasp of the enhanced possibilities thus opened up not only for real-time live synthesis, but also in practical terms as a realistic proposition for live performances in different venues. Lippe was to complete one further work using the 4X, *Paraptra* (1991) for stereo tape, based on processed harp and guitar sounds, but by this stage his primary preoccupation was exploring the creative potential of the Workstation.

As noted in Chapter 3, the IMW, and its commercial derivative the ISPW, consisted of a NeXT computer acting as a command and control host device, connected to a network of Intel i860 processor boards that were used for fast front-end computing tasks. In engineering terms this environment was a marked improvement on that associated with the 4X, since it reduced what used to be a three-stage architecture, with all the additional problems of internal communication, to one consisting in hardware terms of just two segments. In the case of the 4X an intermediate control system for scheduling events had to be inserted between the 4X and the host computer. In the IMW the architecture of the i860 made it possible for the real-time scheduling functions to be implemented entirely within the DSP environment. Thus, in software terms, once the instructions had been loaded into the latter, the network of i860 processors became entirely self-sufficient, the NeXT computer acting simply as a graphics-based monitoring console.

The associated NeXT computer, otherwise known as the NeXT Cube, had been launched in 1988 as one of a series of advanced computer workstations specifically developed as compact alternatives to older more traditional minicomputers such as the PDP-11. Although, as was the case for rivals such as the Silicon Graphics and Sun workstations, the NeXT was primarily intended for applications such as computer-aided graphic design, the facilities provided for high-speed communication with other devices directly via its own internal communications bus, known as the NextBus, made it especially attractive as a host for the i860 system. Moreover, the architecture of the latter made it possible to communicate command and control data entirely via MIDI.

Each IMW/ISPW board consisted of two i860 processors, each with a fast local memory of 32 megabytes, a considerable improvement on earlier systems such as the DMX-1000, which had a maximum on-board memory capacity of just 4 kilobytes. Furthermore, the NextBus could accommodate up to three IMW/ISPW boards, this modular arrangement allowed up to six digital signal processors to operate in parallel. Each processor could access the local memories of the other i860 processors within the system, thus creating a powerful computing environment.[18] Each board hosted a pair of analog-to-digital and digital-to analog converters, the complete Workstation thus providing facilities for up to six channels of audio. In due course a special interface card was developed to accommodate eight channels of both analog and digital I/O. In common with other advanced computer workstations, the NeXT was based on UNIX, an environment originally pioneered by Bell Telephone Laboratories for the PDP-11. This allowed almost all of the associated processes and control functions to be written in the C programming language, which, along with its various extensions and derivatives, has underpinned the development of computer music applications to the present day. In the case of both the IMW and the ISPW systems, however, standard UNIX could not provide the level of performance necessary at an operating system level to handle audio communications between the i860 DSPs and the host computer in real time.[19]

In order to overcome this hurdle, an additional control layer, known as the CoProcessor Operating System (CPOS), was introduced. Perhaps uniquely, this extra control sub-layer was resident in the i860 part of the system, thus reversing the usual master-slave relationship when executing DSP-intensive tasks.[20] In terms of applications software, two programs achieved particular prominence from the outset, ANIMAL and Max. ANIMAL (ANIMAted Language), developed by Eric Lindemann, was primarily intended as a development tool for graphics applications, in particular the design of graphics-driven user interfaces for controlling music applications on the IMW.[21] However, in the current context it is the further development of Max for the Workstation that is of particular interest.[22]

In Chapter 3 reference is made to the development of the FTS (Faster Than Sound) extension to Max for sound processing, the precursor of both Max/MSP and also Puckette's Pd (Pure Data). Lippe was to play an important role both in terms of the practical implementation of FTS on the Workstation and the subsequent use of Max/FTS in the context of real-time synthesis.

279

Moreover, the corresponding enhancements to the working environment led him finally to engage with the possibilities of live processing in a performance context. The resulting work, *Music for Clarinet and ISPW*, was thus an important landmark both in terms of the evolution of Max as a composing environment and also Lippe's own creative development, thus providing an important reference point for his subsequent musical repertory, up to and including *Music for Tuba and Computer* (2008), the work selected for close study in this chapter.

Music for Clarinet and ISPW was commissioned in 1990 by the Center for Computer Music and Music Technology (CCMMT), Kunitachi College of Music, Tokyo. Lippe completed an initial version of the work at IRCAM before relocating to CCMMT in 1991 to continue its composition as part of a visiting fellowship. A series of public presentations of the work in progress were undertaken, starting with four performances at IRCAM in April 1991 and finishing with a further presentation in Tokyo in January 1992. Unfortunately, arrangements for a full-scale Tokyo premiere of the completed work ran into a number of practical difficulties and this landmark event took place instead in New York in March 1992.

Two features of the Workstation merit closer scrutiny at this stage. The first of these concerns the design of a graphics-based user interface and data editing facility by Puckette. This editor, known as EXPLODE, was implemented as an external "object" for Max, and was thus accessible to the user from within the graphics-based Max environment.[23] Although the prototype version used parameters derived directly from MIDI performance data, specifically time, pitch, velocity, duration, and audio channel, this was soon extended to embrace performance events triggered directly from audio signals. Lippe was to make an important contribution to the further research necessary in this challenging context, testing and refining a pitch detection algorithm developed by Puckette for use with EXPLODE.[24] In writing a study for clarinet specifically for this purpose, he also usefully prepared the ground for *Music for Clarinet and ISPW*.[25] Important refinements in the algorithm included a facility to extract variations in pitch as a continuous control function that could be used in a manner similar to that of a pitch bend function in MIDI, supported by an envelope tracking facility.[26] Lippe and Puckette describe the techniques employed as follows (see also Figure 8.2):

> The procedure for score following is rather simple: enter a score into a computer in some form, and then play the score as real-time input to the computer (either via a MIDI interface or a microphone and acoustic analysis), comparing the computer's stored score to the musician's playing on a note by note basis. If the comparison being made between the two is successful, the computer advances in the data base (the stored score) in parallel with the player, triggering electronic events at precise points in the performance score. In theory, one or many parameters can be followed, but with one interesting exception, we have settled on pitch.

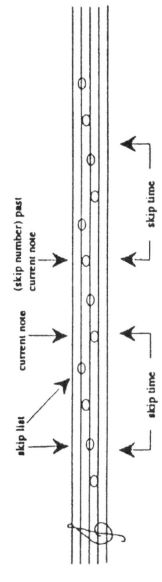

Figure 1. A "score" (the phrase a-b-c-d repeated three times), indicating a possible state for the score follower. Incoming notes can match either an element of the skip list, or a note on or past the "current note", but not past the end of the second "skip time" interval (the tenth note in this example). At this point, the notes b and d would be eaten by the skip list; the notes a and c would match the fifth and seventh notes, respectively.

FIGURE 8.2

Score follower.[27]

The score following algorithm's state consists of a pointer to the "current" note, and a set of pointers to prior notes which have not been matched (the "skip list"). There are two free parameters: the "skip number" (a non-negative integer) and the "skip time" (in units of time.) The "current note" is the note immediately after the furthest note (in the ordering of the data base) that has been matched. The score follower is started by setting the current note to the first note of the data base. Once the last note has been matched, the current note is undefined (but matching can still continue if there are notes in the skip list.) When a live note is played, the follower attempts to match it with a note in the data base; the matched note must have the same pitch as the live one (alternatively, if the live notes might have octave errors such as from a pitch tracker, matches can be accepted between notes that differ by an octave.) First, a match is sought from the skip list. For the match to be valid the skipped note may not be more than the skip time prior to the current note (the time being taken from the data base); that is, the follower will not back up more than that amount. (We can thus drop old notes from the skip list to control its size.)

If no match is found from the skip list, the search is continued starting at the current note. First, a fixed number of notes are examined, given by the skip number. Then, starting from the last such note, the search is continued for all notes that lie within the skip time. If a match is found at or past the current note, the current note and skip list are updated. In figure 1, a possible score follower state is shown, indicating which notes are matchable at a given time. Typical choices are one or two for the skip number, and .1 to .3 seconds for the skip time. The skip number is primarily relevant in slow, melodic passages where no two notes might be within the skip time of each other in the data base; it represents the number of mistakes of omission the player may make before the follower gets lost. (From the point of view of the score follower, the player "jumps ahead" to the next correct note that is played.) The skip number is best kept small because a wrong or extra note can cause the follower to jump forward; the greater the skip number, the greater the number of possibilities for matching the incorrect note.[28]

The second feature to be considered here is the practical characteristics of FTS. Although there are some differences in terms of the additional features provided when Max/FTS is directly compared with a more recent version of Max/MSP, the key operating principles are essentially identical. Although some significant programming challenges had to be solved, from the user point of view extending the library of MIDI control functions provided by Max to embrace audio functions was, from a conceptual point of view, entirely straightforward. Parallels may be drawn with the functional characteristics of a voltage-controlled synthesizer, where a network of interconnections between audio signal generators and processors is linked to a second network of control signals that regulate the operation of the former in real time. The distinction between these two components is secured by using a tilde (~) suffix to all the library components that directly handle audio signals.[29] Figure 8.3 shows the specification of a simple enveloped oscillator implemented in FTS as one component of a chain of polyphonic oscillators illustrates the way in which audio and control functions are thus combined.[30]

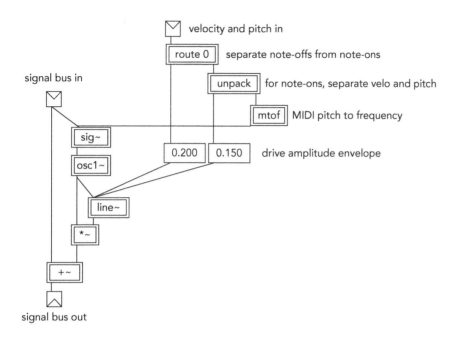

signal bus in

velocity and pitch in

route 0 — separate note-offs from note-ons

unpack — for note-ons, separate velo and pitch

mtof — MIDI pitch to frequency

sig~

0.200   0.150 — drive amplitude envelope

osc1~

line~

*~

+~

signal bus out

283

By the time Lippe started work on *Music for Clarinet and ISPW* in early 1990, over forty signal processing objects had been developed for FTS, embracing a wide range of signal processing tasks such as sampling, filtering, pitch tracking, level detection, reverberation, delay lines, cross-synthesis, spatialization, and analysis/resynthesis techniques such as phase vocoding.[32] Further contributions to the development of this repertory of DSP objects were made by Zack Settel, who had joined IRCAM initially on a composing fellowship in 1986, coincidentally the same year as Lippe. He too was to take an increasing interest in developing new tools for Max/FTS, and his collaboration with Lippe and Puckette led to an important performing partnership, known as the Convolution Brothers.[33]

This repertory of DSP functions was explored and extended by Lippe in two important respects. Firstly, he made extensive use of a time-stretching and pitch-transposing algorithm that allowed independent control of the two parameters, developed by Puckette. A key stimulus here was his growing interest in the spectral possibilities of processing vocal sounds. Secondly, he made significant use of granular synthesis techniques, building upon the pioneering work of Barry Truax, Curtis Roads, and Iannis Xenakis, discussed in Chapter 2. The parallels that can be drawn with Truax are especially significant in terms of the use of tendency masks to shape the granulations, in turn influenced by his earlier period of study at the Institute of Sonology. Notable similarities extend to the design of his graphic user interface for the ISPW, which he describes as follows:

Using Max on the ISPW, I have constructed an interface for controlling granular sampling in real time. All the parameters mentioned above, including onset time into the sampled sound, pitch, envelope description, maximum amplitude, grain duration, rate of grain production, overlap of grains, and spatial location of each grain are all controllable in real time for each grain that is calculated. Max also allows for real time switching from one sampled sound to another; either by reading elsewhere in memory, loading sound files from disk, or sampling anew (all of which can be done while the granular reading continues to take place). A control panel allows for the setting of parameter values via sliders and number boxes, and parameters can be independently changed over time via automation. Independent granular sampling tasks can run at the same time. Since the point of departure for this work in granular sampling grew out of experimentation with "time-stretching" of sampled sounds, each task originally produced a single stream of grains. Multiple, simultaneous grain attacks were a later development. (The number of tasks and the number of overlapping grains within a task are limited by real-time constraints.) A recent addition to the system allows for real-time mixing and sampling of the granular output of simultaneous tasks, which then may be reused as sample tables for other granular sampling tasks. This "recursive" approach offers exponential increases in densities, and a musically reflexive dimension (the ability to recall earlier musical material) which can be pertinent.[34]

Perhaps even more fundamentally at the process level, similarities with the granular processes used for time stretching in Truax's later works can also be identified in Lippe's commentary on the work:

My initial experiments with granular sampling were extremely simple and employed a single stream of grains. The auditory result of randomly choosing onset times into a stored sound, while producing grains at the original pitch of the sound, is fairly statistical. Using phrases of clarinet music, one has the impression with certain phrases that, for example, an entire 10-second phrase is sounding simultaneously. This is not surprising, since any onset is just as possible as any other, and, since, in using 20 millisecond grain durations with overlaps of 5 milliseconds between successive grains, more than 60 grains are produced each second. (Increasing the overlap time between grains will greatly increase the density of grains per second.) One sampled clarinet phrase, in particular, made up of approximately 5 seconds of rapid short notes, and then a 5-second held note was noteworthy because of the omnipresence of the long note in this statistical sound mass. It was immediately obvious that the musical content of the stored sounds being operated on was not a trivial aspect of the procedure, and that mapping algorithmic calculations onto the stored sound might produce more successful results if the musical content of the sound was taken into account.[35]

This granular-based technique usefully augmented Puckette's essentially phase vocoder–based approach to time-stretching for the ISPW, and Lippe was to make extensive use of this enhancement in *Music for Clarinet and ISPW*.[36] This work was an important milestone in the development of Lippe's musical repertory and merits closer scrutiny. His composing strategy was based on the following operational principles:

> Due to the large number of parameters and the much larger number of values needed for each parameter in granular techniques, it is obvious that algorithmic mappings can be extremely useful, if not necessary. . . . Since the ISPW offers tools for real-time audio signal analysis of acoustic instruments for the extraction of musical parameters, another level of control over the granular sampling comes directly from the performers, giving musicians a degree of expressive control over the electronic transformations. In *Music for Clarinet and ISPW* the sampled sounds used for granular sampling are taken directly from the performed score, either sampled on-the-fly during performance, or prerecorded and loaded into memory during performance. Continuous pitch and amplitude tracking of a performance offers musically relevant data which can be used to control aspects of an electronic score [see Figure 8.4], and perceptually create coherence between the instrument and electronics. In the clarinet piece, continuous pitch data taken from the clarinet is often used to control the pitch of grains, and continuous amplitude data controls the windowing of the tendency masks of certain parameters. In a composition in progress, additional control of parameters is being attempted via spectral analysis, thus allowing for timbral control of the sampling by way of instrumental color changes.[37]

285

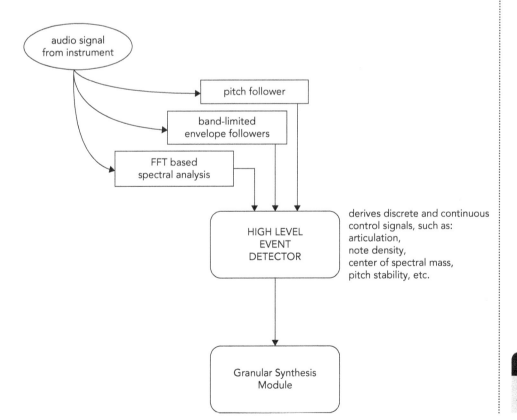

FIGURE 8.4

Flow diagram for real-time feature extraction.[38]

Three versions of his time-stretching algorithm were developed; *Trevor,* *PLAY-RAND*, and *Trevor_back*. *Trevor_back* reverses the direction of sampling through the data file, and *PLAY-RAND* introduces random parameters in terms of data extraction and granulation.[39] In terms of more standard signal processing techniques, extensive use is made of the frequency shifting, flanging, harmonizing, frequency and amplitude modulation, noise modulation, reverberation, and spatial distribution. The ways in which these techniques are applied, however, include a number of novel features, reflecting the nature and scope of the materials that are thus embraced.[40]

The live performance of the clarinet is of primary importance in this context, involving both acoustic feature detection and the insertion of performance control parameters. The basic configuration of the detection system is shown in Figure 8.5, using a refinement of the acoustic component of the dual MIDI/ acoustic tracker system described earlier:

The performance data extracted from the clarinet has a dual purpose. Firstly, to synchronize individual note-events with the score previously loaded into the computer, and secondly, to use the discrete variations in pitch and

286

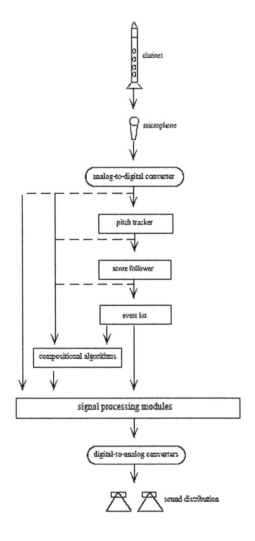

FIGURE 8.5

Acoustic feature extraction and performance control system.[41]

amplitude as control functions for a matrix of real-time digital signal processing tasks. The latter are subject to algorithmically determined selection and triggering procedures, extending not only to the live processing of the clarinet sound, but also the selection and processing of prerecorded sound events. The score-following algorithm was designed by Puckette, building on his previous work in this context.[42] Even at this relatively late stage in the development of his technique, however, the complexity of the processes involved still created opportunities for performance errors, and these remain material risks even in the context of present-day score-following facilities. Lippe eventually concluded that, for this work at least, it would be better to abandon the score-following method of triggering events and rely instead on manual intervention by the performer via a foot-pedal, or optionally that of a second party using the computer keyboard.[43]

The complexity of the techniques employed in *Music for Clarinet and ISPW* are by now self-evident, but at the same time they provide an important milestone in the development of computer music works involving a live performer. In now turning to a subsequent Lippe work for detailed study in the context of analysis and resynthesis, our understanding of the creative and technical issues that arise can be usefully enhanced.

Inside *Music for Tuba and Computer*

Commissioned by the Zentrum für Kunst und Medientechnologie (ZKM) in Karlsruhe at the initiative of the tuba player Melvyn Poore, *Music for Tuba and Computer* was composed in 2008 and created on January 31, 2009, in ZKM's *Kubus* hall, along with two other works by Agostino Di Scipio and Poore himself. Lippe's composition is part of a long lineage of works for solo instrument and live electronics, of which *Music for Clarinet and ISPW* was the starting point. *Music for Flute and ISPW* (1994), *Music for Contrabass and Computer* (1995), *Music for Piano and Computer* (1996), and *Music for Alto Saxophone and Computer* (1997) were all composed using the ISPW—at IRCAM for *Music for Flute*, and at the Hiller Computer Music Studios of the State University of New York at Buffalo for the three other works.[44] The subsequent works, *Music for Hi-Hat and Computer* (1998), *Music for Cello and Computer* (1999), *Music for Marimba and Computer* (2004), and *Music for Snare Drum and Computer* (2007), did not involve the ISPW, but all continued to make use of the Max environment for the live interaction and digital sound processing.[45] For the composer, this lineage does not result from the advance planning of a particular series:

[Since the early 1990s,] a majority of [my] pieces are for single instruments and electronics. And, in terms of where [*Music for Tuba and Computer*] fits into the sequence of pieces, I am not sure if I have ever mapped out a sequence initially, so that it is not following in some line that is logical at all. I think, in fact, it may be that it partially could be a reaction, to a certain degree, to the piece that was made prior to it, or the couple of pieces that were made prior to it. . . . Usually, with every piece, I am trying to think, well, what can I do that I did not do in the last few pieces?[46]

However, Lippe mentions one important specificity of *Music for Tuba and Computer*, related to the interaction between the instrumentalist and the computer, and resulting from the creative process at ZKM:

There is a lot more, let us say, real-time control for the player. . . . In this [piece], there are some very . . . specific directions for how to produce responses from the computer that might be considered proper responses. And one of the reasons for this piece having a more intimate relationship, in some ways, between the performer and the computer, is that a lot of the compositional work on the piece was done in the presence of the performer. There was a very close interaction for this piece between myself and Melvyn Poore. . . . He would try some things, and he was always ready to play some things, test things out, and then he would go back in his studio, and I would continue to work.[47]

The properties of the solo instrument chosen for a particular piece have, of course, fundamental implications for the composer's orientations in researching digital processes, all the more as the pitch, amplitude, and, more importantly, spectrum of the instrument are continuously used to shape the electroacoustic part of the work:

In developing some convolution cross-synthesis ideas, certain instruments respond better to certain kinds of synthetic crossings with sounds than other instruments. For instance, crossing timpani with, let us say, a noise burst, works quite well. . . . Crossing maybe a violin with a noise burst makes less sense. . . . A lot of that has to do with questions of spectral intersection between two sounds. . . . There is some work I did in [*Music for Tuba and Computer*] with . . . compression and expansion of FFT bins, and. . . . I was surprised that it worked as well as it did with tuba, because the tuba spectrum is rather poor, in terms of number of harmonics. . . . The effect was rather subtle, but quite, I think, remarkable.[48]

You can watch videos of our interviews with Cort Lippe in the accompanying software, which includes several presentations where the composer discusses his compositional ideas and processes, and discusses excerpts of Music for Tuba and Computer. *Demonstration Video 8.1 shows how to access these resources and play longer excerpts of these interviews.* ▶

General form and materials

As with most of Cort Lippe's works for soloists and computer, the program notes for *Music for Tuba and Computer* present the modalities of interaction between the instrument and the live electronics as an essential factor in shaping the musical discourse:

> Formally, the piece is in two sections, and the instrument/computer relationship moves on a continuum between the poles of an extended solo and a duo. Musically, the computer part is sometimes inseparable from the tuba part, but serves rather to amplify the tuba in multiple dimensions and directions; while at the other extreme of the continuum, the computer part also has its own independent musical voice.[49]

Music for Tuba and Computer has an approximate duration of 16′30″, and the two sections last 7′30″ and 9′00″, respectively.[50] The work starts with the tuba playing a low D (see Figure 8.6).

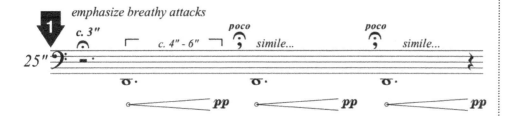

This pitch is held for the opening two-thirds of the first section; the tuba player is required to operate dynamic and timbre variations with "mouth shape, harmonics, and consonant multiphonics."[52] At bar 14 (approx. 3′30″), the instrumentalist must begin singing into the tuba and play long durations with circular breathing:

> I have a . . . rather simple and easily perceivable goal in the first section, in which the player continues to play this one note, but complicates the note with circular breathing, and shaping of the mouth in different ways, singing into the tuba, so this one note becomes actually much more than a single note, although it is dominated by the continually held low D. One of the hard things, I think, compositionally, is, how do you break from something like that, and when do you break from it? How do you get away from something you have been sitting on for quite a long time in a piece? . . . I just started adding notes, gradually. But the first note you add is kind of shocking, in a certain way.[53]

At bar 21 (approx. 5′05″) the tuba starts deviating from the low D within a range of less than one tone, and new pitch classes then appear, starting with an F. From bar 24 to the end of the first section, the tuba alternates short, fast, large-range motifs with low "pedal tones" (see Figure 8.7).

FIGURE 8.7

Bar 24 of *Music for Tuba and Computer*, starting the alternation between short motifs and low pedal tones.[54]

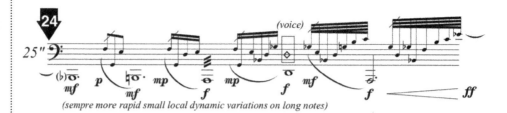

(*sempre more rapid small local dynamic variations on long notes*)

Gradually, these low pedal tones exhaust all twelve pitch classes of the chromatic scale; a low A-flat, an octave and a tritone down from the initial D, only appears as the final pedal tone of section 1, and leads into section 2. A-flat, one octave higher, is also the final note of the second section, and the dyad D/A-flat can be seen as the two main pitch poles of the piece.

Although the spectrum of the tuba, or more generally the solo instrument, is at the forefront of Lippe's electroacoustic research, his approach to writing is very different from that of spectralism as developed by composers such as Gérard Grisey or Tristan Murail:

> Often, in pieces where I am making use of the spectrum of the instrument in the electronic part, I tend to do something different in the instrumental part. . . . It is often thought that spectralists make use of information based on analysis of instruments, or natural sounds . . . or even [frequency modulation], which Tristan Murail made use of in instrumental music. So, it is [in my case] going in the other direction: the spectral exploration ends up being in the computer part, and the actual *écriture*, or musical notes for the instrument, are based on other kinds of interests.[55]

The following sections focus on the computer environment implemented for the performance of *Music for Tuba and Computer*, before presenting the interactions between the tuba part and the live electronics through the chronology of the work.

The digital environment for the performance of *Music for Tuba and Computer*

Implemented in Max, the computer program developed by Cort Lippe for his tuba piece takes the digitized acoustic output of the instrument as audio input, and interacts with it through a network of dynamically interconnected modules acting as generators and processors. As discussed in more detail later, both types of modules can be controlled with parameters derived from the real time analysis of the sound produced by the tuba.

Generators
- A large oscillators module with two 48-oscillator banks and a third submodule including Phase-Aligned Formant synthesis (PAF).
- Two samplers, respectively named "Sampler S" and "Sampler T."
- A synthesizer named "Toto."

Processors
- A harmonizer.
- A noiser/phaser module.
- A bank of frequency shifters.
- A large set of fast Fourier transform (FFT) processors, with several submodules and additional sources for cross-synthesis.
- A simple reverberation.
- A bank of allpass filters.
- A "spatialization" module, involving phasing with complex modulation.
- A stereo output module, including two parallel Leslie effects.

> You can use Presentation 1 of the accompanying software, "Interactive structural map," to listen to a simulation of performance while visualizing the tuba, the generators, the processors, and how they are dynamically interconnected in Music for Tuba and Computer, as presented in Demonstration Video 8.2. ▶

The sigmund~ object and the oscillators module

The oscillators module, used in many different ways from the beginning of *Music for Tuba and Computer* through to the first quarter of the second section, consists of three submodules: two banks of forty-eight oscillators, and a "Fundamental" module mostly involving Phase-Aligned Formant synthesis. Like most generators and processors in Lippe's piece, the oscillators are used in conjunction with a real-time signal analysis engine, developed by the composer around Miller Puckette's sigmund~ external object for Max.[56] Sigmund~ is defined as a "sinusoidal analysis and pitch tracking" object,[57] and "analyses an incoming sound into sinusoidal components, which may be reported individually or combined to form a pitch estimate."[58] In Lippe's implementation, sigmund~ is configured to output five types of information, all computed from the built-in analysis based on a real-time fast Fourier transform of 2048 points:

- "Notes" are output as floating-point Midi pitch numbers from sigmund~ every time a new note event is detected in the input signal.
- "Pitch" is also a floating-point Midi pitch value, but is continuously estimated and output. The output interval corresponds to the hop size of the FFT, set to 1,024 samples in Lippe's program, that is, half the FFT size. At the normally operating sampling frequency of 44,100 Hz, this means the information is output every 46.44 milliseconds.

- "Envelope" is the continuously estimated and output level of the incoming signal.
- "Tracks" are continuously estimated frequency and amplitude values for forty-eight sinusoidal peaks. The peaks are "arranged into maximally continuous tracks"[59] over time, and are output with a flag indicating whether the information belongs to a new track, to a continued track, or to an empty track.
- Finally, "peaks" are also continuously estimated frequency and amplitude values for forty-eight sinusoidal peaks; however, unlike "tracks," they are arranged in decreasing order of amplitude.

While the three first types of data—notes, pitch, and envelope—are propagated toward most generators and processors of the real-time environment, as will be discussed in the presentation of each of these modules, sinusoidal tracks and peaks are only used to control the oscillators module, and most significantly its two oscillator banks, making the link between the spectral analysis of the live tuba sound and the resynthesis particularly strong. For Lippe, there is little value in passing the analysis of the incoming signal directly to the oscillator banks: "just to simply resynthesize the sound of the tuba is of course less interesting than creating some other kind of processing result from the computer part."[60] Indeed, the sinusoidal components information is only used as a basis for a variety of subsequent manipulations. For instance, nonsinusoidal wavetables are often used for the resynthesis with the oscillator banks:

> The typical way to do analysis/resynthesis is that you resynthesize with a bank of sine wave oscillators. . . . [But] the idea [in *Music for Tuba and Computer*] of using harmonic signals, with a couple more harmonics, meant that each harmonic [generated] its [own] set of harmonics in that way. So, it is a much richer kind of result than just the sine wave result, because [in this latter case] what you put in is what you get out. If you have adequate analysis/resynthesis, and you put an instrument in, you get that instrument out, or maybe a slightly watered down version of that instrument. But using harmonic tables, with multiple overtones, you can get a much richer signal out than the original input.[61]

Before examining the several processes involved in the oscillators module, you can familiarize yourself with a straightforward analysis/resynthesis of a tuba sound, using Presentation 4 of the accompanying software, "Spectral analysis and resynthesis," and vary it using the tables mentioned by the composer, as shown in Demonstration Video 8.3. ▶

The first bank of the oscillators module is driven from the forty-eight sinusoidal tracks output by the sigmund~ object. In a typical analysis/resynthesis situation, the frequency and amplitude values of each track pass with minimal processing to each oscillator of the bank.[62] A first technique used by Cort Lippe to diverge from such a conventional use is the decoupling of the resynthesized amplitudes from those estimated by sigmund~. When the continuously received amplitudes are blocked, the oscillators are only updated in terms of frequencies, with the amplitudes remaining at their most recent value. Although the frequencies are still derived from the spectrum of the tuba, their decoupling from the corresponding amplitudes is sufficient to create, perceptually, an impression of randomization in the resynthesis. Such a glittering effect can be heard in the first seconds of *Music for Tuba and Computer*, where the arbitrarily amplified spectral components of the tuba contrast strikingly with the steady low pitch of the instrument itself.

A submodule named "Gumbo," when active, applies the spectral envelope of the live tuba to the amplitudes of the forty-eight oscillators of the first bank. This technique, also found with the same name and a very similar implementation in Philippe Manoury's *Pluton*, relies on the continuous recording of the FFT magnitudes of the tuba signal into a buffer.[63] These magnitudes are then used as a control for the amplitudes of the resynthesis oscillators: for instance, a sinusoidal component with a frequency of 1,000 Hz will have a great amplitude if a lot of spectral energy is present at the frequency bin corresponding to 1,000 Hz in the analysis of the tuba sound recorded in the Gumbo buffer; the same sinusoidal component will have an amplitude of zero if no energy can be found at that frequency bin in the buffer. This second case should theoretically never occur in a conventional and artifact-free case of analysis/resynthesis, as it is expected that if a partial is estimated at a given frequency, then some energy is present at that frequency in the Gumbo buffer. However, such a correspondence is not necessarily applicable in *Music for Tuba and Computer*, as several mechanisms, including the decoupling of amplitudes mentioned above, imply that the spectral contents derived from sigmund~ do not necessarily correspond to the spectral contents of the Gumbo buffer. Besides, the Gumbo implementation, as in *Pluton*, allows for the recorded spectral envelope to be compressed or stretched, in which case the correspondence becomes irrelevant. A reactivity factor also sets the rate at which new amplitudes are applied, whether abruptly or smoothly.

Another submodule named "Chapo," only used in bars 14 to 17 of section 1, is also used to apply a spectral envelope to the amplitudes of the first bank of oscillators (the Gumbo and the Chapo module are never used simultaneously). Unlike that of Gumbo, the spectral envelope of Chapo is prewritten in a table. The envelope is continuously moving across the frequency axis on the basis of the envelope information output by sigmund~ and a constant portamento value, creating an effect of spectral glissandi over the sinusoidal components.[64]

Alongside the Gumbo and Chapo submodules, a spectral snapshot system is implemented so that the frequency and amplitude values of the sinusoidal components can be held for a certain duration: this technique is used through most of section 1, as a snapshot is taken in bar 6 and held through to bar 26. Over this period, the variations in the behavior of the first oscillator bank do not rely on the sinusoidal decomposition of the live tuba spectrum, but on the spectrum captured at the beginning of bar 6. As previously mentioned, the oscillator bank can also play nonsinusoidal waves; in the patch for *Music for Tuba and Computer*, a set of fifteen wavetables is available, fourteen of which are actually used in the piece:

> Most of the tables I use happen to be different weights of harmonics. There are a couple of . . . more inharmonic tables, but they have to be used judiciously, because you can really create a very, very thick texture out of something that is inharmonic like that. . . . Some of them are used in other pieces, but because of the small number of harmonics in the actual tuba, I felt much more comfortable using richer signals than sine waves for the resynthesis.[65]

Finally, a frequency multiplying factor can be used to multiply the frequencies as output by sigmund~, before being sent to the Gumbo and Chapo submodules and, ultimately, to the oscillator bank.

The second bank of the oscillators module is not driven by continuous tracks, but by the forty-eight peaks output by sigmund~. It is much simpler than the first bank, in that it has no Gumbo or Chapo submodule, and the rest of its implementation is similar to that of the track-driven bank. The resynthesis can be made with sine waves or one of the fifteen wavetables available in the program; a frequency multiplying factor is also implemented and varied through the piece. The spectral snapshot mechanism works slightly differently: when the snapshot is taken, the frequencies of the sinusoidal peaks are held, but not the amplitudes. Those are still passed to the resynthesis bank, but are smoothed over a longer time (100 milliseconds rather than 5 milliseconds). In Lippe's piece, a spectral snapshot for the second oscillator bank is taken in bar 2 and held through to bar 21.

The third submodule of the oscillators generator is named "Fundamental": it is driven by the peak that matches the pitch estimated by sigmund~. In practice, this fundamental-driven synthesis is only active in section 1 between bars 15 and 24, and during that period the frequency and amplitude of the fundamental peak are those of the snapshot taken at bar 2 by the first oscillator bank submodule. The synthesis engine consists of two objects: a phase modulation object and a Phase-Aligned Formant object. In the modulation object, a sinusoidal oscillator is phase modulated with another sinusoid, the frequency of which is set with the pitch output by sigmund~; the modulation amount is controlled with the tuba amplitude envelope. The other object implements PAF synthesis, a technique developed by Miller Puckette and "subject of a 1994 patent owned by IRCAM."[66] Its author presents it as follows:

> Sounds—especially but not exclusively speech—are often described in terms of their fundamental pitch and several *formants*, or peaks in the spectral envelope. A formant's contribution to the perceived timbre of the sound is roughly determined by the formant's peak strength, center frequency, and bandwidth. One can approximately describe a sound's spectral envelope by locating its most important peaks and representing them as formants. . . . The PAF (*Phase-Aligned Formant*) generator . . . is an inexpensive method for generating sounds with a desired pitch and set of formants.[67]

In the implementation for *Music for Tuba and Computer*, the pitch of the PAF object is set with the fundamental frequency received as a result of the snapshot taken at bar 2; the center frequency and the bandwidth are either set with numeric values, or modulated with the tuba amplitude envelope as delivered by the sigmund~ object.

> *You can engage aurally with the two oscillator banks and the fundamental-driven synthesis of the oscillators module and their associated techniques as described above by exploring further Presentation 4 of the accompanying software. Demonstration Video 8.4 guides you through these features and provides aural examples related to their implementation in* Music for Tuba and Computer. ▶

The two samplers S and T

The two samplers, simply labeled "ssamp" and "tsamp" in Lippe's Max patch, both implement sample playback, each in specific ways. Sampler S has eight loop players and can access prerecorded samples from a reservoir of forty buffers, numbered 1 to 40. Each of these samples corresponds to a tuba note, all semitones of the chromatic scale being represented from D#1 to F#4. Sampler S is active in the second section of *Music for Tuba and Computer*, starting at event 9. In our interviews, Lippe mentions its function in event 18:

> Late in the piece, a kind of . . . climactic denouement . . . there are a great number of processes that are all taking place at the same time. There is some FFT processing . . . [and] there is a kind of sampler playback, that goes between eight different samples, rhythmically mixing between them. That takes place in the background . . . moving from pitch to pitch, based on pitches that the tuba player played.[68]

The mix of the eight samples is handled with a two-dimensional surface on which a point defines the balance between all eight sounds. In Lippe's patch, the eight buffers are represented around this surface. If the point is at the center of the surface, all sounds are mixed with an equal level. If the point is toward an edge of the surface, it tends to emphasize the nearest samples. The position of the point, and consequently the mix of the eight samples, is automated with a Lissajous trajectory: its horizontal and vertical coordinates are defined with two independent sine waves, the frequency, amplitude, and phase of which are varied through section 2. As evoked by Lippe, new notes detected by sigmund~ in the live tuba signal assign the sample corresponding to the estimated pitch to one of the eight loop players, successively; at any time, the output of sampler S is therefore a harmony made of the most recent eight pitches played by the live tuba.

Sampler T, only used from event 14 of section 2, has two distinct functions: the first is that of playing a 1.5 minute tuba sequence previously recorded by Melvyn Poore and named "melvyn-samp"; this sequence is looped during all the period of activity of the sampler. The second function of sampler T is to play samples from Cort Lippe's previous tuba piece, *Solo Tuba Music*, premiered by Mel Culbertson in 1987. The composer mentions them, again in the context of event 18 of the second section:

> There is also a playback of some . . . very short samples of extended techniques of solo tuba that I took from a piece I wrote some years ago for solo tuba. . . . A kind of a memory of an earlier piece in a certain way, using techniques that are not used in [*Music for Tuba and Computer*].[69]

In events 18 and 19, some specific pitches—defined as "hotspots"—trigger the playback of three of these short samples, chosen randomly in a reservoir of nineteen recordings from the composer's earlier piece.

> *Presentation 5 of the accompanying software, "Samplers," enables you to explore samplers S and T, their recorded sounds, and their modes of interaction with the live tuba. You can also use Presentation 16 to watch the interview with Cort Lippe quoted above, where he discusses event 18 of section 2 and shows his real-time software in action. Finally, you can also use Presentation 1 to scrutinize the samplers' activity in the context of the musical work. Demonstration Video 8.5 shows how to use these interactive resources.* ▶

The Toto synthesizer

The Toto synthesizer does not have variable parameters; it implements several techniques, including frequency modulation, multistage ring modulation, and the Karplus-Strong algorithm, involving a delay line with filtered feedback as a method for string synthesis, taking the tuba signal and the pitch information from sigmund~ as inputs.[70] It is active from events 7 to 19 of the first section, and from events 15 to 20 of the second section.

Demonstration Video 8.6 shows how to explore the Toto synthesizer using Presentation 6 of the accompanying software. ▶

Harmonizer, noiser/phaser, frequency shifters

These three processor modules can take either the live tuba or its resynthesis as inputs, and can send their output signals toward the FFT processors, the reverberation, the spatialization, and the stereo output.

The harmonizer consists of four parallel lines implementing a variable time delay to transpose its incoming signal; each line can be set in terms of transposition amount, and also a constant delay time, allowing for arpeggio-like effects. The transposition amounts can either be set with static or dynamic values in midicents[71] (6,000 midicents being defined as no transposition), or mapped to the amplitude envelope provided by sigmund~. In *Music for Tuba and Computer*, the harmonizer appears three times. In section 1, it processes the resynthesis from events 14 to 19; each line first ramps its transposition amount from 6,000 midicents to 8,071, 7,933, 8,333, and 8,589 midicents, respectively, then remains constant at these values, and then ramps its transposition amount again upward by ten semitones (reaching 9,071, 8,933, 9,333, and 9,589 midicents, respectively). In section 2, the transpositions are set with the amplitude of the tuba. From events 5 to 7, the harmonizer transposes both the tuba and the resynthesis; from events 17 to 20, it transposes the tuba only. In both cases, these amplitude-driven transpositions are passed to the FFT processes.

The two components of the noiser/phaser module both rely on four delay lines and oscillators reading, at different frequencies, a wavetable with rich spectral contents. In the case of the noiser component, eight wavetable players are combined to modulate the output amplitude of four lines delaying the input signal by short constant times (25, 21, 17.7, and 9.3 milliseconds, respectively). This leads to an aperiodic amplitude modulation of the four delayed signals, and is close to white noise when the base frequency for the wavetable players is at its maximum; this frequency can itself be set with a specific value or mapped to the amplitude envelope of the tuba. The four delay lines of the phaser component have their time varied, each with one dedicated wavetable player, leading to, as the name of the component indicates, a phasing effect. The noiser/phaser module is active through most of section 1, appearing at event 3 and deactivated at event 1 of the second section; it then reappears at event 14 until the end of the piece.

The frequency shifters module consists of four parallel lines, each with controls for the amount of frequency shift, the level of the positive sidebands, and the level of the negative sidebands. An automation mechanism can be activated to modulate the positive sidebands level asynchronously, at a certain speed. The frequency shifters module is active from event 18 of section 1 to event 7 of section 2, and then from events 16 to 20 of the second section.

In the accompanying software, you can use Presentation 8, "Frequency shifters," Presentation 9, "Harmonizers," and Presentation 10, "Noiser/Phaser," to explore these three simple processes individually. And you can use the interactive structural map of Presentation 1 to investigate their instantiations in Music for Tuba and Computer, as shown in Demonstration Video 8.7. ▶

The FFT processors

The FFT processors module appears at the beginning of section 2; it includes a variety of different spectral techniques, which are activated, interconnected, and parameterized dynamically through the section. One of these techniques is named "reverse noise reduction" by Cort Lippe:

A strange use of the idea of noise reduction is reverse noise reduction, in which the noisy parts of playing are amplified, and the pitch aspects of [it] are reduced. [At the beginning of section 2] there are some very, very low . . . pitches that are pedal tones on the tuba. And I have asked that the player emphasizes the breath of the attacks and decays of the notes, and also tries to vary the timbre slightly, as well as just a slight variation of the pitch. It is an example of something that looks relatively simple, but there are lots of demands on the player. And what I want to do is, take away some of the signal processes that are going on, and just focus on this idea of amplifying the noise.[72]

The reverse noise reduction appears at the beginning of section 2 until the end of event 5; it is reactivated from events 11 to 19 with further spectral processing. The magnitude threshold below which the frequency-domain signal passes and is amplified can be varied dynamically; an automation can also vary it periodically with an adjustable speed.

There are two independent lines of cross-synthesis in the FFT processors module. As defined by Julius Orion Smith III,

cross-synthesis is the technique of impressing the spectral envelope of one sound on the flattened spectrum of another. A typical example is to impress speech on various natural sounds, such as "talking wind."[73]

In Lippe's patch for *Music for Tuba and Computer*, it is the spectral envelope of the live tuba that is impressed on several types of sources. In the first line of cross-synthesis, the carrier signal is a sawtooth wave, the pitch of which is randomly changed, making in events 8 and 9 a "tuning game" in which the tuba player searches for consonances between the instrument and the cross-synthesis, as described more specifically below, in the analysis of section 2. The second line of cross-synthesis impresses the spectral envelope of the live tuba on four distinct sources. Three of these carriers are encapsulated inside the FFT module: a noise generator, the playback of the "melvyn-samp" sequence previously mentioned as also used with the sampler T, and a frequency modulation engine controlled with the pitch and envelope output by sigmund~. The fourth carrier is the signal output by sampler S, starting at event 9.

Five spectral processors, statically chained in series, rely on data recorded in buffers and interpolated in a similar way as that of sampler S, albeit for very different purposes. The first processor reorders the FFT bin indexes in such a way that the data recorded at a given bin index is in most cases read back at a lower bin index, in effect compressing the spectrum: a "phasing sound is produced by compressing and expanding the timbre of the tuba itself."[74] The second processor is a spectral filter, scaling the magnitude of each frequency bin by an interpolated random value between 0 and 1. Then, a spectral delay with feedback spreads the signal over time, with per-bin interpolated values assigned to both the delay time and the feedback amount. The fourth process scales the phase differences of the first sixty-four frequency bins, considerably blurring the spectrum of the incoming sound. Finally, a spectral spatializer distributes each frequency bin independently across the left and right channels: it creates "a very light left and right movement; it is not extremely audible spatialization, but the sound continues to shift very subtly."[75]

For each of these five processes, the data associated with the transformation of each frequency bin is stored in eight buffers arranged around a two-dimensional surface; as with sampler S, the interpolation between these eight buffers depends on the position of a point on the central surface. This position can be set manually using the graphical user interface associated with each process, which Lippe used for experimenting with the processes in the compositional period; however, during the performance itself, all interpolation positions are automated with Lissajous movements, with independent sinusoidal functions controlling the horizontal and vertical coordinates of each process's interpolation point, exactly as with the interpolated mix of sampler S.

The reverse noise reduction, the two cross-synthesis engines, and the five per-bin processors[76] can be interconnected dynamically with many controls for the levels internal to the overall FFT module, as recapitulated below:

– The main input, taking signals from the live tuba, sampler T, the Toto synthesizer, the harmonizer, the noiser/phaser module, and the frequency shifters, can be routed toward the series of five per-bin processors, and is always sent to the reverse noise reduction and the two cross-synthesis lines.

- – The secondary input, taking signals from the noise generator, the sound file player, the frequency modulation, and sampler S, can be directly routed toward the output of the overall module, and is always used as the carrier for the second cross-synthesis.
- – The reverse noise reduction can be directly sent to the overall output, or processed further with the five per-bin modules.
- – Likewise, the result of the first cross-synthesis process, taking a sawtooth waveform as the carrier, can be directly sent to the overall output, or processed further with the five per-bin modules.
- – The result of the second cross-synthesis process can be sent to all five per-bin modules, or just to the per-bin stereo panner.
- – The output of the series of five per-bin processes goes to the overall output of the FFT module with an adjustable level control.

An automated process, active from events 16 to 18 of section 2, controls, periodically and with an adjustable speed, the levels of the reverse noise reduction sent to the overall output and of the second cross-synthesis process sent to the per-bin stereo panner.

You can explore aurally all of these FFT processes independently with Presentation 15 of the accompanying software, "Fast Fourier transform processes." In the video of Presentation 13, Cort Lippe demonstrates the five per-bin processes in action. And you can use the parameter panels and parameter envelopes of Presentation 1 to investigate the dynamic evolution of all values through the chronology of section 2. Demonstration Video 8.8 introduces you to all these features, and you are encouraged to explore them further. ▶

Allpass filters and reverberation

Both the allpass filters and the reverberation modules amplify their input signals over time on the basis of delay lines with feedback. The first module comprises two parallel lines, each with three allpass filters chained in series; the delay times and amounts of feedback are adjustable. The module takes its input signal from the resynthesis oscillators, and is only active from events 4 to 6 of the first section; an automated mechanism turns the input level on for 200 milliseconds at randomized periods between two and three seconds. This "otoa-machine," along with relatively long delay times (between 128 and 780 milliseconds) and significant feedback amounts, transform the incoming resynthesis bursts into quickly decaying rhythmic motifs.[77]

The reverberation module is active through the entire piece. It can take signals from the live tuba and almost all the other modules, with the exception of the allpass filters, the spatialization, and the stereo output; it can direct its own output to these two latter modules. The signal processing engine consists of early reflections, longer echoes, and a reverberation with adjustable decay time. In *Music for Tuba and Computer*, the input and output levels are constant at their maximum value, and only the decay time is occasionally varied; its value is always high, making the room effect clearly perceptible.

> *Presentations 11, "Allpass filters," and 12, "Reverberation," enable you to listen to these two processes and experiment with their parameters. You can also use Presentation 1 to observe and listen to them in the context of the piece, for instance with the automatically set level from the oscillators to the allpass filters, as Demonstration Video 8.9 explains.* ▶

Spatialization and stereo output

Although *Music for Tuba and Computer* was commissioned by a leading institution for the spatialization of sound, Cort Lippe did not consider space as a fundamental attribute during the compositional process; rather, he made use of ZKM's Klangdom, a forty-seven-loudspeaker hemisphere installed in the *Kubus* hall for the diffusion of the premiere.[78] "I did not work on the spatialization until the piece was done. The spatialization was all after the fact, it was just a way to present the piece."[79] In general, the composer's focus on instruments and live electronics impacts his approach to sound in space: "this whole idea of keeping the performer central, which is important to me, means that I don't explore space as much as I would really like to."[80] Cort Lippe's Max patch for the real-time performance of the piece has a two-channel output. During the premiere, he made use of ZKM's Zirkonium software to make a site-specific projection of both the amplified tuba and the electronic part across the *Kubus* hemisphere:

> It was actually quite pleasurable . . . and very easy to work with their system, and I could do all the kinds of things that are interesting to do with sound, in terms of moving it around, in different kinds of pathways. . . . But I was still worried about the centrality of the performer, and I was able to come up with a scheme that I was comfortable with, that allowed me to do these complicated trajectories of the electronic sound, by instantiating the performer in such a way that as things got more complicated in terms of trajectories, I could insure that the performer would still be central to the experience. . . . A lot of the more complex movements in this

301

particular setup takes place as the tuba is playing more dynamically. . . . I was able to use a real-time envelope follower on the performer in order to directly control the number of speakers the performer would be amplified in. . . . As the performer played louder, the number of loudspeakers started to increase. . . . The most important thing was that this increase was in volume, in the sense of space, not in the sense of amplitude.[81]

Within the performance patch itself, there is no assumption about diffusion in a specific location. Each of the already presented generators and processors has three output channels: one mono, and one stereo. Almost every module can forward its mono output to a spatialization module and its stereo signal to a global stereo output module.[82] The spatialization module decomposes its incoming signal into real and imaginary components thanks to a Hilbert transform; the resulting complex signal is then processed with two parallel complex modulation engines, which direct their output signals to the left and right inputs of the global stereo module, respectively. The complex signals are modulated with one low-frequency oscillator with two out-of-phase outputs. The global stereo output module simply passes each of its input channels into a dedicated Leslie cabin effect simulator; the rotation frequency of each channel can be adjusted independently.

> You can use Presentation 17 of the accompanying software, "Spatialization," to experiment with both the spatialization module and the stereo output module, as shown in Demonstration Video 8.10. ▶

Global control of the digital environment

Like Philippe Manoury's *Pluton* and Jonathan Harvey's *Fourth String Quartet*,[83] the behavior of the digital environment for Cort Lippe's *Music for Tuba and Computer* is managed by electronic events—twenty-six in section 1, twenty-two in section 2—which trigger series of commands, typically handling the activation of the generators and processors, the amount of signal sent from one module to another, module parameter values, and specific processes such as taking a snapshot for the spectral analysis operated with sigmund~, or automated control over amplitudes, or Lissajous figures interpolating between FFT per-bin parameters, to name but a few examples from the processes detailed above. In the score of the tuba piece, each of these events is clearly identifiable with a numbered black arrow.[84]

A significant difference from Manoury's and Harvey's works is that each event is associated with a recommended duration, both written on the score and set in the Max patch. The tuba player can use a computer screen to monitor a progress bar indicating the time remaining to the next event; as Lippe explains, the screen "acts as a conductor".[85] According to the score, "events are triggered by the computer operator";[86] in practice, they can be triggered by the tuba player with a simple MIDI pedal, or automatically with the patch progressing toward the following event when the specified duration has elapsed.

Instrumental and electronic interactions through *Music for Tuba and Computer*
Section 1

Music for Tuba and Computer starts with a quiet, low D pedal tone played by the tuba; the first oscillator bank produces distinctive glittering sine tones, which appear and decay together with the instrumental sound. Both the instrument and the synthetic tones are reverberated. Low D tones are repeated, settling the pitch polarization for the first section; at event 2 the fourth tone is attacked more firmly, and its spectral content is recorded as a snapshot to be used by the second oscillator bank from events 3 to 21. At event 3 the tuba progressively increases the durations of the notes, as required by the score, and a slight phasing effect is applied to both the tuba and the resynthesis by the noiser/phaser module. The second oscillator bank, resynthesizing the previously recorded snapshot with sine waves, is also activated.

At event 4 the tuba player is asked to "begin slight timbre changes via mouth shape, harmonics, and consonant multiphonics";[87] the allpass filters start capturing and amplifying short bursts of the resynthesis, the timbre of which is also varied through the event by successive changes in the harmonic content of the wavetables used by the second oscillator bank. At event 5 a dramatic *sforzando* low D of the tuba breaks the initial quietness of the piece; it projects the rich texture of the resynthesis, itself shaped rhythmically with the allpass filters. The sforzando note is repeated; at event 6 a second spectral snapshot of the tuba is taken, freezing the forty-eight frequencies and amplitudes used for the first oscillator bank. The complex modulation of the spatializer module is also activated. The amplitude and density gradually decay, and the frozen timbre of the second spectral snapshot, modulated by the tuba via the Gumbo module with a low reactivity, can be heard emerging in the background.

303

You can watch Cort Lippe presenting the first minutes of the opening section by watching the video in Presentation 7 of the accompanying software, "Introduction to Music for Tuba and Computer." You can use Presentation 1 to listen to the piece and explore the modules and their parameters as they evolve and contribute to the electroacoustic part. Demonstration Video 8.11 explains how to operate these features for the first six events of section 1, and you are encouraged to use these resources further as you read through the following text on the remainder of the piece. ▶

After a brief pause, event 7 starts with a long low D tone; the allpass filters are deactivated, and the Toto synthesizer is introduced, providing a raw electronic counterpart to the live tuba. Through to event 8, the tension increases, with the tuba playing progressively louder and shorter pedal tones, always with small dynamic variations, and with the Gumbo spectral expansion being increased at each event, brightening the frozen timbre of the first oscillator bank. At event 14 the harmonizers are activated and operate an upward glissando of the transpositions of the resynthesis; the tuba player adds a vocal component to the pedal tones. At event 15 the Chapo module is activated, alternating with the Gumbo module. This creates abrupt spectral downward glissandi when the tuba player breathes. The fundamental-driven synthesis, at first augmented with modulation, also contributes to the significant intensification of the electronic part. At event 17 the Leslie effects on both channels of the overall stereo output are activated and accelerate quickly, maximizing the entropy of the electronics. At event 18 a new upward glissando of the harmonizer transpositions, along with the appearance of frequency-shifters and the Phase-Aligned Formant synthesis, leading to a climax at event 19; at this point, the electroacoustic part seems to have reached autonomy, and appears emancipated from the tuba from which it originated.

Following this climax, the electronic texture seems to dissolve itself during event 19; the PAF synthesis is controlled with slowly varying dynamics of the live tuba and modulated with the frequency shifters with automated levels, and the Leslie effect slows down and disappears, along with the Toto synthesizer. The PAF dominated texture is held with sustained tuba tones through to event 21, where the instrumentalist starts deviating from the D pitch pole; the pitch variation becomes prominent and is emphasized with tremolos. The spectral snapshot of the second oscillator bank is unfrozen, and at event 23 the frequency multiplier for the corresponding resynthesis glissandos downward.

At event 24 the PAF synthesis decays quickly, and the frequency multiplier for the first oscillator bank glissandos upward. From then on, the tuba starts playing short phrases, with fast motifs in the middle range alternating with low pedal tones. The electronic transformations are back to the type of relationship they had with the instrument in the opening: although timbrally very distinct from the instrument, they are clearly synchronized to it, and no independent texture can be heard anymore. At event 26 the tuba motifs, and consequently its electronic counterparts, become quieter, shorter, and less dense, and the final low A-flat leads into the following section.

Section 2

While the tuba plays tremolos in the extreme low range with, as the score requests, "breathy attacks and decay into breath," the FFT module is activated, starting with the reverse noise reduction with varying thresholds through to event 5, emphasizing the noises emitted by the tuba player.[88] The tuba still resonates through the two oscillator banks with extreme frequency, multipliers and then through the frequency shifters. From event 3, the tuba starts playing short motifs, still in the low range, progressively expanding into virtuosic sequences, culminating in loudness and density at event 7, before slowing down and finally pausing at event 8. During this first period of the second section, the temporal and spectral densification is enhanced with the reappearance at event 5 of the harmonizer, the transpositions of which are mapped to the amplitude envelope of the tuba, and with cross-synthesis between the tuba and white noise (from event 3) and frequency modulation synthesis (from event 5). From event 5, the result of the cross-synthesis is itself processed with the Lissajous-automated spectral panning; from event 6, the live tuba—both directly and via its harmonized transpositions—is itself transformed with the automated FFT per-bin phasing.

Event 8 opens a contrastingly quiet and steady sequence of 2.5 minutes, in which Lippe implements a tuning game. The tuba player must start slow, with *legato* phrases using pitches in the middle range of the instrument; this triggers a random pitch for a sawtooth wave, itself cross-synthesized with the tuba. If the tuba is in dissonance with the cross-synthesized sawtooth, the player must play an ascending or descending chromatic line, searching for a consonant interval. When the consonance is found, long durations must be played, and consonances must be kept by playing intervals such as octaves, fifths, fourths, or thirds. If a dissonance reappears, the player is asked to move off quickly to another note. A phrase is terminated with a long consonant decrescendo followed with a one-second silence, which retriggers a new random pitch for the sawtooth, enabling the player to start a new phrase following the same principle. At event 9 the tuning game continues, and automations for the interpolations of the FFT per-bin processes are activated in succession: first, the bin reordering, followed sixteen seconds later with the bin phasing and thirty-two seconds later with the bin filtering. At this point, sampler S is activated and cross-synthesized with the live tuba. At event 10 the tuning game ends, but the tuba continues playing phrases with the same character; the spectral processes are enriched further with the automated interpolations of the spectral delay with feedback.

At event 14 the tuba plays quick motifs in the middle range alternating with low sforzando pedal tones; these low notes act as "hotspots" that trigger specific modules to be processed with the FFT. This first occurs with the noiser/phaser module, then at event 15 with the Toto synthesizer, at event 16 with the frequency shifters, and at event 17 with the harmonizer, the transpositions of which depend on the amplitude envelope of the hotspot notes. In events 18 and 19, the same hotspots principle continues, but now in an open form: the player is asked to play materials *ad libitum* from events 14 to 17; as the score requires:

> [T]he notes with fermati should get longer and longer in duration while their dynamics of sustain should become more and more varied. At the same time, the

rhythms of the short notes should gradually become more staccato and faster, with shorter durations.[89]

In addition to triggering specific modules, the hotspots also trigger random samples from Lippe's earlier tuba piece, and the output of both samplers is sent to the stereo output and the spatialization, contributing to the overall dramatization of the musical discourse.

> In Presentation 18 of the accompanying software, "Playing with hotspots," Cort Lippe explains and demonstrates the hotspots principle. You can also explore Presentation 19, "Tuning game and hotspots," to interact yourself with the two open form sequences of Music for Tuba and Computer: the tuning game of events 8 and 9, and the hotspots starting at event 14. Demonstration Video 8.12 shows how to use these interactive resources. ▶

At event 20 the tuba returns to fixed sequences written on the score, and both the instrumental and the electronic parts start to quiet. The triggering of old tuba samples is deactivated, and that of the hotspot-bound modules is terminated at event 21, where the tuba player plays dynamic variations on the final low A-flat, before the final spectral resonances slowly decay toward the end of the piece.

Conclusions

Through the sixteen minutes of *Music for Tuba and Computer*, Cort Lippe pursues his long-term engagement with the interactions between solo instruments and live electronics, by shaping a musical form in which the centrality of the performer is constant, but in dialogue with a large variety of articulations with the electroacoustic counterpart. While the start of the piece establishes the timbral contrast between the instrument and the real-time processes, it makes clear that the first is the origin of the latter; the electronics are then constantly developed according to movements between emancipation and resynchronization. Whether in a situation of extended solo or in a virtual duo, the electronics are always closely informed by the live performance, and in particular by the spectral attributes of the instrument. The openness provided in some parts of the second section gives the performer an opportunity both to create the musical discourse and to explore the behavior of the augmented instrument with an extended freedom. In the fixed parts, the many dynamic and timbral variations required by the score indications offer a chance to constantly explore all the expressive dimensions of the digital environment created by the composer for his performers.

Natasha Barrett
Hidden Values—The Lock

Contexts for *Hidden Values—The Lock*

The early evolution of spatial technologies

The electroacoustic works of Natasha Barrett provide an interesting perspective on the innovative ways in which modern digital technology may be used in the production of electroacoustic music, in particular the use of spatial projection as a primary component of the compositional process. Her interests in the creative possibilities of this sonic characteristic have taken Barrett to the forefront of developments in this context, and her distinctive use of the advanced techniques that have been developed for this purpose provide an interesting point of focus for this chapter.

The location of sounds, whether auditioned through headphones or loudspeakers, has been integral to the development of the medium, from the early works composed by the post–World War II pioneers to the present day. Until the advent of commercial multitrack tape recorders in the late 1950s, most composers were limited to the possibilities of stereo sound imaging, and several of the earliest works were realized using just a single channel of audio.[1] Even in the latter case, however, an important consideration was the sense of perspective that can be created using a combination of amplitude and added reverberation to distinguish between sounds that are in close proximity and those that are located further away. In a stereophonic environment the ability to manipulate the location of sounds between the two loudspeakers extends this listening perspective to two dimensions: left to right, and front to back.[2]

Whereas in the case of broadcasts and recordings of classical music the intention is usually to reproduce as near as possible the sonic characteristics experienced by an audience in a concert venue, the world of electroacoustic music has been bound by no such conventions. The early stereo works of Luciano Berio at the Radio Audizioni Italiane (RAI) electronic studio in Milan, founded by Berio and Bruno Maderna in 1955, are especially interesting in this context for his use of three-position imaging in many works: left speaker, right speaker, and dead center (an illusion created by applying the same signal levels to both loudspeakers simultaneously).[3] The desire to explore the possibilities of spatial projection during the 1950s led some pioneering composers to seek ways and means of increasing the number of playback channels available in performance by synchronizing the audio outputs of two or more tape machines. Such an arrangement required significant practical ingenuity, a notable early example being the system developed at the Westdeutscher Rundfunk (WDR) electronic studio in Cologne for Karlheinz Stockhausen's four-channel work *Gesang der Jünglinge* (1955–1956). In this case, two stereo tape recorders were electromechanically coupled together using tape with sprocket perforations down one edge.[4] This experimental technique was developed further in *Kontakte* (1959–1960), scored for live piano, percussion, and a four-channel electronic tape.

The development of sound diffusion systems for performance

With the introduction of multitrack tape recording toward the end of the 1950s and the subsequent development of increasingly sophisticated facilities for mixing and sound diffusion, interest in the creative possibilities of spatial projection gathered pace. By the late 1970s several sound diffusion systems had been developed specifically for concert performances of electronic music, notably the Gmebaphone developed by the Groupe de Musique Expérimentale de Bourges in 1973 for its annual festival of electroacoustic music, and the Acousmonium (1974), a sound diffusion system developed by the Groupe de Recherches Musicales (GRM), allowing the projection of sound in performance using up to forty-eight discrete channels, projected over eighty loudspeakers.

The Acousmonium was influential in the design of a further system originally intended specifically for the diffusion of stereo works over multiple loudspeakers, first developed by Jonty Harrison in 1982. Known as BEAST (Birmingham ElectroAcoustic Sound Theatre), this system accommodates a variable number of loudspeakers, expandable from a minimum core of eight units. Four of these loudspeakers are located in an arc toward the front of the stage, the inner two providing a narrower than usual stereo image, and the outer two an expanded or "wide" stereo image. The other four are located toward the corners of the listening area, two at the front and two at the back further back, elevated on stands to create an immersive perspective enhanced with a vertical dimension.[5] More recently this system has expanded to accommodate the projection of multiple channels, embracing a variety of formats.[6]

Until the early 1980s, sound diffusion systems were based for the most part on analog design principles, and although these served such interests well, the associated technologies were subject to some practical limitations. It was the emergence of digital recording and signal processing software as the decade advanced that finally unlocked the true potential of spatial projection as a compositional tool. By the time Barrett was establishing her credentials as an electroacoustic music composer in the mid-1990s, powerful and increasingly versatile resources for such purposes were becoming generally available for composers and performers.

John Chowning

A useful starting point for the study of the advanced spatialization techniques that have emerged from the digital domain is the pioneering work of John Chowning. Whereas his primary legacy in a technical context is the development of frequency modulation (FM) synthesis, his initial engagement with the possibilities of computer music specifically focused on the spatial positioning of sound images. His interest in such possibilities was stimulated by concert experiences while studying composition in France from 1959 to 1962. He observes:

> Some concerts included electroacoustic—the *Domaine musical* at the *Théâtre de l'Odéon* and the *Groupe de recherches musicales* (GRM) presented concerts at the French Radio that were exclusively electroacoustic. Some of the music composed for 4-channels was, quite literally, head turning.[7]

As noted in Chapter 1, one of the first practical steps Chowning took to enhance his installation of MUSIC IV at Stanford University in 1964 was to commission a matrix of four digital-to-analog converters, thus creating a means of exploring the projection of sounds within a quadraphonic listening environment.[8] A revealing account of this voyage of discovery is recorded in an article he published in 2011:

> While much was understood in the early 1960s about stereo imaging in the azimuthal dimension, I was unable to find convincing information about distance or the radial dimension. Even nowadays there seems to be no agreement as to the perceptual cues for distance. . . . I knew from careful listening that reverberation must be an important component of distance perception, but I was unable to determine in what way. Music IV did not have any "reverb" unit generators, but it did have delay. Beginning on the IBM 7094/PDP-1 system and then moving to the PDP-6/10, I built reverberators using re-circulating delay units (comb filters). . . . By

309

1967 I had completed the spatial processing system that would allow me to place a sound at a discrete location outside the perimeter of a square where there was a loudspeaker at each of its corners. In the following year I achieved a graphic solution to controlling the Doppler shift in frequency as a function of radial velocity. While I had understood that to properly model the Doppler effect required variable delay lines, it was an option that was not practical because of the computational limits.

The program to control the movement of sounds through an illusory space was largely complete by 1968. I had generated a number of simple geometrical sound paths in order to evaluate the strength of the illusions. Of course, the azimuth (perceived angle) of the source was highly sensitive to the listener position within the listener space. But as long as the listener was not very close to one of the loudspeakers, the spatial distortion did not seem to destroy the illusion. Having four channels in a surround configuration seemed to produce effective illusions even for poor listener positions, as the direct signal could move through two or three of the channels even when the listener was just next to one of the four speakers. My conception of the spatial processing system evolved as I gradually learned about perception, the physics of sound and reverberant spaces. The perception of distance seemed not so sensitive to the listener's position relative to the loudspeakers. While subtle and easily covered, the distance cue seemed to me to be more robust than the azimuthal cue. The direct signal's amplitude decreases in inverse proportion to an increase in distance. The amount of reverberation must remain more or less constant, however, providing for a distinction between a sound whose amplitude decreases because of an increase in distance as opposed to a decrease in musical dynamic, in which case the reverberation decreases in the same proportion as does the direct signal. There is a point where the overall intensity of the reverberation is equal to the intensity of the direct signal.[9]

Chowning's exploration of sound imaging within a surround sound environment at a time when the medium of computer music was still very much in its infancy was truly groundbreaking. However, the limited processing power of computers at the time served as a major constraint for his investigations in this context. His reference to the Doppler frequency shift characteristic that occurs in the natural acoustic environment when sound sources physically move in relation to the listener (for example, the rise in the perceived pitch of an emergency vehicle as it approaches, followed by the reverse effect as it departs into the distance) is a crucial consideration in this context, and his pioneering work on the algorithms required to achieve this element of realism were to prove of considerable significance. He first explored the creative possibilities of spatial imaging in *Sabelithe* (1971), but at this stage he had not perfected the necessary algorithms. These were first successfully implemented for *Turenas* (1972) and also feature in *Stria* (1977).[10]

Surround sound techniques

A comprehensive survey of the various spatialization techniques that have been used in the composition and performance of electronic and computer music over the years is beyond the scope of the current study.[11] However, a number of key features merit closer scrutiny. As already noted, there are some important differences between listening environments that are constrained to imaging of sounds in front of an audience, as if on a conventional concert platform, and those that extend to surround sound perspectives. Cinemagoers regularly experience the aural enhancements made possible by Dolby surround sound systems and some also can enjoy these effects at home using domestic versions of the system. The latter context is significant since it provides a possible gateway for the wider public to access electroacoustic works that make use of spatial techniques that extend beyond a purely stereophonic perspective.[12]

Whereas for the most part Dolby techniques are used in the cinema simply to add additional sound components along the sides and rear of the listening area from time to time when the visual content invites an immersive aural perspective, the availability of these additional discrete sound channels facilitates a more proactive approach to surround sound imaging should this be desirable.[13] With the introduction of Dolby Atmos in 2012, the possibility of locating sound images that appear to originate from points above the listening audience has also become a viable proposition, and useful parallels can be drawn with the more sophisticated audio spatialization systems that have been developed for composers such as Natasha Barrett.

It has already been noted that the fixed projection of quadraphonic electroacoustic works using four loudspeakers at each corner of a performance venue usefully extends a conventional stage-based stereo perspective into one that facilitates a surround sound experience. There are, however, some drawbacks to such an arrangement, notably the inability to secure the accurate location and movement of sounds within the resulting 360° perspective. Composers exploring the possibilities of stereo imaging soon become aware of what has been described as the "hole in the middle" characteristic, where, for example, simply panning a sound from the left-hand speaker to the right-hand one does not result in a consistent perspective of a sound smoothly traversing the listening area. Uncertainties as regards both position and perceived amplitude arise from either side of the midpoint, hence the term used to describe the phenomenon. Using four loudspeakers positioned at the four corners of the listening area actually compound these shortcomings, leading to similar uncertainties between each of the four loudspeakers.

Increasing the number of loudspeakers from four to eight, suitably arranged in a circle, significantly diminishes this shortcoming in terms of acoustic mapping, and a number of composers over the years have successfully

311

made use of such octophonic playback environments. However, long before such developments achieved their full potential, investigations were under way into other methods of both coding and reproducing sounds in a three-dimensional listening environment, starting with a technique known as Ambisonics.

Over the years this spatialization technique has evolved into a powerful and versatile resource, facilitating the accurate movement of sound images within an immersive listening area that embraces both horizontal and vertical coordinates. Moreover, unlike more traditional approaches to multiple speaker environments, the techniques used to control the spatial positioning of the sounds do not require the speakers to be positioned according to predetermined configurations in terms of both the precise number of speakers to be employed and their physical location surrounding the listening area. Further, the spatial coding technique does not involve the use of conventional amplitude panning techniques to distribute sounds between loudspeakers, the amplitude and positioning information being coded instead in terms of vectors, to be interpreted and decoded directly by the chosen playback system. For composers, a key implication is that once a work has been encoded it may be decoded differently according to the number and location of the loudspeakers in a given concert situation, a flexibility not otherwise easily available. The functional characteristics of the specific implementation of Ambisonics encoding developed at IRCAM during the early 2000s are integral to the later study of *The Lock* from *Hidden Values*, by Natasha Barrett, and the circumstances associated with the birth and early development of the technique merit closer study.

Ambisonics

The birth of Ambisonics is associated with the discoveries of three pioneers during the early 1970s.[14] These were Duane Cooper in the United States, and Michael Gerzon and Peter Fellgett in England.[15] Although Cooper's 1972 paper established some important key principles in terms of developing a matrix-based coding of stereo recordings, in the first instance for broadcasting purposes, it was Fellgett and more particularly Gerzon who are to be credited with developing this approach to the point where the full potential of this technique for capturing and reproducing spatial characteristics could be productively explored as a compositional tool.[16]

As is the case for all advanced spatialization systems of this type, the underlying mathematics associated with the coding and decoding processes for Ambisonics are necessarily complex, but for current purposes it is sufficient to limit the discussion to the scope and nature of the primary principles thus involved. In a keynote article on surround sound psychoacoustics published in 1972, Gerzon notes the following:

> There are a number of different mechanisms by which the ears localize sounds, including several low-frequency, mid-frequency, and high-frequency mechanisms, as well as information derived from the reverberation of sounds. With only a few

transmission channels available, one cannot hope to satisfy them all, but most existing "discrete" and "matrix" systems do not satisfy more than one or two criteria. . . . To design surround-sound systems we do not need to understand the full intricacies of the sound processing mechanisms in the ears and brain. As far as engineering is concerned, all we need know is what type of stimulus (*i.e.* sound field information) is needed to create a given subjective impression, and then we can design apparatus to produce a stimulus of the required type. . . . However, it is [also] necessary to have a description of the required stimulus that is simple enough mathematically to handle in detailed calculations. Otherwise we will only be able to design a system by guessing a circuit configuration and then "number crunching" the data in a computer to see whether it will work. As there are many millions of possible system configurations, it is extremely unlikely that such a design procedure would happen to hit upon the best possible result, or even something approximating to it. . . . In commercial "discrete" practice, the process of assigning positions in the sound field to the available channels, known as "encoding," is done using four channels. Sounds not in the four corner positions are, in this procedure, assigned to just those two of the four channels representing corner directions adjacent to the desired direction. This only handles distant sounds in a horizontal direction, and it is by no means evident that this is the best way of assigning such a sound field to four channels. Similarly, it is not evident, and not in fact true, that feeding these channel directly to a square of speakers gives an optimum recreation of the original sound field. Thus, any surround-sound system gives rise to two distinct but related psychoacoustic questions:

- Is a given method of encoding the sound field ever capable of good subjective recreation of the sound field? That is, does the encoding method used permit the possibility of designing some decoder giving good results?
- Given a good method of encoding, what is the best design of decoder for use with a given layout of loudspeakers?[17]

The latter issues go straight to the heart of the challenges that have to be addressed in this context. In the case of systems such as Ambisonics, the primary consideration is the ways in which our ears receive and decode audio signals arriving from different directions, and how these characteristics can most convincingly be simulated. This requires an understanding of the features that determine listening in terms of the head-related transfer function, or HRTF. This, for example, involves two components in terms of the comparisons to be made between aural information simultaneously received by each ear, the interaural level differences (ILD), and the interaural time differences (ITD). Such characteristics, along with filtering by the body itself, contribute largely to how the brain decodes the spatial location of incoming sounds.

Whereas direct modeling of the physical characteristics of these responses using headphones can produce convincing results, the use of loudspeaker configurations to the same ends has proved altogether more problematic. The key issue during the early stages of Ambisonic development was how to produce convincing sound imaging using conventional listening facilities. The use of enhanced spatialization in FM broadcasting was a particular interest of Fellgett, and in 1974 he established some important guidelines that are still relevant to the more advanced Ambisonic configurations in use today. He notes:

> It follows that the highest fidelity in sound reproduction requires that the directionality of sound should mimic both the direct and reverberant sound of the concert hall. This not just a matter of a vague splash of delayed echoes, but of a relationship between directionality and time-delay which gives specific information: this information is what we shall mean directly by ambience. Systems capable of reproducing it will be called "ambisonic."[18]

His suggested system configuration is shown in Figure 9.1, and he describes it this way:

> It is first necessary to characterize the sound-field at a given place in the room where the performance is taking place. The sound field at a point can conveniently be characterized in terms of spherical harmonics representing the sound field pressure and its derivatives. . . . The 0th order is equivalent to the sound-field pressure alone, and gives simply mono without directional information. The [first] three spherical harmonics of order 1 are equivalent to the three Cartesian components of particle velocity vx, vy and vz. Higher orders of spherical gradients represent non-redundant combinations of higher gradients; they are of potential interest for the future but need not be considered for the purpose of current developments.

In practical terms these parameters translate into a capture system ideally consisting of an integrated matrix of four microphone capsules, one with an omnidirectional response characteristic, known as the "W" signal, and the other three with bipolar or figure-of-eight response characteristics, capturing the Cartesian coordinates in the three associated planes of directional capture; front-back (the "X" signal), left-right (the "Y" signal), and up-down (the "Z" signal). Known as B-format signals, these individual channels of audio data are then recorded on separate recording tracks for subsequent decoding and reproduction via a matrix of loudspeakers, arranged around the listener.

Translating theory into practice, however, proves to be no easy task. Designing a microphone that meets the above specification is all but impracticable, since the sounds arriving at each capsule are impeded by the physical presence of the others. One solution, pioneered by Calrec UK in 1978, was marketed as the Soundfield microphone, consisting of a tetrahedral arrangement of four capsules. The resulting audio data thus captured, known as A-format signals,

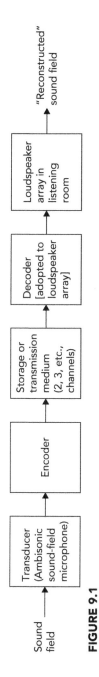

FIGURE 9.1

General Ambisonic configuration suggested by Peter Fellgett.[19]

are then electronically converted into an equivalent B-format.[20] This technique, indeed, forms the basis of the multi-capsule Ambisonic microphones widely used today, and is an essential component of the audio capture techniques used by composers such as Barrett.

Back in the 1970s, Ambisonics appeared to have an attractive future as an enhancement for domestic listening environments, but this necessitated a further interim coding process reducing B-format signals to just two channels for transmission via conventional media such as FM radio and vinyl records.[21] Even in contexts where B-format signals are recorded using several discrete recording tracks, the design of suitable decoders and associated loudspeaker configurations has proved challenging. In practice a quadraphonic arrangement of four loudspeakers, one in each corner of the listening area, is generally considered the minimum requirement, and although the vertical as well as the horizontal components of audio data can often be convincingly reproduced in this manner, it soon became clear to Ambisonic pioneers that truly periphonic 360° sound reproduction requires a more sophisticated methodology, expanding the number of channels used for both data capture and reproduction over multiple loudspeakers.

The closing remarks of Fellgett above referring to higher orders of spherical gradients confirm that he was fully aware of this requirement for achieving truly accurate spatial imaging. Such an outcome, however, required the development of more sophisticated digital recording and sound processing technologies, leading in turn to an enhancement known as higher order Ambisonics. The techniques associated with the latter extension were used in the composition of *Hidden Values* and will subsequently be studied in more detail.

The IRCAM Spatializer (Spat)

Whereas Ambisonics was arguably the most successful surround sound format to emerge from the pre-Dolby era, by the late 1980s work on other techniques that have also become significant for composers was gathering pace. Common to all of these developments is the increasingly sophisticated use of computer-based spatial imaging, in more advanced contexts associated with elaborate configurations of the associated loudspeakers encapsulating the listening area. In 1991 IRCAM started work on a spatialization project in collaboration with Espaces Nouveaux that was to become especially significant for subsequent work in this area. At the time the primary focus of attention was the IRCAM Music Workstation and the Max graphical programming environment.[22] Prior work with the 4X, not least in the context of performing Boulez's *Répons*, had stimulated considerable interest in the possibilities of spatial projection, and perhaps mindful of the distinctive features of systems such as the Acousmonium used for the performance of GRM works in Radio France, it was timely to launch such an initiative. The inspiration for the project was prior research on room acoustics carried out by the room acoustics laboratories at IRCAM and Télécom Paris. Known as the Spatialisateur, or Spat, the resulting computer-controlled spatialization system provides a fully periphonic listening environment based on a versatile series of digital signal processing algorithms specially developed for the spatialization and reverberation of sounds.[23]

Initially, the real-time signal processing requirements were too demanding even for the IRCAM Music Workstation, and a system was specially constructed for the purpose. This was known as the Station d'Informatique Musicale (SIM), based on a pair of i860 processors and hosted by a NeXT computer. This remained in service until the end of 1994. By the end of the decade, general increases in computing power made it possible to integrate Spat with the all-software Max (Max/MSP) environment, and thus make it available to a much wider circle of potential users. In the latter format, Spat provides a comprehensive library of Max objects and abstractions for real-time spatial projection. Such advances, however, do not diminish the requirement for a suitably comprehensive array of loudspeakers, suitably configured and positioned to reproduce accurately the desired spatial characteristics. Although a number of researchers have contributed to the development of Spat, credit for the design of the signal processing algorithms as implemented in Max is due to Jean-Marc Jot and Olivier Warusfel, who were also largely responsible for the design of the earlier prototypes.[24]

What sets Spat apart from other spatialization systems is that it can be configured to reproduce spatial characteristics that are entirely user-defined. This facility not only allows these characteristics to be modified to accommodate the response characteristics of different acoustic environments, it also allows different spatial methodologies to be applied. For example, Ambisonic encoding and decoding are embedded in Spat as one of the options, and as will be seen in the subsequent analysis of *The Lock*, this configuration is central to the composition and performance of the three pieces that make up Barrett's *Hidden Values*. The Max module **Spat~** can be viewed schematically as in Figure 9.2.

The library of modules that make up **Spat~** is divided into two categories of objects: DSP objects that provide the signal processing functions, and high-level control objects that can be used to control several DSP parameters simultaneously.

Signal processing is divided into four primary stages. The first, known as the Source module, is concerned with preprocessing incoming audio data to provide the two signals that are required for the next processing stage. These consist of what is known as the "face" signal that contains the acoustic information generated by the source in the direction of the listener, and the "omni" signal that contains the acoustic information radiated by the source in all directions. The former is used by the next module, known as the Room Effects module, to reproduce the directly received sound, and the latter to provide an input to the chosen room reverberation algorithm.

318

The generation of these two signals allows for a number of processing modifications to be introduced, notably "pre-delay" characteristics if so required, to reproduce the time lags that result from individual signals arriving at the ear of the listener from sources located at different differences. Use of a variable "pre-delay" characteristic thus creates the all-important Doppler function associated with moving sources. Further modifications can be made if so desired, for example changes to the spectral characteristics of applied signals.

The Room effects module provides the core artificial reverberation characteristics, receiving the two signals generated by the first module and providing three groups of output signals: center, the signal containing the direct sound; sides, two signals, left and right, providing the first-order room reflections; and surround, the signals containing the more diffuse later reflections. The number of signals thus generated can be varied according to the context.

The response of the Room effects module is divided into four time quadrants:

- Direct: The direct sound provides the zero time reference (0 ms) for the description of the artificial room effect that follows it.
- Early: This section contains the discrete early reflections, shared between the two sides signals of Room. The date and intensity of each reflection can be controlled individually.
- Cluster: This section contains a denser pattern of diffuse later reflections which are equally shared between the surround signals.
- Reverb: This section contains the later, more diffuse reverberation, divided into uncorrelated signals of equal energy sent to the surround outputs.

The next module, Directional distribution, is the panning module. It receives the outputs from all three groups of signals generated by the Room effects module and is used to direct the signals to the output channels, for reproduction via the associated array of loudspeakers. The control interface consists of two sections. The first, known as source localization, can be used to vary the positioning of the center channel sound image between the loudspeakers.[26] The second, known as loudspeaker configuration, allows the two early reflection signals to rotate, adding a further variable component to the positioning of sounds.

The final module, Output equalization, provides the final decoding process, allowing corrections and/or modifications to be made to both spectral and temporal characteristics, if necessary to rectify any shortcomings encountered in different concert hall situations.

Three further methods of periphonic spatialization have proved of particular significance for computer music applications. The first of these, pioneered by Augustinus J. Berkhout in 1988, is known as Wave Field Synthesis, or WFS, and like Ambisonics it is an option available within Spat. A key characteristic of this method is the replication as accurately as possible of the wave fronts generated by sound sources within the auditorium, thus creating virtual images where the starting point is their actual physical location in the listening area, achieved by generating the required acoustic wave components from a surrounding array of loudspeakers.[27]

Although this approach makes the positioning of the listener in the listening area somewhat less critical than would otherwise be the case, the realism of the results depends very much on the number of speakers available to synthesize the resulting wave fields, in an ideal situation involving upward of perhaps fifty or more speakers in a concert auditorium. It is possible within Spat to combine techniques of spatialization, and indeed, in the case of the first movement of *Hidden Values*, Natasha Barrett augments her use of Ambisonics with a WFS component, involving four arrays each of sixty-four speakers. WFS will work with smaller speaker configurations, although in such circumstances its potential advantages over alternative spatialization techniques are materially reduced.

Vector base amplitude panning (VBAP)

The second method, pioneered by Ville Pulkki in 1997, is known as vector base amplitude panning, or VBAP. This method is based on a reworking of the conventional principles of amplitude panning in terms of vectors, which in turn facilitate the use of relatively simple and computationally efficient equations for the positioning of virtual sound sources within the listening area. Although VBAP techniques have been further developed and extended over the years, the fundamental characteristics remain the same. Pulkki notes the following in the context of the original version, which could be configured to use a maximum of eight suitably positioned loudspeakers:

319

VBAP has three important properties:

1. If the virtual source is located in the same direction as any of the loudspeakers, the signal emanates only from that particular loudspeaker, which provides maximum sharpness of the virtual source.

2. If the virtual source is located on a line connecting two loudspeakers, the sound is applied only to that pair, following the tangent law. The gain factor of the third loudspeaker is zero.

3. If the virtual source is located at the center of the active triangle, the gain factors of the loudspeakers are equal.

   The loudspeakers may be in arbitrary two- or three-dimensional positioning. VBAP gives a maximum localization sharpness that can be achieved with amplitude panning since it uses at any one time the minimum number of loudspeakers needed: one, two, or three. The number of virtual sound sources or loudspeakers is not limited by the method.

   By using VBAP it is possible to make recordings for any loudspeaker configuration or create recordings that are independent of loudspeaker placement. Multiple virtual sources can be positioned in two- or three-dimensional sound fields, even with very complex loudspeaker configurations.[28]

The freedom to use arbitrary configurations therefore has some practical advantages. Just three loudspeakers, for example, are sufficient to generate an extension of stereo sound images with both horizontal and vertical location of sounds, as seen in Figure 9.3.

If further speakers are then added to the rear of the listening area, it becomes possible to produce sound images with a full 360-degree periphonic

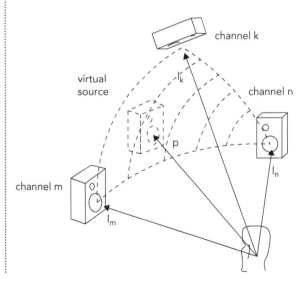

FIGURE 9.3

Virtual source in a three-loudspeaker VBAP configuration.[29]

320

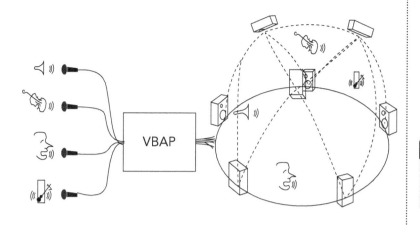

FIGURE 9.4

Full 360-degree periphonic spatialization in a VBAP configuration.[30]

spatialization, as demonstrated in Figure 9.4. In 2000 Pulkki developed a Max version of VBAP, and like Ambisonics this is also available as an option within Spat.

These Spat options provide composers with a powerful repertory of tools, each offering a distinctive and essentially unique set of spatialization tools. VBAP is essentially a versatile extension of traditional amplitude panning techniques, and some composers prefer this approach to locating and manipulating sound images. Barrett has been less persuaded by this method, concentrating instead on Ambisonics and WFS. An alternative to VBAP, distance-based amplitude panning (DBAP), which has also been implemented as a Max option available in Spat, was developed in 2009. The basic difference in this approach is that the actual position of the loudspeakers is the starting point for generating the associated imaging parameters, with no regard to where listeners are situated.[31]

Natasha Barrett and spatial projection

Barrett's career as an electroacoustic music composer dates back to her studies as an undergraduate and, subsequently, a postgraduate student at City University, London, supervised in the latter context by Denis Smalley, with an interpolated master's year at the University of Birmingham studying with Jonty Harrison. In the latter context she came into direct contact with the techniques of spatializing stereo works over multiple loudspeakers developed by BEAST, and this experience was to prove important in stimulating her interests in spatial projection as a core element of her electroacoustic compositions. Similarly, Smalley's association with the aesthetics of the Groupe de Recherches Musicales (GRM) provided an important gateway to engaging with the techniques of acousmatic composition.

As noted earlier, the timing of her academic studies, with the completion of her doctorate in 1997, could not have been more appropriate for facilitating her subsequent engagement with the possibilities of spatial projection. A key landmark in this chronology of technical developments was to be the 2000 International Computer Music Conference held in Berlin, which embraced workshops, papers, listening sessions, and a spirited debate on the relative merits of spatialization techniques such as Ambisonics and VBAP. In an article written in the same year for the online journal of the Canadian Electroacoustic Community (CEC) *eContact!*, Barrett provides an interesting insight into her creative thinking during the years leading up to her doctorate, embracing some of her very earliest electroacoustic compositions:

> Here I summarize my current compositional intentions and how they have changed over the past five years. The clearest change, or more accurately "clarification," has concerned the methods I use to create and control musical structure. Attempts to capture aspects of the physical and natural world, either as main or minor factors in the composition, are common to many of my works. The trend has been to capture these aspects in both intrinsic and extrinsic materials, most recently with methods that are non-conflicting and integral to both sound and structure in a non-compromising fashion. . . .
>
> In *Puzzle Wood* (1995) sound sources and transformations were chosen partly for their implication of wind, landscape and energy. This work was an attempt to create a landscape by layering foreground, mid- and background sound materials. At the time, it seemed inappropriate to use sharp articulations and silences because our perception of the world consists of an uninterrupted stream of information. During the composition process the intention of creating a landscape became absorbed, and partly obscured, by concepts concerning the structural grouping of elements for perceptual purposes. . . .
>
> In *Earth Haze* (1995) the intention was also to evoke a natural environment through the selection of sound materials and computer transformations. One of the differences between *Earth Haze* and *Puzzle Wood* is that in *Earth Haze* these intentions were the main focus of the composition. Many sound materials were selected to evoke the natural environment through aural recognition of the sounding material. Source sounds were also selected to create connotative contrast. "Natural" sounds, where only the material is suggested, such as the sound of stones knocking together, are thus relatively abstract, while sounds originating in an "urban" source (where the complete sounding body and mechanism is suggested, such as dustbin lorries and traffic), provided connotative and extra-musical contrast. . . .
>
> The structural use of space is designed to reinforce the evocative aspects of the work. The use of close-microphone studio recorded source sounds are intended to connect acoustically or connotatively to the implications of space and distance inherent to environmental source material, and to other materials that have undergone certain transformations. Reverberation effects are not included because of the need to imply an "expanse" rather than a "room." . . . [The] repeated contrast of small and large spaces marks a point of arrival to the divergence of sound transformation and musical structure. In retrospect, whether such connections between sound materials and spatial dispositions are evident enough to define the hierarchical and temporal organization of structure for the ear, is under question.[32]

These reflections on the possibilities of spatial projection provide important clues to the underlying aesthetic that was to underpin her subsequent repertory of compositions, which have embraced both multichannel tape works and also installation-based projects.

The first work to attract significant public attention was *Little Animals*, completed in 1997. Although still restricted to the functional characteristics of a conventional stereo environment, Barrett was concerned to explore the relationships that may be established between sonic components that are readily identifiable with the natural sound world and those that lie beyond our human experience. In the context of spatialization, she notes:

Five aspects of the spatial sound palette used in *Little Animals* form a continuum between musical and extramusical implication. At one extreme exists "real" space; in other words, the illusion of space achieved through the application of reverberation and filtering effects, stereo positioning, or through the recording of a source sound in a space other than an acoustically dead recording studio. The application of filtering and spectral stretching techniques result in "timbral" or "spectral" space: namely, the implication of width and depth through the relationship of frequency components.

Resonant filtering techniques can further emulate the sustain characteristic of reverberation at the expense of detail in the amplitude envelope. Convolution produces a similar effect, which can result in reverberation characteristics with high pitch coloration. There therefore exists a smooth transition between real space and the implication of spatial attributes. The implication of space encounters further abstraction in the concept of "time space." In this instance, expectations concerning the behavior of physical objects in the real world, such as the time delay between action and response connections in a sound allusion, result in the experience of stimulation and response relationships in the composition.

The final feature of the spatial sound palette involves a sense of "total realism," where the perception of realism is a combination of sound and spatial qualities. Describing sound as real or synthetic may appear contradictory, as all sound is "real," and any computer manipulation may disrupt both the natural acoustic resonance and any association with real-world physical behavior. I use these terms to separate sound qualities that suggest a "real" acoustic source from those qualities that lack acoustic reality.

A real acoustic source is one that appears to be produced by a resonating body or volume of air. Such sound is characterized by attention to small details, irregularities, instability, and change in spectral evolution. To our perception, a synthetic sound (often sounding as if it were created by computer synthesis) appears to lack these characteristics. The transition from real to synthetic qualities is a continuous and relative scale where the perceived strength of each is often dependent on the musical context.[33]

323

At this time the only practical means of enhancing the spatial perspective in concert situations was the live diffusion of electroacoustic material over multiple loudspeakers in the manner of BEAST, and Barrett actively researched these possibilities during her studies at Birmingham and City universities both in terms of *Little Animals* and other works dating from this period, notably *Buoyant Charm* (1997, revised 2001), a work for mixed instrumental ensemble and acousmatic sound. Here the diffusion possibilities are further enhanced through the use of live electroacoustic processing of instrumental sounds. In her PhD thesis she notes:

> A work open to interpretation embodies the excitement of the "unknown." Different performers and different performances result in different musical interpretations. The diversity of the variation depends on the number and the nature of the live elements. Live work, using one instrumental performer, sound diffusion and live signal processing, contains three independent interpretation strategies, each of which has different degrees of variability, while a work written for many instrumental performers is not necessarily open to wider interpretation possibilities than the solo work. In *Buoyant Charm*. . . . I found the interpretation invariant, despite the different styles of score notation and the number of performers involved. Sections comprising graphical or improvisatory notations were performed as consistently as sections involving traditional notation. This result occurs because many performers need to maintain the sense of ensemble during passages of improvisation where a soloist may exercise more freedom. Compared to mixed instrumental electroacoustic work, the performance of acousmatic music over a sound-diffusion system has few interpretation possibilities. This difference is due to the fixed nature of tape music, where varying performance results from a combination of the performance space, the speaker placement and the sound diffuser's spatial placement of sound.[34]

Circumstances were materially to affect Barrett's further engagement with the possibilities of acousmatic music and the role of spatialization in her creative process. In 1998 she was awarded a grant from the Research Council of Norway to work at Norsk nettverk for Teknologi, Akustikk og Musikk (NoTAM) in Oslo. The opportunities opened up by her work at NoTAM were considerable, and at the end of the residency a year later she decided to stay in Norway, taking up a post at the music conservatoire in Tromsø. In 2000 she became a freelance composer, making Oslo her permanent place of residence.

Her move to Norway, however, had one material drawback in terms of the limited access she could secure to large-scale diffusion facilities, necessitating a major review of the ways in which she could develop her interests in spatialization, working in studio environments that were generally limited to no more than four playback channels.[35] It was at this point that she first became aware of the possibilities of Ambisonics, marking the start of an engagement with its features that has continued to the present day.

Her early experiences were much as described in the earlier consideration of the technique, generating or capturing sound images in A-format, and converting them into a B-format, ready for multichannel decoding. However, she soon realized that a simple first-order implementation of the technique had a number of shortcomings, especially when Ambisonics is used for concert performances—in particular that it is not possible to locate the loudspeakers in the exact positions anticipated by the decoding algorithms. The resulting errors in the location of sound images become even more problematic if three-dimensional rather than two-dimensional spatial imaging is attempted.[36]

The solution for Barrett lay in the implementation of the earlier-mentioned higher order Ambisonics formats (HOAs), allowing the more accurate positioning and dynamic movement of sounds in both pantophonic and periphonic contexts. In the 1990s more sophisticated coding and decoding matrices were still very much in the early stages of development; furthermore, the processing power of desktop computers, even models such as the Apple PowerMac G3 and its immediate successors, was still insufficient to execute higher order Ambisonic processing in real time. Her initial engagement with HOA techniques thus involved significant delays between entering the spatialization coordinates and waiting for the computations to complete before auditioning and evaluating the results. Her own description of the basic principles of higher order Ambisonics provides a useful starting point for a more detailed study of their application in the composition of *The Lock*:

> Without entering too deeply into a technical description, ambisonics is a system of sound reproduction based on the spherical harmonics of the sound field. The more spherical harmonics, or in other words the higher the order of representation (high order ambisonics, or HOA), the greater the spatial resolution over a larger listening area. Basic ambisonic encoding (rather than recording) involves the directional encoding of plane waves and neglects the near field effect of finite distance sources. In the real world, when a sound is located in near-field the wave-front curvature depends on the sound's distance. The curvature effects how the listener perceives parallax, relative and absolute distance. Soundfield recordings capture the real sound field, but with a low spatial resolution and a small sweet spot. HOA allows some control over these acoustic (rather than extrinsic) distance cues, and combined with the spatial resolution over a large listening area we may ask why not work in as high order as possible? [37]

While there is no theoretical limit to the higher orders of coding and decoding that may be implemented, there is an exponential relationship between the extent of these functions and both the number of loudspeaker channels and the intensity of the associated computations that are required. Whereas today the processing power of most computers is sufficient for real-time HOA applications involving several orders of encoding, the continuing practical challenges of providing the corresponding configuration of loudspeakers and channel decoders in suitably dimensioned listening areas should not be underestimated.

Barrett's first Ambisonics piece, *The Utility of Space*, was completed in 2000. For this she used a second-order, nine-channel HOA format, decoded to a hexagonal matrix of six Ambisonic channels, along with a stereo layer containing different sound materials to be interpreted over any other available loudspeakers, depending on the diffusion context. A stereo version of the piece was also produced for an associated commercial CD. As her work expanded to embrace 3D spatialization, the complexities of her HOAs were further expanded as well. By the mid-2000s she had embraced twelve- and sixteen-channel HOA formats as well as more conventional multichannel configurations and commercial formats such as Dolby 5.1. Works such as *Deep Sea Creatures, Mobilis in Mobili*, and *Trade Winds*, completed in 2006, are all available in multiple formats. *Trade Winds* was in many respects a landmark work, commissioned by NoTAM with funds from the Norwegian Cultural Council and the Norwegian Composers' Fund. The original concert format is a sixteen-channel source comprising second-order Ambisonics and conventional spatialization techniques, with accompanying video material created by Marianne Selsjord. As the composer notes, unlike a conventional video, this material is not intended for direct viewing. It is designed to create lighting effects and imagery drawing on the listeners' conscious and subconscious connection to sound imagery. The work is a fifty-seven-minute electroacoustic composition inspired by this vast expanse of sea. Barrett unleashes the musical potential of acoustic recordings from a hundred-year-old sailing ship, interviews from a retired Norwegian captain, and recordings from above and within harbor, shore, and open oceans around the world. The music takes the listener on a journey from culture into nature, through storm, fables, ugliness, and beauty in a way unheard before.[38]

In parallel with these developments, the techniques she applied not only to capture and/or directly synthesize audio materials, but also to process these digitally, became progressively more sophisticated. Barrett had used Max during the 1990s to provide MIDI control of processing functions, and the launch of Max/MSP opened up an important portal to a repertory of entirely computer-based signal processing applications, leading her to develop her own external processing objects. The resulting integration of these software-based resources with those required for Ambisonics thus created a powerful and increasingly versatile toolbox for her composing, working in the first instance in her personal studio in Oslo. As her experience and knowledge of Ambisonics increased, she came to understand the potential of combining HOA with other spatial projection methods, including the direct generation of both mono and stereo images. Indeed, the distinctive characteristics of her works are materially reinforced by such context-specific combinations of these different techniques.

In a similar vein, the extension of her spatialization techniques to embrace installation works provides a further important dimension to her creative repertory. Starting with her earliest four-channel installation works, *Mimetic Dynamics* (1999) and *Rain Forest Cycle* (2000), and then *Displaced: Replaced II* (2002), a sound and video installation with interactive graphics and sound controlled by real-time weather conditions and using full three-dimensional, first-order Ambisonics decoded over a cubic array, a succession of increasingly sophisticated installations were to follow, including *Boundary Conditions* (2004), involving a spatial sound and architectural installation using second-order Ambisonics, and *Adsonore* (2004), based on the characteristics of the human immune system. By 2007 she was making use of third-order Ambisonics, and three years later she was creating fully interactive three-dimensional installations, starting with *Crush* (2010). The latter format was also especially useful for two-dimensional works, since the minimum loudspeaker requirements are those required for conventional octophonic works, involving eight loudspeakers arranged in a circle.

One further landmark development in terms of the use of spatialization as an integral part of her compositional process merits particular attention in terms of progress toward the composition of the *Hidden Values* at IRCAM in 2012. In 2008 she secured a Giga-Hertz award from the Center for Art and Media (ZKM) in Karlsruhe in recognition of her composition of *Sub Terra* (2008), a concert work spatialized over fourteen loudspeakers and three associated installation pieces designed as preparatory listening experiences for the former.[39] The award enabled Barrett to take up a residency at ZKM, leading to the composition of *Kernel Expansion*, completed in 2009.

Exploring the possibilities of sound diffusion and spatialization were key elements of the creative objectives of ZKM from its foundation in 1989. In 1991 Sabine Schäfer and Sukandar Kartadinata developed a MIDI-based computer-controlled sound diffusion system known as Topoph, developed in cooperation with the University of Karlsruhe. The current Klangdom system was initiated in 2003 by a group of software and hardware engineers under the direction of Ludger Brümmer, and subsequently installed in the Cube theater of ZKM. This spatialization environment consists of a dome arrangement of forty-seven loudspeakers controlled by a diffusion system and interactive software known as Zirkonium. The latter facility allows the accurate positioning of sound images within the listening area, supported by a smaller twenty-four-loudspeaker configuration located in the main composition studio.[40] A key element of the design philosophy was the design of a user interface that allowed maximum flexibility in terms of the available modes of diffusion and their application:

> At its core, all Zirkonium does is give the user a model of a room, let her place virtual sound sources in the space, and route sound to speakers to realize this request.

327

When so described, it sounds simple, but there are many design decisions involved. As with the hardware, flexibility and pragmatism were the guiding principles in making these decisions. Thus, we defined the goal of offering this functionality in a minimalist way. This resulted in an acousmatic system. For many uses, this is sufficient. In other situations, Zirkonium can also be used as a basic building block and extended with simulations. The philosophy of pragmatism and flexibility manifests itself in many places. Zirkonium uses VBAP for spatialization, but it also defines an interface to allow for use of other algorithms, such as Ambisonics. Zirkonium does not add reverb, distance cues, and simulation of movement artefacts (e.g., Doppler shift), but it does support the user in doing this herself. . . . Furthermore, Zirkonium has been designed to be used in other spaces, not just at ZKM. Users may define their own loudspeaker configurations that describe their local environment. And realizing that the environment itself may not always be at the disposal of the artist, Zirkonium can simulate speaker configurations for headphone listening.[41]

The Klangdom system allowed Barrett to explore the true potential of periphonic sound imaging, developing further the hybrid spatialization techniques that were to become central to the subsequent realization of *Hidden Values* at IRCAM, combining in this instance materials synthesized using higher (third) order Ambisonics with conventional first-order recordings of acoustic sources. Her sound sources were recorded using a stereo A-format microphone (Soundfield SPS200) and a combination of two separate cardioid (Neumann KM140) microphones, and two omni-directional (DPA 4060) microphones, providing six channels of source recording. Her experiences using this advanced ZKM system allowed her to identify and clarify some important issues that have to be addressed in such contexts. She notes, for example:

Recorded ambisonic sources address some challenges concerning complex real-world features, yet introduce their own set of problems: normal B-format transformations (zoom, mirror, rotation, "tape" transposition) are insufficient, and other modifications risk losing channel coherence even though some A-format transformations have been suggested to preserve spatial impression. Often it is desirable to focus on space, spectrum, morphology or extrinsic identity of specific elements of a complex scene. In this case it is more effective to isolate the element (or record a similar source out of context) and resynthesize the spatial location, preferably in HOA. Therefore, even before decoding issues enter into the process it is necessary to combine recorded sources with HOA synthesized materials. Furthermore, mixing two or more Soundfield recordings, containing complex environmental information where the microphone location has changed, is often problematic; the recordings contain different spatial pictures that when mixed tend to cancel out. . . .

In tests in the Klangdom, the vertical dimension was problematic. The volume of the elevated source appeared to fluctuate depending on spectral content and image size, regardless of loudspeaker distance compensation, and often the spatial image appeared to collapse. It can be speculated that the loudspeaker locations were problematic for the decoding matrix and that spatial distortion was enhanced by strong floor reflections (which vary depending on audience and seating arrangements). Therefore, instead of full 3D, the encoding involved horizontal layers of first-order and third-order materials, each decoded for one of three vertically displaced loudspeaker subgroups. Although not the same as a full 3D decoding this was found to be an acceptable compromise.[42]

The interest stimulated by *Kernel Expansion*, and Barrett's critical evaluations of the challenges faced in realizing her creative objectives, provided the stimulus for IRCAM's subsequent invitation to Barrett for a research residency, focusing in particular on the practical, perceptual, and compositional uses of higher order Ambisonics. As her resulting IRCAM research report notes, this work explored three main technical areas: very high-order synthesized Ambisonics sound-fields in two dimensions up to the twelfth order and three dimensions up to the 9th order; near-field compensated higher order Ambisonics; and higher-order recorded sound-fields.

Specific attention was focused on the following musical considerations: distance information, enhanced spatial precision, detailed recorded sound-fields to capture accurate real-world spatial relationships and the control of sound points, and motions and masses in relation to both timbre and "extra-musical" meaning. The work was carried out in IRCAM's Studio-1 installed with a twenty-four-loudspeaker hemisphere, and in the Espace de Projection, installed with a seventy-five-loudspeaker three-dimensional shoebox shaped array. Ambisonics synthesis was carried out using existing and specially implemented methods in IRCAM's Spatialisateur.[43] The residency period was for three months, carried out part-time over seven months during 2011–2012, and the creative outcome was the suite of three pieces, *Hidden Values*, of which the final piece, *The Lock*, is now studied in detail.

Inside *Hidden Values—The Lock*

Premiered at IRCAM's Espace de Projection on November 29, 2012, *Hidden Values* is a twenty-two-minute acousmatic triptych described by Natasha Barrett as "a musical-drama played in space and a spatial-timbral composition."[44] The overall work is articulated around the notion of invention, as the composer explained in an intent statement:

> Every year, new inventions push the boundaries of science and enrich our understanding of the natural world. Ancient and seemingly minor inventions have also shaped our societies and affect our everyday in a multitude of ways. A single object can connect to the history of the world, yet the utility of these simple devices go unnoticed.[45]

Each individual piece of *Hidden Values* focuses on a specific invention: the first part is *The Umbrella* (4′22″), an object that metaphorically "protects and saves, defends and deflects, covers and disguises."[46] The second part, *Optical Tubes* (6′44″), explores "how it would have been for objects to appear in focus as you moved toward or away from them."[47] The third part, specifically investigated in the analysis that follows, is *The Lock* (8′48″):[48]

> The invention of the lock and key can be traced back over 4,000 years. The theme of the lock and key and its metaphors, have been used throughout literary and dramatic history. Locked doors provide safety in a modern world. A lock hides secrets from prying eyes, locks people in, locks people out, represents power and ownership.[49]

The Lock is the most dramatic piece of *Hidden Values*, while the two others explore thematic and spatialization concepts in a more abstract way. As Barrett explains:

> I am still working with the idea of a musical form, where I have sections, where there is a clear change and then a development. I am always thinking about development; I am not interested in stringing things together because they sound nice. I always go back and actually work out, if I have a sound here, what meaning does that have later on? And in this piece [*The Lock*], [I am thinking about drama and its musical development in space]. But in the other [two] pieces, I am thinking less about the dramatic meaning and more about that I have this type of sound, and it has developed in this sort of way. How can I take that even further? At what point do I need to come back? I am thinking much more on an abstract musical basis than a dramatic basis.[50]

> *You can use the accompanying software to watch videos of our interviews with Natasha Barrett, where she discusses several aspects of her creative process, both generally and particularly on* Hidden Values, *and comments on musical excerpts of* The Lock. *Demonstration Video 9.1 presents this feature and shows an excerpt of Presentation 17 with the composer expanding on the specificity of* The Lock *within the overall work.* ▶

The musical materials of *The Lock*

For *Hidden Values*, Barrett chose two contrasting categories of source materials: voice and percussion. *The Lock* itself "plays out a drama between two forces: one represented by the female voice, the other by percussion instruments."[51] The two types of source materials were recorded by Barrett, working with Evdokija Danajloska, a composer and soprano, and Gilles Durot, a percussionist with Ensemble InterContemporain. All the materials heard in *the Lock* are derived, by selection and processing, from these primary recordings;

there is no use of additional recordings or synthesis. The composer explains her interest for such materials:

> Voiced sounds are clear in their source. Through sound transformations the identity of the person may change, but only in extreme temporal-spectral distortion will we be able to disguise the vocal nature of the source. Voiced sounds are therefore interesting in terms of our understanding distance cues that relate to sound identity and spectrum: changing the spectrum changes our understanding of source distance rather than source identity.[52]

On the other hand, "percussion sounds are in many ways the opposite of the voice."[53] For the composition of *Hidden Values*, Barrett defined her percussive repertory with pragmatic concerns in mind:

> I chose a practical selection of metal, wood and skin instruments portable enough to move between the chosen recording locations. Even before computer manipulation a percussion sound may already confuse the listener of its identity and instead we hear the gesture and the energy behind the articulation. Performed gesture and energy, along with ease of transformation and abstraction were important to the work in terms of spatial gestures and to the continuum between abstract sound masses and concrete points.[54]

In this analysis of *The Lock*, the materials are actually divided into three main types: those derived from vocal-only recordings, those derived from percussion sequences, and those derived from mixed recordings, where both Danajloska and Durot can be heard performing at once. For each of these three main types, three degrees of transformation are considered: "source" materials are direct excerpts from the recorded sequences; "processed" materials are sounds that were derived from the sources with some form of digital processing; and "abstract" materials are also derivations from the sources, but the extent to which they have been transformed is such that their origin is difficult or impossible to recognize, or that the resulting material acquires an autonomous identity, spectromorphologically distinct from its corresponding source file.[55]

> These two levels of categorization of the materials of The Lock (vocal, percussive, and mixed on the one hand; source, processed, and abstract on the other hand) are used in several interactive aural presentations of the accompanying software. At this stage of the chapter, it is useful to refer to Presentation 4, "Genealogies of materials," which provides sound examples from each category, also showing derivation links from one sound to another. Demonstration Video 9.2 shows how to access and engage with this interactive explorer. ▶

Whether vocal, percussive, or mixed, most musical sequences for *Hidden Values* were performed by Danajloska and Durot, on the basis of Barrett's "musical

331

sketches, descriptions of gestures, personas or behaviours,"[56] and recorded in several locations in central Paris:[57] indoor recordings were made in IRCAM's Studio 5 and the main large foyer of Centre Georges-Pompidou, and some sequences were recorded outdoors, in the areas adjacent to the two buildings. All recordings involved complex arrays of microphones: an Eigenmike and a Soundfield microphone, both placed in a central location; spot microphones on percussion instruments; a lapel microphone and a medium-distance microphone for the soprano. For the sequences recorded within the Centre Pompidou, four omnidirectional microphones were placed in the corners of the foyer.[58]

> *You can use the paradigmatic chart of Presentation 16 in the accompanying software to listen to the different sound files resulting from the recording of a same sequence with different microphones. For instance, in section 1C of* The Lock, *eleven excerpts from the percussion sequence labeled "sequence_13," recorded in the foyer of Centre Pompidou, are played simultaneously: four files from one of the omnidirectional microphones located in the corners; six files from the percussion spot microphones (one on the bowl, one on the temple block, one on the crotales, one on the chimes, one on the tom, and one on the cymbal); and one B-format file from the central Soundfield microphone. Demonstration Video 9.3 shows how to retrieve and listen to these sound files or others.* ▶

Overall, many different sequences were recorded, of which the following were eventually included in *The Lock*:[59]

Voice materials:
- hum-seq1
- open-seq (open-seq1, open-seq3, and open-seq4)
- what-seq (what_seq_long, what-seq2, whatseq3)
- close-voice-tense1
- DPA 406034
- DPA 406035
- sequence_35

Percussion materials:
- sequence_12
- sequence_13
- sequence_18
- sequence_34
- sequence_43
- sequence_46
- sequence_tom_up_bottom

Mixed materials:
- sequence_49
- sequence_50
- sequence_51
- sequence_52
- perc-voice-roar-voice
- perc-voice-angry-play4-voice
- sequence_perc-voice-amgrey-play4
- sequence_code1

Taking once again the example of "sequence_13" from the percussion materials, nine source recordings, all of a duration of 7′13″, can be found in Barrett's archive: five are recordings from the percussion spot microphones ("bowl_13.wav," "chimes_13.wav," "crotales_13.wav," "temple block_13.wav," and "tom _14.wav"); the other four are recordings from the four omnidirectional microphones located in each corner of the Centre Pompidou foyer ("DPA 7_11.wav," "DPA 8_11.wav," "DPA 15 _12.wav," "DPA 16_11.wav").[60]

If the percussion sequences can be clearly identified in all nine recordings, different parts of the percussion set are more prominent in the spot microphone files, while the DPA recordings retain a much more substantial amount of the atmosphere of the large foyer, including background noise, from which a drill notably emerges on several occasions. From this raw material, six out of nine sound files were eventually included in *The Lock*: only one of the four DPA recordings was actually used ("DPA 7_11.wav"); for all of these six files, only a twenty-second segment was selected for *The Lock* out of the original seven minutes.

In addition to these source recordings, two files in the composer's archive result from simple transformations of other source recordings, absent from the archive (likely named "cymbal_13.wav" and "soundfield_12.wav"): "cymbal_13biteq.wav" is a short nineteen-second excerpt slightly equalized, and "soundfield_12bit.wav" is probably a simple twenty-four-second excerpt from the corresponding source recorded with the Soundfield microphone, with little or no further processing. In turn, slightly shorter excerpts of these two files were included in the final work.

A similar pattern of derivations of the source materials was applied to all the categories listed above, to different extents, resulting in various quantities of sound files. Many different processes and techniques were used, from simple extractions, application of gain envelopes, or sound reversal, to more complex operations such as micro-editing to condense percussion motifs, time-varying tape transposition, granulation, spectral filtering, time-stretching, or pitch-shifting. As Barrett explains, her approach to sound transformation is closely intermingled with her work on spatialization:

333

I [frequently] transform a sound in parallel to its spatial movement. So, often I am using filtering and modulation effects, which transform a sound with the same dynamic gesture as its motion. I am not using pitch-shifting in the way of using Doppler, but I might be using a modulation which has a dynamic profile similar to the gestural spatial profile. It gives you a feeling of transformations occurring through space and time, rather than just a sound being transformed into something else.[61]

You can listen to more of the composer's account on her use of processing sound and its relation to spatialization in the video of Presentation 14. Although a detailed description of the processes used in Hidden Values and The Lock is beyond the scope of this analysis focusing on spatialization techniques, you can nonetheless explore the source, processed, and abstract materials further by using the paradigmatic representation of Presentation 16, as shown in Demonstration Video 9.4. ▶

Barrett's software environment for the playback and spatialization of materials

A performance of *The Lock* requires two essential software applications: Steinberg's Nuendo for sequencing, and Cycling '74's Max, including objects from the Spat library, for live spatialization. All the sound files are arranged and played back in Nuendo; they can be categorized according to three main types. At the top are four mono tracks making one layer of A-format sound files;[62] below are six four-channel tracks holding a variety of Ambisonic B-format recordings; and finally, sixty-two mono tracks labeled "to spat N"[63] contain sound files that are subject to real-time spatialization in Max, using IRCAM's Spatialisateur.

All the sound files are passed to the thirty-eight inputs of the composer's Max patch via the Jack Audio Connection Kit software.[64] The A-format sound files were composed by processing offline A-format sources with a convolution reverberation in which were loaded three-dimensional A-format impulse responses recorded by Barrett herself in different spaces. The first four tracks of B-format files are merged into one four-channel stream (Max inputs 35 to 38), in turn decoded in Max to loudspeaker-bound signals using the Harpex algorithm developed by Svein Berge in collaboration with Barrett;[65] the two other B-format tracks are merged into another four-channel stream (Max inputs 31 to 34) and then decoded with the Harpex object. The thirty remaining inputs (1 to 30) receive signals from the sixty-two Spat tracks of the Nuendo session; each of these thirty signals are processed by the spat.spat~ Max object, which also receives commands enabling the individual spatialization of each of these thirty sources, as described in more detail shortly.

In addition to these audio tracks—A-format, B-format, Spat tracks—the Nuendo session contains seven MIDI tracks, which send messages to a MIDI receiver in Max for the real-time spatialization: one track contains MIDI note messages, triggering specific spatial configurations or processes; six others contain CC (control change) messages, enabling the continuous control of the positioning of some sources in the three-dimensional listening space.[66]

In Presentation 3 of the accompanying software, Natasha Barrett presents and discusses the software configuration she uses as a working and performance environment. You can also use the Interactive Structural Chart of Presentation 1 to visualize and play the different types of audio materials as arranged in the composer's Nuendo session and spatialized in her Max patch. Demonstration Video 9.5 shows how to operate these interactive presentations. ⏵

Through the organization of her working environment, Barrett makes a distinction between pre-spatialized elements—the A-format and B-format files—and sounds that are spatialized in real-time—those arranged on the mono Spat tracks. About the pre-spatialized B-format sounds, she explains:

These are Ambisonics-recorded sound files . . . actually in this instance just B-format—I have also used Eigenmike recordings in other parts of this piece [*Hidden Values*], but here [in *The Lock*] we have just the B-format to capture a complex scene—a complex picture, which is very difficult to actually compose, because it contains so many elements. It would take a lot of work to [construct the scene] artificially. So, these are complex scenes, recorded.[67]

On the other hand, the sounds of the sixty-two Spat tracks are all passed from Nuendo to the central processor of IRCAM's Spat—the Max external named spat.spat~. The spatialization processes involved, which are computed in real-time during the performance,[68] are now the object of further attention.

Three-dimensional positioning and movements operated by IRCAM's Spatialisateur

Natasha Barrett's Max patch for the real-time spatialization of *The Lock* includes a thirty-input spat.spat~ object that encodes thirty incoming sound sources as mono signals in 3D Ambisonics. The Ambisonic signals are subsequently decoded to loudspeaker signals with a spat.decoder~ object. In addition to audio signals, the spat.spat~ object receives messages from the main Spat graphical user interface object: spat.oper.[69]

Sound source positioning

At the beginning of a performance of *The Lock*, the spat.oper object is initialized with a number of parameters (global source presence and distance attenuation rules, aperture, yaw centered toward the listener, Doppler effect activated, room effect turned off[70]). During the performance itself, the processes taking place in Max all ultimately affect the positioning of some or all of the thirty source signals in the three-dimensional space. The positions of each source are provided with either Cartesian coordinates—in the x, y, z format—or navigational coordinates—in the azimuth, distance, elevation format.[71]

You can use Presentation 6 of the accompanying software, "Single source spatialization," to load a mono sound file from The Lock or from your personal library, and position it in the three-dimensional field using our dedicated graphical user interface. As with the spat.oper object in Max, the position of the source is represented with a colored circle that you can drag around the listener.

Since this chapter on Hidden Values focuses on 3D spatialization, the accompanying software provides an advanced loudspeaker setup interface. It is expected that the software is used, in the most common case, on a computer with a standard stereo sound card and a pair of loudspeakers or headphones. In this case, the spatial positions of the sound objects of The Lock are encoded binaurally so that the user can perceive them in the best possible way, including on the front-rear and up-down axes. All the interactive aural presentations that focus on spatialization also include a visualization interface, enabling the user to observe the spatial positions and movements accurately, thus compensating for the aural limitations imposed by a standard two-channel hardware configuration.

Nonetheless, the accompanying software has been designed to accommodate both standard two-channel configurations and more advanced studio setups, so that the spatialization in The Lock can also be investigated in a multichannel environment, such as a ring of eight loudspeakers—where the perception of positions on the front-rear axis will be enhanced—or even three-dimensional layouts as can be found in institutions such as IRCAM or some universities.[72]

Demonstration Video 9.6 shows how to setup the accompanying software according to your listening environment, whether it is a computer with stereo loudspeakers or headphones, or a studio with more than two loudspeakers, arranged in 2D or in 3D. The Demonstration Video then illustrates how to use Presentation 6 and position a single source in the virtual three-dimensional field, regardless of your hardware configuration. ▶

Through the chronology of *The Lock*, some values of the MIDI note track of the Nuendo session are sent to Max in order to trigger an immediate repositioning of all the thirty Spat sources at once. The composer explains this technique:

Often, I will load a completely new spatial picture to suddenly swap from one thing I have setup, which is quite stable and has been there for a couple of minutes . . . to a completely new arrangement of items in the picture. It is like a spatial cut, actually.[73]

Playback of prerecorded trajectories

The positioning of some sources can also be set by continuous MIDI control change messages, also transmitted from Nuendo to Max: this MIDI data defines specific trajectories with x and y coordinates evolving over time.[74] In our interviews, Barrett takes the example of a processed vocal sound object from the "open-seq4" category appearing in section 1A[75] at 0'28", and details how the trajectory was defined alongside the modulation applied to the voice:

> I am simply taking this vocal sound and I am moving it through the space. But you can clearly hear that it is not just a single vocal sound . . . it is not just one constant sound that is moving. There is quite a lot of processing going on. . . . not in real-time, but pre-processed in Nuendo. . . . As the sound moves, space would normally modulate the sound, so you would hear a transformation. . . . I have rendered that transformation to a sound file, simply for CPU [purposes] and organization to keep track of things.[76]

The compositional writing of such trajectories is primarily made by experimenting with gestures using a mouse, while the sound file is being played:

> I do not draw it first of all in Nuendo, because you could say, I am going to draw, have a linear transformation, from this point to this point. But if we want to give the impression that the sound has a velocity, then you need to accelerate and decelerate it a little bit. It is maybe not what it is in reality, but things do not move at a constant speed; they [would] sound very robotic and artificial. So, to give that sort of sense of gesture . . . you could say there is gesture in the space, and . . . for me this comes actually from sound diffusion performance. . . . Motion has a gesture, motion is not a straight line going at a constant speed.[77]

Recording three-dimensional movements with a mouse is not trivial, and as the composer has noted,[78] at the time of composition of *Hidden Values* she would record the trajectories on the horizontal plane first, and if necessary record the vertical position afterward.

> *Presentation 7 of the accompanying software, "Recording and playback of trajectories," enables you to play sound files and record trajectories in a similar way, either by interacting with the graphical representations of the horizontal and vertical planes, or by drawing directly onscreen. The interactive structural chart of Presentation 1 and the paradigmatic representation of Presentation 16 both have coloring options enabling you to visualize the specific sounds of the work that are*

controlled with MIDI tracks. The paradigmatic representation also displays the times at which the positions of all sources are reset. Demonstration Video 9.7 guides you through these features of the accompanying software. ▶

Sound images

Many of the mono sound files arranged on the sixty-two Spat tracks of the Nuendo session are single, independent sources: whether static or dynamically controlled in space, they are positioned individually, such as the "open-seq4" processed vocal sound discussed above. But many other of these mono sound files are in fact grouped as sound images:

> I have a series of mono tracks and multichannel tracks. The mono tracks are normally single mono sounds, but often they will be split. So maybe I have a four or five channel multichannel recording, which I then will distribute on four or five tracks. It looks like it is mono, but it is actually not. It is a multichannel recording, which I am playing back on those tracks simultaneously, and then spatializing as a sound image.[79]

Several images appear clearly as superimposed mono sound files in the composer's Nuendo session. For instance, at the very beginning of section 1B, the Spat tracks 20 to 23 play four simultaneous fragments of percussion materials from the "sequence_46" recordings: they all contain the same double-attack motif played on the temple-block, recorded from four different spot microphones: close to, respectively, the chimes, the crotales, the cymbal, and the temple-block itself. These fragments are positioned by the Spat close to each other, at a similar distance behind the listener, but slightly spread on the left-to-right axis.

In some other cases, images are not only composed with sound files from different recording positions; the sound processing made during the composition may also differ significantly across the sound files of the same image. At the beginning of section 2A, some mixed materials from the "perc-voice-roar-voice" category are played simultaneously; their musical origin is identical, but their pre-performance processing has resulted in different spectral profiles; making sound images with complex distributions of space and timbre.

In the accompanying software, Presentation 9, "Image spatialization," enables you to load several sounds from The Lock at once, and to position each of them individually to experiment with the spatialization of sound images. You can also load your own sound files to investigate this process further. The paradigmatic representation in Presentation 16 enables you to locate images and to play each of its constituent sound files individually, and the interactive structural chart of Presentation 1 provides a visualization for the exact spatial positions of sound images. Demonstration Video 9.8 shows how to use these interactive presentations. ▶

Some sound images are static, as the position of their sound components is constant; others are dynamically spatialized. The playback of prerecorded trajectories described above can apply to individual sources, as well as sound images; some images are also controlled with processes implemented in the composer's Max patch: these are rotations, transpositions, and randomization.

Rotations

The first of these higher-level spatialization processes appears toward the beginning of the piece, and reappears at the very end. Three tracks, 11, 12, and 13, contain processed and abstract materials from the vocal "hum-seq1" category, made of humming melodic motifs recorded by Evdokija Danajloska. The sounds appearing on the three rotated tracks are time-stretched and, for some of them, heavily filtered versions of the original recordings. They are located above the equator (by an elevation angle of about 22 degrees), at a constant distance of 1.4 meters from the listener, and are rotated clockwise around the listener at a speed of five rotations per minute. Barrett explains this process and its application to the opening section of *The Lock*:

> I am not sending any control information in Nuendo; what I have done is to start a process, which involves these three sounds rotating as an image. . . . Something which I have learnt maybe the hard way over many years is that sound images are not made of mono points, or a mono point, or one moving trajectory. Images . . . have a size, they have a sense of mass, they have a shape. So that is why I have at least three sounds here, spaced apart, so you don't hear a mono point moving around. You hear a voice, maybe you think that is a person, but at least you feel that there is actually an image.[80]

The video of Presentation 5, "Discussions around excerpts of The Lock,*" provides the context for this quotation, with Barrett playing this excerpt and soloing the three rotated tracks. You can also use Presentation 1 to play the same excerpt yourself; a menu enables you to highlight the rotated sound files, which you can also solo and mute. Finally, Presentation 11, "Spatialization processes: Image rotations," enables you to play with the rotation process itself, with access to its different parameters, as shown in Demonstration Video 9.9.* ▶

Image transpositions

Another spatialization process operated in Max is the transposition of sound sources from their current position by a certain amount. In Nuendo, some of the MIDI tracks contain control change values that are interpreted by the Max patch as transposition values across the x (left-right) and y (front-rear) axes, and applied to several sounds at once, resulting in image transpositions. This technique actually complements the previously mentioned use of control change values for the playback of prerecorded trajectories, which in several cases is applied to sound images. Both of these techniques—MIDI tracks providing position values directly and MIDI tracks providing transposition amounts from the current position—enable the composer to implement movements of entire images through the listening space. She discusses the example of an image built from drum scrape sounds from the "sequence_tom_up_bottom" materials in section 1B:

> Here . . . I have three versions of this scraping drum, which I am moving to make a big, fat image, which is also quite important when it comes to the motion of the sound. . . . If I have got three sounds, and I move them in Cartesian—rather than polar—coordinates, this means that the angular relationships are constant, so as they come towards you, it then sounds like [the image] is getting bigger.[81]

You can use Presentation 12, "Spatialization processes: Image transpositions," to experiment with the transposition of sound images in Cartesian coordinates. And again, Presentation 1 enables you to locate the sound files affected by this process and to listen to them both in the context of the work or isolated from the other sounds. Demonstration Video 9.10 shows how to operate these features of the accompanying software. ▶

Spatial randomization

The randomization of spatial positions is only used in one short passage of *The Lock*, at the climax of the end of section 1C. A processed vocal phrase from the "what_seq_long" category, as well as some of the "sequence_12" percussion sequences, including significantly distorted ones, are affected. While the randomization engine is active, some random values are generated at a regular period of 448 milliseconds, and these values affect the distance, azimuth, and elevation of the Spat sources 3, 4, 5, 6, 7, and 9.[82] The arbitrary repositioning of these materials, themselves having a very dynamic character, contributes to the general instability of the end of the first section.

Presentation 13, "Randomization of spatialization," enables you to experiment with this technique, as shown in Demonstration Video 9.11. ▶

Spatialization and dramatization in the structure of *The Lock*

Together with the opposition between vocal and percussive material, the articulation of spatialization plays a crucial role in the shaping of *The Lock*. Natasha Barrett assesses how her research into advanced technologies of sound in space is inseparable from her conception of the composition:

Without the spatialization, there would not be an interesting structure to this piece. The structure hinges on two things. It hinges on the dramatic interplay of the two actors here, a soprano and a percussionist . . . and how they interact. But this interaction does not work without the space [component], because they interact in space. Their whole drama is [thus] setup as a spatial play. *The Lock* is about locked doors, about one character being locked inside, and breaking out, or a door which can open and reveal something awful . . . or something fantastic there; so, the whole idea of what a locked door can imply, this [means] separation of space. And then opening the door [means] the mixing of space. So, space is integral to the way the sound materials are then developed, it has been integral to the way the sound materials were recorded to start off with. Also, this was an underlay that determined how I composed the sound materials, or composed the sketches for the performers to play, which I then recorded as sound sources. So, the sketches for the soprano and the percussionist, they were not just improvising, they were playing little scores, and ideas I had given to them. Those ideas were anticipating what I could do spatially with the musical structure.[83]

The nearly nine-minute structure of *The Lock* can be considered as being made of two large sections, each divided into three subsections, named 1A to 2C in this study.

Section 1
The Lock begins with the exposition of two contrasting materials, both derived from the "hum-seq1" vocal recordings, but considered by the composer as representing the two main categories: the second material has been processed in such a way that it has become abstract, and its deep, bass texture is perceptually closer to the drum rubs appearing later in the piece than to the original humming voice.[84] These two opening materials are also opposed spatially: the unprocessed voice is at the front and slightly to the left of the listening space, while the abstract percussion-like texture is behind the listener. Barrett describes her intention: "I have defined these two zones—voice [at the front], percussion [at the back]."[85] After half a minute, another vocal sound appears: the "open-seq4" onomatopoeia already mentioned, moving from left to right at the front of the scene. Some additional bass texture fragments appear statically at the back, and more short vocal materials come into play with different trajectories, animating the front of the scene:

Now the little voice ["open-seq4"] has moved, it is still only over there [at the front]. It is not coming into our space. We are looking at a scene, with the voice. And the percussion is still behind us, in a back scene. . . . You could say, dramatically, the voice is sort of happy, in its little safe space.[86]

One minute in, a sound image with three strongly processed versions of the "hum-seq1" recording appears, slowly rotating around the listener and therefore starting to take over the back scene, having previously been reserved for the percussion-like textures.

> *Three presentations of the accompanying software are particularly useful to refer to through this paragraph on the structure of* The Lock. *In the video of Presentation 15, "Spatialization and structure," Barrett discusses her use of space through the chronology of the piece, as quoted above. The paradigmatic representation of Presentation 16 enables you to locate materials according to their categories or spatial processes, while highlighting the distribution of such categories through the chronology of* The Lock. *And the interactive structural chart of Presentation 1 gives you access to the combined sequencer and spatialization view for the entire piece, facilitating the interactive exploration of each section. Demonstration Video 9.12 shows how to operate these features for Section 1A, and you are encouraged to use these resources as you read the following text concerning the remaining sections.* ▶

Starting at 1′18″, section 1B introduces unambiguous percussion materials, with a loud and sudden double-attack motif on the temple-block, both on the reverberated A-format tracks and as a four-item image on the Spat tracks, located behind the listener. The overall scene momentarily gets a more agitated character, and after another double-attack motif, now on the tom, settles down and leaves room for long, sustained textures derived from vocal materials: "hum-seq1," "open-seq1," and an "open-seq3" sound moving slowly moving from left and right in front of the listener.[87] These are complemented with the slowly rotating "hum-seq1" image, and some sparse punctuations from the unprocessed percussion kit. At 1′42″, a processed drum rub image appears, combining both a B-format recording and two Spat sources. Initially moving behind the listener, its movements seem to threaten the vocal area; at 2′07″, this new material is reinforced as its image is populated with up to six sound sources, some of them adventuring across the initially established transversal frontier. At 2′25″, a third reverberated double-attack motif, played on the tom, increases the dramatic tension: the drum rub now takes over the entire space, and the vocal materials now sound endangered, as if struggling against the percussive intrusion. By the end of the subsection, the "close-voice-tense" material and its choking, guttural noises push this struggle to a climax, and the percussion characters seem to have now settled, with prominent sound images from the "sequence_34" and "sequence_43" categories. Barrett gives her reading of this subsection:

> The drum [rub] is coming in, and it is going to push the voice out. . . . Now [after the tom double-attack motif], it has really come inside [the central listening space]. The voice actually does not get out quite yet.[88]

The sustained processed "hum-seq1" texture suddenly stops at 3′04″, leaving room for a long sequence of sparse percussion materials ("sequence_43"). This new material is present both as a sound image on six Spat tracks, statically positioned behind the listener, and as an A-format recording from the Soundfield microphone; this latter recording introduces a significant amount of ambient noise from the foyer of Centre Pompidou, making a striking spatial contrast as section 1C begins. All the materials—voice and percussion—are now heard in a broader context, recalling the environmental characteristics of the recordings. The soprano is heard singing "what" on a B-format fragment of the "what_seq3" category, and itself marks a spatial shift. As Barrett indicates, "now the voice is out of the picture. It is the first time we hear it very distant."[89] On the other hand, "the percussion is now the dry [element], in the space with us."[90] Some granulated voices then appear, and a very dense percussion motif from the "sequence_44" materials punctuates the soundscape, introducing a chaotic sequence, filled with fragments of sung voice, percussion, and background noises captured during the indoor recordings, notably a drill heard along with the "sequence_13" percussion sequence:

> Whenever you hear this very intense percussion, where you are inside it, from a dramatic point of view this is the percussion taking over. And it also takes over the space, the voice does not have a place there. And I think this is interesting just to point out how you can use space to push things out. You actually occupy the space. The space is now too full for anything else to be there, and for it to make sense. And the voice could struggle: if you put the voice in, she would have to shout.[91]

This dense sequence reaches its climax with an abstract granulated image, derived from the vocal "what-seq2" recordings, quickly moving from the front to the back of the listening space, while the two only spoken phrases of *The Lock* are pronounced, in French: first "*Ne fais pas ça*" (Do not do that), whispered very closely right in front of the listener, and "*Remettez-moi les clés*" (Hand over the keys), commandingly articulated from a certain distance.

Section 2

After a brief silence, section 2 starts at 4′48″ with a processed drum scrape image moving around the listener from the back area to the front, soon joined with similarly moving materials from the mixed recordings, containing several declinations of the "what" word and some rubs and attacks on the tom. The first minute of section 2A is sparse and articulated, and the composer comments on it as follows:

> Now, [about] the processing on the voice and the processing on the drum, there are similarities in the morphology of the sounds, and how they are behaving in space. They are trying to mimic each other, spatially and through spectromorphology. . . . They are trying to come together; of course, it is very difficult because one is voice

and one is percussion, but their contours, their envelopes are quite similar. . . . It is the first time when actually now they are acting together, in the same space.[92]

During the first period of this section, some B-format fragments seem intermittently to open the door to an outer space. The space progressively becomes denser, and from 6′11″ new developments start with punctuations with the fast, tight percussion motif previously heard in section 1C.

The transition toward section 2B is marked by the freezing of the tail of a "what" glissandoing motif at 6′48″, announcing the voice taking over again among the developments initiated in section 2A. Several harmonic, sustained vocal textures, onomatopoeias, and sung fragments occupy and saturate the scene, entirely surrounding the listener:

> Here is the first time the voice has completely taken over. So now, it has pushed the percussion out: we are inside this very rich vocal spectrum. And that also reflects back to the beginning: before, spatially you had this quite beautiful, I think, voice singing at one point in space, clearly a person, an image. And now [in section 2B] she has been able to go back to this overdramatically, she has been able to go back to her expression of a sung voice, rather than these short, quite ugly, types of gestures, but she is taking up the whole space. So spatially, she is taking over, the voice is taking over, and you are now inside that.[93]

Among this saturation of the listening space by the singing voice, a vocal "open-seq4" fragment signals the re-exposition of the voice-based materials heard in section 1A; and section 2C can be seen as a recapitulative coda, also reintroducing the processed "hum-seq1" image rotating around the listener. But the global spatial distribution of these initial materials makes, as has been the case through the whole chronology of *The Lock*, its own dramaturgic statement:

> We do not go right back to the beginning. Now, we are more with the voice, the voice is in the space, rather than looking out on the scene, that is the transformation. . . . You do not get the voice there [at the front] and the percussion here [at the back] anymore . . . so you could say the voice has won in some ways, because now the voice has come, finally, into your space. It is calm, it is expressing the same musical motif, but . . . it is in control again, it has found peace and calm, and you are inside, with the voice.[94]

Conclusions

Through its nearly nine minutes, *The Lock* results from Natasha Barrett's long-term experience with advanced three-dimensional spatialization of sound, by presenting a strong dramaturgy where the vocal and percussive materials are characterized in such a way that the consideration of space is fully integrated to all the dimensions of the creative process and the musical work. The residency at IRCAM proved to be an ideal working context for her to explore systematically the most recent advances in 3D Ambisonics: Markus Noisternig, a researcher on the *Acoustic and Cognitive Spaces* team of the institute, remembers the collaboration:

> You know Ambisonics has these very many decoding schemes, from in-phase maximum energy back to maximum velocity vector, cross-over frequencies and whatever you can use as a parameter to shape the decoder. And then together with the Institute of Electronic Music in Graz we developed a special decoder . . . which we called an energy-preserving decoder . . . where we tried to keep the energy fluctuation as low as possible when you move the sound around the audience. . . . Thibaut Carpentier, who is the developer of our research group, implemented all the different Ambisonics decoders that you can find in the literature. Which gave us the possibility, together with Natasha, to listen to the same scene with different decoding settings. . . . We found [a] very nice parameter set which actually works very well, so that you can nicely produce in the production studio and then go down to the concert room and get some very nice results which she was happy with.[95]

Working in a collaborative environment also facilitated the use of a large range of technologies. Wave field synthesis was not considered for *The Lock*, but Barrett took advantage of its availability in the Espace de Projection for the opening movement of *Hidden Values—The Umbrella*:

345

> A second composer in residence, the same period, the same year, was Rama Gottfried. . . . He was working with the entire system, so Wave Field Synthesis and Ambisonics in parallel. And of course, there was also a very nice exchange between Natasha and Rama. So, we listened together to the Wave Field Synthesis, and she liked the idea of these focused sound sources in front of the array, especially for the first movement, for the rain drops. It worked quite well in Ambisonics, but she thought it might be nice to get this little flavor of Wave Field Synthesis also in her piece.[96]

This indeed exemplifies Barrett's general approach to the technology: its exploration is always connected to aesthetic concerns; her research on the three-dimensional spatialization of sounds and images is fundamentally motivated by musically conceived ideas. The close integration of compositional approaches to space raises the question of their perception by the audience and the concert hall configurations. Here is the composer's account:

> I think that Ambisonics overcomes the transferability problem much better than other multichannel systems, because Ambisonics is scalable. . . . But of course, when you are thinking about spatial precision, and clarity, what we are hearing here [in studio 1 at IRCAM] is very clear, and it is unlikely that most listeners in the concert [hall] will ever hear it as clearly as this. But there is still a lot of information that

comes out in the concert. . . . What do we lose and what do we still keep hold of? And I think in all compositions which involve space as a structural element, there are some spatial gestures for example, or scenes, or spatial behaviors which are strong, and they survive in all contexts.[97]

Through the dramatic nature of the composition, both as process and as outcome, *The Lock* perhaps illustrates best among *Hidden Values* Natasha Barrett's implementation of 3D audio technologies to achieve sound images, trajectories, and spatialized spectromorphologies, providing the audience with an aesthetically striking experience of the articulation of sounds in their listening space.

Conclusion

The individual chapters of *Inside Computer Music* prepare the ground for an enhanced perspective that has the potential to develop new and arguably unique insights into the evolution of the medium in a variety of creative contexts. Although the scope of this investigation has been necessarily constrained by the choice and number of works studied, the outcomes are encouraging in this context. The criteria applied in selecting these works and the techniques employed in their analysis are extensively discussed in the Introduction, and the extent to which the desired objectives have been achieved is now a matter for considered reflection. It is important to acknowledge that the outcomes of these nine analyses are only the first steps in a voyage of discovery that needs to be developed significantly further before any substantive conclusions may be drawn. Nonetheless, in setting out to address the research questions identified at the outset, a number of pertinent issues have emerged to underpin further work in this regard.

One of our key aims in this project was to investigate how far technological innovation has influenced musical creativity in computer music and generated new musical potential for composers. A sample of just nine works cannot hope to provide a full or even representative sample of all that has happened in computer music since the early 1960s. Indeed, there are whole areas we have not attempted to cover, such as popular music, improvisation, live coding, or multimedia works, to name just a few, and the field continues to evolve in exciting new directions. It is hoped, nonetheless, that the chosen focus has provided a new and hopefully innovative perspective that usefully prepares the ground for further investigations in related contexts. Different composers among the group we studied have engaged with technology in different ways.

Some have been very directly involved in the development and programming of new algorithms (e.g., Chowning, Truax, Wishart, Lippe). Some have worked closely with developers in the creation of new resources, playing a significant role in technical innovations but not directly creating these themselves (Manoury, Harvey, Barrett). Manoury's collaboration with Miller Puckette in the production of *Pluton* in fact led to the latter's initial development of software (Max) that continues to evolve and play a major role in the creation and performance of much computer music (including several of the later works we have examined here, and indeed Max is the basis for our own software produced to accompany this publication).

Others have used preexisting resources exploring their new musical potential (Westerkamp, Dhomont') without being directly involved in the scientific development themselves. In reality, the categories are not this clear-cut; rather, for the most part, it is a spectrum of engagement with varying types of technical involvement across the range, and in some cases the level of technical involvement by a composer varies from work to work. Nonetheless, whatever form the interrelation of technology and creativity has taken, the clear indication from the works we have analyzed is that technology does potentially open up significant new ways of creating and shaping music. This can be much more than simply realizing existing musical ideas in a new format: working with new technologies enables composers to conceive music in new ways, though this is not to deny that there are also often important continuities with previous developments.

In the works we have examined, for example, we have seen how timbre can take on much greater significance in the structuring of music, as seen in Chowning's use of his FM algorithm together with a pioneering programming language to shape both the timbre and formal structure of *Stria*; Truax's development of software to enable him to control long passages of music in terms of subtle multilayered timbral and textural transformations; or the differing uses and metamorphoses of prerecorded sounds by Dhomont, Westerkamp, and Wishart, which helped them to form their works in innovative and distinctive ways. An example is Westerkamp's evocation and poetic transformation of a natural soundscape through the course of a work and Dhomont, among other things, using recordings to create subtle cross-references between works, both his own and those of Guillaume de Machaut and Pierre Schaeffer.

Wishart's formation of an extended musical work from digital metamorphoses of a single source is at once radically new and a following of tradition. It is traditional in deriving material from motivic transformations, indeed taking this to an extreme rarely if ever found in acoustic music, but radically new in that the transformations here are not just in terms of melodic or harmonic variation, but also involve digital audio processing, leading to timbral and textural changes that are central to the sonority and formation of the work. Timbral manipulation as a structural feature is also evident in the works involving live instrumental performance. This is to be found, for example, in Lippe's sophisticated use of frequency-domain processing of the sounds played live by a soloist, and the role this processing plays not just in coloring the music but also in helping to structure the work.

Spatialization is another distinctive characteristic that features in almost all of the works we have studied. The physicality of instruments and performers limits the role of spatialization in acoustic music, though with notable exceptions, ranging from the use of *cori spezzati* in St. Mark's Venice in the sixteenth century to Luigi Nono's *Prometheus* or Karlheinz Stockhausen's *Sternklang* in the twentieth. Computer-generated music does not face the same physical constraints, especially with increasingly large arrays of loudspeakers in both two and three dimensions. Software and technology for sound spatialization has evolved rapidly in recent years, and continues to do so. Barrett's *The Lock* provides an example of the current state of the art, making use of high order Ambisonics and skillfully distributing multiple recordings (recorded from different spatial perspectives) of source sounds around the virtual acoustic space. Harvey's *Fourth String Quartet* demonstrates a sophisticated use of spatialization in conjunction with live performance with different layers of amplified and processed material moving in patterned and rhythmic spatial movements, linked to notated motifs in the instrumental parts.

The above summarizes just some of the multiple and diverse ways in which technology offers new opportunities to composers to expand their creative concept of music. There is much more beyond the works we have studied, and the range of possibilities continues to expand. But as development continues, it is important to take stock of what has been achieved to date. It is important on a number of different levels: historically as a record of developments that will become more difficult to access as time passes and the earlier technologies become obsolete; musically and analytically in developing a deeper understanding of the ideas underlying these works, an understanding that can only be fully gained by examining the technical and the musical hand-in-hand; and compositionally so that the lessons of earlier generations of composers working with computers can be passed on and developed by future generations.

Our conclusion is that technology has indeed had a significant and highly creative influence on the composition of new musical works. Most notably, as we have seen, it has opened up the potential for the creative exploration of a much wider range of sounds, enabled the manipulation of timbre to become a highly significant shaping force in music, and facilitated the integration of spatial positioning and movement into musical structure.

Composers and performers of computer music now enjoy access to a wide range of powerful and extremely versatile technical resources. Such has been the pace of development that as a consequence the provenance of many of the associated synthesis and signal processing techniques has long since disappeared from immediate view, raising the stakes considerably in terms of how best to gain a thorough understanding of their true creative potential and their full significance in the formation of works in the repertoire. As will now be becoming clear from the earlier chapters, their development has evolved over many stages, ranging in context from important initiatives pursued across the years in major research institutions such as Stanford, MIT, and IRCAM, to those attributable to key individuals working further afield, such as Trevor Wishart. It is also important not to overlook the significance of parallel activities in the commercial sector, which have similarly embraced an extensive spectrum of techniques for the production of computer music.

Our belief and experience is that technology can, and indeed should, not only change the way composers and performers work, but also transform the ways in which this repertoire is studied. The methodology of our investigation has therefore embraced technology (the software that accompanies this text) as an integral element of our research and its dissemination. How can words or diagrams alone convey the meaning and significance of something that is dynamic, temporal, and aural? How can the musical potential of an abstract scientific algorithm be conveyed by verbal description alone?

Creating software models of such algorithms has enabled us to understand more fully the context in which the composers worked, comprehend the opportunities and limitations they faced, and get closer to experiencing their working methods. Direct engagement with the music as sound is also, we believe, essential for gaining a deeper understanding of this music (perhaps of any music?). Analyzing by interactively engaging with the sounds, trying out alternatives, comparing passages aurally through interactive aural structural charts, or simulating the composer's process of creation provides a level of insight not possible simply through reading.

The FM techniques used by Chowning to compose *Stria*, studied in Chapter 1, for example, can only be intensively explored in a purely software environment, enabling direct interaction with all the different parameters. Hardware implementations in commercial synthesizers necessarily impose a number of practical limitations. Similar problems arise in seeking to explore the techniques encountered in pioneering systems that combined synthesis and signal processing software with custom-designed hardware such as IRCAM's 4X discussed in Chapter 3, or GRM's SYTER discussed in Chapter 5. Given that most of these original systems are now consigned to the museum, the development of entirely software-based simulations of their functional characteristics is essential to developing a full understanding of these technologies and the works created with them.

Accessibility is only the first step in embarking on such a voyage of discovery. The question still remains how best to explore the associated sound synthesis and signal processing resources in ways that will enable a thorough understanding of their use in the past by different composers and their creative potential for the future. This brings the argument full circle to the fundamental issues that have underpinned this project right from the outset. Whereas some of these techniques can be studied in a relatively straightforward manner, others are inherently more complicated. A notable example of the scope and extent of the challenges to be overcome in the latter context is provided by reflecting further on granular methods of sound production, studied in Chapter 2. A number of software-based granular systems have been developed over the years, following the pioneering work of Roads and Truax. However, without further instruction provided in a suitably "hands-on" environment, few are likely to grasp the full potential of this intrinsically complex technique. The detailed discussion of Truax's *Riverrun* provides an example of how such challenges can be profitably addressed.

Software has also enabled us to incorporate video recordings of interviews with the composers, and in some cases with the technical teams with whom they worked. Although we have included transcriptions of short passages in the text, this is no substitute for hearing and seeing the individuals in person. So the integration of technology and creativity is equally as vital to our investigation as it is to the works we have studied. To gain the most from this volume, we urge readers to watch the video demonstrations alongside reading the text and then interact with the technologies and the works by using the software itself. In this way, the interaction of technology and creativity will be most fully experienced on multiple levels.

Whereas it is hoped that the whole is greater than the sum of the parts in terms of the resulting body of knowledge that can be acquired from studying the contents of each chapter in turn, in situations where a more selective approach is taken by the reader, we have endeavored to ensure the resulting perspectives are suitably self-contained and securely located in the wider context. It remains to be seen how an understanding of the medium of computer music can be further enhanced by extending the methodologies that have been explored in these chapters to embrace further key works that have shaped and influenced its evolution from the middle of the last century to the present day.

Notes

Introduction

1. See Michael Clarke. 2013. "Analysing Electroacoustic Music: An Interactive Aural Approach," *Music Analysis*, 31(3): pp. 347–380.

2. A series of intermediary publications by the authors document in more detail the approach taken and the process of designing and developing the applications. See Michael Clarke, Frédéric Dufeu, and Peter Manning. 2013. "Introducing TaCEM and the TIAALS software," *Proceedings of the 2013 International Computer Music Conference—Perth, Australia* (San Francisco: International Computer Music Association): pp. 47–53; Michael Clarke, Frédéric Dufeu, and Peter Manning. 2014. "From Technological Investigation and Software Emulation to Music Analysis: An integrated approach to Barry Truax's *Riverrun*," *Proceedings of the 2014 International Computer Music Conference—Athens, Greece* (San Francisco: International Computer Music Association): vol. 1, pp. 201–208; Michael Clarke, Frédéric Dufeu, and Peter Manning. 2016. "Using Software Emulation to Explore the Creative and Technical Processes in Computer Music: John Chowning's *Stria*, a Case Study from the TaCEM Project," *Proceedings of the 2016 International Computer Music Conference—Utrecht, The Netherlands* (San Francisco: International Computer Music Association): pp. 218–223. A comparative work on two specific case studies was also produced: Michael Clarke, Frédéric Dufeu, and Peter Manning. 2015. "Les relations entre technologie et créativité dans l'analyse des musiques électroacoustiques: Une étude comparative de *Riverrun* de Barry Truax et *Imago* de Trevor Wishart," *Musurgia*, XXII(1): pp. 27–44.

3. Thomas Licata, ed. 2002. *Electroacoustic Music: Analytical Perspectives* (Westport, CT: Greenwood Press); Mary Simoni, ed. 2006. *Analytical Methods of Electroacoustic Music* (New York: Routledge); Simon Emmerson and Leigh Landy, eds. 2016. *Expanding the Horizon of Electroacoustic Music Analysis* (Cambridge, UK: Cambridge University Press); Miller Puckette and Kerry Hagan, eds. 2020. *Between the Tracks: Musicians on Selected Electronic Music* (Cambridge, MA: MIT Press).

4. Peter Manning. 2013. *Electronic and Computer Music*, 4th ed. (New York: Oxford University Press); Roger Dean, ed. 2009. *The Oxford Companion of Computer Music* (New York: Oxford University Press); Curtis Roads. 2015. *Composing Electronic Music: A New Aesthetic* (New York: Oxford University Press).

5. See Susan Bruce, ed. 2008. *Three Early Modern Utopias: Utopia, New Atlantis, and The Isle of Pines* (Oxford: Clarendon Press).

6. The technical processes of electrical sound production can be traced back to a pioneering development in America, launched in 1897 by Thaddeus Cahill. Known as the Dynamophone or Telharmonium, this system consisted of a commercial electrical power generator fitted with special inductors connected directly to the revolving shafts of the dynamo. It was, however, the invention of the thermionic valve in 1906 by Lee de Forest that established the key principles necessary to engage with the true potential of electronic sound production and signal processing.

7. For a fuller perspective on the development of electronic music from the turn of the 20th century to 1945, see Manning, *Electronic and Computer Music*, pp. 3–16.

8. Ibid., pp. 19–98.

9. For an informative introduction to the early evolution of the digital computer, see Brian Randell, ed. 2013. *The Origin of Digital Computers: Selected Papers* (New York: Springer).

10. Konrad Zuse is now considered to have achieved a major landmark in this context with his development of an electro-mechanical and also programmable computer based on binary coding during 1936–1938, known as the Z1, in Germany. However, the subsequent work of the mathematician Alan Turing during the 1940s in Cambridge, UK, arguably earns him the title of the true pioneer of digital computing, albeit with a considerable debt to a Hungarian American mathematician, John von Neumann.

11. Notwithstanding these practical challenges, pioneers were to make important advances not only in terms of computer music, but also in other branches of the arts and literature, including film. See Hannah B. Higgins and Douglas Kahn. 2012. *Mainframe Experimentalism: Early Computing and the Foundations of the Digital Arts* (Berkeley: University of California Press).

12. Westerkamp's interest in soundscape composition was stimulated by her engagement with the World Soundscape Project based in SFU, thus coming into direct contact with Truax who also made important contributions to the associated repertory subsequent to the composition of *Riverrun*.

Chapter 1

1. Although it was possible to transmit a number of speech-quality calls in such a manner, using different frequency bands within the available audio spectrum, problems of crosstalk and other associated artifacts severely limited what was possible in this regard.

2. For a more complete study of the early development of mainframe computers and their role in the birth of computer music, see Peter Manning. 2013. *Electronic and Computer Music*, 4th ed. (New York: Oxford University Press): pp. 181–196.

3. Programming a computer in assembler code involves the use of a mnemonic representation of the machine-level instructions specific to the computer concerned.

4. Claude Shannon and Warren Weaver. 1949. *The Mathematical Theory of Communication* (Urbana: University of Illinois Press).

5. Max Mathews. 1963. "The Digital Computer as a Musical Instrument," *Science*, 142(3592): pp. 553–557.

6. Ibid., p. 554. The quality of digital audio depends on both key parameters, the sampling rate determining the bandwidth and the number of binary bits used to quantize each sample value the degree of residual noise that is generated. For a comprehensive introduction to the principles of digital audio, see Manning, *Electronic and Computer Music*, pp. 245–260.

7. Although only intended as an overview, the above schematic reveals the limited fidelity of his initial synthesis system, the 5 kHz smoothing filter defining the maximum possible bandwidth, resulting from a sampling rate of just 10 kHz. By the end of the decade other documentation indicates that the sampling rate for Music N systems had been generally upgraded to 20 kHz, but this was well short of the bandwidth required for high-quality sound production.

8. The development of real-time environments for generating computer music will be considered in later chapters.

9. See, for example, Curtis Roads and Max Mathews. 1980. "Interview with Max Mathews," *Computer Music Journal*, 4(4): pp. 15–22.

10. Hannah Higgins and Douglas Kahn, eds. 2012. *Mainframe Experimentalism* (Berkeley: University of California Press): p. 132.

11. James Tenney. 1963. "Sound-Generation by Means of a Digital Computer," *Journal of Music Theory*, 7(1): pp. 24–70.

12. In Music IV and subsequent versions, all wavetable functions are called directly using a "Fn" descriptor, where "n" is a reference number to a function definition that is inserted in the "score." The "Pn" descriptor, involving an additional data coding step, was dispensed with.

13. See Roads and Mathews, "Interview with Max Mathews."

14. Tenney, "Sound Generation by Means of a Digital Computer," p. 51.

15. Victor Lazzarini. 2013. "The Development of Computer Music Programming Systems," *Journal of New Music Research*, 42(1): pp. 97–110. Later Music N programs were to provide more extensive libraries of resources.

16. Such a mixed programming environment was to prove invaluable to several other initiatives that were to follow, especially during the 1970s and early 1980s. See, for example, the discussion of Barry Truax's *Riverrun* in Chapter 2.

17. For a detailed perspective on Risset's early contributions to computer music, see Jean-Claude Risset. 1964. "Computer Music Experiments 1964– . . . ," *Computer Music Journal*, 9(1): pp. 11–18.

18. Risset's association with Schaeffer's Groupe de Recherches Musicales (GRM) is considered in Chapter 5 (Dhomont).

19. Risset, "Computer Music Experiments 1964– . . . ," p. 11.

20. Mathews, "The Digital Computer as a Musical Instrument."

21. The knowledge and experience thus acquired was to prove invaluable to the support he subsequently provided for GRM and IRCAM in the context of both Music V and Music 10.

22. For a detailed description of the work, see Risset, "Computer Music Experiments 1964– . . . ," pp. 14–16.

23. Jean-Claude Risset. 1994. "Sculpting Sounds with Computers: Music, Science, Technology," *Leonardo*, 27(3): pp. 257–261.

24. It has been more generally assumed that the first piece to make use of this technique is Chowning's *Sabelithe*, composed in 1971. However, personal communication with Chowning has confirmed that Risset's *Mutations* was indeed the first completed work so to do, albeit perhaps in a less evident manner. FM synthesis had featured in an earlier sketch of *Sabelithe* realized in 1967, but this version was never completed.

25. Risset's absence for military service (1965–1967) created a timely opportunity for Chowning to start his own investigations in terms of dynamic control. Interestingly, one of his projects was concerned with controlling the spatial projection of sound in space. A number of the composers that feature in this project have engaged with techniques of spatialization, and key aspects of their contributions in this regard will be considered further in Chapter 9 in the context of Natasha Barrett's *Hidden Values*.

26. A personal communication with Chowning confirms these circumstances.

27. John Chowning. 1973. "The Synthesis of Complex Audio Spectra by Means of Frequency Modulation," *Journal of the Audio Engineering Society*, 21(7): pp. 526–534. This article was also published in *Computer Music Journal*, 1(2): pp. 46–54, and in a reformatted

355

digital version, dated February 13, 1977, at https://ccrma.stanford.edu/sites/default/files/user/jc/fm_synthesispaper-2.pdf, accessed April 3, 2020. For clarity, the sequence of diagrams that follow are reproduced from the latter version of the article.

28. https://ccrma.stanford.edu/sites/default/files/user/jc/fm_synthesispaper-2.pdf .

29. Ibid.

30. Ibid.

31. Given the coding similarities, it is easy to implement the examples given in the article using Csound.

32. Chowning, "The Synthesis of Complex Audio Spectra."

33. Since I = d/m, d = I x m. As Chowning notes, the bandwidth is related directly to the modulation index (and only indirectly to the deviation), thus I = P7 x P6. In order to achieve the envelope characteristic for the modulating oscillator the numeric difference between the two indices is first calculated, coded as (P8 – P7) x P6, and then used as the range value for the chosen envelope function. The result is then used to modulate the starting index value, P7 x P6, by adding the two components together before feeding the result to the amplitude input of the modulating oscillator.

34. Chowning, "The Synthesis of Complex Audio Spectra."

35. Ibid.

36. The amplitude cancellation or reinforcement that occurs when several sidebands have the same absolute frequency must be considered with a specific attention to initial conditions. If the carrier and/or the modulation frequencies are modified over time and then are set back to their initial values, the resulting timbre may differ, as the phase alignment between carrier and modulator will have, in most cases, been changed along with the variations in frequency.

37. As will be seen in due course, the evolution of Max, from its initial beginnings as a MIDI-only implementation of research first carried out at IRCAM by Miller Puckette, to its commercial MIDI plus audio version Max/MSP and video extension known as Jitter, has a material bearing on the study of several of the works to be considered in subsequent chapters. Since 2012 the generic term Max has become the official descriptor for marketing purposes, but to avoid possible confusion when studying compositions completed prior to this date the descriptors Max and Max/MSP will be used.

38. John Chowning. 2011. "*Turenas*: The Realisation of a Dream," paper presented at Journées d'Informatique Musicale, Université de Saint–Étienne.

39. See Note 25.

40. Most of the characteristics of Music 10 can be explored using Csound. See, for example, Richard Boulanger, ed. 2000. *The Csound Book* (Cambridge, MA: MIT Press).

41. See video in Presentation 15, "Chowning's compositional process and career," of the accompanying software, at 4′18″.

42. Kevin Dahan and Olivier Baudouin have previously worked on reconstructing the algorithmic and the synthesis programs used for the composition of *Stria*. See Kevin Dahan. 2007. "Surface Tensions: Dynamics of *Stria*," *Computer Music Journal*, 31(3): pp. 65–74. Also, Olivier Baudouin. 2007. "A Reconstruction of *Stria*," *Computer Music Journal*, 31(3): pp. 75–81. Some aspects of our emulation have been adapted from Dahan's Csound code, as published on a DVD accompanying *Computer Music Journal*, 31(4).

43. See, for instance, Edward A. Lowman. 1971. "An Example of Fibonacci Numbers Used to Generate Rhythmic Values in Modern Music," *Fibonacci Quarterly*, 9(4): pp. 423–426.

44. Each number in the sequence is the sum of the previous two numbers.

45. See video in Presentation 2 ("The shaping of *Stria*") of the accompanying software, at 3′51″.

46. See video in Presentation 2 of the accompanying software, at 17′35″.

47. The change of amplitude of different sidebands as the modulation index alters is complex and intuitively unpredictable, but can be calculated using Bessel functions.

48. As Bruno Bossis noted in his 2005 article on *Stria*, "[the use of two parallel modulators] allows for even more complex spectra, without increasing modulation indices, which would reduce the relative importance of the carrier frequency in the output signal." Bruno Bossis, "*Stria* de John Chowning ou l'*oxymoron* musical: Du nombre d'or comme poétique," in Évelyne Gayou, ed. 2005. *John Chowning. Portraits Polychromes* (Paris: Ina-GRM, TUM–Michel de Maule): p. 99. Translated from the French by the authors.

49. These thirty-three events are distributed across the six sections of *Stria* as follows: 3, 9, 5, 9, 5, 2.

50. The first of these twenty-six variables is the index of the global procedure to be called. To generate *Stria*, Chowning always used 2 as input to call the "event2" procedure, the most elaborate of the three he wrote in SAIL ("event0," "event1," "event2").

51. The "event type" variable was not implemented as a parameter in the emulation of Presentation 10, as Chowning always called the "event2" procedure (see previous note). The "event begin time" variable was not implemented, as irrelevant in the context of generating one single event. The "constant first sideband" variable was implemented by Chowning to enable constant first upper or lower sidebands across all the elements of one given event, but was in fact never used in *Stria*.

52. As the recursion is called when the value read from the table distributing elements in the chronology of the event equals 0.42, theoretically several recursive calls could happen in each event, even with only one level of recursion. However, Chowning commented out a line of code so that once a recursion has occurred, no additional recursion is possible within the considered event.

53. This permutation is one of several possible depending on parameters of the SAIL algorithm: it applies when the frequency space is inferior to 1 (resulting from a negative power for frequency space) and when division of frequency space is set to 0 (resulting in nine divisions of the space as opposed to eighteen).

54. The original code for this reverberation was lost and the algorithm we use in our emulation is based on Kevin Dahan's estimate derived from information from the composer and fine-tuned by listening tests and used in his 2007 Csound emulation. See Dahan, "Surface Tensions: Dynamics of *Stria*," as well as the DVD accompanying *Computer Music Journal*, 31(4).

55. By using the "Sort data vertically according to parameter values" menu in the Presentation inspector.

56. Charles Dodge and Thomas A. Jerse. 1997. *Computer Music Synthesis, Composition and Performance*, 2nd ed. (London and New York: Schirmer): p. 126.

57. *Computer Music Journal*, 31(4): Accompanying DVD.

58. Charles Dodge and Thomas A. Jerse, *Computer Music Synthesis, Composition and Performance*, p. 126. However, it is not clear how this diagram was generated. The number of blocks that are identified do not correspond to the number of events in any of the versions of the work. For a detailed presentation of the available sources on *Stria* and the different versions of the work, see Laura Zattra. 2007. "The Assembling of *Stria* by John Chowning: A Philological Investigation," *Computer Music Journal*, 31(3): pp. 38–64.

357

Chapter 2

1. Dennis Gabor. 1946. "Theory of Communication," *Journal of the Institute of Electrical Engineers Part III*, 93: pp. 429–457.

2. Claude E. Shannon and Warren Weaver. 1949. *The Mathematical Theory of Communication* (Urbana: University of Illinois Press).

3. Iannis Xenakis. 1955. "La crise de la musique sérielle," *Gravesaner Blätter*, 1: pp. 2–4.

4. Iannis Xenakis. 1971. *Formalized Music: Thought and Mathematics in Composition* (Bloomington: Indiana University Press; rev. ed., New York: Pendragon Press, 1992).

5. Ibid., pp. 43–44.

6. See Chapter 1 for further information on the Music N family of synthesis programs, including Music V.

7. Curtis Roads. 1978. "Automated Granular Synthesis of Sound," *Computer Music Journal*, 2(2): pp. 61–62.

8. Ibid., p. 61.

9. See Curtis Roads. 2001. *Microsound* (Cambridge, MA: MIT Press).

10. For a detailed account of Le Caine's pioneering work in this area, see Gayle Young. 1984. "Hugh Le Caine: Pioneer of Electronic Music in Canada," *HSTC Bulletin: Journal of the History of Canadian Science, Technology and Medicine/HSTC Bulletin: revue d'histoire des sciences, des techniques et de la médecine au Canada*, 8(1): pp. 20–31. The key exhibit at EXPO '67 was a prototype programmable synthesizer, using serial algorithms to generate note sequences. See Hugh Le Caine and Gustav Ciamaga. 1967. "A Preliminary Report on the Serial Sound Structure Generator," *Perspectives of New Music*, 6(1): pp. 114–118.

11. IRCAM (the Institut de Recherche et Coordination Acoustique/Musique), founded in Paris by Pierre Boulez in the 1970s, was soon to eclipse these initiatives in terms of computing power with the purchase of a much larger mainframe computer, a PDP-10, and the legacy of these developments in terms of music software is studied elsewhere.

12. The concept of byte addressing, where units of 8 binary bits can be combined to make the now familiar configurations of 16, 32, and 64 bits, was still relatively new at the time, and the PDP-15 followed the more traditional word format, using a basic unit of 18 bits. The ability to partition each word into different groupings of bits, however, brought many programming advantages, especially where memory was restricted.

13. With the introduction of MIDI during the early 1980s, it became possible to use SSP to generate performance data for external sound generators.

14. Truax was directly influenced by Dr. Otto Laske, the cognitive musicologist with whom he studied at Utrecht, and with whom he collaborated on the OBSERVER software to study musical problem solving within an interactive computer music environment. See Barry Truax. 1999. "Sonology: A Questionable Science Revisited," in Jerry Tabor, ed., *Otto Laske: Navigating New Musical Horizons* (Westport, CT: Greenwood Press): pp. 21–36.

15. Barry Truax. 1976. "For Otto Laske: A Communicational Approach to Computer Sound Programs," *Journal of Music Theory*, 20(2): pp. 227–300.

16. Ibid., p. 236.

17. In the case of a conventional performance, the issue of interpretation is of course an additional consideration, but the score remains the ultimate arbiter as to the intentions of the composer.

18. He was also aware of other initiatives, such as the work of Lejaren Hiller and Leonard Isaacson using an ILLIAC computer to generate traditional score data for works such as the *Illiac Suite* (1956) and Hubert Howe's work with composing arrays during the 1960s, but these were not to prove directly relevant to his own work.
19. Barry Truax. 1973. "The Computer Composition—Sound Synthesis Programs POD4, POD5 & POD6," *Sonological Reports No. 2* (Utrecht, Institute of Sonology): Section I.
20. Truax, "For Otto Laske," pp. 261–262.
21. With the subsequent introduction of stereo sound distribution in the non-real-time version POD7, the frequency limits reduced to between 58 and 6,005 Hz.
22. His pioneering implementation of real-time FM synthesis resulted in the composition of his quadraphonic work *Tape VII "The Journey to the Gods"* from *Gilgamesh*, in 1973.
23. Truax created experimental stereo versions of both POD4 and POD5, described in *Sonological Reports No. 2*, but the limitations of the entirely software-based computing facilities at the Institute of Sonology materially restricted their practical value. The development of resources capable of fully supporting such a composing environment depended on technical advances that only became possible subsequent to his return to SFU.
24. Truax, "The Computer Composition," Section IV.
25. This post resulted from an invitation from Raymond Murray Schafer in the first instance to collaborate on the newly established World Soundscape Project. This development and the significance of Truax's contributions to its development are considered in Chapter 4, in the context of the composer study focusing on the work of Hildegard Westerkamp.
26. Barry Truax. 1978. "Computer Music Composition: The Polyphonic POD system," *IEEE Computer*, 11(8): pp. 40–50.
27. Ibid., p. 44.
28. Constructed from a quarter wave representation of 2,048 values.
29. It is relevant to note that all of Truax's POD compositions were composed in a quadraphonic (four channel) configuration.
30. See Dean Walraff. 1979. "The DMX-1000 Signal Processing Computer," *Computer Music Journal*, 3(4): pp. 44–49.
31. As an option an additional memory bank could be purchased for generating effects such as reverberation. This, however, was much slower than the main memory bank and could therefore not be used for primary processing functions.
32. FORTRAN IV was used both for PODX and his subsequent granular synthesis programs.
33. Barry Truax. 1985. "The PODX System: Interactive Compositional Software for the DMX-1000," *Computer Music Journal*, 9(1): pp. 29–38.
34. Barry Truax. 1988. "*Sequence of Earlier Heaven*: The Record as a Medium for the Electroacoustic Composer," *Leonardo*, 21(1): pp. 25–28.
35. References to Gabor's theories in the writings of Truax were now to become increasingly significant.
36. The earlier-mentioned implementation of granular synthesis techniques using Music 11 at MIT in 1981 was especially influential in this context. See: Curtis Roads. 1985. "Granular Synthesis of Sound," in Curtis Roads and John Strawn, eds., *Foundations of Computer Music* (Cambridge MA: MIT Press): pp. 145–159.
37. See Barry Truax. 1988. "Real-Time Granular Synthesis with a Digital Signal Processor," *Computer Music Journal*, 12(2): pp. 14–26.

38. This was not a variable parameter in Truax's granular synthesis programs, given the processing implications, not least the number of simultaneous voice streams.

39. Truax, "Real-Time Granular Synthesis," p. 15.

40. *Riverrun* is a case in point here, dispensing with any use of tendency masks.

41. For a detailed description of GSAMX, see Barry Truax. 1994. "Discovering Inner Complexity: Time Shifting and Transposition with a Real-Time Granulation Technique," *Computer Music Journal*, 18(2): pp. 38–48.

42. *Documentation DVD #1* (CSR-DVD 0801) can be ordered at: sfu.ca/~truax/order.html.

43. "Strand" is not a term Truax employs; it is used here to clarify the discussion of *Riverrun*'s structure.

44. Authors' diagram.

45. Ibid.

46. Ibid.

47. Ibid.

48. Ibid. The accompanying software for this chapter can be used in an octophonic format by using the corresponding menu in the Audio Settings, at the right of the main window, and reproduce the spatialization configuration of *Riverrun* in an appropriately equipped studio.

49. As found, for instance, in Mara Helmuth. 2006. "Barry Truax's *Riverrun*," in Mary Simoni, ed., *Analytical Methods of Electroacoustic Music* (New York: Routledge): pp. 187–238.

50. However, it should be noted that placing ramps on the center value and range creates progressions identical to a tendency mask.

Chapter 3

1. See Peter Manning. 2013. *Electronic and Computer Music*, 4th ed. (New York: Oxford University Press): pp. 207–216.

2. See Chapter 2.

3. Although there have been some changes over the years to reflect new interests and technical developments, the research groupings at IRCAM have broadly retained their original remit. The current classifications are as follows: Acoustic and Cognitive Spaces, Perception and Sound Design, Sound Analysis–Synthesis, Music Representations, Analysis of Musical Practices, and Sound Music Movement Interaction. These groupings are in turn associated with the following projects: Sound Synthesis and Processing, Composition, Design and Mediation, Gesture and Interaction, Indexing and Search Engines, and Sound Spatialization.

4. Jonathan Harvey was a composer who for many years saw significant advantages in continuing to work in such a manner, and the reasons that informed this choice are considered further in Chapter 7.

5. The arguments that were put forward for floating-point data formats are complex and certainly with hindsight open to some debate. At the time the accuracy of integer representations of audio data samples was generally limited to a resolution of just sixteen bits, which can indeed create potentially serious problems if audio data is subject to material in this format changes in amplitude levels. With the subsequent introduction of twenty-four-bit integer resolutions, as discussed below, the arguments for using floating-point formats to preserve numerical accuracy became less persuasive, especially when the increased demands on data processing were considered. Such considerations were especially critical in those contexts requiring a real-time mode of

operation. Fortunately, subsequent improvements in computing speeds were progressively to eliminate this potential drawback of the alternative format.

6. See comments in Gerhard Eckel, Xavier Rodet, and Yves Potard. 1987. "A Sun-Mercury Music Workstation," *Proceedings of the 1987 International Computer Music Conference—Champaign/Urbana, Illinois* (San Francisco: International Computer Music Association): pp. 159–165.

7. Hal G. Alles and Peppino (Giuseppe) di Giugno. 1977. "A One Card 64 Channel Digital Synthesiser," *Computer Music Journal*, 1(4): pp. 7–9.

8. Interesting parallels can be drawn here with the progression from additive to FM synthesis pioneered by John Chowning and the subsequent evolution of the techniques in Barry Truax's granular synthesis programs. See Chapters 1 and 2.

9. For an introduction to the 4X, including its use in the composition of *Répons*, see Pierre Boulez and Andrew Gerzso. 1988. "Computers in Music," *Scientific American*, 258(4): pp. 44–50.

10. The component AMD 2901 four-bit slices were identical to those used in the DMX-1000.

11. Although di Giugno continued to make improvements to the 4X during the decade, he was aware of the limitations of its integer-based processor, even with a twenty-four-bit resolution, drawing public attention to this deficiency as early as 1983. His desire to develop a floating-point version operating at a higher sampling rate, however, was never fully realized, work ceasing with a prototype version known as the 5A. See Giuseppe di Giugno and Eugenio Guarino. 1983. "Un processore rapido floating–point," *Atti del 5° Colloquio Di Informatica Musicale* (Ancona): pp. 36–42.

12. In the late 1980s, miniaturization was taken a stage further in terms of a suitably modified version of the 4X controlled by an Apple Macintosh. See later discussion on the birth of Max.

13. See Michel Starkier and Philippe Prevot. 1986. "Real Time Gestural Control," *Proceedings of the 1986 International Computer Music Conference—The Hague* (San Francisco: International Computer Music Association): pp. 423–426.

14. Emmanuel Favreau, Michael Fingerhut, Olivier Koechlin, Patrick Potacsek, Miller Puckette, and Robert Rowe. 1986. "Software Developments for the 4X Real-Time System," *Proceedings of the 1986 International Computer Music Conference—The Hague* (San Francisco: International Computer Music Association): pp. 369–374.

15. Boulez was to continue working on modifications to *Répons* for many years. For a fuller perspective, see Jean–Jacques Nattiez. 1993. *Le Combat de Chronos et d'Orphée*, (Paris: Christian Bourgois éditeur).

16. The spatial distribution of the processed sounds was controlled via a special computer-controlled diffuser known as the Halophone, developed at the Heinrich-Strobel-Stiftung in Freiburg. See Andrew Gerzso. 1984. "Reflections on *Répons*," *Contemporary Music Review*, 1(1): pp. 23–34.

17. Barry Vercoe subsequently developed a real-time version of Csound, initially for an ultra-fast DSP processor but subsequently for generic implementation as workstations and desktop computers became increasingly more powerful. See Barry Vercoe and Dan Ellis. 1990. "Real-Time CSOUND: Software Synthesis with Sensing and Control," *Proceedings of the 1990 International Computer Music Conference—Glasgow, UK* (San Francisco: International Computer Music Association): pp. 209–211.

18. Nyssim Lefford and Barry Vercoe. 1999. "An Interview with Barry Vercoe," *Computer Music Journal*, 23(4): pp. 9–17.

19. See Joshua Bloch and Roger Dannenberg. 1985. "Real-Time Computer Accompaniment of Keyboard Performances," *Proceedings of the 1985 International Computer Music Conference—Simon Fraser University, Vancouver* (San Francisco: International Computer Music Association): pp. 279–289; and Barry Vercoe and Miller Puckette. 1985. "Training the Synthetic Performer," *Proceedings of the 1985 International Computer Music Conference—Simon Fraser University, Vancouver* (San Francisco: International Computer Music Association): pp. 275–278.

20. See Chapter 8.

21. The initial version of this software was demonstrated at the 1984 International Computer Music Conference, Paris, hosted by IRCAM. A video of this demonstration can be located at https://www.youtube.com/watch?v=vOYky8MmrEU, accessed April 3, 2020.

22. IRCAM subsequently designed and built a special flute using a MIDI-based detection system. See Damien Pousset, *La flûte-MIDI, l'histoire et quelques applications, mémoire de maîtrise* (Université Paris–Sorbonne, 1992).

23. See Barry Vercoe and Miller Puckette, "Training the Synthetic Performer."

24. Max Mathews and Joseph Pasquale. 1981. "RTSKED: A Scheduled Performance Language for the Crumar General Development System," *Proceedings of the 1981 International Computer Music Conference—North Texas State University* (San Francisco: International Computer Music Association): p. 286.

25. For a more detailed account of this evolution of Max at IRCAM, see Miller Puckette. 2002. "Max at Seventeen," *Computer Music Journal*, 26(4): pp. 31–43.

26. The development of mass-produced desktop computers was materially to affect the future of the computer industry, and this early example of their ability to challenge the exclusivity of traditional mainframe and minicomputer technologies was at least initially unsettling to some, both in IRCAM and elsewhere.

27. For a revealing and very personal perspective on these formative influences, see Philippe Manoury. 1995. "Entretien avec Jean-Pierre Derrien", at http://www.philippemanoury.com/?p=349, accessed April 3, 2020.

28. Philippe Manoury. 1984. "The Arrow of Time," tr. Tod Machover and Nigel Osborne, *Contemporary Music Review*, 1(1): pp. 131–145.

29. Ibid., p. 140.

30. Ibid.

31. FTS (Faster Than Sound) was an audio signal processing extension to Max developed at IRCAM by Puckette specifically for the i860 processors used in the ISPW; see Miller Puckette. 1991. "FTS: A Real-Time Monitor for Multiprocessor Music Synthesis," *Computer Music Journal*, 15(3): pp. 58–67. In 1991 work began on developing versions of FTS that would work in other computing environments, leading to a new Java-based version developed by François Déchelle, known as jMax. The better-known derivative, MSP, was developed and released by Cycling '74 in 1998 as an extension to the commercial version of Max, originally launched by Opcode in 1990, the combined package being known as Max/MSP, more recently simply as Max.

32. Unlike Max/MSP, Pd is an open source program, freely available to the wider community.

33. It should be noted that another work for the 4X was completed and performed at IRCAM in the same year, *Aloni*, by Thierry Lancino. This was scored for ensemble and children's choir. Both of these works received their first performance in April 1987.

34. *Jupiter* has received significant attention in terms of the production of commentaries and text-based analyses, a notable example being Andrew May. 2006. "Philippe

362

Manoury's *Jupiter*," in Mary Simoni, ed., *Analytical Methods of Electroacoustic Music* (London: Routledge): pp. 145–185. However, most accounts concentrate on the later versions of the piece, and thus underplay the significance of the 4X in facilitating the original version.

35. Philippe Manoury, program note for *Jupiter*, http://brahms.ircam.fr/works/work/10482/, accessed April 3, 2020. Translated from the French by the authors.

36. Jean-Baptiste Barrière. 1987. "Musical Production at IRCAM in 1986–87: A Studio Report," *Proceedings of the 1987 International Computer Music Conference—Champaign/Urbana, Illinois* (San Francisco: International Computer Music Association): pp. 57–64.

37. The components of the "orchestra" are extensively described in Andrew May, "Philippe Manoury's *Jupiter*." It must be noted, however, that subsequent versions of the piece, such as the Pd version, include several refinements and extensions, both musical and technical.

38. Philippe Manoury, "Les partitions virtuelles" (1997), article available online at http://www.philippemanoury.com/?p=340, accessed April 3, 2020.

39. Miller Puckette, "Max at Seventeen," p. 34.

40. Miller Puckette. 1988. "The Patcher," *Proceedings of the 1988 International Computer Music Conference—Cologne* (San Francisco: International Computer Music Association): pp. 420–429.

41. Philippe Manoury. 1997. translated by Nick Le Quesne, in liner notes of Philippe Manoury, *La partition du ciel et de l'enfer. Jupiter*, CD, Musidisc France, Accord, 465 307-2: p. 8.

42. Philippe Manoury, "*Pluton*," online notice, http://brahms.ircam.fr/documents/document/21518/, accessed April 3, 2020. Translated from the French by the authors.

43. Translation from video of Presentation 2 of the accompanying software, "The form of *Pluton*," from 0′58″ to 1′55 ″.

44. The pianist for both the 1988 and 1989 versions of *Pluton* was Ichiro Nodaira.

45. Program note for the final version: http://brahms.ircam.fr/works/work/10493/, accessed April 3, 2020. Translated from the French by the authors.

46. Patrick Odiard. 1995. "De la confrontation à la conjonction: À propos de *Sonus ex machina*," *Les cahiers de l'Ircam. Compositeurs d'aujourd'hui*, no. 8, *Philippe Manoury*: p. 50.

47. Ibid., Translated from the French by the authors.

48. Ibid., p. 52.

49. Ibid., pp. 52–53.

50. Ibid., p. 50.

51. For further indications on the musical materials of *Pluton*, but also of *Jupiter* and *La partition du ciel et de l'enfer*, see Patrick Odiard, "De la confrontation à la conjonction."

52. Although the digital environment for *Pluton* was originally implemented for the 4X system, the source for the analysis presented in this chapter is a subsequent Max patch developed by Serge Lemouton. This patch is named PLUTON2008_agora and was kindly provided to the authors by Alain Jacquinot at IRCAM in 2009.

53. As Miller Puckette points out in the video interviews of the accompanying software, the use of the term "harmonizer" is improper, as the module has only one line of pitch shifting.

54. This sampling algorithm was named "Trevor," as it was initially being tested with a sample from Wishart's *Vox 5*. See Chapter 8.

55. A midicent is a hundredth of a semitone.

56. Philippe Manoury. 2003. "*Pluton* by Philippe Manoury," in Marc Battier, Bertrand Cheret, Serge Lemouton, and Philippe Manoury, eds., *PMA LIB. Les musiques électroniques de Philippe Manoury/The electronic music of Philippe Manoury*, CD-ROM (Paris: IRCAM —Centre Georges Pompidou): p. 6.

57. Events 1, 3, 5, 7, and 9 activate the metronomes; events 2, 4, 6, 8, and 10 stop them.

58. This effect is particularly audible when the periods of the metronomes are relatively short, such as in event 9 of section VE, where the three periods are 377, 194, and 212 milliseconds.

59. 6,000 midicents means no transposition, 4,800 means transposition one octave down (12 x 100 midicents below 6,000), 7,200 means transposition one octave up (12 x 100 midicents above 6,000). The intervals of this sequence of section IIA are thus: two octaves up (8,400), one octave and a minor sixth up (8,000), one major sixth up (6,900), one fourth up (6,500), one tritone up (6,600), one major second up (6,200), one major sixth down (5,100), one minor third down (5,700), and one minor sixth up (6,800).

60. Manoury, "*Pluton* by Philippe Manoury," p. 11.

61. As Puckette remarks in the video of Presentation 7 of the accompanying software (at 7′35″), parameters with a lower-case "o" (such as oto2 or oto4) refer to the first oscillator module (fft-oscs1), while parameters with an upper-case "O" (such as Oto2 or Oto4) refer to the second oscillator module (fft-oscs2).

62. This simple output command is the message "bang" in Max.

63. For instance, if the user-defined value is 100 milliseconds, the first glissando will last 100 milliseconds, the second 200 milliseconds, the third 300 milliseconds, and the twelfth 1,200 milliseconds.

64. As noted in the video of Presentation 7 of the accompanying software (at 24′25″), a third mode is available for Gumbo slides, outputting all glissandi simultaneously, but this third mode is never used in *Pluton*.

65. Puckette notes in the video of Presentation 7 of the accompanying software (at 1′10″) that "the piece was premiered at [a sampling frequency of] 32 kHz, and the original FFT size was 512 [samples]," meaning the FFT analysis was performed every 16 milliseconds (with no overlap-add), and the width of each frequency bin was 62.5 Hz. In the implementation of the Max patch investigated in this study, the sampling frequency is 44.1 kHz, and the FFT size is 1,024 samples—hence, the FFT analysis is performed every ca. 23.22 milliseconds, and the width of each frequency bin is about 43.07 Hz.

66. Manoury, "*Pluton* by Philippe Manoury," p. 19.

67. Video of Presentation 7 of the accompanying software, 16′00″ to 16′21″.

68. Manoury, "*Pluton* by Philippe Manoury," p. 20.

69. More generally, the spatialization module does not send any signal back to the digital environment: its four outputs are sent directly to the hall loudspeakers.

70. As well as VA, which is entirely a piano solo with no electronics.

71. Manoury, "*Jupiter* by Philippe Manoury," in Marc Battier, Bertrand Cheret, Serge Lemouton, and Philippe Manoury, eds., *PMA LIB. Les musiques électroniques de Philippe Manoury/The electronic music of Philippe Manoury*, CD-ROM (Paris: IRCAM—Centre Georges Pompidou): p. 8.

72. "Stage output" is the terminology of the authors.

73. On four corners front-left, front-right, rear-left, and rear-right.

74. It is important to note, however, that this autonomy is ideal and only true assuming a smooth operation of the digital environment. In practice, because of the difficulties to

implement a perfectly robust score follower, it is recommended that a computer operator is present during the concert to trigger events manually if the score follower fails.

75. In the Max patch studied here, the score is stored in a bank of "detonate" objects, the successors to the "explode" object for Max (see Miller Puckette. 1990.) "Explode: A User Interface for Sequence and Score Following," *Proceedings of the 1990 International Computer Music Conference—Glasgow, UK* (San Francisco: International Computer Music Association): pp. 259–261.

76. Philippe Manoury et al. 2008. "PLUTON2008_agora.maxpat," Max patch for the performance of Pluton. Document provided by the Creation and Diffusion department at IRCAM.

77. This command in fact repeats the setting, as rgate had already been set to zero in event 3.

78. Manoury et al., "PLUTON2008_agora.maxpat."

79. Markov sequences are named after the Russian mathematician Andreï Markov (1856–1922), who elaborated the formalism of Markov chains.

80. Manoury, "*Pluton* by Philippe Manoury," p. 20.

81. Philippe Manoury. 1993. *Pluton* pour piano avec capteurs Midi et système de synthèse et de traitement audionumérique en temps réel, score, Paris, Durand, p. 25. Translated from the French by the authors.

82. As named by the composer in the score, p. 27. Translated from the French by the authors.

83. Ibid., p. 26.

84. There are two parallel modules for both the audio recording into the Trevor sampler and for the Markov recording and playback; for instance, the audio contents of the R1 sequence is recorded into the first eight-voice sampler (opening chord) and the second sampler (closing chord). The A3 sequence only activates the first Markov matrix; if played immediately after R1, A3 would therefore only trigger the playback of the opening chord of R1. The A4 sequence only activates the second matrix; the three other Markovian sequences (A1, A2, A5) activate both matrixes at once.

85. Philippe Manoury. 1998. *Pluton*, CD, Ondine, ODE 888-2.

86. This is incidentally the exact same order as that of the simulation files provided with the program examined in this study, which is given as example in Presentation 1 of the accompanying software.

87. Philippe Manoury, *Pluton*, score. p. 26.

88. May, "Philippe Manoury's *Jupiter*," p. 180.

Chapter 4

1. For a detailed account of the birth and early development of the World Soundscape Project, see Keiko Torigoe. 1982. "A Study of the World Soundscape Project" (MFA diss., York University, Toronto, Ontario).

2. Raymond Murray Schafer, *The Composer in the Classroom* (1965) and *Ear Cleaning* (1967).

3. Raymond Murray Schafer. 1969. *The New Soundscape* (Vienna: Universal Edition) and Schafer. 1970. *The Book of Noise* (Wellington, New Zealand: Price Milburn.

4. Hildegard Westerkamp. 1993. Interview with Andra McCartney, in Andra McCartney. 1999. "Sounding Places: Situated Conversations through the Soundscape Conversations of Hildegard Westerkamp" (PhD diss., York University, Toronto, Ontario): pp. 149.

5. This two-record set contained sounds captured on the shoreline and in the harbor, as well as signals and other distinctive sounds from the city. In addition, an illustrated talk by Schafer and the sound recordists was included with a further track narrated by Schafer, providing examples of good and bad acoustic design in Vancouver. Subsequently, the recordings were re-released on CD, along with a companion CD providing a further series of field recordings of Vancouver sounds. Known as the Soundscape Vancouver '96 project, the resulting sound documents were made by Robert MacNevin and Scott Morgan between 1991 and 1995, and this second CD, which also includes comparisons with the 1973 recordings, was curated by Truax and Westerkamp. See https://www.sfu.ca/~truax/vanscape.html, accessed April 3, 2020.

6. See Simon Emmerson. 1986. "The Relation of Language to Materials," in Simon Emmerson, ed., *The Language of Electroacoustic Music* (London: Macmillan).

7. Barry Truax. 1996. "Soundscape, Acoustic Communication and Environmental Sound Composition," *Contemporary Music Review*, 15(1): pp. 49–65.

8. A case might be made for citing *Okeanos* as the very first soundscape composition. However, as a work that predates even the first group recording projects of the WSP, its status in this context is open to debate. The choice of sound material does not in itself ensure that the complex issues that were to arise in terms of an associated aesthetic were either anticipated of fully engaged with. Nonetheless, the work is of formative significance.

9. Raymond Murray Schafer. 1977. *The Tuning of the World: Towards a Theory of Soundscape Design* (Toronto: McClelland & Stewart; 2nd ed., Rochester, VT: Destiny Books, 1994).

10. Barry Truax. 1977. *Handbook for Acoustic Ecology* (Vancouver: A.R.C. Publications).

11. Ibid., p. iv.

12. His book *Acoustic Communication*, for example, provides a useful context for a more detailed scrutiny of its acoustic ecology in terms of the nature of sound, listening, soundscape, and the impact of technology on acoustic communication. See Barry Truax. 1984. *Acoustic Communication* (New York: Ablex Publishing Corporation; 2nd ed., Westport, CT: Ablex, 2001).

13. Barry Truax. 2002. "Genres and Techniques of Soundscape Composition as Developed at Simon Fraser University," *Organised Sound*, 7(1): pp. 5–14.

14. Barry Truax. 2000. "The Aesthetics of Computer Music: A Questionable Concept Reconsidered," *Organised Sound*, 5(3): pp. 119–126.

15. Truax, "Soundscape, Acoustic Communication and Environmental Sound Composition."

16. Ibid.

17. The sentence is a quotation from the Indian mystic Kirpal Singh in *Naam or Word*. A later version of the piece ends with a poem by Norbert Ruebsaat, "When There Is No Sound."

18. Hildegard Westerkamp. 1993. Interview with Andra McCartney (1993), in McCartney, "Sounding Places," p. 151.

19. Hildegard Westerkamp. 2002. "Linking Soundscape Composition and Acoustic Ecology," *Organised Sound*, 7(1): pp. 51–56.

20. Hildegard Westerkamp. 1974. "Soundwalking," *Sound Heritage*, 3(4). A revised version (2001) can be found in Angus Carlyle, ed. 2007. *Autumn Leaves, Sound and the Environment in Artistic Practice* (Paris: Double Entendre): pp. 49–54.

21. Ibid.

22. Hildegard Westerkamp. 1978. *Fantasie for Horns I*, program note.

23. This event, held annually from 1971 until 2009, was arguably the most significant competition during this period for aspiring composers of electronic and computer music to achieve international recognition.

24. Hildegard Westerkamp. 1981. *A Walk through the City*, program note.

25. The definitive version of *Streetmusic* consists solely of a two-channel tape. However, a special version was also conceived as a work for any portable instrument and two-channel tape, along with a companion work, *Windmusic*, for any wind instrument and two-channel tape. See McCartney, "Sounding Places," p. 161.

26. Hildegard Westerkamp. 1982. *Streetmusic*, program note.

27. Hildegard Westerkamp. 1983. *Cool Drool*, revised program note.

28. Hildegard Westerkamp. 1987. "Listening and Soundmaking: A Study of Music-as-Environment" (MA diss., Simon Fraser University, Vancouver, British Columbia), pp. 35–55.

29. Hildegard Westerkamp. 1985. *His Master's Voice*, program note.

30. Hildegard Westerkamp. 1990. *Breathing Room*, program note.

31. http://wfae.net/, accessed April 3, 2020.

32. Hildegard Westerkamp, program note for *Beneath the Forest Floor*, consulted on the composer's website, https://www.hildegardwesterkamp.ca/resources/PDFs/program-notes-pdf/Beneath-the-Forest-Floor.pdf, accessed April 3, 2020.

33. Ibid.

34. Transcription from video of Presentation 2 of the accompanying software, "Contexts for *Beneath the Forest Floor*," from 2′28″ to 4′15″.

35. Transcription from video of Presentation 3 of the accompanying software, "Shaping the musical work," from 1′02″ to 2′01″.

36. Transcription from video of Presentation 2 of the accompanying software, from 4′44″ to 4′50″.

37. Ibid., from 5′01″ to 5′23″.

38. Transcription from video of Presentation 3 of the accompanying software, from 17′27″ to 18′15″.

39. Transcription from video of Presentation 5 of the accompanying software, "From the natural environment to the studio," from 5′47″ to 6′52″.

40. Note from Hildegard Westerkamp's archive for *Beneath the Forest Floor*, document "Beneath_Notes to Materials1," sound file index 3.

41. Westerkamp's archive, document "Beneath_Notes to Materials1," sound file index 67 ("Thrush amb. 1′27″").

42. For this research, the composer kindly provided the authors with five archive folders, containing, respectively, 72, 71, 79, 59, and 12 sound files. Each folder also includes a scan of her handwritten notes on each of the sound files. In this chapter, we refer to the sound files by their archive folder, numbered 1 to 5, and their name.

43. For convenience, the expression "Phuit bird" is used as an onomatopoeic description for the bird's call in these recordings.

44. For consistency with the composer's terminology as used in her archive, we identify the squirrel at Romeo's as "Squirrel 1" and the squirrel from Lighthouse Park as "Squirrel 4."

45. Transcription from video of Presentation 2 of the accompanying software, from 0′29″ to 1′25″.

46. The entire field recording is not present in the archive provided by Westerkamp, but the thirty-four-second excerpt containing the four thrush calls is, and can be listened

to in Presentation 1 of the accompanying software. The file is in folder 1, "ID75_trush_4calls_not gated.wav."

47. Archive folder 1, "ID74_trush_4calls_gated.wav."

48. Archive folder 1, "ID53_winter wren_peeps_eq_gated_edited closer.wav."

49. Transcription from video of Presentation 6 of the accompanying software, "Working with technology," from 2′34″ to 3′42″.

50. The intermediary file is not in the composer's archive; it is therefore not possible to know whether the transposition was operated after the reversal or conversely.

51. Transcription from video of Presentation 3 of the accompanying software, from 6′22″ to 8′09″.

52. Ibid., from 18′37″ to 19′19″.

53. From "ID06_raven_C_var.speed_0.10.6.wav" in folder 1 to "ID12_ravenCarm_I.6_delay.wav" in folder 3.

54. It remains unknown whether the stereo delay used by Westerkamp had a feedback parameter; no feedback can be heard in the examples mentioned here.

55. Transcription from video of Presentation 6 of the accompanying software, from 4′02″ to 4′06″.

56. The three transposed versions are in folder 4: "ID22_thrush_ID21_var.speed0.07.wav," "ID23_thrush_ID21reverb_var.speed0.42.wav," and "ID24_thrush_ID21reverb_var.speed0.31.wav." The subsequent mix of these three files used in the final piece is, also in folder 4, "ID27_mix_ID22–24.wav."

57. As Curtis Roads defines it, the Doppler shift effect was "first described by the astronomer [Christian] Doppler," and is "a change in pitch that results when the source and the listener are moving relative to each other. A common example is heard when standing next to a train track as a train approaches at high speed and then passes. As the train moves closer, the wave fronts of the sound reach us more quickly, causing the pitch to be raised. When the train passes we hear the pitch shift downwards." Curtis Roads. 1996. *The Computer Music Tutorial* (Cambridge, MA: MIT Press): pp. 463–464.

58. Transcription from video of Presentation 6 of the accompanying software, from 12′53″ to 13′12″. From the discussion immediately preceding this excerpt of the interview, it appears plausible that the sampler was the Akai S700, a twelve-bit rack version released in 1987.

59. Transcription from video of Presentation 6 of the accompanying software, from 10′09″ to 11′32″.

60. Which corresponds to a playback speed of 1.56 percent, which amounts to playing the sound sixty-four times slower.

61. Folder 1, "ID03_raven_Carmanah.wav."

62. Folder 3,"ID28_ravenCarm_I.9_looped0.07.wav."

63. Folder 4, "ID02_ravenCarm_start of piece_looped.wav."

64. In another analysis of *Beneath the Forest Floor*, Frédérick Duhautpas, Antoine Freychet, and Makis Solomos provide their transcriptions of the pitches and harmonies generated from the winter wren twitters, heard in the opening section, and from the thrush calls, heard in the transition from the Water section through to the end of the work. See Frédérick Duhautpas, Antoine Freychet, Makis Solomos, "*Beneath the Forest Floor* de Hildegard Westerkamp: Analyse d'une composition à base de paysages sonores," *Analyse musicale*, 76: pp. 34–42. For another analysis of *Beneath the Forest Floor*, see Leigh Landy. 2020. "On Hildegard Westerkamp's *Beneath the Forest Floor* (1992)," in Miller Puckette and Kerry Hagan, eds., *Between the Tracks: Musicians on Selected Electronic Music* (Cambridge, MA: MIT Press).

65. Transcription from video of Presentation 13 of the accompanying software, "Musical parameters and form," from 0′35″ to 1′52″.
66. Transcription from video of Presentation 3 of the accompanying software, from 2′41″ to 3′07″.
67. Both located in folder 4 of the archive.
68. Folder 4, "ID39_creeksection_w.thrushcord to end.wav."
69. Transcription from video of Presentation 6 of the accompanying software, from 13′14″ to 13′53″.
70. Transcription from video of Presentation 14 of the accompanying software, "Listening to the materials of *Beneath the Forest Floor*," from 18′49″ to 20′11″.
71. The timings provided in this analysis are those of the work as published on CD: Hildegard Westerkamp. 2010. *Transformations*, CD, Montreal, empreintes DIGITALes, IMED 1031.
72. "On entend le son de corbeau à la vitesse normale plusieurs fois dans la pièce, mais il est impossible pour l'oreille de faire le lien avec le son transformé." Duhautpas, Freychet, and Solomos, "*Beneath the Forest Floor* de Hildegard Westerkamp, p. 35. Translated from the French by the authors.
73. Transcription from video of Presentation 3 of the accompanying software, from 3′48″ to 6′05″.
74. Ibid., from 8′19″ to 9′29″.
75. Hildegard Westerkamp, long version of the program note for *Beneath the Forest Floor*, n.p. Document kindly provided to the authors by the composer.
76. Transcription from video of Presentation 3 of the accompanying software, from 14′42″ to 15′01″.
77. Hildegard Westerkamp, long version of the program notes.
78. Ibid.
79. Ibid.
80. Transcription from video of Presentation 6 of the accompanying software, from 4′43″ to 5′33″.

Chapter 5

1. Here the issues of terminology, discussed in the Introduction, require further study in context. The descriptor "electroacoustic music" was established by Pierre Schaeffer and his associates in the context of the underlying aesthetic principles that shaped and influenced the development of the Groupe de Recherches Musicales (GRM), and in so doing the composing style of Dhomont. In embracing the evolution of the associated technologies explored by the GRM and the detailed study of their use in *Phonurgie*, useful insights are thus provided into the technical and creative synergies that have underpinned this genre, subsequently to be explored by other composers, notably in Europe.
2. For further information on the birth and early development of *musique concrète*, see Peter Manning. 2013. *Electronic and Computer Music*, 4th ed. (New York: Oxford University Press): pp. 19–38.
3. Rosemary Mountain and Francis Dhomont. 2006. "From Wire to Computer: Francis Dhomont at 80," *Computer Music Journal*, 30(3): pp. 10–21.
4. These recorders manufactured by Studer, known as the G36, were valve-based machines widely used in broadcasting.

5. Studer launched the A77 Revox in 1967, followed in 1978 by the B77 series. These recorders used entirely solid-state electronics including an oscillator-based capstan control system. The Mark II version of the B77 included a built-in variable speed control facility allowing the pitch to be varied within a range of +/− 2 semitones (extendable to +/− 7 semitones via an optional external control facility). However, all these models from the very first A77 could be modified to allow continuous variable speed control from a stationary mode to almost twice the normal playback speed.

6. Pierre Schaeffer. 1966. *Traité des objets musicaux* (Paris: Éditions du Seuil).

7. CNRS, originally founded in 1939, became the primary national research center for France after the end of the Second World War, with research divisions in many major cities, including Marseille. Ironically, Jean-Claude Risset had joined CNRS as a young research associate in 1963 before relocating to the United States to work with Max Mathews at Bell Labs from 1965 to 1969 (see Chapter 1). However, it was to be a further sixteen years, including a period at both IRCAM and GRM, before he returned to CNRS as director of research and development in electroacoustic music.

8. Francis Dhomont. 1996. "Is There a Québec Sound?," *Organised Sound*, 1(1): pp. 23–28.

9. These programs were described as a radiophonic opera, *La coquille à planètes*.

10. For a fuller perspective on Schaeffer's pioneering development of *musique concrète,* see Karine Le Bail and Martin Kaltenecker, eds. 2012. *Pierre Schaeffer: Les constructions impatientes* (Paris: CNRS Editions).

11. For a comprehensive introduction to the four key phases in the development of GRM, see Daniel Teruggi. 2007. "Technology and *musique concrète*: The Technical Developments of the Groupe de Recherches Musicales and Their Implication in Musical Composition," *Organised Sound*, 12(3): pp. 213–231.

12. The RTF had started to acquire tape recorders in 1949 and the studio was able to gain limited access to a single machine in 1950. The reliability of the early recorders, however, left much to be desired, and even in 1951, following the wholesale replacement of the disk-cutting lathes with more recent models, there were still some residual concerns.

13. For further information on the Morphophone and the Phonogènes, including photographs, see Peter Manning, "La Musique Concrète et ses Appareils," in Le Bail and Kaltenecker, *Pierre Schaeffer: Les constructions impatientes*, 140–151.

14. Pierre Schaeffer. 1952. *À la recherche d'une musique concrète* (Paris: Éditions du Seuil): pp. 114–116.

15. For a full critique on his adoption of the descriptor "acousmatic" and the issues arising, see Marc Battier. 2007. "What the GRM Brought to Music: From *musique concrète* to Acousmatic Music," *Organised Sound*, 12(3): pp. 189–202.

16. As a further illustration of the challenges faced over the years with terminology, whereas as already noted, the origins of the term "electroacoustic music" can similarly be traced to the French-based listening tradition associated with GRM, it has long since taken on generic proportions for many commentators that potentially at least embrace all electronic works that are auditioned via a loudspeaker and/or headphones.

17. For a more detailed explanation of this technique, see Manning, *Electronic and Computer Music*, pp. 71–72.

18. The studio was designed by Henri (Enrico) Chiarucci, who also during the 1960s developed some additional electronic processing devices to supplement the resources of the synthesizers.

19. Peter Zinovieff was subsequently to use a pin matrix system for his EMS range of commercial synthesizers, starting with the VCS3, launched in 1969.

20. Although interest was subsequently to decline in the face of increasing attractive digital alternatives, the Coupigny synthesizer remained in use until the early 1990s.

21. It should also be noted that Xenakis left GRM in 1963 to pursue his ideas elsewhere in Paris, establishing his own rival research and development center, EMAMu, in 1966, renamed CEMAMu (Centre d'Études de Mathématique et Automatique Musicales) in 1972.

22. Daniel Teruggi. 1998. "Le système SYTER: Son histoire, ses développements, sa production musicale, ses implications dans le language électroacoustique d'aujourd'hui" (PhD diss., Université Paris 8): p. 108.

23. For a discussion of the most significant hybrid systems developed during the late 1960s and early 1970s, see Manning, *Electronic and Computer Music*, pp. 207–216.

24. Progress, however, was far from straightforward. A subsequent move to the music department at the Centre Universitaire de Marseille-Luminy in 1972 terminated the necessary access to a suitable computer and it was not until 1974 that he was able once again to install Music V on a slow but serviceable Telemecanique T1600 computer.

25. Teruggi, "Le système SYTER," pp. 117–118.

26. Ibid., pp. 125–133.

27. See Chapter 3.

28. These microprocessors were also used in the design of the DMX-1000. See Chapter 2.

29. See Jean-François Allouis. 1978. "Use of High Speed Microprocessors for Digital Synthesis," *Proceedings of the 1978 International Computer Music Conference—Northwestern University, Illinois* (San Francisco: International Computer Music Association): pp. 26–28. Also published in (1979) *Computer Music Journal* 3(1): pp. 14–16.

30. See the respective discussions in Chapters 2 and 3.

31. Jean-François Allouis and Jean-Yves Bernier. 1982. "The SYTER Project Sound Processor Design and Software Overview," *Proceedings of the 1982 International Computer Music Conference—Venice* (San Francisco: International Computer Music Association): pp. 232–240.

32. Ibid.

33. The PDP-11/60 was equipped with a vector graphic GT40 display screen and light pen, but these resources were considered too rudimentary at the time for SYTER.

34. Essentially the same model of computer used by Barry Truax to develop his GSX and GSAMX programs for the DMX-1000 at Simon Fraser University in Canada.

35. The commercial versions used a clone of the 11/73, known as Bull SMS90.

36. See Teruggi, "Le système SYTER," pp. 240–278.

37. Ibid., p. 252.

38. For a complete list, see Teruggi, "Technology and *musique concrete*," p. 226.

39. This version was the result of a collaboration between Vinet and Yann Geslin, by this stage managing a SYTER system located in the Paris Conservatoire.

40. Teruggi, "Le système SYTER," pp. 302–303.

41. The top of the range Macintosh FX with a 68030 processor running at 40 MHz being a possible exception.

42. Hugues Vinet and Daniel Teruggi. 1991. "GRM Report," *Proceedings of the 1991 International Computer Music Conference—Montreal* (San Francisco: International Computer Music Association): pp. 82–85.

43. Apple Computer, Installation Manual for GRM Tools Version 1.5 (1994).

371

44. For confirmation of this mode of composing, see: Mountain and Dhomont, "From Wire to Computer."

45. Évelyne Gayou. 2007. *GRM: Le groupe de recherches musicales: Cinquante ans d'histoire* (Paris: Librairie Arthème Fayard): p. 215.

46. For a detailed analysis of *Points de fuite*, see: Stéphane Roy. 1996. "Form and Referential Citation in a Work by Francis Dhomont," *Organised Sound*, 1(1): pp. 29–41.

47. There are some interesting connections here with the techniques of soundscape composition discussed by Barry Truax in Chapter 4.

48. Liner notes of Francis Dhomont. 2001. *Cycle du son*, CD, empreintes DIGITALes, IMED 0158. Marc Battier highlights the importance of the upheaval, both in terms of sound research and instrumental absence: "With his *Étude aux chemins de fer*, realized with recordings made at the Batignolles station . . . Pierre Schaeffer composed the first of his five *Études de bruits*. The era that started then, from 1948, with *musique concrète*, is characterized with a paradox: music, from now on, exists without any instrument. Withdrawing the instrument is the corollary to research on new sound sources." Translated from Marc Battier. 1995. "Une nouvelle géométrie du son: Le paradoxe de la lutherie électronique," *Les cahiers de l'Ircam. Recherche et musique*, no. 7, *Instruments*: pp. 50–51.

49. *AvatArsSon* is dedicated to "the inventors of the treasure": Dhomont mentions in the liner notes of *Cycle du son* the names of François Bayle, Luciano Berio, Michel Chion, Denis Dufour, Luc Ferrari, Pierre Henry, Ivo Malec, Bernard Parmegiani, Guy Reibel, Jean-Claude Risset, Pierre Schaeffer, Karlheinz Stockhausen, Daniel Teruggi, Edgard Varèse, Iannis Xenakis, Christian Zanési, and evokes "others too numerous to name."

50. Translation by the authors from video of Presentation 5 of the accompanying software, "*Phonurgie* within the *Cycle du Son*," from 0′14″ to 0′58″.

51. For a detailed analysis of *Novars*, see Andrew Lewis. 1998. "Francis Dhomont's *Novars*," *Journal of New Music Research*, 27(1–2): pp. 67–83.

52. Gayou, *GRM*, p. 219.

53. Lewis, "Francis Dhomont's *Novars*."

54. Liner notes of Francis Dhomont, *Cycle du son*, CD.

55. Regarding the variety of transformation means of these sources, *Phonurgie* can be linked to Manoury's *Pluton* and the number of digital processes applied in real time to the piano; however, all of these processes were implemented by Manoury and his collaborators in one unique environment, Max and the 4X, while Dhomont typically explores a wider range of available technologies. Besides, his explorations are not limited by any real-time constraints, as his work is for fixed media.

56. Translated by the authors from video of Presentation 18 of the accompanying software, "Creative approaches to technology," from 0′29″ to 1′55″.

57. According to Dhomont, these transformations were obtained by playing Schaeffer's objects through the reverberation and the phasing of two Lexicon units, the PCM 60 and PCM 70 digital reverb processors (private conversation, December 2015).

58. Annette Vande Gorne mentions that "[before using] the Pro Tools software . . . [the mixing process] started on an eight-track analog recorder." Translated by the authors from Annette Vande Gorne. 2006. "Catalogue commenté des œuvres de Francis Dhomont," in Gayou, Évelyne, ed., *Francis Dhomont. Portraits polychromes* (Paris, Ina-GRM): p. 114.

59. These categories and descriptions are directly translated after a document provided by Francis Dhomont. The category names all appear as such in his Pro Tools session.

60. See, for instance, the TARTYP (Tableau Récapitulatif de la Typologie) in Schaeffer, *Traité des objets musicaux*, p. 459.

61. See also Arturo Parra. 2002. *Parr(A)cousmatique*, CD, empreintes DIGITALes, IMED 0264.

62. At the Festival International de Musique Actuelle de Victoriaville (Quebec), on May 15, 1998.

63. Video of Presentation 8 of the accompanying software, "Field recordings," from 0′51″ to 1′40″.

64. Due to incomplete documentation of the creative process of *Phonurgie*, it is not possible to track back all the environments and specific transformations used by the composer for this or other works. The information delivered here was established by interrogating several types of information, such as the composer's personal documentation and his own archive.

65. Apart from the simple transformations mentioned earlier, there are two notable exceptions to this general difficulty of recognizing a particular source. The recording of pigeon wings is clearly recognizable as such; for the informed listener, the direct quotation of Pierre Schaeffer's third object from the *Étude aux objets* can also be detected easily. It is also worth mentioning that a listeners who know *Novars* would certainly recognize the Machaut-based texture present in *Phonurgie*; however, they could not guess that this texture is derived from the *Messe* without having read this extra-musical information published by Dhomont, for instance on concert program notes.

66. A form of granulation, the word "brassage" is frequently encountered in the terminology of computer music. See Chapter 6 for a further discussion of this technique, as used by Trevor Wishart.

67. In a session with SYTER dated 1997, as documented in the composer's notes.

68. Private conversation, December 2014.

69. The intermediary sound file, after coloration, can be listened to against its source in Presentation 9 of the accompanying software, "Successive sound transformations." This harmony can also be heard, with several transposition processes, in the first minute of "À l'orée du conte" and of "La muraille d'épines," respectively the second and seventh movements of *Forêt profonde*.

70. Dhomont's documentation mentions, for this "T1" material, the use of SYTER's ETIR4 jointly with speed variation. It is therefore possible that both the transposition and the time-stretching were done in one go, as ETIR4 includes FOUR transpositions for the stretched result.

71. As mentioned in note 70.

72. As written in the SYTER instrument reference, ACCHAR "can be used as a bank of harmonizers, echo room, arpeggio generator, and more generally to generate complex masses from simple elements." Translated from Teruggi, "Le système SYTER," p. 391.

73. Translated by the authors from Denis Dufour and Thomas Brando, "Quelques définitions," online glossary for the website of AECME (Association des Enseignants de Composition en Musique Électroacoustique), http://www.aecme.org/definitions, accessed April 3, 2020.

74. Video of Presentation 13 of the accompanying software, "Studio 123 and SYTER," from 0′23″ to 1′38″.

75. Archive of Francis Dhomont documenting the use of SYTER for *séquences-jeu* recorded from Pierre Schaeffer's *Étude aux objets* in 1988. This figure is reproduced with kind permission of the composer.

76. Video of Presentation 15 of the accompanying software, "Working in the studio and at GRM," from 5′30″ to 7′13″.

77. Private conversation, December 2014.

78. Sliders are named "*réglettes*" in the French terminology of SYTER.

79. In SYTER, these parameters are labeled as follows: NIVEAU/ENTRÉE, REINJ, DIR/HAR, DELAIS, RATIO1, RATIO2, RATIO3, RATIO4, DELAI1, DELAI2, DELAI3, DELAI4.

80. Two–dimensional sliders are named "*sticks.*"

81. The user can exclude any of the parameters from the interpolation process; these parameter values then remain constant during the interpolation.

82. The International Computer Music Conference was held in Paris that year.

83. Translated by the authors from Teruggi, "Le système SYTER," pp. 268–270.

84. Ibid., p. 394.

85. Private conversation, December 2014.

86. "Varvit" is the contraction of "*Variation de vitesse*" (speed variation).

87. The input screen is named "Lecture" in the terminology of SYTER.

88. Translated by the authors from Teruggi, "Le système SYTER," p. 386.

89. Sections 1 and 2, and sections 3 and 4, overlap. The headers labeled "1/2" and "3/4" represent these transitions: they start at, respectively, the beginning of sections 2 and 4, and finish at, respectively, the end of sections 1 and 3.

90. Transcribed from Francis Dhomont's personal analytical notes on *Phonurgie*.

91. Ibid.

92. Ibid.

93. Ibid.

94. Ibid.

95. This is visible in the "Chronological" category ordering in Presentation 16. By order of appearance, the categories of the first section are "Sch1," "Boul2," "Cloch," "Boul1," "Turbo," "Punch," "Porte," "AKS iter," "Elem. LdS," "Sch0," and "Porte SY."

96. Although Dhomont grouped punctuating objects and excerpts of this *séquence-jeu* as one single category ("Sch1"), the paradigmatic chart in Presentation 16 of the accompanying software makes the distinction between "Sch1" and "Sch1."

97. Cf. the text to footnote 54: "the allusions to the origins melt away before the original propositions; filiation is not renounced, but here the child, finally grown, reveals its identity."

98. Indeed, in terms of comparing studio technologies and their resultant influence on creativity, one might include a third studio based in Paris at the time of the composition of these two works, established by Xenakis, first as Centre d'Études de Mathématique et Automatique Musicales (CEMAMu), subsequently as Les Ateliers UPIC, and finally renamed Centre for the Composition of Music Iannis Xenakis (CCMIX). See Chapter 2.

Chapter 6

1. Martin Atkins, Andrew Bentley, Tom Endrich, Rajmil Fischman, David Malham, Richard Orton, and Trevor Wishart, "The Composers Desktop Project," *Proceedings of the 1987 International Computer Music Conference—Champaign/Urbana, Illinois* (San Francisco: International Computer Music Association, 1987): pp. 146–150.

2. See Chapter 1.

3. Early PCs and the original Apple Macintosh were limited to a maximum of just 128 kilobytes of programmable memory. The Atari 1040 ST released in 1986 offered 1,024 kilobytes and quickly became the preferred machine for the CDP. Later versions such as the TT030, Mega ST, and Falcon, released respectively in 1990, 1991, and 1992, offered up to 4 megabytes of memory, expandable in the case of the Falcon to a maximum capacity of 14 megabytes.

4. The Sony PCM system consisted of two components, the PCM decoder and interface and an associated Betamax video tape recorder. Unfortunately, this format soon became obsolete in the face of competition from the alternative VHS format, which gave inferior results in this context.

5. Ironically, as noted in Chapter 3, IRCAM was subsequently to withdraw its existing mainframe computer, a PDP-10, and with it Music V. This was to have material implications for Trevor Wishart's initial engagement with the facilities at the institution.

6. A version was also produced in due course for the high-end Silicon Graphics (SGI) Workstation, allowing institutional CDP users to use the software in a much faster processing environment.

7. There are also a number of associated articles and interviews, including Internet-based materials, that add useful further information, and this commentary draws upon these also where relevant.

8. Trevor Wishart. 1985. *On Sonic Art*, (York, England: Imagineering Press).

9. Trevor Wishart, ed. Simon Emmerson. 1996. *On Sonic Art* (Amsterdam: Harewood).

10. Trevor Wishart. 1994. *Audible Design: A Plain and Easy Introduction to Practical Sound Composition* (York, England: Orpheus the Pantomime): pp. 100–112.

11. The descriptions of his software in *Audible Design* are usefully augmented by an unpublished article that appeared shortly before he started work on *Imago*: Trevor Wishart. 2000. "Computer Sound Transformation: A Personal Perspective from the U.K.", subsequently made available on his personal website, http://www.trevorwishart.co.uk/transformation.html, accessed April 3, 2020.

12. Trevor Wishart. 2012. *Sound Composition*, (York, England: Orpheus the Pantomime).

13. Nicolas Marty. 2011. "'Creavolution' with Trevor Wishart," interview by Nicolas Marty, *JMM: The Journal of Music and Meaning* 10: pp. 81–107.

14. Wishart, *Sound Composition*, pp. 43–44.

15. James Moorer. 1978. "The Use of the Phase Vocoder in Computer Music Applications," *Journal of the Audio Engineering Society* 26(1–2): pp. 42–45.

16. Ironically, IRCAM was subsequently to embrace such techniques of analysis and resynthesis on a grand scale with the development of its now widely used program AudioSculpt.

17. Mark Dolson. 1986. "The Phase Vocoder: A Tutorial," *Computer Music Journal* 10(4): pp. 14–27.

18. His work at IRCAM composing this work is described in Trevor Wishart. 1988. "The Composition of *Vox-5*," *Computer Music Journal*, 12(4): pp. 21–27.

19. http://www.composersdesktop.com/, accessed April 3, 2020.

20. In the interview with Matteo Milani referenced below, Wishart observed that "[t]he original ports onto the Atari ran very slowly: e.g. doing a spectral transformation of a 4 second stereo sound might take 4 minutes at IRCAM, but took 2 days on the Atari. However, on your own system at home, you could afford to wait."

21. Wishart, *Audible Design*, pp. 8–9.

22. Matteo Milani. 2009. "Chemistry of Sound," (Interview with Trevor Wishart), *Digimag Magazine*, 41, http://www.digicult.it/digimag/issue–041/trevor-wishart-chemistry-of-sound/, accessed April 3, 2020.

23. *Globalalia*, premiered in 2004, is an interesting companion to *Imago* in terms of the choice of source sound material. Instead of a single sound source, it uses an extensive repertory of 134 speaking voice samples in twenty-six different languages, recorded from television stations available on the Internet. See Wishart, *Sound Composition*, pp. 114–129.

24. Yiorgos Vassilandonakis. 2009. "An Interview with Trevor Wishart," *Computer Music Journal*, 33(2): pp. 8–23.

25. Readers are also directed to Wishart's own account of this work in Wishart, *Sound Composition*, pp. 100–113.

26. Richard Dobson's contributions to the CDP have included Soundshaper, an alternative graphic user interface to that used for Sound Loom.

27. Wishart, *Audible Design*, p. 96.

28. For example, the EMS 3000 Vocoder, or the Moog 16 Channel Vocoder.

29. Wishart, "The Composition of *Vox-5*."

30. Wishart, "Computer Sound Transformation."

31. These processing techniques are considered further in Chapter 5 in the context of Francis Dhomont's work at GRM, leading to the composition of *Phonurgie*.

32. Wishart, "Computer Sound Transformation."

33. Ibid.

34. Ibid.

35. Ibid.

36. Ibid.

37. The contributions of Miller Puckette to the development of computer music are in many respects without parallel, certainly in a technical context, and these are considered further in other chapters.

38. Wishart, "Computer Sound Transformation."

39. Ibid.

40. Ibid.

41. Ibid.

42. Ibid.

43. Three sound files in the archive are in fact dated from 2003; having been generated much after the creation of *Imago*, they are being ignored in this study.

44. In particular, text files document most of the mixes made by the composer, and can inform on the individual sound components merged to a larger-scale sound file.

45. Although a stereo to mono conversion can seem anecdotal from a musical point of view, it is important to consider in tracking a creative process based on Sound Loom, as some of the processes involved can only be operated on mono files, such as all the phase vocoder based transformations, as well as the waveset distortions.

46. The dates on which no file has been generated are here ignored for simplicity.

47. In the terminology of Sound Loom, "recycling" consists into taking a processed sound file as the basis for the next step of transformation.

48. The transposition ratios for the nineteen chords can be found in text files of the archive, named "chord0.txt" to "chord18.txt": (0) 0, −9, −16; (1) 0, −8, −15; (2) 0, −6, −15; (3) 0, −5, −15; (4) 0, −9, −15; (5) 0, −8, −14; (6) 0, −6, −14; (7) 0, −5, −14; (8) 0, −7, −14; (9) 0, −5,

−11; (10) 0, −6, −16; (11) 0, −8, −17; (12) 0, −5, −13, −23; (13) 0, −8, −18; (14) 0, −9, −19; (15) 0, −11, −17; (16) 0, −6, −20; (17) 0, −11, −21; (18) 0, −7, −23.

49. As documented in the "stack.txt" text file generated on April 23: the transpositions in semitones are 5, 0, -7, and -12.

50. In the terminology of Sound Loom, a mix file is a text file describing how the source sounds are used to make the resulting mix.

51. In order of appearance in the work: "opening.wav" (September 8), "uber_dddd_eeee. wav" (August 25), "ub_ed_transit_ub_sea.wav" (September 2), "ubermix_clink3xx_to_ sea.wav" (25 August), "post_uber_sea_a.wav" (September 10), "ffgggg.wav" (August 21), "gamelphrase_edited" (September 10), and "imago_end" (September 13).

52. Wishart, *Sound Composition*, pp. 100–112.

53. Video of Presentation 2 of the accompanying software, 2′29″ to 3′05″.

54. Transcribed from Trevor Wishart's archives, with kind permission from the composer.

55. The quoted sound categories appearing in the rest of this analysis are the composer's terminology, as found in the diffusion score for *Imago*, reproduced as an appendix to Wishart, *Sonic Composition*.

56. Authors' analysis.

57. Figure 6.3 displays abbreviated versions of the sound file names, with paths and extensions removed. Where file names have a "_cop" suffix, they are in fact exact copies of the original. Transcribed from Trevor Wishart's archives, with kind permission from the composer.

58. Transcribed from Trevor Wishart's archives, with kind permission from the composer.

59. The ordering in the mix file may indicate the order in which the composer decided to add the sound files to the resulting mix.

60. The timings given in these texts are those corresponding to the published recording of *Imago*. The timings given in the composer's diffusion score as found in Wishart, *Sound Composition* do not entirely correspond to those of the published recording.

61. Wishart, *Sound Composition*, p. 111.

62. Wishart, diffusion score of *Imago*: pp. 4–5.

Chapter 7

1. Harvey's list of works completed at IRCAM include the following commissions: *Mortuos Plango, Vivos Voco* (1980); *Bhakti* (1982); *Ritual Melodies* (co-commission with South East Arts, UK, 1989–1990); *Advaya* (1994); *Fourth String Quartet* (co-commission with Ars Musica and the Ultima Festival, 2003); *Two Interludes and a Scene for an Opera* (2003); *Wagner Dream* (co-commission with De Nederlandse Opera, the Holland Festival, and Grand Théâtre de Luxembourg, 2003–2007); *Speakings* (co-commission with BBC Scottish Symphony Orchestra and Radio France, 2008).

2. In the UK, study for a PhD in composition was unknown at this time. This threshold was crossed in the late 1960s by the University of York, soon to be followed by the University of Durham, signaling a major change in the status of composition as an area for advanced academic research. For Harvey's thesis, see Jonathan Harvey. 1965. "The Composer's Idea of his Inspiration," E-thesis, University of Glasgow, UK. Also see Michael Downes, ed. 2000. *Jonathan Harvey, Music and Inspiration* (London and New York: Faber and Faber).

3. For a detailed commentary on Stockhausen and the early development of *Elektronische Music* at Westdeutscher Rundfunk, Cologne, see Peter Manning. 2013. *Electronic and Computer Music*, 4th ed. (New York: Oxford University Press: pp. 39–67.

4. Harvey indeed was subsequently to write a book on Stockhausen's works. See Jonathan Harvey. 1976. *The Music of Stockhausen* (London and New York: Faber and Faber).

5. Arnold Whittall. 1999. *Jonathan Harvey* (London: Faber and Faber): p. 10.

6. Notes from discussions between the composer and Peter Manning at the 1972 EMS workshop, Stockholm. These notes also provide important clues as to why his earlier encounter with Zinovieff's MUSYS system, discussed below, proved less than fruitful, since a primary attraction of the EMS-1 system was its ability to process composing algorithms in addition to time-sequenced synthesis instructions.

7. Truax also attended the EMS workshop, but for good reason the career paths of the two composers, in particular the choice of Truax to develop his own facilities at Simon Fraser University, Vancouver, rather than work at large institutions such as IRCAM or Stanford (CCRMA), were to remain essential independent. Peter Manning also attended this workshop, and was thus able to become acquainted at first hand with the formative ideas of both composers in terms of electronic and computer music.

8. It is interesting to note in this context that in his putative study *Time Points*, the one parameter he did not subject to serial procedures was that of timbre.

9. Two other hybrid systems from the same period allowed means of such a direct interaction, the first, known as GROOVE (Generated Real-time Output Operations on Voltage-controlled Equipment), developed by Max Mathews at Bell Labs in 1970, and MUSYS III, developed by Peter Zinovieff and his associates at his private London studio in 1969. For further information on all three systems, see Manning, *Electronic and Computer Music*, pp. 207–215.

10. In 1963 Hugh Davies, later to direct the studio at Goldsmiths College, established a temporary studio in the Department of Physics, University of Oxford, mainly used to prepare sound effects for plays. A further studio based on a Moog synthesizer was established in the late 1960s at the University of Manchester, but the venture was not sustained at this time.

11. Winter investigated the possibility of installing Music V on the Cardiff University mainframe computer in the early 1970s, but he abandoned the idea because of the practical difficulties encountered in negotiating suitable access. The initiative in this context then passed to the Music Department at the University of Durham, where Peter Manning, with assistance from Barry Vercoe, installed Music 360 in 1974 on the IBM 360 mainframe computer shared by the Universities of Durham and Newcastle. Discussions were held with Harvey in 1975 with a view to his possible use of this resource, but similar operational difficulties made such an arrangement impractical and the project was soon abandoned.

12. The prototype research for the Synthi 100 control computer was carried out by Peter Eastty, an engineering graduate from the University of Durham who made important contributions in terms of developing prototype hardware for the Durham studio before moving to work for Peter Zinovieff. His subsequent move to IRCAM to work with Giuseppe di Giugno on the design of the 4CED system terminated further work on the Synthi project. See also Chapter 3 (Manoury).

13. Mike Greenhough, Ian Bowler, and Stephen Morris. 1985. "The Electronic Music Studio at University College Cardiff," *Proceedings of the 1985 International Computer*

Music Conference—Simon Fraser University, Vancouver (San Francisco: International Computer Music Association): pp. 415–418.

14. Marcus West. 1982. "'Sequemuse'—A Hybrid Computer-Music System," *Interface*, 11: pp. 47–60.

15. See Chapter 2.

16. Although the materials produced at EMS were entirely synthetic, and a VCS 3 synthesizer is used as a live performance component in *Inner Light 3*, Harvey became particularly interested in the possibilities of processing acoustic materials, and it is in this context that his long association with IRCAM was to produce rich dividends in the digital realm.

17. Pamela Alcorn. 1992. "Perspectives of Electroacoustic Music: A Critical Study of the Electroacoustic Music of Jonathan Harvey, Denis Smalley and Trevor Wishart" (Durham theses, Durham University, UK): pp. 151–154. Available at Durham E-Theses Online: http://etheses.dur.ac.uk/1201/, accessed April 3, 2020.

18. Jonathan Harvey, program note for *Inner Light 3* (IRCAM repository), http://brahms. ircam.fr/works/work/9027/, accessed April 3, 2020.

19. Jonathan Harvey. 1981. "*Mortuos Plango Vivos Voco*: A Realisation at IRCAM," *Computer Music Journal*, 5(4): pp. 22–24.

20. Ibid. p. 23.

21. See Xavier Rodet and Gerald Bennett. 1980. "Synthèse de la voix chantée par ordinateur," in *Conférences des Journées d'études* (Paris: Festival International du Son, 1980): pp. 73–91; and Xavier Rodet, Yves Potard, and Jean-Baptiste Barrière. 1984. "The CHANT Project: From the Synthesis of the Singing Voice to Synthesis in General," *Computer Music Journal*, 8(3): pp. 15–31.

22. Harvey, "*Mortuos Plango Vivos Voco*: A Realisation at IRCAM."

23. Jonathan Harvey. 1986. "The Mirror of Ambiguity," in Simon Emmerson, ed., *The Language of Electroacoustic Music* (London: Macmillan): p. 177.

24. A detailed analysis of this work carried out by Michael Clarke was a major stimulus for the project that has underpinned this book, and readers interested in studying the evolution of the novel techniques that have been explored in this context are directed to this earlier publication and its accompanying software. See Michael Clarke. 2006. "Jonathan Harvey's *Mortuos Plango, Vivos Voco*," in Mary Simoni, ed., *Analytical Methods of Electroacoustic Music* (New York: Routledge): pp. 111–143.

25. Jonathan Harvey, Denis Lorrain, Jean-Baptiste Barrière, and Stanley Haynes. 1984. "Notes on the realization of *Bhakti*," *Contemporary Music Review*, 1(1): pp. 111–129.

26. Ibid., p. 113.

27. For an extensive analysis and critical commentary on *Bhakti*, see John Palmer. 2001. Bhakti *for Chamber Ensemble and Electronics: Serialism, Electronics and Spirituality* (Lewiston, NY: Edwin Mellen Press, 2001).

28. Alcorn, *Perspectives of Electroacoustic Music*, p. 164.

29. For a comprehensive account of the evolution of both synthesizers, see Manning, *Electronic and Computer Music*, pp. 223–227.

30. The original Fairlight I used monophonic eight-bit samples at a sampling rate of 16 kHz, associated with just 16 Kbytes of memory per voice.

31. Jonathan Harvey. 1986. "*Madonna of Winter and Spring*," *Musical Times*, 127(1720): pp. 431–433. There are some interesting comparisons to be made between the techniques employed in the composition of the electronic components of *Madonna of Winter and Spring* and those adopted by Philippe Manoury for *Pluton*. See Chapter 3.

379

32. Jonathan Harvey. 1999. "The Metaphysics of Live Electronics," *Contemporary Music Review*, 18(3): pp. 79–82.

33. Ibid.

34. See Xavier Rodet and Pierre Cointe. 1984. "FORMES: Composition and Scheduling of Processes," *Computer Music Journal*, 8(3): pp. 32–50.

35. See Xavier Rodet, Yves Potard, and Jean-Baptiste Barrière. 1984. "The CHANT Project: From the Synthesis of the Singing Voice to Synthesis in General, *Computer Music Journal*, 8(3): pp. 15–31.

36. Jan Vandenheede and Jonathan Harvey. 1985. "Identity and Ambiguity: The Construction and Use of Timbral Transitions and Hybrids," *Proceedings of the 1985 International Computer Music Conference—Simon Fraser University, Vancouver* (San Francisco: International Computer Music Association): pp. 97–102.

37. Jan Vandenheede. 1992. "Jonathan Harvey's *Ritual Melodies*," *Interface*, 21(2): pp. 149–183.

38. Harvey, "The Mirror of Ambiguity," pp. 185–186.

39. Vandenheede, "Jonathan Harvey's *Ritual Melodies*, p. 163.

40. For a detailed account of the evolution of these programs, see Manning, *Electronic and Computer Music*, pp. 395–416.

41. For an account of an early initiative in this context, see Jamie Bullock and Lamberto Coccioli. 2005. "Modernising Live Electronics Technology in the Works of Jonathan Harvey," *Proceedings of the 2005 International Computer Music Conference—Barcelona* (San Francisco: International Computer Music Association); and Jamie Bullock and Lamberto Coccioli. 2006. "Modernising Musical Works Involving Yamaha DX-based Synthesis: A Case Study," *Organised Sound*, 11(3): pp. 221–227.

42. It is interesting to note that once again Harvey did not explore the resources of the 4X, presumably on the grounds that the difficulties to be faced in using this unique facility for works involving live electronics in venues other than IRCAM far outweighed the potential benefits. Ironically the very developments that were to produce the tools he required, notably Max/MSP, were well underway at IRCAM by the time he had completed *Ritual Melodies*. See Chapter 3.

43. See Chapter 9.

44. An earlier version of this analysis was presented in a lecture-recital given by Michael Clarke together with the Arditti Quartet and Gilbert Nouno, organized by the Institute of Musical Research in London in January 2012, a video of which can be accessed online via the companion website for this book.

45. Ibid.

46. Ibid.

47. See, for instance, Thibaut Carpentier, Markus Noisternig, and Olivier Warusfel. 2015. "Twenty Years of IRCAM Spat: Looking Back, Looking Forward," *Proceedings of the 2015 International Computer Music Conference—Denton, Texas* (San Francisco: International Computer Music Association): pp. 270–277; and Chapter 9.

48. Gaston Bachelard. 1943. *L'air et les songes: Essai sur l'imagination du movement* (Paris: Librairie José Corti). English translation quoted by Harvey. 1988. Gaston Bachelard, *Air and Dreams: An Essay on the Imagination of Movement*, translated from the French by Edith Farrell and Frederick Farrell (Dallas: Dallas Institute Publications).

49. Jonathan Harvey. 2004. "The Genesis of Quartet no. 4," in Jonathan Cross, ed., *Identity and Difference: Essays on Music, Language and Time* (Leuven: Leuven University Press): pp. 43–53.

50. Bachelard, *L'air et les songes*, quoted by Harvey in "The Genesis of Quartet no. 4," p. 48.

51. Ibid., p. 52.
52. Ibid., p. 52.
53. Ibid., p. 48.
54. The bardo passages are not marked as such in the score.
55. See Suzanne Jozek. 2016. *Jonathan Harvey: ". . . towards a Pure Land": Stationen einer kompositorischen Reise* (Mainz, Germany: Schott) for more extensive discussion of the influence of Buddhism on Harvey's work, including the *Fourth Quartet*.
56. Two Spat units are used in the work.
57. In some rare occurrences, the playback of prerecorded sound files is involved.
58. At the very end of the piece, one of the granulators also sends its signals directly to the six loudspeakers, with no processing by the Spat modules.
59. Harvey, "The Genesis of Quartet no. 4," p. 44.
60. The loop buffers, the phase vocoders, the Brownian granulators. The reverberation and harmonizers rely on shorter-term memories.
61. Harvey, "The Genesis of Quartet no. 4," p. 47.
62. Ibid., p. 51.
63. Ibid., p. 48.
64. Or a keystroke from the computer.
65. Terminology by the authors.
66. Granulation has featured prominently in other work studied in this book. Barry Truax's *Riverrun*, for example, used synthesized grains exclusively to produce the sonorities for the work. In later works, Truax has used granulation of prerecorded sounds. Likewise, granulation was one of the techniques used by Trevor Wishart to transform the single prerecorded source sound used in *Imago*. Here, Jonathan Harvey uses granulation techniques in the context of live performance to transform sounds stored in a buffer in real time during the concert.
67. Harvey, "The Genesis of Quartet no. 4," p. 46–47.
68. See Nathan Wolek. 2002. "Granular Toolkit v1.0 for Cycling74's Max/MSP," *Journal SEAMUS*, 16(2): pp. 34–46.
69. From event 7.
70. Harvey, "The Genesis of Quartet no. 4," p. 46.
71. With the only exception of the grains from the multichannel granulator used at the very end of cycle 5, which distributes the grains directly to the loudspeakers, without going through the Spatializer units.
72. Nicolas Donin. 2006. "Spatialization as a Compositional Tool and Individual Access to Music in the Future: Jonathan Harvey in Conversation with Nicolas Donin," *Circuit*, 16(3): pp. 75–82.
73. Ibid., p. 77. Emphases are from the quoted text.
74. The *Fourth String Quartet* can be played with both loudspeaker configurations. As noted by the composer while discussing spatialization using IRCAM's Spat, "the independence of the speakers is very important. The fact that you can have 4, 6, 8 or 20 speakers, or any number you like: the sound is *between* the speakers. It doesn't come from *this* speaker or *that* speaker. It is always calculated to use the speakers to locate itself. You're never conscious in my experience of any one particular speaker. You're always conscious of sound being somewhere around you . . ." (Donin, "Spatialization as a Compositional Tool," pp. 76–77. Emphases are from the quoted text).
75. Harvey experimented with a number of different interfaces for such control in different works; since 2003, the *Quartet* has been played using Wacom and Lemur tablets; the

381

most recently used device is the iPad, as demonstrated by Gilbert Nouno and Arshia Cont in the videos of the accompanying software.

76. Harvey, "The Genesis of Quartet no. 4," pp. 45–46.

77. Transcription from Jonathan Harvey's sketch in Figure 7.3.

78. Harvey, "The Genesis of Quartet no. 4," p. 52.

79. See also the discussion in Chapter 3 on Philippe Manoury's *Pluton* and Chapter 8 on Cort Lippe's *Music for Tuba and Computer.*

80. Transcription from video of Presentation 16 of the accompanying software, "Demonstration of the performer's interface," from 10′13 ″ to 11′24″.

81. Transcription from video of Presentation 11 of the accompanying software, "The use of techniques through the *Quartet* cycles," from 32′17″ to 33′06″.

82. Transcription from video of Presentation 11 of the accompanying software, from 30′15″ to 31′21″.

Chapter 8

1. Cort Lippe. 1996. "Real-Time Interactive Digital Signal Processing: A View of Computer Music," *Computer Music Journal*, 20(4): pp. 21–24.

2. Essentially the same version of the program subsequently to be installed at IRCAM.

3. See Chapter 2 for further information on developments at the Institute of Sonology during the early 1970s.

4. Paul Berg. 1979. "PILE: A Language for Sound Synthesis," *Computer Music Journal*, 3(1): pp. 30–41.

5. The Institute of Sonology acquired a DMX-1000 front-end processor for the PDP-15 in 1984, and this transformed the working environment for real-time synthesis applications, leading, for example, to a new real-time version of PILE, known as Pile4.

6. Cort Lippe. 1982. *8110 K: A Composition Report* (Utrecht: Institute of Sonology).

7. A significant influence on Lippe was Denis Lorrain's detailed critique on the stochastic techniques of Xenakis published in 1980. See Denis Lorrain. 1980. "A Panoply of Stochastic 'Cannons,'" *Computer Music* Journal, 4(1): pp. 53–81.

8. Lippe, *8110 K: A Composition Report.*

9. It was some years before a solution was found to these problems, using a specially designed sixty-four-voice hardware synthesizer as a front-end processor for version C of UPIC. A more significance advance in this context, however, was the introduction of a PC-based version of the system in 1991. See (1) Jean-Michel Raczinski and Gérard Marino. 1988. "A Real Time Synthesis Unit," *Proceedings of the 1988 International Computer Music Conference—Cologne* (San Francisco: International Computer Music Association): pp. 90–100; and (2) Gérard Marino, Jean-Michel Raczinski, and Marie-Hélène Serra. 1990. "The New UPIC System," *Proceedings of the 1990 International Computer Music Conference—Glasgow, UK* (San Francisco: International Computer Music Association): pp. 249–252.

10. Cort Lippe. 1986. *Music for Bass Clarinet and Tape* program note.

11. Cort Lippe and Miller Puckette. 1991. "Music Performance Using the IRCAM Workstation," *Proceedings of the 1991 International Computer Music Conference—Montreal* (San Francisco: International Computer Music Association): pp. 533–536.

12. Cort Lippe. 1988. "A Technical Description of *Pluton* by Philippe Manoury," *IRCAM Annual Report* (Paris: IRCAM). Lippe had also contributed to the technical production of Manoury's first 4X piece, *Jupiter*, completed in 1987.

13. Lippe also provided significant technical support for other 4X-based works realized and performed during the later 1980s, including the opera *Valis* by Tod Machover (1987), *Antara* by George Benjamin (1987), and a reworking of *Répons* by Boulez for a performance in the Festival of Avignon (1988).

14. Lippe, "Real-Time Interactive Digital Signal Processing."

15. Cort Lippe. 1991. "Real-Time Computer Music at IRCAM," *Contemporary Music Review*, 6(1): pp. 219–24.

16. Conversation with Cort Lippe, January 2015.

17. Cort Lippe. 1989. *Music for Harp and Tape*, program note.

18. For more detailed information on the design of the IMW, see Eric Lindemann, François Déchelle, Bennett Smith, and Michel Starkier. 1991. "The Architecture of the IRCAM Musical Workstation," *Computer Music Journal*, 15(3): pp. 41–49.

19. The NeXT was based on three processors, a Motorola 68030 central processing unit, a Motorola 68882 floating-point unit, and a Motorola 56001 digital signal processing chip.

20. For a detailed explanation of CPOS, see Eric Viara. 1991. "CPOS: A Real-Time Operating System for the IRCAM Musical Workstation," *Computer Music Journal*, 15(3): pp. 50–57. Interestingly, Miller Puckette did not make use of this facility, preferring instead to concentrate on developing his own solutions to real-time audio communications in the context of FTS.

21. Eric Lindemann. 1990. "ANIMAL—A Rapid Prototyping Environment for Computer Music Systems," *Proceedings of the 1990 International Computer Music Conference—Glasgow, UK* (San Francisco: International Computer Music Association): pp. 241–244.

22. It should be noted, however, that the design features of ANIMAL were to prove influential on Puckette in the subsequent development of his Pd program, as an alternative to Max/MSP.

23. Miller Puckette. 1990. "EXPLODE: A User Interface for Sequencing and Score Following," *Proceedings of the 1990 International Computer Music Conference—Glasgow, UK* (San Francisco: International Computer Music Association): pp. 259–261.

24. Cort Lippe and Miller Puckette. 1991. "Musical Performance using the IRCAM Workstation," *Proceedings of the 1991 International Computer Music Conference—Montreal* (San Francisco: International Computer Music Association): pp. 533–536.

25. See Cort Lippe, Zack Settel, Miller Puckette, and Eric Lindemann. 1991. "The IRCAM Musical Workstation: A Prototyping and Production Tool for Real-Time Computer Music," *Proceedings of the 9th Italian Colloquium of Computer Music* (Genoa: Associazione di Informatica Musicale Italiana).

26. As noted in Chapter 2, research into techniques of score following was initiated at IRCAM by Barry Vercoe in 1983, and one of Puckette's first projects on joining the institution two years later was to work with Vercoe developing and refining the associated algorithms. It is also important to recognize the important contributions to these techniques by Roger Dannenberg in this context, working at Carnegie Mellon University. The same software was also used to produce a revised version of Manoury's *Pluton* for the ISPW.

27. Ibid., p. 185.

28. Miller Puckette and Cort Lippe. 1992. "Score Following in Practice," *Proceedings of the 1992 International Computer Music Conference—San Jose, California* (San Francisco: International Computer Music Association): pp. 182–183.

383

29. For a detailed account of the functional characteristics of FTS, see Miller Puckette. 1991. "FTS: A Real-Time Monitor for Multiprocessor Music Synthesis," *Computer Music Journal*, 15(3): pp. 58–67.

30. Miller Puckette. 1991. "Combining Event and Signal Processing in the MAX Graphical Programming Environment," *Computer Music Journal*, 15(3): pp. 68–77.

31. Ibid., p. 73.

32. Cort Lippe. 1993. "A Composition for Clarinet and Real-Time Signal Processing: Using Max on the IRCAM Signal Processing Workstation," *Proceedings of the 10th Italian Colloquium of Computer Music* (Genoa: Associazione di Informatica Musicale Italiana): pp. 428–432.

33. See Zack Settel and Cort Lippe. 1994. "Real-Time Timbral Transformation: FFT-based Resynthesis," *Contemporary Music Review* 10(2): pp. 171–179.

34. Cort Lippe. 1994. "Real-time Granular Sampling Using the IRCAM Signal Processing Workstation," *Contemporary Music Review*, 10(2): pp. 149–155.

35. Ibid., p. 154.

36. Lippe, "A Composition for Clarinet and Real-Time Signal Processing."

37. Ibid.

38. Ibid., p. 429.

39. Trevor Wishart was working at IRCAM at the time, developing materials for his piece *Vox 5* (see Chapter 6), and Lippe initially tested out the routine using one of Wishart's sound samples, hence the name. Interestingly, there is a similarity in organizational terms to the way in which the time-stretching algorithms of Wishart's Sound Loom were subsequently configured.

40. Philippe Manoury also made extensive use of the *Trevor* algorithms in *Pluton*. For further information see Chapter 3.

41. Lippe, "A Composition for Clarinet and Real-Time Signal Processing," p. 429.

42. Puckette and Lippe, "Score Following in Practice."

43. See David Wetzel. 2006. "A Model for the Conservation of Interactive Electroacoustic Repertoire: Analysis, Reconstruction, and Performance in the Face of Technological Obsolescence," *Organised Sound*, 11(3): pp. 273–284.

44. The only piece involving several instrumentalists during this period was *Music for Sextet and ISPW* (1993), for flute, bass clarinet, violin, cello, trombone, and piano.

45. Additionally, Lippe composed *Trio for Clarinet and Two Computers* (2002), which stands out from this lineage as it involves an electroacoustic performer: "the software interface allows the computer operator (in this case [Lippe]) to perform on the computers as another musician, musically reacting to the clarinet and the computer responses to the clarinet." Cort Lippe and Esther Lamneck, program note for *Trio for Clarinet and Two Computers*, consulted on the composer's website: https://www.cortlippe.com/uploads/1/0/7/0/107065311/clarinettrio-notes.pdf, accessed April 3, 2020.

46. Transcription from video of Presentation 2 of the accompanying software, "Composing for solo instrument and live electronics," from 1′13″ to 2′22″.

47. Ibid., from 2′55″ to 4′45″.

48. Transcription from video of Presentation 20 of the accompanying software, "The creative use of technology," from 3′25″ to 6′04″.

49. Cort Lippe, program note for *Music for Tuba and Computer*, consulted on the composer's website: https://www.cortlippe.com/uploads/1/0/7/0/107065311/lippe-tubanotes.pdf, accessed April 3, 2020.

50. These durations are given on the basis of the recording by Melvyn Poore used in the accompanying software. The recording available from Cort Lippe's website at https://www.cortlippe.com/uploads/1/0/7/0/107065311/lippe-tubaaudio.mp3 (accessed April 3, 2020) also lasts about 16′30″; the score mentions a duration of 16 minutes.

51. Cort Lippe. 2008. Score of *Music for Tuba and Computer*, p. 1, reproduced with the kind permission of the composer. Downloadable from https://www.cortlippe.com/uploads/1/0/7/0/107065311/lippe-tubascore.pdf (accessed April 3, 2020).

52. Ibid.

53. Transcription from video of Presentation 2 of the accompanying software, from 26′04″ to 27′15″.

54. Score of *Music for Tuba and Computer*, p. 5.

55. Transcription from video of Presentation 21 of the accompanying software, "On form, pitch, rhythm and spectrum," from 14′20″ to 15′13″.

56. The sigmund~ object and its documentation can be downloaded from Ted Apel's website, at http://vud.org/max/, accessed April 3, 2020. The sigmund~ object is a successor to Puckette's fiddle~ external object for Max. See Miller S. Puckette, Theodore Apel, and David D. Zicarelli. 1998. "Real-Time Audio Analysis Tools for Pd and MSP," *Proceedings of the 1998 International Computer Music Conference—University of Michigan, Ann Arbor* (San Francisco: International Computer Music Association): pp. 109–112.

57. Max help file for the sigmund~ external, as downloaded from http://vud.org/max/, accessed April 3, 2020.

58. Ibid.

59. Ibid., subpatcher "sinusoid-tracking."

60. Transcription from video of Presentation 7 of the accompanying software, "Introduction to *Music for Tuba and Computer*," from 5′19″ to 5′29″.

61. Transcription from video of Presentation 20, from 7′14″ to 8′11″.

62. In Cort Lippe's patch, the "track" flag is used to handle frequencies and amplitudes sent to the oscillator bank: when a new track is detected, the corresponding oscillator first jumps immediately to the new frequency, and then glissandos smoothly (over 5 milliseconds) to the following frequency values of the continued track.

63. See the discussion of Philippe Manoury's *Pluton* in Chapter 3.

64. Incidentally, the Chapo technique also appeared in another early work with live electronics by Manoury realized with the assistance of Cort Lippe: *Jupiter*, for flute and 4X—the first piece of the *Sonus ex machina* cycle. The Chapo spectral envelope, used in sections VI and XII of *Jupiter*, was applied to oscillators, and controlled with the pitches of the flute. See Philippe Manoury, "*Jupiter* by Philippe Manoury," in Marc Battier, Bertrand Cheret, Serge Lemouton, and Philippe Manoury, eds. 2003. *PMA LIB. Les musiques électroniques de Philippe Manoury/The Electronic Music of Philippe Manoury*, CD-ROM (Paris: IRCAM—Centre Georges Pompidou): pp. 17–22.

65. Transcription from video of Presentation 20, from 8′13″ to 9′04″.

66. Miller Puckette. 2007. *The Theory and Technique of Electronic Music* (Singapore: World Scientific): p. 160.

67. Miller Puckette. 1995. "Formant-Based Audio Synthesis Using Nonlinear Distortion," *Journal of the Audio Engineering Society*, 43(1): pp. 41–43.

68. Transcription from video of Presentation 16 of the accompanying software, "Superposition of FFT processes," from 0′00″ to 0′52″.

69. Ibid., from 1′17″ to 1′46″.

70. See Kevin Karplus and Alex Strong. 1983. "Digital Synthesis of Plucked-String and Drum Timbres," *Computer Music Journal*, 7(2): pp. 43–55.

71. A midicent is a hundredth of a semitone.

72. Transcription from video of Presentation 14 of the accompanying software, "Fast Fourier transform reverse noise reduction," from 0′02″ to 1′09″.

73. Julius Orion Smith III. 2011. "Cross-synthesis," in *Spectral Audio Signal Processing*, https://ccrma.stanford.edu/~jos/sasp/Cross_Synthesis.html, online book edition, accessed April 3, 2020.

74. Transcription from video of Presentation 13 of the accompanying software, "Fast Fourier transform processing," from 1′37″ to 1′45″.

75. Ibid., from 2′15″ to 2′27″.

76. Technically, all spectral processes of the FFT module perform operations on each frequency bin of the frequency-domain signal; however, only these five processes have independent parametric values for each bin. For convenience, they are therefore named "per-bin processors" in the rest of this chapter and in the accompanying software.

77. Terminology of Cort Lippe's Max patch for *Music for Tuba and Computer*; "otoa" designates the amount of signal going from the resynthesis oscillators ("o") to the allpass filters ("a").

78. See Chandrasekhar Ramakrishnan, Joachim Goßmann, and Ludger Brümmer. 2006. "The ZKM Klangdom," *Proceedings of the New Interfaces for Musical Expression Conference (NIME'06), Paris*: pp. 140–143.

79. Transcription from video of Presentation 22 of the accompanying software, "Space and acoustics," from 8′55″ to 9′08″.

80. Ibid., from 2′40″ to 2′48″.

81. Ibid., from 4′38″ to 7′05″.

82. The only two exceptions are the FFT processors and the allpass filters, which can only send their stereo signals to the stereo output module—they never send their mono signal to the spatialization module.

83. See Chapters 3 and 7.

84. As with Manoury's and Harvey's works, the commands corresponding to each event are stored in qlist objects. When a specific event is triggered, the contents of the qlist object at the corresponding event index is queried. Each command is prefixed with a specific keyword defining its destination in the Max program: for instance, a "otor 127" command will set the amount of signal from the oscillators module ("o") to the reverberation module ("r") to a value of 127. A "revfb 100" will set the reverberation feedback to a value of 100.

85. Transcription from video of Presentation 7, from 0′22″ to 0′23″.

86. Score of *Music for Tuba and Computer*, performance notes, (n.p.).

87. Ibid., p. 1.

88. Ibid., p. 5.

89. Ibid., p. 9.

Chapter 9

1. Where works were performed live, using multiple sound sources directed to different loudspeakers, early experience of multichannel sound diffusion was also gained. Although such situations were rare, the work of Pierre Schaeffer and his associates in Paris during the later 1940s and early 1950s developing *musique concrète* is of particular

interest in this context. See Peter Manning. 2013. *Electronic and Computer Music* (New York: Oxford University Press): pp. 20–38.

2. There is, however, an important distinction to be made between three-dimensional projection that is auditioned in a manner essentially external to the simulated acoustic space, as is the case with conventional stereophony, and one that is truly immersive, where the listener is surrounded by three or more loudspeakers, or indeed in certain circumstances listening via headphones. This significance of this distinction will be considered further in due course.

3. See Peter Manning. 2006. "The Significance of *Techné* in Understanding the Art and Practice of Electroacoustic Composition," *Organised Sound*, 11(1): pp. 81–90.

4. The work was originally conceived as a five-channel work, with an additional loudspeaker mounted in the ceiling, and the practical difficulties of achieving the further synchronization necessary led to the abandonment of this enhancement.

5. See Jonty Harrison. 1998. "Sound, Space, Sculpture: Some Thoughts on the 'What,' 'How' and 'Why' of Sound Diffusion," *Organised Sound*, 3(2): pp.117–127.

6. See Scott Wilson and Jonty Harrison. 2010. "Rethinking the BEAST: Recent Developments in Multichannel Composition at Birmingham ElectroAcoustic Sound Theatre," *Organised Sound*, 15(3): pp. 239–250.

7. John Chowning. 2014. "Mathews' Diagram and Euclid's Line—Fifty Years Ago," *Proceedings of the 2014 International Computer Music Conference—Athens* (San Francisco: International Computer Music Association): pp. 7–10.

8. The significance of this pioneering work should not be underestimated.

9. John Chowning. 2011. "*Turenas*: The Realisation of a Dream" (paper presented at Journées d'Informatique Musicale, Université de Saint-Etienne). Available online at https://ccrma.stanford.edu/sites/default/files/user/jc/turenas-_the_realization_of_a_dream.pdf, accessed April 3, 2020.

10. There is an interesting reciprocal relationship here between the influence of Risset on Chowning in the context of FM synthesis, also discussed in Chapter 1, and Chowning's influence on Risset in terms of the use of dynamic spatial projection, to be found in works such as *Songes*, composed at IRCAM. See Lev Koblyakov. 1984. "Jean-Claude Risset—*Songes* (1979)," *Contemporary Music Review*, 1(1): pp. 171–173.

11. For a useful introduction to the early history of spatialization, up to the mid-1990s, see Curtis Roads. 1996. *The Computer Music Tutorial* (Cambridge, MA: MIT Press): pp. 449–492.

12. Increasing awareness of the creative potential of domestic surround sound systems has indeed led some composers to produce Dolby-encoded versions of their multichannel works.

13. Whereas the original Dolby 5.1 configuration consisted of three speakers at the front and two speakers either side of the listening area, the more sophisticated Dolby 7.1 extends the immersive perspective with two further speakers positioned toward the rear (the .1 descriptor in each case refers to an additional "sub-woofer" speaker available at the front to enhance low frequencies).

14. For a detailed account of Fletcher's pioneering work in this context, see Stephen H. Fletcher. 1992. *Harvey Fletcher 1884–1981: A Biographical Memoire* (Washington DC: National Academy of Sciences).

15. Arguably a fourth perspective is attributable to a project on surround sound for FM broadcasting involving James Gibson, Richard Christensen, and Allen Limberg. See James J. Gibson, Richard M. Christensen, and Allen L. R. Limberg. 1972. "Compatible

FM Broadcasting of Panoramic Sound," *Journal of the Audio Engineering Society*, 20: pp. 816–822.

16. See: Duane H. Cooper and Takeo Shiga. 1972. "Discrete-Matrix Multichannel Stereo," *Journal of the Audio Engineering Society*, 20: pp. 346–360.

17. Michael Gerzon. 1974. "Surround-Sound Psychoacoustics: Criteria for the Design of Matrix and Discrete Surround Sound Systems," *Wireless World*, 80: pp. 483–486.

18. Peter Fellgett. 1974. "Ambisonic Reproduction of Directionality in Surround Sound Systems," *Nature,* 252: pp. 534–538.

19. Ibid., p. 535.

20. The University of York, UK, played a significant role in the development of Ambisonics in association with Calrec. See, for example, David G. Malham and Anthony Myatt. 1995. "3-D Sound Spatialization Using Ambisonic Techniques," *Computer Music Journal*, 19(4): pp. 58–70.

21. This coding technique, known as C-format or UHJ, removes any inclusion of vertical information, reducing the reproduction possibilities to a purely horizontal plane of projection. In addition, the accuracy of the spatial location of sound images is materially reduced.

22. See Chapters 3 and 8.

23. IRCAM/Espaces Nouveaux, *Spatialisateur—User Manual* (Paris: IRCAM—CNRS UMR STMS, 1995–2012).

24. See Jean-Marc Jot and Olivier Warusfel. 1995. "Spat~: A Spatial Processor for Musicians and Sound Engineers," http://articles.ircam.fr/textes/Jot95a/, accessed April 3, 2020.

25. The figure and the description that follows is directly derived from the IRCAM *Spatialisateur—User Manual.*

26. As the manual notes, this is an extension of techniques first pioneered by Chowning and cited earlier in the chapter.

27. See Augustinus J. Berkhout, Diemer de Vries, and Peter Vogel. 1993. "Acoustic Control by Wave Field Synthesis," *Journal of the Acoustical Society of America*, 93(5): pp. 2764–2778.

28. Ville Pulkki. 1997. "Virtual Sound Source Positioning Using Vector Base Amplitude Panning," *Journal of the Audio Engineering Society*, 45(6): pp. 456–466.

29. Ville Pulkki. 2000. "Generic Panning Tools for MAX/MSP," *Proceedings of the 2000 International Computer Music Conference—Berlin* (San Francisco: International Computer Music Association), n.p., Figure 1.

30. Ibid., Figure 2.

31. Trond Lossius, Pascal Baltazar, and Théo de la Hogue. 2009. "DBAP—Distance-Based Amplitude Panning," *Proceedings of the 2009 International Computer Music Conference-Montreal* (San Francisco: International Computer Music Association): pp. 489–492. For a detailed comparison of the differences between VBAP and DBAP, see Dimitar Kostadinov, Joshua D. Reiss, and Valeri Mladenov. 2010. "Evaluation of Distance Based Amplitude Panning for Spatial Audio," *Proceedings of the IEEE International Conference on Acoustics, Speech, and Signal Processing*.

32. Natasha Barrett, "Musical Structure, Shifting Perspectives and Composition," *eContact!*, 3(3): http://cec.sonus.ca/econtact/wea2/MusicalStructure.htm, accessed April 3, 2020. Document revised by the composer in 2019 and provided to the authors.

33. Natasha Barrett, "Little Animals: Compositional Structuring Processes," *Computer Music Journal*, 23(2): pp. 11–18.

34. Natasha Barrett. 1997. "Structuring Processes in Electroacoustic Composition" (PhD diss., City University, UK): p. 107.

35. Conversation with the composer, IRCAM, April 2015. She continues to compose in her own studio using four-channel playback facilities that are sufficient in an Ambisonic context to allow her to code the diffusion algorithms necessary for concert situations where the required number of speakers channels for accurate imaging is available.

36. Felipe Otondo. 1999. "Creating Sonic Spaces: An Interview with Natasha Barrett," *Computer Music Journal*, 31(2): pp. 10–19.

37. Natasha Barrett. 2010. "Ambisonics and Acousmatic Space: A Composer's Framework for Investigating Spatial Ontology," *Proceedings of the Sixth Electroacoustic Music Studies Network Conference, Shanghai*.

38. Natasha Barrett, program note for *Trade Winds*: http://www.natashabarrett.org/tw.html, accessed April 3, 2020.

39. Given the length of the concert work *Kongsberg Silver Mines*, originally one of the three installation pieces was performed at the Giga-Hertz award concert. This reworking of the piece as a self-contained composition allowed her to explore the potential of the 43-loudspeaker "Klangdom" diffusion system. Interestingly Trevor Wishart received the main Giga-Hertz prize in the same year for *Imago*, also performed in the same concert.

40. See Ludger Brümmer, Götz Dipper, David Wagner, Holger Stenschke, and Jochen Arne Otto. 2014. "New Developments for Spatial Music in the Context of the ZKM Klangdom: A Review of Technologies and Recent Productions," *Divergence Press*, 3. Online journal, http://divergencepress.net/2014/12/01/2016-11-20-new-developments-for-spatial-music-in-the-context-of-the-zkm-klangdom-a-review-of-technologies-and-recent-productions/, accessed April 3, 2020.

41. Chandrasekhar Ramakrishnan. 2009. "Zirkonium: Non-Invasive Software for Sound Spatialisation," *Organised Sound*, 14(3): pp. 268–276.

42. Natasha Barrett. 2010. "*Kernel Expansion*: A Three-Dimensional Ambisonics Composition Addressing Connected Technical, Practical and Aesthetical issues," *Proceedings of the 2nd International Symposium on Ambisonics and Spherical Acoustics, Paris*.

43. Natasha Barrett. 2012. "The Perception, Evaluation and Creative Application of High Order Ambisonics in Contemporary Music Practice," *IRCAM Composer in Research Report*.

44. Barrett, "The Perception, Evaluation and Creative Application of High Order Ambisonics," p. 4.

45. Natasha Barrett. 2012. "*Hidden Values* (2012) 22′00," online notice, http://www.natashabarrett.org/Hidden_values.html, accessed April 3, 2020.

46. Ibid.

47. Ibid.

48. In the version premiered at IRCAM, *The Lock* and *Optical Tubes* were respectively the second and third parts of *Hidden Values*; their order in the triptych was subsequently reversed by the composer. In this writing, we refer to *The Lock* as the third part of the work, according to the updated ordering.

49. Barrett. 2012. "*Hidden Values* (2012) 22′00."

50. Transcription from video of Presentation 17 of the accompanying software, "*The Lock* within *Hidden Values*," from 1′53″ to 2′38″.

51. Barrett. "*Hidden Values* 22′00."

52. Barrett, "The Perception, Evaluation and Creative Application of High Order Ambisonics," p. 4.

389

53. Ibid. A dichotomy between voice and percussion can also be found in Martin Laliberté, "Archétypes et paradoxes des nouveaux instruments," in Hugues Genevois and Raphaël De Vivo, eds. 1999. *Les nouveaux gestes de la musique* (Marseille: Éditions Parenthèses): p. 121: "musical instruments of our century . . . like traditional acoustic instruments, are situated between two essential poles, two complementary archetypes: the voice and the percussion." Translated from the French by the authors.

54. Barrett, "The Perception, Evaluation and Creative Application of High Order Ambisonics," p. 4.

55. This categorization between source, processed, and abstract is the musicological elaboration of the authors. While determining that a sound file is a source material is generally unproblematic, thanks to the composers' archive and her labeling, the distinction between processed and abstract is of course subjective, and is discussed on the basis of listening examples in forthcoming Demonstration Videos.

56. Barrett, "The Perception, Evaluation and Creative Application of High Order Ambisonics," p. 4.

57. Additional recordings of percussion instruments were also made by just the composer in Oslo.

58. Barrett, "The Perception, Evaluation and Creative Application of High Order Ambisonics," pp. 4–5.

59. The labeling of these sequences is that of the authors, on the basis of Barrett's naming of source tracks and stems in her Nuendo session.

60. For unclear reasons, the suffix numbers vary from microphone to microphone (13 in most cases, 11 for three of the DPAs, 12 for another DPA, 14 for the tom). These numbering differences are consistent across all sequences in the composer's archive: for instance, "sequence_12" includes "chimes_12.wav," "crotales_12.wav," "temple block_12.wav," and "tom _13.wav. In all cases, the authors have labeled the sequences with the most commonly used suffix, as in the example of "sequence_13," which corresponds to "bowl_13.wav," "chimes_13.wav," "crotales_13.wav," and "temple block_13.wav."

61. Transcription from video of Presentation 14 of the accompanying software, "Processing sound in a spatialization context," from 0′39″ to 1′17″.

62. As mentioned earlier, A-format sound files are made with the four signals directly captured by the four microphones of a Soundfield microphone. In Barrett's Nuendo session, each A-format channel is located on one of four mono tracks.

63. N being a number from 1 to 30: one for each input of IRCAM's Spat hosted in Max. For clarity these 62 tracks are named Spat tracks in the rest of this text. The Nuendo Spat tracks numbered from 1 to 30 are mapped to Spat's inputs 1 to 30 with strict numeric correspondence. Tracks 31 to 62 are mapped to Spat's inputs with no particular order; the mapping can be observed specifically using Presentation 1 of the accompanying software.

64. The Jack software allows audio signals to be passed from the outputs of an application to the inputs of another. See http://www.jackaudio.org, accessed April 3, 2020.

65. See for instance, Svein Berge and Natasha Barrett. 2010. "High Angular Resolution Planewave Expansion," *Proceedings of the Second International Symposium on Ambisonics and Spherical Acoustics*, Paris: pp. 4–9.

66. The composer would now use the Open Sound Control (OSC) protocol rather than MIDI for such control messages, but this option was not available at the time of composing *Hidden Values*.

67. Transcription from video of Presentation 3 of the accompanying software, "The global software environment," from 1′54″ to 2′22″.

68. It is important to note that this consideration of real-time spatialization is mostly computational, as opposed to performative: the spatial movements are calculated by Max, but there is no user interaction on these processes. From one performance to another, these movements will mostly be identically reproduced, with the very local exception of some involving randomization.

69. The visualization of the thirty sources as green circles, appearing in several videos of our interviews with Natasha Barrett in the accompanying software, is provided by the spat. oper object.

70. The composer reported to us that, while the room effect of Spat is indeed turned off for the performance of *The Lock*, it was useful during the compositional process to operate tests with the effect activated, especially in contrast to the Ambisonics convolution reverberation.

71. In the coordinate system provided by the Spat, the x axis is left-right, y is front-rear, and z is up-down. Values are provided in meters, where 0 is the listener's position; positive values are for right, front, up, and negative values are for left, rear, down. In the azimuth, distance, and elevation format, the azimuth angle in degrees gives the direction on the horizontal plane; a value of 0 corresponds to a point located in front of the listener; a value of 90 corresponds to a point located to the right side. The elevation, also in degrees, gives the direction on the vertical plane; a value of 0 corresponds to no elevation and a value of 90 corresponds to a point located exactly above the listener. The distance from the listener is provided in meters. See Jean-Marc Jot et al. 2012. *Spatialisateur: User Manual* (Paris, IRCAM-Centre Pompidou): pp. 22–25.

72. For instance, the SPIRAL studio at the University of Huddersfield, where the accompanying software for this chapter has been developed, has three rings of eight loudspeakers surrounding the listener; each ring is at a different height, and a twenty-fifth loudspeaker is located exactly above the listener.

73. Transcription from video of Presentation 5 of the accompanying software, "Discussions around excerpts of *The Lock*," from 19′27″ to 19′43″.

74. The MIDI CC tracks for *The Lock* do not affect the z coordinate of the sources controlled with this mechanism: their vertical position is constant at the equator (0 meter).

75. The definition of sections is that of the authors.

76. Transcription from video of Presentation 5 of the accompanying software, from 2′09″ to 2′54″.

77. Ibid., from 5′32″ to 6′22″.

78. Ibid., from 45′33″.

79. Transcription from video of Presentation 3 of the accompanying software, from 1′00″ to 1′28″.

80. Transcription from video of Presentation 5 of the accompanying software, from 4′30″ to 5′17″.

81. Ibid., from 20′14″ to 20′55″.

82. The azimuth randomization for source 4, containing a distorted percussion sequence, also occurs every 448 milliseconds, but is desynchronized from the other random changes by a delay of 300 milliseconds, thus increasing the chaotic characteristics of the spatial reimaging.

83. Transcription from video of Presentation 15 of the accompanying software, "Spatialization and structure," from 0′00″ to 1′46″.

84. In our interviews, this second material of the opening of *The Lock* is named "the bass" by Barrett: "the bass connects to the percussion, but it is abstract." Transcription from video of Presentation 15 of the accompanying software, from 2′00″ to 2′03″.

85. Transcription from video of Presentation 15 of the accompanying software, from 2′11″ to 2′14″.

86. Transcription from video of Presentation 15 of the accompanying software, from 2′47″ to 3′09″.

87. In the light of Barrett's explanations on the dramatic interplay between voice and percussion, this back and forth movement at the front of the scene can be seen as defensive, this vocal element seeming to protect its territory before percussion materials start taking it over.

88. Transcription from video of Presentation 15 of the accompanying software, from 7′02″ to 7′20″.

89. Ibid., from 7′54″ to 7′58″.

90. Ibid., from 7′59″ to 8′03″.

91. Ibid., from 8′31″ to 8′59″.

92. Ibid., from 14′13″ to 15′26″. Following this particular quote, it is worth noting that, with the exception of the "noise_fill_pomp_bform" fragment containing residual noise with neither actual percussion nor voice contents and appearing at the beginning of section 1C, materials from the mixed voice and percussion recordings only appear from the beginning of section 2, whether they are presented as direct sources, as processed, or as abstract sounds.

93. Transcription from video of Presentation 15 of the accompanying software, from 19′31″ to 20′06″.

94. Ibid., from 26′41″ to 27′20″.

95. Transcription from video of Presentation 19 of the accompanying software, "Interview with Olivier Warusfel and Markus Noisternig," from 2′18″ to 3′37″.

96. Ibid., from 4′29″ to 5′07″.

97. Transcription from video of Presentation 20 of the accompanying software, "The concert and the audience," from 0′48″ to 2′24″.

Bibliography

Alcorn, Pamela. 1992. "Perspectives of Electroacoustic Music: A Critical Study of the Electroacoustic Music of Jonathan Harvey, Denis Smalley and Trevor Wishart" (Durham theses, Durham University, UK).

Alles, Hal G., and Peppino (Giuseppe) di Giugno. 1977. "A One Card 64 Channel Digital Synthesiser," *Computer Music Journal*, 1(4): pp. 7–9.

Allouis, Jean-François. 1978. "Use of High Speed Microprocessors for Digital Synthesis," *Proceedings of the 1978 International Computer Music Conference—Northwestern University, Illinois* (San Francisco: International Computer Music Association, 1978): pp. 26–28. Also published in *Computer Music Journal*, 3(1): pp. 14–16 (1980).

Allouis, Jean-François, and Jean-Yves Bernier. 1982. "The SYTER Project Sound Processor Design and Software Overview," *Proceedings of the 1982 International Computer Music Conference—Venice* (San Francisco: International Computer Music Association): pp. 232–240.

Atkins, Martin, Andrew Bentley, Tom Endrich, Rajmil Fischman, David Malham, Richard Orton, and Trevor Wishart. 1987. "The Composers Desktop Project," *Proceedings of the 1987 International Computer Music Conference—Champaign/Urbana, Illinois* (San Francisco: International Computer Music Association): pp. 146–150.

Bachelard, Gaston. 1943. *L'air et les songes: Essai sur l'imagination du movement* (Paris: Librairie José Corti).

Barrett, Natasha. 1997. "Structuring Processes in Electroacoustic Composition" (PhD diss., City University, UK).

Barrett, Natasha. 1999. "Little Animals: Compositional Structuring Processes," *Computer Music Journal*, 23(2): pp. 11–18.

Barrett, Natasha, "Musical Structure, Shifting Perspectives and Composition," *eContact!*, 3(3): http://cec.sonus.ca/econtact/wea2/MusicalStructure.htm, accessed April 3, 2020.

Barrett, Natasha. 2010. "Ambisonics and Acousmatic Space: A Composer's Framework for Investigating Spatial Ontology," *Proceedings of the Sixth Electroacoustic Music Studies Network Conference, Shanghai*.

Barrett, Natasha. 2010. "*Kernel Expansion*: A Three-Dimensional Ambisonics Composition Addressing Connected Technical, Practical and Aesthetical Issues," *Proceedings of the 2nd International Symposium on Ambisonics and Spherical Acoustics*, Paris.

Barrett, Natasha. 2012. "*Hidden Values* (2012) 22'00," online notice, http://www.natashabarrett.org/Hidden_values.html, accessed April 3, 2020.

Barrett, Natasha. 2012. "The Perception, Evaluation and Creative Application of High Order Ambisonics in Contemporary Music Practice," *IRCAM Composer in Research Report*.

Barrière, Jean-Baptiste. 1987. "Musical Production at IRCAM in 1986–87: A Studio Report," *Proceedings of the 1987 International Computer Music Conference—Champaign/Urbana, Illinois* (San Francisco: International Computer Music Association): pp. 57–64.

Battier, Marc. 1995. "Une nouvelle géométrie du son: Le paradoxe de la lutherie électronique," *Les cahiers de l'Ircam. Recherche et musique*, no. 7, *Instruments*: pp. 43–56.

Battier, Marc. 2007. "What the GRM Brought to Music: From *Musique Concrète* to Acousmatic Music," *Organised Sound*, 12(3): pp. 189–202.

Baudouin, Olivier. 2007. "A Reconstruction of *Stria*," *Computer Music Journal*, 31(3): pp. 75–81.

Berg, Paul. 1979. "PILE: A Language for Sound Synthesis," *Computer Music Journal*, 3(1): pp. 30–41.

Berge, Svein, and Natasha Barrett. 2010. "High Angular Resolution Planewave Expansion," *Proceedings of the Second International Symposium on Ambisonics and Spherical Acoustics*, Paris: pp. 4–9.

Berkhout, Augustinus J., Diemer de Vries, and Peter Vogel. 1993. "Acoustic Control by Wave Field Synthesis," *Journal of the Acoustical Society of America*, 93(5): pp. 2764–2778.

Bloch, Joshua, and Roger Dannenberg. 1985. "Real-Time Computer Accompaniment of Keyboard Performances," *Proceedings of the 1985 International Computer Music Conference—Simon Fraser University, Vancouver* (San Francisco: International Computer Music Association): pp. 279–289.

Bossis, Bruno. 2005. "*Stria* de John Chowning ou l'*oxymoron* musical: Du nombre d'or comme poétique," in Évelyne Gayou, ed., *John Chowning: Portraits Polychromes* (Paris: Ina-GRM, TUM–Michel de Maule): pp. 87–115.

Boulanger, Richard, ed. 2000. *The Csound Book* (Cambridge, MA: MIT Press).

Boulez, Pierre, and Andrew Gerzso. 1988. "Computers in Music," *Scientific American* 258(4): pp. 44–50.

Bruce, Susan, ed. 2008. *Three Early Modern Utopias: Utopia, New Atlantis, and The Isle of Pines* (Oxford: Clarendon Press).

Brümmer, Ludger, Götz Dipper, David Wagner, Holger Stenschke, and Jochen Arne Otto. 2014. "New Developments for Spatial Music in the Context of the ZKM Klangdom: A Review of Technologies and Recent Productions," *Divergence Press*, 3. Online journal, http://divergencepress.net/2014/12/01/2016-11-20-new-developments-for-spatial-music-in-the-context-of-the-zkm-klangdom-a-review-of-technologies-and-recent-productions/, accessed April 3, 2020.

Bullock, Jamie, and Lamberto Coccioli. 2005. "Modernising Live Electronics Technology in the Works of Jonathan Harvey" *Proceedings of the 2005 International Computer Music Conference—Barcelona* (San Francisco: International Computer Music Association).

Bullock, Jamie, and Lamberto Coccioli. 2006. "Modernising Musical Works Involving Yamaha DX-Based Synthesis: A Case Study," *Organised Sound*, 11(3): pp. 221–227.

Carpentier, Thibaut, Markus Noisternig, and Olivier Warusfel. 2015. "Twenty Years of IRCAM Spat: Looking Back, Looking Forward," *Proceedings of the 2015 International Computer Music Conference—Denton, Texas* (San Francisco: International Computer Music Association): pp. 270–277.

Chowning, John. 1973. "The Synthesis of Complex Audio Spectra by Means of Frequency Modulation," *Journal of the Audio Engineering Society*, 21(7): pp. 526–534.

Chowning, John. 2011. "*Turenas*: The Realisation of a Dream," paper presented at Journées d'Informatique Musicale, Université de Saint-Étienne, May 25–27, 2011.

Chowning, John. 2014. "Mathews' Diagram and Euclid's Line—Fifty Years Ago," *Proceedings of the 2014 International Computer Music Conference—Athens* (San Francisco: International Computer Music Association): pp. 7–10.

Clarke, Michael. 2006. "Jonathan Harvey's *Mortuos Plango, Vivos Voco*," in Mary Simoni, ed., *Analytical Methods of Electroacoustic Music* (New York: Routledge): pp. 111–143.

Clarke, Michael. 2013. "Analysing Electroacoustic Music: An Interactive Aural Approach," *Music Analysis*, 31(3): pp 347–380.

Clarke, Michael, Frédéric Dufeu, and Peter Manning. 2013. "Introducing TaCEM and the TIAALS software," *Proceedings of the 2013 International Computer Music Conference—Perth, Australia* (San Francisco: International Computer Music Association): pp. 47–53.

Clarke, Michael, Frédéric Dufeu, and Peter Manning. 2014. "From Technological Investigation and Software Emulation to Music Analysis: An Integrated Approach to Barry Truax's *Riverrun*," *Proceedings of the 2014 International Computer Music Conference—Athens, Greece* (San Francisco: International Computer Music Association): vol. 1, pp. 201–208.

Clarke, Michael, Frédéric Dufeu, and Peter Manning. 2016. "Using Software Emulation to Explore the Creative and Technical Processes in Computer Music: John Chowning's *Stria*, A Case Study from the TaCEM Project," *Proceedings of the 2016 International Computer Music Conference—Utrecht, The Netherlands* (San Francisco: International Computer Music Association): pp. 218–223.

Clarke, Michael, Frédéric Dufeu, and Peter Manning. 2015. "Les relations entre technologie et créativité dans l'analyse des musiques électroacoustiques: Une étude comparative de *Riverrun* de Barry Truax et *Imago* de Trevor Wishart," *Musurgia*, XXII(1): pp. 27–44.

Cooper, Duane H., and Takeo Shiga. 1972. "Discrete-Matrix Multichannel Stereo," *Journal of the Audio Engineering Society*, 20: pp. 346–360.

Dahan, Kevin. 2007. "Surface Tensions: Dynamics of *Stria*," *Computer Music Journal*, 31(3): pp. 65–74.

Dean, Roger, ed. *The Oxford Handbook of Computer Music* (New York: Oxford University Press, 2009).

Dhomont, Francis. 1996. "Is There a Québec Sound?," *Organised Sound*, 1(1): pp. 23–28.

Dodge, Charles, and Thomas A. Jerse. 1997. *Computer Music Synthesis, Composition and Performance*, 2nd ed. (London and New York: Schirmer).

Dolson, Mark. 1986. "The Phase Vocoder: A Tutorial," *Computer Music Journal*, 10(4): pp. 14–27.

Donin, Nicolas. 2006. "Spatialization as a Compositional Tool and Individual Access to Music in the Future: Jonathan Harvey in Conversation with Nicolas Donin," *Circuit*, 16(3): pp. 75–82.

Downes, Michael, ed. 2000. *Jonathan Harvey, Music and Inspiration* (London and New York: Faber and Faber).

Dufour, Denis, and Thomas Brando, "Quelques définitions," online glossary for the website of AECME (Association des Enseignants de Composition en Musique Électroacoustique), http://www.aecme.org/definitions, accessed April 3, 2020.

Duhautpas, Frédérick, Antoine Freychet, and Makis Solomos. 2015. "*Beneath the Forest Floor* de Hildegard Westerkamp: Analyse d'une composition à base de paysages sonores," *Analyse musicale*, 76: pp. 34–42.

Eckel, Gerhard, Xavier Rodet, and Yves Potard. 1987. "A Sun-Mercury Music Workstation," *Proceedings of the 1987 International Computer Music Conference—Champaign/Urbana, Illinois* (San Francisco: International Computer Music Association): pp. 159–165.

Emmerson, Simon. 1986. "The Relation of Language to Materials," in Simon Emmerson, ed., *The Language of Electroacoustic Music* (London: Macmillan).

Emmerson, Simon, and Leigh Landy, eds. 2016. *Expanding the Horizon of Electroacoustic Music Analysis* (Cambridge, UK: Cambridge University Press).

Favreau, Emmanuel, Michael Fingerhut, Olivier Koechlin, Patrick Potacsek, Miller Puckette, and Robert Rowe. 1986. "Software Developments for the 4X Real-Time System,"

Proceedings of the 1986 International Computer Music Conference—The Hague (San Francisco: International Computer Music Association): pp. 369–374.

Fellgett, Peter. 1974. "Ambisonic Reproduction of Directionality in Surround Sound Systems," *Nature*, 252: pp. 534–538.

Fletcher, Stephen H. 1992. *Harvey Fletcher 1884–1981: A Biographical Memoire* (Washington, DC: National Academy of Sciences).

Gabor, Dennis. 1946. "Theory of Communication," *Journal of the Institute of Electrical Engineers Part III*, 93: pp. 429–457.

Gayou, Évelyne. 2007. *GRM: Le groupe de recherches musicales: Cinquante ans d'histoire* (Paris: Librairie Arthème Fayard).

Gerzon, Michael. 1974. "Surround-Sound Psychoacoustics: Criteria for the Design of Matrix and Discrete Surround Sound Systems," *Wireless World*, 80: pp. 483–486.

Gerzso, Andrew. 1984. "Reflections on *Répons*," *Contemporary Music Review*, 1(1): pp. 23–34.

Gibson, James J., Richard M. Christensen, and Allen L. R. Limberg. 1972. "Compatible FM Broadcasting of Panoramic Sound," *Journal of the Audio Engineering Society*, 20: pp. 816–822.

Di Giugno, Giuseppe, and Eugenio Guarino. 1983. "Un processore rapido floating-point," *Atti del 5° Colloquio Di Informatica Musicale* (Ancona): pp. 36–42.

Greenhough, Mike, Ian Bowler, and Stephen Morris. 1985. "The Electronic Music Studio at University College Cardiff," *Proceedings of the 1985 International Computer Music Conference—Simon Fraser University, Vancouver* (San Francisco: International Computer Music Association): pp. 415–418.

Harrison, Jonty. 1998. "Sound, Space, Sculpture: Some Thoughts on the 'What,' 'How' and 'Why' of Sound Diffusion," *Organised Sound*, 3(2): pp.117–127.

Harvey, Jonathan. 1965. "The Composer's Idea of his Inspiration" (E-thesis, University of Glasgow, UK).

Harvey, Jonathan. 1975. Program note for *Inner Light 3* (IRCAM repository), http://brahms.ircam.fr/works/work/9027/, accessed April 3, 2020.

Harvey, Jonathan. 1976. *The Music of Stockhausen* (London and New York: Faber and Faber).

Harvey, Jonathan. 1981. "*Mortuos Plango Vivos Voco*: A Realisation at IRCAM," *Computer Music Journal*, 5(4): pp. 22–24.

Harvey, Jonathan. 1986. "The Mirror of Ambiguity," in Simon Emmerson, ed., *The Language of Electroacoustic Music* (London: Macmillan).

Harvey, Jonathan. 1986. "*Madonna of Winter and Spring*," *The Musical Times*, 127(1720): pp. 431–433.

Harvey, Jonathan. 1999. "The Metaphysics of Live Electronics," *Contemporary Music Review*, 18(3): pp. 79–82.

Harvey, Jonathan. 2004. "The Genesis of Quartet no. 4," in Jonathan Cross, ed., *Identity and Difference: Essays on Music, Language and Time* (Leuven: Leuven University Press): pp. 43–53.

Harvey, Jonathan, Denis Lorrain, Jean-Baptiste Barrière, and Stanley Haynes. 1984. "Notes on the Realization of *Bhakti*," *Contemporary Music Review*, 1(1): pp. 111–129.

Helmuth Mara. 2006. "Barry Truax's *Riverrun*," in Mary Simoni, ed., *Analytical Methods of Electroacoustic Music* (New York: Routledge): pp. 187–238.

Higgins, Hannah B., and Douglas Kahn. 2012. *Mainframe Experimentalism: Early Computing and the Foundations of The Digital Arts* (Berkeley: University of California Press).

Jot, Jean-Marc, and Olivier Warusfel. 1995. "Spat~: A Spatial Processor for Musicians and Sound Engineers," http://articles.ircam.fr/textes/Jot95a/, accessed April 3, 2020.

Jozek, Suzanne. 2016. *Jonathan Harvey: ". . . towards a Pure Land": Stationen einer kompositorischen Reise* (Mainz: Schott).

Karplus, Kevin, and Alex Strong. 1983. "Digital Synthesis of Plucked-String and Drum Timbres," *Computer Music Journal*, 7(2): pp. 43–55.

Koblyakov, Lev. 1984. "Jean-Claude Risset—*Songes* (1979)," *Contemporary Music Review*, 1(1): pp. 171–173.

Kostadinov, Dimitar, Joshua D. Reiss, and Valeri Mladenov. 2010. "Evaluation of Distance Based Amplitude Panning for Spatial Audio," *Proceedings of the IEEE International Conference on Acoustics, Speech, and Signal Processing*.

Laliberté, Martin. 1999. "Archétypes et paradoxes des nouveaux instruments," in Hugues Genevois and Raphaël De Vivo, eds. *Les nouveaux gestes de la musique* (Marseille: Éditions Parenthèses): pp. 121–138.

Landy, Leigh. 2020. "On Hildegard Westerkamp's *Beneath the Forest Floor* (1992)," in Miller Puckette and Kerry Hagan, eds., *Between the Tracks: Musicians on Selected Electronic Music* (Cambridge, MA: MIT Press).

Lazzarini, Victor. 2013. "The Development of Computer Music Programming Systems," *Journal of New Music Research*, 42(1): pp. 97–110.

Le Bail, Karine, and Martin Kaltenecker, eds. 2012. *Pierre Schaeffer: Les constructions impatientes* (Paris: CNRS Editions).

Le Caine, Hugh, and Gustav Ciamaga. 1967. "A Preliminary Report on the Serial Sound Structure Generator," *Perspectives of New Music*, 6(1): pp. 114–118.

Lefford, Nyssim, and Barry Vercoe. 1999. "An Interview with Barry Vercoe," *Computer Music Journal*, 23(4): pp. 9–17.

Lewis, Andrew. 1998. "Francis Dhomont's *Novars*," *Journal of New Music Research*, 27(1–2): pp. 67–83.

Licata, Thomas, ed. 2002. *Electroacoustic Music: Analytical Perspectives* (Westport, CT: Greenwood Press).

Lindemann, Eric. 1990. "ANIMAL—A Rapid Prototyping Environment for Computer Music Systems," *Proceedings of the 1990 International Computer Music Conference—Glasgow, UK* (San Francisco: International Computer Music Association): pp. 241–244.

Lindemann, Eric, François Déchelle, Bennett Smith, and Michel Starkier. 1991. "The Architecture of the IRCAM Musical Workstation," *Computer Music Journal*, 15(3): pp. 41–49.

Lippe, Cort. 1982. *8110 K: A Composition Report* (Utrecht: Institute of Sonology).

Lippe, Cort. 1988. "A Technical Description of *Pluton* by Phillipe Manoury," *IRCAM Annual Report* (Paris: IRCAM).

Lippe, Cort. 1991. "Real-Time Computer Music at IRCAM," *Contemporary Music Review*, 6(1): pp. 219–24.

Lippe, Cort. 1993. "A Composition for Clarinet and Real-Time Signal Processing: Using Max on the IRCAM Signal Processing Workstation," *Proceedings of the 10th Italian Colloquium of Computer Music* (Genoa: Associazione di Informatica Musicale Italiana): pp. 428–432.

Lippe, Cort. 1994. "Real-Time Granular Sampling Using the IRCAM Signal Processing Workstation," *Contemporary Music Review*, 10(2): pp. 149–155.

Lippe, Cort. 1996. "Real-Time Interactive Digital Signal Processing: A View of Computer Music," *Computer Music Journal*, 20(4): pp. 21–24.

397

Lippe, Cort. 2008. Program note for *Music for Tuba and Computer*, https://www.cortlippe.com/uploads/1/0/7/0/107065311/lippe-tubanotes.pdf, accessed April 3, 2020.

Lippe, Cort, and Esther Lamneck. 2002. Program note for *Trio for Clarinet and Two Computers*, https://www.cortlippe.com/uploads/1/0/7/0/107065311/clarinettrio-notes.pdf, accessed April 3, 2020.

Lippe, Cort, and Miller Puckette. 1991. "Music Performance Using the IRCAM Workstation," *Proceedings of the 1991 International Computer Music Conference—Montreal* (San Francisco: International Computer Music Association): pp. 533–536.

Lippe, Cort, Zack Settel, Miller Puckette, and Eric Lindemann. 1991. "The IRCAM Musical Workstation: A Prototyping and Production Tool for Real-Time Computer Music," *Proceedings of the 9th Italian Colloquium of Computer Music* (Genoa: Associazione di Informatica Musicale Italiana).

Lorrain, Denis. 1980. "A Panoply of Stochastic 'Cannons,'" *Computer Music Journal*, 4(1): pp. 53–81.

Lossius, Trond, Pascal Baltazar, and Théo de la Hogue. 2009. "DBAP—Distance-Based Amplitude Panning," *Proceedings of the 2009 International Computer Music Conference—Montreal* (San Francisco: International Computer Music Association): pp. 489–492.

Lowman, Edward A. 1971. "An Example of Fibonacci Numbers Used to Generate Rhythmic Values in Modern Music," *Fibonacci Quarterly*, 9(4): pp. 423–426.

Malham, David G., and Anthony Myatt. 1995. "3-D Sound Spatialization using Ambisonic Techniques," *Computer Music Journal*, 19(4): pp. 58–70.

Manning, Peter. 2013. *Electronic and Computer Music*, 4th ed. (New York: Oxford University Press).

Manning, Peter. 2006. "The Significance of *Techné* in Understanding the Art and Practice of Electroacoustic Composition," *Organised Sound*, 11(1): pp. 81–90.

Manning, Peter. 2012. "La musique concrète et ses appareils," in Karine Le Bail and Martin Kaltenecker, eds. *Pierre Schaeffer: Les constructions impatientes* (Paris: CNRS Editions): pp. 140–151.

Manoury, Philippe. 1984. "The Arrow of Time," tr. Tod Machover and Nigel Osborne, *Contemporary Music Review*, 1(1): pp. 131–45.

Manoury, Philippe. 1987. Program note for *Jupiter*, http://brahms.ircam.fr/works/work/10482/, accessed April 3, 2020.

Manoury, Philippe. 1989. Program note for the final version of *Pluton*, http://brahms.ircam.fr/works/work/10493/, accessed April 3, 2020.

Manoury, Philippe. 1995. "Entretien avec Jean-Pierre Derrien", http://www.philippemanoury.com/?p=349, accessed April 3, 2020.

Manoury, Philippe. 1995. "*Pluton*," online notice, http://brahms.ircam.fr/documents/document/21518/, accessed April 3, 2020.

Manoury, Philippe. 1997. *La partition du ciel et de l'enfer. Jupiter*, CD, Musidisc France, Accord, 465 307-2.

Manoury, Philippe. 1997. "Les partitions virtuelles", article available online at http://www.philippemanoury.com/?p=340, accessed April 3, 2020.

Manoury, Philippe. 2003 "*Jupiter* by Philippe Manoury," in Marc Battier, Bertrand Cheret, Serge Lemouton, and Philippe Manoury, eds. *PMA LIB. Les musiques électroniques de Philippe Manoury/The Electronic Music of Philippe Manoury*, CD-ROM (Paris: IRCAM—Centre Georges Pompidou).

Manoury, Philippe. 2003. "*Pluton* by Philippe Manoury," in Marc Battier, Bertrand Cheret, Serge Lemouton, and Philippe Manoury, eds. *PMA LIB. Les musiques électroniques de*

Philippe Manoury/The Electronic Music of Philippe Manoury, CD-ROM (Paris: IRCAM—Centre Georges Pompidou).

Marino, Gérard, Jean-Michel Raczinski, and Marie-Hélène Serra. 1990. "The New UPIC System," *Proceedings of the 1990 International Computer Music Conference—Glasgow, UK* (San Francisco: International Computer Music Association): pp. 249–252.

Marty, Nicolas. 2011. "'Creavolution' with Trevor Wishart," interview by Nicolas Marty, *JMM: The Journal of Music and Meaning*, 10.

Mathews, Max. 1963. "The Digital Computer as a Musical Instrument," *Science*, 142(3592): pp. 553–557.

Mathews, Max, and Joseph Pasquale. 1981. "RTSKED: A Scheduled Performance Language for the Crumar General Development System," *Proceedings of the 1981 International Computer Music Conference—North Texas State University* (San Francisco: International Computer Music Association).

May, Andrew. 2006. "Philippe Manoury's *Jupiter*," in Mary Simoni, ed., *Analytical Methods of Electroacoustic Music* (London: Routledge): pp. 145–185.

McCartney, Andra. 1999. "Sounding Places: Situated Conversations through the Soundscape Conversations of Hildegard Westerkamp" (PhD diss., York University, Toronto, Ontario).

Milani, Matteo. 2009. "Chemistry of Sound," (Interview with Trevor Wishart), *Digimag Magazine*, 41, http://www.digicult.it/digimag/issue–041/trevor-wishart-chemistry-of-sound/, accessed April 3, 2020.

Moorer, James. 1978. "The Use of the Phase Vocoder in Computer Music Applications," *Journal of the Audio Engineering Society*, 26(1–2): pp. 42–45.

Mountain, Rosemary, and Francis Dhomont. 2006. "From Wire to Computer: Francis Dhomont at 80," *Computer Music Journal*, 30(3): pp. 10–21.

Murray Schafer, Raymond. 1977. *The Tuning of the World: Towards a Theory of Soundscape Design* (Toronto: McClelland & Stewart; 2nd ed., Rochester, VT: Destiny Books, 1994).

Nattiez, Jean-Jacques. 1993. *Le Combat de Chronos et d'Orphée* (Paris: Bourgois).

Odiard, Patrick. 1995. "De la confrontation à la conjonction: À propos de *Sonus ex machina*," *Les cahiers de l'IRCAM. Compositeurs d'aujourd'hui*, no. 8, *Philippe Manoury*: pp. 39–66.

Otondo, Felipe. 2007. "Creating Sonic Spaces: An Interview with Natasha Barrett," *Computer Music Journal*, 31(2): pp. 10–19.

Palmer, John. 2001. Bhakti *for Chamber Ensemble and Electronics: Serialism, Electronics and Spirituality* (Lewiston, NY: Edwin Mellen Press).

Pousset, Damien. 1992. "La flûte-MIDI, l'histoire et quelques applications," in *Mémoire de Maîtrise* (Université Paris-Sorbonne).

Puckette, Miller. 1988. "The Patcher," *Proceedings of the 1988 International Computer Music Conference—Cologne* (San Francisco: International Computer Music Association): pp. 420–429.

Puckette, Miller. 1990. "EXPLODE: A User Interface for Sequence and Score Following," *Proceedings of the 1990 International Computer Music Conference—Glasgow, UK* (San Francisco: International Computer Music Association): pp. 259–261.

Puckette, Miller. 1991. "FTS: A Real-Time Monitor for Multiprocessor Music Synthesis," *Computer Music Journal*, 15(3): pp. 58–67.

Puckette, Miller. 1991. "Combining Event and Signal Processing in the MAX Graphical Programming Environment," *Computer Music Journal*, 15(3): pp. 68–77.

Puckette, Miller. 1995. "Formant-Based Audio Synthesis Using Nonlinear Distortion," *Journal of the Audio Engineering Society*, 43(1): pp. 41–43.

Puckette, Miller. 2002. "Max at Seventeen," *Computer Music Journal*, 26(4): pp. 31–43.

Puckette, Miller. 2007. *The Theory and Technique of Electronic Music* (Singapore: World Scientific).

Puckette, Miller S., Theodore Apel, and David D. Zicarelli. 1998. "Real-Time Audio Analysis Tools for Pd and MSP," *Proceedings of the 1998 International Computer Music Conference Conference—University of Michigan, Ann Arbor* (San Francisco: International Computer Music Association): pp. 109–112.

Puckette, Miller, and Kerry Hagan, eds. 2020. *Between the Tracks: Musicians on Selected Electronic Music* (Cambridge, MA: MIT Press).

Puckette, Miller, and Cort Lippe. 1992. "Score Following in Practice," *Proceedings of the 1992 International Computer Music Conference—San Jose, California* (San Francisco: International Computer Music Association): pp. 182–185.

Pulkki, Ville. 1997. "Virtual Sound Source Positioning Using Vector Base Amplitude Panning," *Journal of the Audio Engineering Society*, 45(6): pp. 456–466.

Pulkki, Ville. 2000. "Generic Panning Tools for MAX/MSP," *Proceedings of the 2000 International Computer Music Conference—Berlin* (San Francisco: International Computer Music Association).

Raczinski, Jean-Michel, and Gérard Marino. 1988. "A Real Time Synthesis Unit," *Proceedings of the 1988 International Computer Music Conference—Cologne* (San Francisco: International Computer Music Association): pp. 90–100.

Ramakrishnan, Chandrasekhar. 2009. "Zirkonium: Non-invasive Software for Sound Spatialisation," *Organised Sound*, 14(3): pp. 268–276.

Ramakrishnan, Chandrasekhar, Joachim Goßmann, and Ludger Brümmer. 2006. "The ZKM Klangdom," *Proceedings of the New Interfaces for Musical Expression Conference (NIME'06), Paris*: pp. 140–143.

Randell, Brian, ed. 2013. *The Origin of Digital Computers: Selected Papers.* Monographs in Computer Science (New York: Springer).

Risset, Jean-Claude. 1985. "Computer Music Experiments 1964–," *Computer Music Journal*, 9(1): pp. 11–18.

Risset, Jean-Claude. 1994. "Sculpting Sounds with Computers: Music, Science, Technology," *Leonardo*, 27(3): pp. 257–261.

Roads, Curtis. 1978. "Automated Granular Synthesis of Sound," *Computer Music Journal*, 2(2): pp. 61–62.

Roads, Curtis. 1985. "Granular Synthesis of Sound," in Curtis Roads and John Strawn, eds. *Foundations of Computer Music* (Cambridge, MA: MIT Press): pp. 145–159.

Roads, Curtis. 1996. *The Computer Music Tutorial* (Cambridge, MA: MIT Press).

Roads, Curtis. 2001. *Microsound* (Cambridge, MA: MIT Press).

Roads, Curtis. 2015. *Composing Electronic Music: A New Aesthetic* (New York: Oxford University Press).

Roads, Curtis, and Max Mathews. 1980. "Interview with Max Mathews," *Computer Music Journal*, 4(4): pp. 15–22.

Rodet, Xavier, and Gerald Bennett. 1980. "Synthèse de la voix chantée par ordinateur," in *Conférences des Journées d'études* (Paris: Festival International du Son): pp. 73–91.

Rodet, Xavier, and Pierre Cointe. 1984. "FORMES: Composition and Scheduling of Processes," *Computer Music Journal*, 8(3): pp. 32–50.

Rodet, Xavier, Yves Potard, and Jean-Baptiste Barrière. 1984. "The CHANT Project: From the Synthesis of the Singing Voice to Synthesis in General," *Computer Music Journal*, 8(3): pp. 15–31.

Roy, Stéphane. 1996. "Form and Referential Citation in a Work by Francis Dhomont," *Organised Sound*, 1(1): pp. 29–41.

Schaeffer, Pierre. 1952. *À la recherche d'une musique concrète* (Paris: Éditions du Seuil,).

Schaeffer, Pierre. 1966. *Traité des objects musicaux* (Paris: Éditions du Seuil).

Settel, Zack, and Cort Lippe. 1994. "Real-Time Timbral Transformation: FFT-Based Resynthesis," *Contemporary Music Review*, 10(2): pp. 171–179.

Shannon, Claude, and Warren Weaver. 1949. *The Mathematical Theory of Communication* (Urbana: University of Illinois Press).

Simoni, Mary, ed. 2006. *Analytical Methods of Electroacoustic Music* (New York: Routledge).

Smith, Julius Orion, III. 2011. "Cross-synthesis," in *Spectral Audio Signal Processing*, https://ccrma.stanford.edu/~jos/sasp/Cross_Synthesis.html, online book, edition, accessed April 3, 2020.

Starkier, Michel, and Philippe Prevot. 1986. "Real Time Gestural Control," *Proceedings of the 1986 International Computer Music Conference—The Hague* (San Francisco: International Computer Music Association): pp. 423–426.

Tenney, James. 1963. "Sound-Generation by means of a Digital Computer," *Journal of Music Theory*, 7(1): pp. 24–70.

Teruggi, Daniel. 1998. "Le système SYTER: Son histoire, ses développements, sa production musicale, ses implications dans le language électroacoustique d'aujourd'hui" (PhD diss., Université Paris 8).

Teruggi, Daniel. 2007. "Technology and *Musique Concrète*: The Technical Developments of the Groupe de Recherches Musicales and Their Implication in Musical Composition," *Organised Sound*, 12(3): pp. 213–231.

Torigoe, Keiko. 1982. "A Study of the World Soundscape Project" (MFA diss., York University, Toronto, Ontario).

Truax, Barry. 1973. "The Computer Composition—Sound Synthesis Programs POD4, POD5 & POD6," *Sonological Reports No. 2* (Utrecht, Institute of Sonology).

Truax, Barry. 1976. "For Otto Laske: A Communicational Approach to Computer Sound Programs," *Journal of Music Theory*, 20(2): pp. 227–300.

Truax, Barry. 1977. *Handbook for Acoustic Ecology* (Vancouver: A.R.C. Publications, 1977).

Truax, Barry. 1992. "Computer Music Composition: The Polyphonic POD system," *IEEE Computer*, 11(8): pp. 40–50.

Truax, Barry. 1984. *Acoustic Communication* (New York: Ablex Publishing Corporation; 2nd ed., Westport, CT: Ablex, 2001).

Truax, Barry. 1985. "The PODX System: Interactive Compositional Software for the DMX-1000," *Computer Music Journal*, 9(1): pp. 29–38.

Truax, Barry. 1988. "Real-Time Granular Synthesis with a Digital Signal Processor," *Computer Music Journal*, 12(2): pp. 14–26.

Truax, Barry. 1997. "*Sequence of Earlier Heaven*: The Record as a Medium for the Electroacoustic Composer," *Leonardo*, 21(1): pp. 25–28.

Truax, Barry. 1994. "Discovering Inner Complexity: Time Shifting and Transposition with a Real-Time Granulation Technique," *Computer Music Journal*, 18(2): pp. 38–48.

Truax, Barry. 1996. "Soundscape, Acoustic Communication and Environmental Sound Composition," *Contemporary Music Review*, 15(1): pp. 49–65.

Truax, Barry. 1999. "Sonology: A Questionable Science Revisited," in Jerry Tabor, ed., *Otto Laske: Navigating New Musical Horizons* (Westport, CT: Greenwood Press): pp. 21–36.

Truax, Barry. 2000. "The Aesthetics of Computer Music: A Questionable Concept Reconsidered," *Organised Sound*, 5(3): pp. 119–126.

Truax, Barry. 2002. "Genres and Techniques of Soundscape Composition as Developed at Simon Fraser University," *Organised Sound*, 7(1): pp. 5–14.

Truax, Barry. 2008. *Documentation DVD #1* (CSR-DVD 0801).

Vande Gorne, Annette. 2006. "Catalogue commenté des œuvres de Francis Dhomont," in Évelyne Gayou, ed., *Francis Dhomont: Portraits Polychromes* (Paris: Ina–GRM): pp. 99–117.

Vandenheede, Jan. 2008. "Jonathan Harvey's *Ritual Melodies*," *Interface*, 21(2): pp. 149–183.

Vandenheede, Jan, and Jonathan Harvey. 1985. "Identity and Ambiguity: The Construction and Use of Timbral Transitions and Hybrids," *Proceedings of the 1985 International Computer Music Conference—Simon Fraser University, Vancouver* (San Francisco: International Computer Music Association): pp. 97–102.

Vassilandonakis, Yiorgos. 2009. "An Interview with Trevor Wishart," *Computer Music Journal*, 33(2): pp. 8–23.

Vercoe, Barry, and Dan Ellis. 1990. "Real-Time CSOUND: Software Synthesis with Sensing and Control," *Proceedings of the 1990 International Computer Music Conference—Glasgow, UK* (San Francisco: International Computer Music Association): pp. 209–211.

Vercoe, Barry, and Miller Puckette. 1985. "Training the Synthetic Performer," *Proceedings of the 1985 International Computer Music Conference—Simon Fraser University, Vancouver* (San Francisco: International Computer Music Association): pp. 275–278.

Viara, Eric. 1991. "CPOS: A Real-Time Operating System for the IRCAM Musical Workstation," *Computer Music Journal*, 15(3): pp. 50–57.

Vinet, Hugues, and Daniel Teruggi. 1991. "GRM Report," *Proceedings of the 1991 International Computer Music Conference—Montreal* (San Francisco: International Computer Music Association): pp. 82–85.

Walraff, Dean. 1979. "The DMX-1000 Signal Processing Computer," *Computer Music Journal*, 3(4): pp. 44–49.

West, Marcus. 1982. "'Sequemuse'—A Hybrid Computer-Music System," *Interface*, 11: pp. 47–60.

Westerkamp, Hildegard. 1987. "Listening and Soundmaking: A Study of Music-as-Environment" (MA diss., Simon Fraser University, Vancouver, British Columbia).

Westerkamp, Hildegard. 1992. Program note for *Beneath the Forest Floor*, https://www.hildegardwesterkamp.ca/resources/PDFs/program-notes-pdf/Beneath-the-Forest-Floor.pdf, accessed April 3, 2020.

Westerkamp, Hildegard. 2002. "Linking Soundscape Composition and Acoustic Ecology," *Organised Sound*, 7(1): pp. 51–56.

Westerkamp, Hildegard. 2007. "Soundwalking," *Sound Heritage*, 3(4). Revised version in: Carlyle, Angus, ed. *Autumn Leaves, Sound and the Environment in Artistic Practice* (Paris: Double Entendre): pp. 49–54.

Wetzel, David. 2006. "A Model for the Conservation of Interactive Electroacoustic Repertoire: Analysis, Reconstruction, and Performance in the Face of Technological Obsolescence," *Organised Sound*, 11(3): pp. 273–284.

Whittall, Arnold. 1999. *Jonathan Harvey* (London: Faber and Faber).

Wilson, Scott, and Jonty Harrison. 2010. "Rethinking the BEAST: Recent Developments in Multichannel Composition at Birmingham ElectroAcoustic Sound Theatre," *Organised Sound*, 15(3): pp. 239–250.

Wishart, Trevor. 1985. *On Sonic Art* (York, England: Imagineering Press).

Wishart, Trevor. 1988. "The Composition of *Vox-5*," *Computer Music Journal*, 12(4): pp. 21–27.

Wishart, Trevor. 1994. *Audible Design: A Plain and Easy Introduction to Practical Sound Composition* (York, England: Orpheus the Pantomime).

Wishart, Trevor. 1996. *On Sonic Art*, ed. Simon Emmerson (Amsterdam: Harewood).

Wishart, Trevor. 2000. "Computer Sound Transformation: A Personal Perspective from the U.K.", subsequently made available on his personal website: http://www.trevorwishart.co.uk/transformation.html, accessed April 3, 2020.

Wishart, Trevor. 2012. *Sound Composition* (York, England: Orpheus the Pantomime).

Wolek, Nathan. 2002. "Granular Toolkit v1.0 for Cycling74's Max/MSP," *Journal SEAMUS*, 16(2): pp. 34–46.

Xenakis, Iannis. 1955. "The Crisis of Serial Music," *Gravesaner Blätter*, 1.

Xenakis, Iannis. 1971. *Formalized Music: Thought and Mathematics in Composition* (Bloomington: Indiana University Press; rev. ed., New York: Pendragon Press, 1992).

Young, Gayle. 1983. "Hugh Le Caine: Pioneer of Electronic Music in Canada," *HSTC Bulletin: Journal of the History of Canadian Science, Technology and Medicine/HSTC Bulletin: revue d'histoire des sciences, des techniques et de la médecine au Canada*, 8(1): pp. 20–31.

Zattra, Laura. 2007. "The Assembling of *Stria* by John Chowning: A Philological Investigation," *Computer Music Journal*, 31(3): pp. 38–64.

Index